STATE
OF
SILENCE

Also by Sam Lebovic

A Righteous Smokescreen
Free Speech and Unfree News

The Espionage Act and
the Rise of America's Secrecy Regime

STATE

OF

SILENCE

Sam Lebovic

BASIC BOOKS

New York

Basic Books
Hachette Book Group
1290 Avenue of the Americas, New York, NY 10104
www.basicbooks.com

Printed in the United States of America

First Edition: November 2023

Published by Basic Books, an imprint of Hachette Book Group, Inc. The Basic Books name and logo is a trademark of the Hachette Book Group.

The Hachette Speakers Bureau provides a wide range of authors for speaking events. To find out more, go to hachettespeakersbureau.com or email HachetteSpeakers@hbgusa.com.

Basic Books copies may be purchased in bulk for business, educational, or promotional use. For more information, please contact your local bookseller or the Hachette Book Group Special Markets Department at special.markets@hbgusa.com.

The publisher is not responsible for websites (or their content) that are not owned by the publisher.

Figures 1, 2, 3, 5, 6, 7, 8, 10, 11, 12, 13, 15, 19, and 20 are courtesy of the Library of Congress.

Print book interior design by Amy Quinn.

Library of Congress Cataloging-in-Publication Data
Names: Lebovic, Sam, 1981– author.
Title: State of silence : the Espionage Act and the rise of America's secrecy regime / Sam Lebovic.
Description: First edition. | New York : Basic Books, 2023. | Includes bibliographical references and index.
Identifiers: LCCN 2023010252 | ISBN 9781541620162 (hardcover) | ISBN 9781541620155 (ebook)
Subjects: LCSH: Espionage—Law and legislation—United States. | United States. Espionage Act of 1917. | Secrecy—Law and legislation—United States. | Official secrets—United States. | Disclosure of information—Law and legislation—United States. | Whistle blowing—Law and legislation—United States. | War on Terrorism, 2001–2009. | Transparency in government—Law and legislation—United States.
Classification: LCC KF9394 .L43 2023 | DDC 345.7302/31—dc23/eng/20230802
LC record available at https://lccn.loc.gov/2023010252

ISBNs: 9781541620162 (hardcover), 9781541620155 (ebook)

LSC-C

Printing 1, 2023

For Em, again and always

CONTENTS

INTRODUCTION

After remaining silent for so long, I started speaking.
—Terry Albury (2021)

B EFORE HE WENT TO PRISON, TERRY ALBURY HAD BEEN AN FBI agent for sixteen successful, if not always entirely happy, years. He had joined the Bureau as an idealistic college graduate in August 2001, hoping to put away sex offenders and child pornographers. After 9/11, Albury embraced the FBI's new focus on counterterrorism, taking seriously his mission to keep Americans safe. As an agent in San Francisco in 2007, he helped arrest a pair of radical Islamists plotting a bombing and received a commendation from FBI director Robert Mueller. He even served a short stint as a counterterrorism investigator in Iraq.[1]

But by the time he moved to Minneapolis, in 2012, Albury was beginning to nurse doubts about his work. He had been involved in too many counterterrorism investigations that went nowhere. They had been opened on the basis of what he called "BS" information— such as a tip from a single, unreliable source—or because of religious or racial prejudice.[2]

1

When Albury arrived in Minneapolis, the FBI's main target was the Somali community. A number of young Somali men had recently left the city to join the militant group Al-Shabab. But when Albury began looking at files opened on the relatives of some of those men, or on local imams, as he participated in community-outreach programs with local mosques—programs that were also a way of recruiting more informants, of starting more surveillance—he frequently found little evidence of terrorism. Yet the surveillance continued, and the files stayed open, sucking up resources and accumulating more irrelevant information. Even if the Bureau turned up nothing, those files would follow the surveilled individuals throughout their lives. Whenever they applied for a passport or a job that required a background check, it would be revealed that they had once been looked at by the FBI. The real impact of his life's work, Albury had come to believe, wasn't protecting Americans from terrorism. Rather, he concluded, "I helped to destroy people."[3]

Albury, himself the son of a political refugee from Ethiopia, was the only Black field agent in Minneapolis. That made it hard to stomach the anti-Somali prejudice that wove its way through the FBI's work in the city, especially after the murder of Michael Brown in 2014 and the eruption of Black Lives Matter protests. "Minneapolis broke me," Albury said later. "It became too hard to ignore the human cost of what we were actually doing."[4]

In 2016 Albury reached out to the *Intercept*, an investigative-journalism website that had made its name publishing disclosures about the security state. He took photos of secret policy documents that outlined the procedures by which the FBI ran its surveillance operations and sent them to the site, which published a series of articles on the "FBI's Secret Rules" in January 2017. Albury didn't see himself as bringing "huge programs to light the public wasn't aware of." What he disclosed were new details about practices that were already the subject of controversy and debate, as well as suspicion among surveilled communities. For instance, one of his most important disclosures was a full and unredacted copy of the Domestic Investigations and Operations Guide, the FBI's internal rulebook.[5]

The *Intercept* articles confirmed that racial and religious profiling was taking place despite FBI rules that banned it. And they raised new questions about the effectiveness and justice of counterterrorism operations. Albury had come to think that these investigations were driven as much by institutional pressures—by the desire of the FBI to be seen to be active—as by any objective threat of domestic terrorism. He seems to have hoped that his disclosures would trigger a public debate about the Bureau, perhaps on the level of the famous Church hearings into FBI abuses in the 1970s, in which it had been revealed that J. Edgar Hoover's FBI had been illegally harassing and intimidating radical activists, including Albury's uncle, who had been a member of the Black Panthers.[6]

That debate never happened. Amid the chaotic opening months of the Trump presidency, there was little public appetite for a close look at the FBI's counterterrorism work.

The FBI, however, was paying very careful attention. It wanted to know who had spilled its secrets. In 2016 it had received a tip-off that the stories were coming when two journalists had filed Freedom of Information Act (FOIA) requests for documents that Albury had disclosed. One of those documents had been seen by only sixteen people in the previous five years. Another had a small highlight mark that identified it. They led the Bureau directly to Albury.

Albury was fired and charged with violating the Espionage Act. There was never any suspicion that he was engaged in espionage as most of us understand the term—there was no suggestion that he was spying for a foreign government or selling secrets for financial gain. His motives were straightforward: "As a public servant, my oath is to serve the interest of society, not the FBI . . . [, and] the public I served had a right to know what the FBI was doing in their name." But his desire to inform the public was completely irrelevant; it wasn't even a possible defense against the charge of espionage. Nor was it necessary for the government to prove that the disclosures had done any actual harm to the nation's security or to the effectiveness of the FBI's work.[7]

The Espionage Act makes it a crime to disclose secret information to those unauthorized to receive it: no excuses, no exceptions. Albury pled guilty to leaking classified information to the press and was sentenced to four years in prison.[8]

Albury is not the only recent victim of the Espionage Act. In the eight years that the Obama administration was in power, it brought espionage charges against eight people for disclosing information to the media. Trump brought six such charges in four years. One case per year may not seem like much. But between 1917, when the Espionage Act was passed, and 2008, a grand total of five such cases had been brought, and only one, in the 1980s, had led to a successful conviction.[9] Yet during the war on terror, Edward Snowden, Chelsea Manning, Thomas Drake, John Kiriakou, Reality Winner, Jeffrey Sterling, and Daniel Hale have all felt the sting of the law.

Moreover, simply counting up the convictions radically understates the power of the law. The Espionage Act serves as the final backstop securing the nation's bloated secrecy regime. No one knows exactly how much information is kept secret by the government. That's part of the problem with secrecy. But by any reckoning, it is a staggering amount. One 2001 estimate suggests that there are 7.5 billion pages of classified information cloistered in the US government—as many pages of secrets as there are pages in all the books on all the shelves in the Library of Congress. By the 2010s, between fifty million and ninety million documents were newly stamped as "secret" every year. Managing them is an expensive business. In 2017, the last year in which this figure was made public, maintaining its secrets cost the United States more than $18 billion.[10]

The power of the Espionage Act lies not just in the cases in which it is used but also in the work it does to protect the secrets of a giant bureaucracy. The law hangs over government employees, threatening to send them to jail for disclosing any information that has been stamped as "secret."

How did the United States end up in this situation? How had a law passed during World War I to prevent foreign spies from stealing secrets become a tool powerful enough to prevent the public from learning what its government is doing?

You won't find an answer by reading the language of the statute. At the heart of the Espionage Act are two sections of the US criminal code, Sections 793 and 794. Section 794 criminalizes what we might think of as traditional espionage—it makes it illegal to collect information for a foreign government. Section 793, the section used to prosecute leakers today, is murkier. It contains six complicated clauses intended to protect secrets by making it illegal to gather or transfer information without authorization. But exactly what they mean, and how they are supposed to work, is very unclear.

For more than a century, lawyers have complained that the Espionage Act is a poorly drafted, deeply confusing law. In the Pentagon Papers case of 1971, which was the first and last time the Supreme Court grappled with the meaning of the sections used to send Albury to jail, Justice John Marshall Harlan called it a "singularly opaque statute."[11] Two years later, a pair of law professors tried to get to the bottom of the mess. After 160 pages of dense legal analysis, they threw up their hands: "The longer we looked, the less we saw . . . the statutes implacably resist the effort to understand."[12]

To understand the law, it is necessary to trace its history. The laws and practices of secrecy emerged in a piecemeal, improvised fashion over many decades. The result is a jerry-rigged and unwieldy regime that keeps too much information secret and that thwarts democratic oversight of national-security and foreign-policy institutions. The pathologies of the present are a product of the past.

This book is the first to tell the whole story of this controversial, confusing law.

The problems with the Espionage Act began with its rushed passage through Congress in 1917. Technically, the Espionage Act was an omnibus law that combined more than a dozen laws relating to foreign relations and defense policy and neutrality. Little attention was paid to what would become Sections 793 and 794, which had been largely copied from an earlier Defense Secrets Act, itself rushed through Congress six years before. As a result, no one really noticed that although Section 793 made it illegal to disclose "information relating to the national defense" to people who weren't authorized to receive it, at no point did the law stop to define what "information relating to the national defense" meant or to delineate any process by which someone might be authorized to access it. At the center of the law was a gaping hole.

What followed were decades of improvisation as courts, politicians, and lawyers tried to make sense of how the laws of secrecy were supposed to work. Sometimes, Congress passed new laws seeking to keep information secret that lawmakers weren't sure was covered by the 1917 law, such as diplomatic code (in 1933) or atomic energy (in 1946) or cryptography (in 1950). In 1950, in the middle of the Cold War spy scare, Congress amended Section 793 itself, although the revisions ended up making the law even more confusing.

More often, the executive branch tried to protect secrets by developing new bureaucratic practices that rounded out the law: by requiring employees in particular agencies to sign confidentiality agreements, for instance, or by asking the press to keep from publishing secret information. The most important of these patches came in 1951, when Harry Truman established the modern classification system—a standardized bureaucratic process to classify information as "Confidential" or "Secret" or "Top Secret." Three-and-a-half decades late, this classification system plugged the biggest hole in the 1917 law. The executive branch now had a process to determine what sorts of information were supposed to be kept away from unauthorized eyes. By the Cold War, a robust secrecy regime had arisen.

Amid the fallout from the controversial war in Vietnam, many of those secrets began to spill. By the 1970s, it turned out that no one was really happy with the secrecy regime, which underwent another round of renovations. Those who were outraged by the secrecy of the state sought the passage of new transparency laws, such as the Freedom of Information Act and new forms of congressional oversight. Those who were more upset that important security information had spilled concluded that the Espionage Act was clearly not up to snuff, and they sought instead to install a suite of new secrecy protections, such as the Classified Information Procedure Act (1980), the Intelligence Identities Protection Act (1982), and internal boards to review the public statements of former intelligence officials. All this was layered on top of the Espionage Act and the classification system, which survived the second half of the twentieth century unchanged.

By 9/11, the nation's secrecy regime was an elaborate patchwork of statutes and executive orders and bureaucratic practices. As the White House waged its war on terror, it would find that the ambiguities of this patched-together legal structure gave it considerable power to develop and deploy an array of secretive policies and programs. Nine decades after it was passed, the Espionage Act at last became a remarkably effective tool for protecting secrets.

Part of the reason that the US secrecy laws are so complicated is that they straddle an unresolved dilemma of democratic life. On the one hand, a democratic government needs the capacity to keep some information secret. You don't want rogue actors getting their hands on the nuclear codes, just as you don't want individual bureaucrats cynically trading secrets for cash. And on a slightly more abstract level, if a democratically elected government has a mandate to administer a program and needs to keep some operational details secret to make that program effective—the names of undercover officers, say, or the schedule for spot audits—then you also want to make sure that no disgruntled employee can undermine the program by spilling the secret: that would amount to a one-person veto. But on the other hand, what makes a democracy democratic is the fact that it rules with the consent of the governed. Such consent is meaningful only if citizens can be fully informed about what their government is doing. The central reason that we so highly value the right to free speech is that it allows the public to educate itself. None of this works if the government can operate in secret. So if someone learns of a secret abuse of power, if they discover that the public is being lied to, then democratic norms require that they share what they learn with their fellow citizens.

In a formal sense, this dilemma is perhaps unresolvable. But a functioning secrecy regime would seek to balance these conflicting priorities—it would find a way to allow for the keeping of a limited number of appropriately held secrets while minimizing the potential for abuse. In theory, that's what the various moving parts of America's secrecy regime are supposed to do.

In reality, the system is a chaotic mess. Overclassification is endemic; transparency measures such as the FOIA are a weak counterweight. When so much information is classified, leaks are inevitable—the temptation to conduct politics by sharing a tip, floating a program, or undermining a rival is too great. Despite the fact that all of those leaks should be criminal according to the letter of the Espionage Act, no one thinks it would be realistic—or desirable—to apply that law literally. Instead, the sweeping provisions of the Espionage Act give the government incredible discretion to prosecute leaks when it so chooses. Such a legal system cannot produce just outcomes; it inevitably bends to the interests of the powerful.

It should be no great surprise that the secrecy regime is as dysfunctional as it is. No master plan guided its growth, and at no point has it been calmly and rationally evaluated. It has been shaped instead by decades of political conflict. Time and again, those who sought to protect the nation from foreign threats claimed the need to police the sorts of information that could circulate in the public sphere. In part, they wanted to prevent foreign spies from accessing valuable information, and the history of the Espionage Act is in no small part the history of spy scares, both real and imagined. But during World War I the Espionage Act was famous not for its secrecy provisions but for another section of the omnibus bill, which was used to send more than a thousand Socialists and radicals to jail on the grounds that their criticism interfered with the war effort just as much as a foreign spy or saboteur would. This heavy-handed censorship regime produced a civil-libertarian backlash that led directly to the rise of our modern understanding of the First Amendment. Supreme Court justice Oliver Wendell Holmes's famous free-speech metaphors—"shouting fire in a crowded theater," "the free trade in ideas"—were both issued in Espionage Act cases in 1919.

The Espionage Act thus helped to produce the first exchanges between two interest groups that would become regular combatants in the twentieth century. The guardians of national security would repeatedly seek new powers to protect their secrets, which often meant threatening the freedoms of the news media: if you wanted to prevent an enemy from learning a valuable secret, you also needed to keep the secret out of the papers. Then civil-liberties groups would rally against the new threat, successfully claiming a First Amendment right not only to criticize the government but also to publish government secrets.

Over time, these clashes between the forces of national security and the forces of free speech produced an uneasy stalemate. Efforts to extend security regulations into the public sphere were repeatedly defeated. Today, Americans are remarkably free to debate government policy, and, by and large, the media are free to publish state secrets if they can get their hands on them. In one sense, the American public sphere is freer than ever before.

Yet because the champions of civil liberties were largely concerned with protecting their autonomy from government overreach, they acquiesced to the power of the state to police its own domain. They did not protest the rise of new secrecy laws and practices anywhere nearly as much as they protested the proposal of new censorship practices. So the security state's desire to control public debate has flowed instead down this path, the path of secrecy.

On one level, the story of the Espionage Act is thus a story of an important, underappreciated evolution in the way the national-security state has sought to police debate in America. Where once the Espionage Act was used as a tool of censorship, today it is used as a tool of secrecy. Where once the state sought to regulate speech, now it is happy to let the public criticize and debate all it wants. What it controls instead is the very information that citizens need to form their opinions.

Although this is, in some sense, a story of evolution, a story of the ways that an old law has come to be used for new purposes, it is also a story of continuity. The state is still using the Espionage Act to silence its critics; it's just that the location of those critics has changed. When the Espionage Act was only a year old, it was used to silence the radical political advocate Eugene Debs, who went to jail for speaking out against what he considered to be an unjust and unnecessary war. A century later, the Espionage Act is used to silence internal critics such as Albury, who went to jail for seeking to inform the public about what he considers to be an unjust and unnecessary security policy.

The result is that a new form of censorship has become more important, one aimed not at the outsider critic of the government but at the insider who can inform the public in the first place. Call someone like Albury or Snowden or Manning what you will—a leaker, a source, a whistleblower, a traitor—they are now the central front in the long-running struggle to bring democratic oversight and control to the security state.

For the historical record makes it quite plain that the Espionage Act has produced a secrecy regime that has grown well beyond any legitimate need to keep information confidential. Public knowledge of matters of national and international significance has been blocked and distorted by the state. Wars have been started in secret. Coups have been engineered. People have been tortured. Millions of people have been subject to surveillance; many of the most committed champions of civil liberties and civil rights have been harassed and intimidated. A corrupt military-industrial complex has channeled billions of taxpayer dollars into private pockets. Foreign policies have been adopted that have led to blowback, costing American lives even as they create pressures for yet more secrecy, yet more security. And when some of these secrets have spilled out, producing momentary controversies that have shaped the history of the Espionage

Act, they have also damaged Americans' faith in their government, fueling the cynicism and rage that roil US politics today.

For more than a century, the Espionage Act has undermined American democracy. It continues to do so today. To understand how this happened, we need to start at the beginning, in the years before World War I, when a rising empire began to worry that foreigners might steal its secrets.

Chapter 1

THE FEAR OF SPIES

In 1917 newspapers criticized the proposed Espionage Act as a threat to their liberties, as this editorial cartoon suggests. Winsor McCay, "Must Liberty's Light Go Out?," *New York American*, May 3, 1917. (Library of Congress)

IT WAS JUNE 14, 1917, AND WOODROW WILSON'S FLAG DAY WASN'T going exactly as planned. The United States had been at war for a little more than two months, and the new holiday was supposed to be a pageant of patriotism. Only the previous year, in the first federally recognized Flag Day, Wilson had marched at the head of a parade of sixty thousand flag-waving Americans, wearing a straw hat and a boutonniere of red, white, and blue carnations. After a twenty-one-gun salute and the unfurling of a giant flag from the Washington Monument, he had delivered a pugnacious address on the need for national unity: "There is disloyalty active in the U.S., and it must be absolutely crushed." That night he had been renominated for the presidency, his party including in its platform an attack on foreigners and foreign-born Americans who were seeking to divide the nation. Wilson's first Flag Day had gone swimmingly.[1]

But on the day of the sequel, it rained torrentially. Huddled under an umbrella held by a Secret Service officer, Wilson delivered his speech to barely one thousand "drenched and bedraggled" patriots. Even Edith Wilson chose to stay in the car. It was an appropriate deflation of this ersatz national holiday, already on its way to becoming the neglected stepchild of the federal calendar. Only the themes of Wilson's speech—loyalty, unity, fear of the foreign—recaptured the mood of the previous year. America had gone to war, he explained, because the Germans had "filled our unsuspecting communities with vicious spies and conspirators and sought to corrupt the opinion of our people." Now the Germans were deploying an army of "agents and dupes" to "undermine the government" and intrigue against the war effort. But they would not win, warned the sodden president, for the United States was dedicated to the cause: "Woe be to the man or group of men that seeks to stand in our way."[2]

The next day, Wilson signed the Espionage Act into law.

To understand the origins of the secrecy laws that the United States still lives with, it is necessary to understand the anxieties of Wilson's era of imperial conflict and racial paranoia. From the American

Revolution through the first decade of the twentieth century, the nation had made do without a law designed to protect its secrets. But then in 1911, Congress hastily enacted a Defense Secrets Act in the midst of a panic about Japanese spies. Six years later, in the weeks after it entered World War I, it radically expanded on that law with the Espionage Act.

These were not carefully drawn laws; they had not been weighed and debated with calm, Olympian detachment. Like the soggy Stars and Stripes of Flag Day II, they were flawed and awkward performances of nationalist fervor, willed into being by the fears of the men who produced them, men who were concerned above all with preserving the hierarchical, imperial world order they believed in. It should be no surprise that the laws that came out of this moment would be poorly suited to balancing secrecy and transparency in anything like a democratic fashion.

Something like an Espionage Act was first proposed in 1907, in a memorandum written by Ralph Van Deman, the founding father of US military intelligence. The case that he made for a new law that would protect the nation's secrets was simple. There were spies everywhere. Spies had recently been arrested in Britain, France, Germany, and Italy. Japanese spies roamed freely in the Philippines, Cuba, and the West Coast of the continental United States. German spies prowled cities up and down the Atlantic seaboard. Other nations had laws against spying; it was time for the US to square up.[3]

Van Deman was not alone in his worries; the decades leading up to World War I were marked by a fear of spies. Subscribers to the *New York Times* read front-page stories about Japanese spies in Manchuria and Copenhagen and Russia and San Diego, about Russian spies in Singapore and Vienna and even in the libraries of New York. "Every nation has spies at work all the time," warned one headline in March 1904. There "are woman spies at all capitals of the nations," added another two months later.[4]

These fears soon translated themselves, as Van Deman had hoped, into new legislation. In 1911 Congress passed a Defense Secrets Act. Passed unanimously and without debate, the Defense Secrets Act was the first peacetime law in US history to try to protect the nation's secrets from foreign eyes. Until now, the government had been content to rely on the Articles of War to punish spying that took place during wartime. The passage of a permanent espionage law was thus a turning point in the history of US democracy—it was the first step on the path to our present secrecy regime. Key sections of the law would be transferred into the Espionage Act six years later, and these remain on the books today.[5]

The timing of these developments raises an important historical question. Why was the need to guard against spies, not even contemplated only decades earlier, now felt so strongly that Congress felt pressed to act not just once, but twice?

It obviously wasn't because spying was a new thing. Scratch a classical civilization, and you'll find a spy story. There are spies in the *Odyssey* and the *Mahabharata*. Moses sent spies into Canaan; Mohammed sent them into Mecca; Judas was an archetypal double agent. Sun-Tzu thought that "secret operations are essential in war," and the earliest known Chinese spy dates to the rise of the Shang dynasty in the eighteenth century BCE. Ever since, political rivalry has always produced both the desire to keep certain information secret and the desire to know the secrets of others. Spies played their part in the intrigues and wars that followed the Reformation, in the Atlantic revolutions of the eighteenth century, in the effort to steal the secret technology of porcelain from the Chinese.[6]

Yet until the early twentieth century, the United States had not felt the need to pass a law to permanently secure its secrets against spies. True, there had been secrecy in the past. The members of the Constitutional Convention had met in secret to establish the very nation itself, and one article of the Constitution they wrote allowed Congress to withhold from publication proceedings relating to diplomacy and military operations as it saw fit. Executive branch negotiations of treaties were also conducted in confidence. The Senate, which had met entirely in secret until 1795, would continue to meet behind closed doors to discuss treaty ratification until 1929.[7]

But treaties leaked frequently, and there had been as yet no serious effort to bureaucratically protect them. The preferred method to keep information from prying eyes was not to criminalize disclosure to the press but to punish the press for publishing secrets it happened to acquire. Moreover, the assumption was that diplomatic secrets had a short life. During the Civil War, Abraham Lincoln began publishing the nation's diplomatic correspondence annually.[8]

Nor were the details of military operations kept secret in anything like a standardized fashion until the end of the nineteenth century. Through the antebellum period, members of the War Department would often label their correspondence "confidential" or "in confidence," but this was an improvised, informal practice, a kind of gentlemanly decorum that created a club of insiders who could be trusted to exchange gossip, ask for favors, and work together. It was not yet a routinized, bureaucratic practice aimed at securing information. As late as the Civil War, the Union Army made do without a formal classification system and tried to keep information from Confederate eyes by regulating the public sphere: preventing newspapers from circulating in military zones, barring certain periodicals from the mail, censoring the telegraph cable, or punishing hostile editors.[9]

It was only in 1869, when it banned taking photographs of forts, that the army began adopting what we might think of as contemporary security practices. Similar orders were issued repeatedly across the late nineteenth century to regulate access to other military locations such as lake and coastal defenses. But only in 1907, when the War Department began trying to standardize the use of the "confidential" label, did these efforts to keep secret the fortifications of particular places begin to migrate to the securing of documents and information. In quick succession thereafter would come both the Defense Secrets Act and new regulations for the classification of information.[10]

The ostensible reason for these new efforts at secrecy was that technological change had made military information both more valuable and more vulnerable. The key to military supremacy, thought generals and politicians, lay in securing advantages in highly sophisticated new forms of weaponry, such as the torpedo, and in being able to plan how to deploy the tools of industrialized war at the most vulnerable points of the enemy. Meanwhile, a revolution in communications and transport technology had shrunk the world, making it easier than ever before to record and circulate information. The camera allowed spies to take new pictures of installations and defenses and documents. The telegraph, the radio, the train, the steamship, and the motorcar all allowed them to roam at will and to communicate their findings over vast distances ever more quickly.[11]

In an era marked by geopolitical rivalry and imperial expansion, it was no surprise that these technological revolutions produced new cultures of espionage and counterespionage. As empires gobbled 8.6 million square miles of Middle Eastern and African and Asian and Pacific Islander land, as they jostled uneasily against one another in a shifting web of rivalries and alliances, they created new bureaucracies to seek information about the world and to shield their own activity from prying eyes. When the United States established new military and naval intelligence divisions in the 1880s, it was acting no differently than the other great powers. Imperial Germany had established a central intelligence bureau in the 1860s; the French and British military each added intelligence branches in the 1870s. The Russian Empire reorganized a host of police and intelligence organizations to create the notorious Okhrana in the 1880s, at around the same time the British established the Special Branch of Scotland Yard and Japan developed its own intelligence operations.[12]

But while the evolution of espionage may have made some new efforts to secure information inevitable, these changes were not sufficient to produce the moral panic about spies that led to the era's sweeping new cultures of security. For most spy operations were far from sophisticated. Even today, open-source information—material gathered from newspapers and public reports and direct observations—is responsible for some 80 percent of all intelligence work.[13] More than a century ago, before the arms race between spies and secrecy had really kicked off, publicly available information was even more valuable. Up until the outbreak of World War I, for instance, European powers gained good intelligence about one another's intentions by making quite simple observations. When the French stopped sending troops to winter on the Italian border, when they stopped funding grain depots in Corsica, it wasn't hard for the Germans to work out that they were no longer planning an invasion of Italy. British interest in Belgium was pretty well telegraphed when the British Army began publishing studies of Belgian roads, rivers, and bridges. On the tense border between the Russian and Austro-Hungarian Empires, intelligence work mostly consisted of reading the newspapers and watching the construction of rail lines and fortifications, which gave a fairly clear picture of military strategy. It was therefore conducted by amateurs—itinerant knife grinders were useful sources—or by military attachés in embassies. Similarly, in the fraught frontiers between expanding empires—on Manchurian plains contested by Japan and China and Russia, in the much romanticized "Great Game" that Russian and English spies played in Central Asia—intelligence work mostly amounted to exploring, to gathering public information, to collaborating with local brigands, and to mapmaking—often done in fancy dress, for colonial cosplay was a favored pastime of the British aristocrats who turned to spy work to spice up their lives of jaded leisure.[14]

Unsurprisingly, such amateur spy work drew in the desperate and the hopeless; efforts to cultivate undercover agents attracted outright fabulists and con artists. In all, the "intelligence" they produced was hardly earth-shattering. French embassies had secret pots of money to hire spies, but as a 1913 parliamentary inquiry concluded, these "salaried secret agents" tended to report "only facts already known or comments of no interest. Most of them are individuals of little personal significance, some are very unreliable, and there are even those who played the role of double-agent." (Fair concerns, we might add, when one considers a character such as Jules De Balasy-Belvata, whose hundreds of reports were full of sensational information that was either useless or entirely fabricated. He sold them to both the French and the German governments for years.)[15]

"It was not often," concluded the head of British military intelligence at the turn of the century, "that a secret agent discovered anything of importance, but it did sometimes happen." Added one of his aides: "Underground intelligence really amounts to very little."[16]

To secure a small class of genuinely secret military information from such spies would not have been particularly difficult. And there was a case to be made that creating new rules about the bureaucratic handling of information was a way of exerting democratic control over a rapidly expanding class of public servants. The first British Official Secrets Act, which was passed in 1889 and would later prove a model for US legislation, was originally known as the "Breach of Official Trust" law and then the "Public Documents" act. Its passage was precipitated less by a fear of foreign spies than by the fact that government documents were being sold to the press by low-level bureaucrats keen to supplement their (admittedly meager) earnings. The law distinguished between acts of espionage and leaks of information without authorization. Such leaks were criminal only if they were against the public interest: selling a secret for personal profit was therefore illegal; whistle-blowing would not have been.[17]

But anxieties about espionage existed on a deeper level; they could not be assuaged by straightforward criminal law. The most famous spy scares of the period were driven as much by fears of cultural and political decline as any objective threat of espionage. In 1894, for instance, a cleaning lady on the payroll of French counterintelligence found confidential French documents in a wastepaper bin in the German embassy. They had been sold to the Germans by an indebted French major. Conservatives pointed the finger instead at Alfred Dreyfus, a Jewish member of the French General Staff who was an appropriate repository for xenophobic conspiracy mongering triggered by the travails of the French Empire. The innocent Dreyfus spent years locked in solitary confinement on Devil's Island; arguments about the Dreyfus affair roiled French politics for a decade. Similarly, during World War I two Russian officers were executed on false charges that they were German spies—their alleged treason proving a useful cover to both explain away Russian military failure and to absorb the fears of an empire on the cusp of revolution.[18]

Amid such dark fantasies of national betrayal, the effort to secure secrets only heightened anxieties about espionage. A feedback loop kicked in. The more information was kept secret, the more valuable it became, which incentivized foreign powers to seek it out, which heightened the fear of spies. For instance, the Dreyfus affair could be traced to a decision by the French to bar Germans from observing their military maneuvers. It was intended to improve French security, but the Germans, robbed of this source of open intelligence, sought out other sources within the state to maintain the flow of information.[19]

Indeed, the creation of agencies committed to securing information actually created a new vulnerability to foreign interference. The most significant instance of espionage in the years leading up to World War I was probably the case of Colonel Alfred Redl, who died by suicide in 1913 when it was discovered that he had been providing the Russians with Austro-Hungarian documents for years. Redl had access to so many secrets, and such a free hand for subterfuge, for a simple reason: he had been responsible for counterintelligence.[20]

There was, and would remain, something curiously self-fulfilling about the cultural logic of spy scares, as events in Great Britain revealed. In 1909 the Committee on Imperial Defense created the Subcommittee on Foreign Espionage, which concluded there was an "extensive system of German espionage" and recommended the creation of a new Secret Service bureau, whose various branches would soon evolve into MI-5 (responsible for counterespionage) and MI-6 (responsible for conducting espionage abroad). The subcommittee also recommended replacing the 1889 Official Secrets Act with a stronger law that would make it easier to control state secrets. Among other changes, the new law put the burden on defendants to prove they had not committed espionage, abolished the public-interest defense, and made it illegal to receive leaked information. It was passed after barely thirty minutes of parliamentary debate, amid a brief war panic triggered by the deployment of a German gunboat to the port of Agadir in Morocco.[21]

But the subcommittee's fear of German spies was, quite literally, a work of fiction. For these were the years in which the spy novel was born. In 1906 more than a million people read William Le Queux's *The Invasion of 1910*, which was published in the high-circulation tabloid the *Daily Mail*. Its tale of a nation riddled with German spies inspired a host of copycats, including Le Queux's own 1909 best-selling work of "faction," *Spies of the Kaiser*, and those of the prolific pulp writer E. Phillips Oppenheim, who wrote 116 spy novels, such as *The Secret*, in which 290,000 German spies had infiltrated England. By 1909, the story had become so formulaic that it was easy for P. G. Wodehouse to write a satirical version—*The Swoop, or How Clarence Saved England*, in which a plucky Boy Scout saves England from no fewer than nine separate invading armies.

These invasion stories had revealingly anxious, defensive plotlines, especially when compared to the aggressive expansionism of the preceding era of British adventure stories. And the genre they birthed would prove remarkably plastic and durable—the lone hero, the besieged nation, and the dark conspiracy could all be adapted to the shifting geopolitics of the twentieth century without losing their basic cultural appeal. In fact, Le Queux's first stabs at the genre featured French spies and a French invasion. When the French and British allied in 1904, he subbed in the Germans.[22]

All these spy stories were preposterous. In the 1890s Germany had thought about drawing up invasion plans and dismissed them as impossible; a 1907 parliamentary investigation, inspired in part by the popularity of invasion stories, had come to the same conclusion. And while it would later become clear that there was, in fact, a small group of German spies in England, they were the same sort of swindlers and hopeless amateurs that dominated espionage elsewhere. One proudly flew the German flag from his houseboat, where his favored espionage technique was to throw parties in which he tried to turn his inebriated guests toward talk of naval affairs. Another was a habitual con man who also tried to sell secrets to the British. A third was a cut-rate dentist and halfhearted pimp who had read some Le Queux novels, concluded that there was easy money in espionage, and volunteered to get the Germans secret information without the faintest idea how to do so. There was "nothing especially secret about the whole business," confessed the German petty officer running the ring.[23]

Nevertheless, alarmist spy stories had major political consequences. Le Queux was well connected socially—to military officers eager to develop new powers, to conservative politicians interested in whipping up security fears, to populist newspaper publishers keen for sensational headlines—and the stories that all these men were spinning created a self-reinforcing cycle of public debate. All that smoke, surely there must be spies? The Subcommittee on Foreign Espionage was created to get to the bottom of things.

The man responsible for presenting evidence of espionage to that committee, Lieutenant Colonel James Edmonds, head of British counterintelligence, was also friendly with Le Queux. To support his sensational claims about German spies, Edmonds produced a long list of suspicious incidents: Germans taking early-morning walks or asking questions about railway bridges, strange Germans renting houses in small towns, people wearing wigs or swearing in German under their breath. Edmonds confessed that a number of his cases were tips from a "well known author," likely Le Queux himself. Many of the others came via letters from self-appointed spy catchers in the public, who were themselves simply amplifying the paranoid fantasies of the storytellers. When the *Weekly News* serialized a Le Queux story, for instance, it simultaneously announced a prize competition that would offer ten pounds to any reader who had information about spies. Edmonds seems to have logged and reported their entries as suspicious cases without even the pretense of further investigation. But the sheer bulk of the reports was convincing. Fiction had become fact. New security bureaucracies and new secrecy laws were created in response.[24]

Yet a sense of security remained elusive. After all, the political order that these men were seeking to secure was that of the British Empire at its zenith. The inequities and exploitation of that empire, the hierarchies of wealth and race and power, all produced a great arc of resistance in the late nineteenth century. The early practitioners of security were directly shaped by it. Two of the early heads of the Army Intelligence Bureau had lost limbs suppressing the Indian Rebellion of 1857. Vernon Kell, who headed up counterespionage after 1909, had witnessed the Boxer Rebellion in China. Scotland Yard's Special Branch had been founded in the 1880s in reaction to an Irish bombing campaign and the global threat of an anarchist movement that was quite taken with the propaganda value of symbolic violence. (In the three decades after 1880, anarchists successfully assassinated heads of state in Austria, Italy, Greece, France, the United States, Spain, Russia—on two occasions—and Portugal, where they killed not only the king but also his heir apparent.)[25]

By the time that Parliament was worrying about German spies, Scotland Yard was increasingly concerned with the threat posed by a diasporic network of radical Indian nationalists, particularly after a wave of bombings in Bombay, attributed to the influence of anarchists in Paris, and the assassination of Sir William Curzon Wyllie of the India Office. The head of counterespionage operations against this new threat was John Wallinger, formerly superintendent of the Bombay Police. Wallinger soon discovered worrying links between Indian nationalists and German intelligence officers, and he began deploying new techniques of counterespionage to meet the threat. Amid the geopolitical turmoil of the period, the anxieties of imperial rule only multiplied.[26]

And, of course, all of this new activity to secure the empire needed to be conducted in secret, for who knew what enemy eyes were watching?

As in the UK, so in the US: the rise of secrecy was intertwined with a fear of spies produced by the anxieties of empire. In 1898, as the United States fought the Spanish Empire en route to the possession of new colonies, it began constructing a new state bureaucracy to secure itself against the new threats that imperial expansion produced. During the Spanish-American War, the Secret Service, until now responsible solely for investigating the counterfeiting of currency, was given $50,000 to sniff out Spanish spies. It spent much of its time hounding Catholic immigrants that it suspected of radicalism. When it did crack a Spanish spy ring orchestrated out of Montreal, it discovered that it had been composed mostly of expatriate Englishmen.[27]

In the long war to suppress Filipino independence fighters, which stretched out for years after the United States took possession of the islands from the Spanish, the US military pioneered new techniques of surveillance and counterintelligence: hundreds of thousands of documents were captured; centralized files were begun on Filipino activists and community leaders and intellectuals. One of the key architects of the system was Van Deman, a hitherto unheralded mapmaker in military intelligence. Based on his experiences in the Philippines, as well as a series of secret mapmaking missions in China, Van Deman began lobbying within the military bureaucracy for vastly expanded espionage and counterespionage activity. He based his new intelligence operations on those of the British. One of his demands was a new espionage act that would keep information secret from foreign spies.[28]

The public advocate for this new secrecy regime was Richmond P. Hobson, representative of Alabama, congressional sponsor of the Defense Secrets Act of 1911, and an apostle of US imperialism. A staunch Methodist and a sanctimonious teetotaler, Hobson had spent his life bouncing from one moral crusade to another. When his peers back at the Naval Academy snuck a verboten cigarette, Hobson so routinely tattled that the entire class ostracized him. It was the stuff of boarding-school nightmares—no one spoke to him for *two years*—but Hobson was unbending. No need for friends, he said: "The highest and truest happiness . . . can come only in the path of rectitude and duty." He would later write the first draft of America's Prohibition law.[29]

Like Van Deman, Hobson's career was made by America's imperial wars at the turn of the century. Serving off the coast of Cuba, he volunteered to head a foolhardy mission to sink the *Merrimac*, an American coal ship, at a choke point at the entrance to Santiago Harbor and thus to trap what remained of the Spanish fleet. It wasn't a good plan, and it went very wrong. Defensive fire from the Spanish ruined both the *Merrimac*'s rudder and some of Hobson's detonators. The explosion that was supposed to sink the ship didn't. The *Merrimac* drifted helplessly away from the choke point, sinking slowly but pointlessly. Hobson and the seven members of his team spent the night bobbing in the water, clinging to an overturned catamaran, before they were captured by the Spanish. After a month in jail, they were released, a little bored, but none the worse for wear. In the interim, the United States had won the war. There hadn't been a need to sink the *Merrimac* after all. US naval superiority had been sufficient to keep the enemy blockaded in the harbor; when the Spanish fleet had tried to break out, it had been sunk.[30]

But the American public was on a slightly desperate search for war heroes—glorious victory in that "splendid little war" had happened so quickly that there was little actual glory to go around. Heroes had to be manufactured, and Hobson was close enough. The botched sinking of the *Merrimac* was compared to the Charge of the Light Brigade and the stand of the Spartans at Thermopylae. "This new bit of history," opined one newspaper in Ohio, "demonstrates that we are a nation of heroes."[31]

Hobson was rapidly promoted and sent on a national speaking tour. Before one of the talks, he was kissed on the cheek by two cousins, which soon became a craze whipped on by a sensationalist press: before speeches, he would be kissed by hundreds of female fans. Hobson, who was considered unbearably handsome by the admittedly mysterious standards of the Progressive Era, was dubbed the "Most Kissed Man in America" and the "Hero of the Merry

Richmond P. Hobson (circa 1898), hero of the *Merrimac*, "most-kissed man in America," and future congressional sponsor of the Defense Secrets Act. (Library of Congress)

Smack." There was a Hobson's Waltz, and a Hobson's Choice cigar, and a candy named, predictably enough, Hobson's Kiss.

The ambitious young man liked the limelight and gave hundreds of speeches on the lecture circuit before running successfully for Congress in 1906. He had just one big, powerful talking point—he wanted the United States to have a big, powerful navy. His reasons were simple. In the early 1890s, at the start of his career as a naval engineer, Hobson had gone to Asia as an observer of the Sino-Japanese War. Struck by the sheer size of the population in China and Japan, intimidated by what he took to be an inherent Asian inclination to hard work, he became convinced that only overwhelming naval superiority would maintain US power in the Pacific. War between the races was coming, "of a magnitude to keep the earth drenched in blood from pole to pole." If the United States wanted access to the markets of Asia, if it wanted to preserve its newly won holdings in the Philippines and Hawaii, if it wanted to prevent a Japanese invasion of the West Coast, it needed to step up to the plate. The "Yellow Peril," warned the handsome naval hero, was a real threat.[32]

Hobson thus became one of the main authors of America's version of the spy scare. As was the case in the German spy scare happening simultaneously in England, fictional fears of Asian invasion were becoming the basis for very real political developments. In 1897 one typical novel—a form of early science fiction more than a spy story—had imagined that a global race war would be triggered by Japanese spies infiltrating Hawaii.[33]

Hobson was saying much the same thing. In 1908 he distilled his many speeches on the Japanese threat into a three-part article that ran in *Cosmopolitan*. As in England, fiction was being laundered into fact. Hobson's articles were "brilliant," proclaimed the middlebrow magazine, and "no work of the imagination": "Captain Hobson is one of the greatest living experts in the science of war, and every move described in these pages is the result of careful study."

Move 1 was already under way: "the swarming of spies" across the West Coast and "our possessions"—Hawaii and the Philippines. (No surprises here, Hobson added: the "Japanese are masters in the inspection and spying out of the naval and military preparations of other nations.") Move 2: the rapid deployment of Japanese forces—200,000 troops would be in Hawaii in two weeks, he said, 500,000 on the West Coast within four months. Move 3: those crack troops—veterans of wars against China and Russia, wielding a terrifying combination of feudal discipline, Asiatic self-sacrifice, and modern weaponry—would unite with the "compact, disciplined Japanese clubs" that immigrant communities had formed on US soil and easily occupy key points across the Pacific. Move 4 was checkmate: the United States would be "thrown open to Chinese and Hindus as well as Japanese, and with the ocean open the white population of the [Pacific] slope would soon be overcome." The race war would be over before the US had even mobilized.[34]

The story, and its sci-fi cousins, reflected the xenophobic paranoia of the time. Fears of Asian immigration were rampant—when the United States barred Chinese immigrants in 1882, Japanese migrants became repositories for all the clichéd nativist fears of slavish, inscrutable Asians. And then in 1905 Japan had the temerity to beat the Russians in a war, a sign that the days of Euro-American military supremacy were numbered. White Americans on the West Coast panicked. In 1906 San Francisco announced it would segregate all

Asian students in its schools, which triggered a diplomatic incident. Japanese protestations looked to nativists like an effort to gin up an excuse for war. Letters poured into the government complaining that Japanese neighbors were acting suspiciously. A mob of angry Californians attacked a Japanese bathhouse and restaurant.

Matters calmed down only when Teddy Roosevelt signed a "gentleman's agreement" with the Japanese government: Japan would be spared the indignity of formal exclusion or segregation, and would in exchange voluntarily restrict the emigration of its citizens to the United States. Hobson was stunned by TR's willingness to sacrifice local control over education to a foreign power: "No free nation in the history of the world has ever suffered such deep, real humiliation as we have suffered at the hands of Japan. We have surrendered the most sacred principle in all the institutions of liberty at the dictation of a power across the Pacific Ocean, a power of an alien race, an oriental absolutism." Such a show of weakness, Hobson thought, simply invited further Japanese intervention.[35]

In 1910, at a time when he was publicly guaranteeing that the United States would be at war with Japan within ten months, Hobson introduced the Defense Secrets Act to Congress. Based loosely on British statutes, the law made it illegal for individuals who were "not lawfully entitled" to information to go to a variety of places connected with the national defense: naval yards, forts, vessels, factories, etc. It also made it illegal to communicate information "connected with the national defense" to someone who lacked authorization to receive it. It was a vague and imprecise law that did not define any of the key terms—what it meant for information to be "connected with the national defense" and how one got authorization to access such information. But the law gave the state new powers to punish individuals with up to a year in prison if they violated it, and up to ten years if they tried to pass information to a foreign government.[36]

To build the case for the law, Hobson mobilized examples of espionage supplied by allies in the intelligence branches of the army and navy. There were stories of spies around the imperial periphery, in Cuba and Panama and especially the Philippines, where engineers had been bribed for photographs of defensive fortifications. A man in Calcutta had found secret blueprints of the forts in Manila Bay, apparently stolen from US files. There were even more reports of Japanese spies on the West Coast, often mailed in by amateur volunteers who had seen—or who had friends who had seen—Japanese men copying records from the Land Office in Los Angeles or mapping the coasts and the borders while pretending to be fishing or prospecting. The details of the incidents remained vague, for military intelligence insisted that they had to be kept secret. But the process was no different from what had happened in England. As Americans began distrusting their Japanese neighbors, they fed their fears to both a conservative press, which spun lurid tales of spies, and to a small cluster of security hawks, who gave them the stamp of official sanction.[37]

It was hardly the most convincing case. Looking over the evidence, the *New York Times* concluded that the threat of espionage was "likely to be much exaggerated." But it was enough to convince Congress that the Defense Secrets Act was "of great and imperative importance and should be enacted into law at the earliest possible date."[38]

In early 1911, Hobson's law passed without congressional debate. It was, for the first time, a sweeping peacetime secrecy law, one that was written broadly to combat a nebulous threat of espionage.

Only five years later, the attorney general was already recommending the passage of a new law to make it illegal to obtain or communicate information relating to the national defense. "The necessity of legislation of this nature against spies is obvious," declared the Wilson administration, because the 1911 act was "incomplete and defective."[39]

The obvious reason for this shift in standards was the outbreak of World War I. As the United States struggled to maintain formal neutrality while providing aid to the Allied war effort, it was inevitable that it would become a setting for covert operations. But as was so often the case, the inflated demands for security far outstripped the actual threat posed by spies.

Even by the low standards of the era, the German espionage campaign in the US was a shambolic, amateurish effort. German spies conducted no political intelligence operations and didn't even try to gain access to secret documents. Instead, they aimed to disrupt the flow of military equipment to the Allies. At first, they did so by creating dummy corporations that would try to buy up supplies so that Allies could not purchase them; they would also pretend to take orders for Allied governments and then fail to deliver them. But in July 1915, the attaché responsible for running these operations accidentally left a briefcase full of plans on a New York subway car, where they were picked up by a watching Secret Service agent and promptly leaked to the press.

Thereafter, the Germans relied mostly on sabotage. They tried to foment strikes at munitions plants and sought to inject livestock bound for Europe with infectious diseases (a plan that did work initially but was easily prevented by heightened security at stockyards). Mostly, they blew things up—most famously the shipping and storage terminal at Black Tom Island in Jersey City, which was a choke point in the logistical chains connecting US industry to the European war. When it erupted at 2 a.m. on July 30, 1916, it shattered windows across Manhattan and into Brooklyn, caused twenty million dollars' worth of damage, killed three people, and injured one hundred more, along with however many of the city's homeless population were living undocumented and uncounted on barges nearby.[40]

Combined with a program to place pro-German propaganda in American newspapers, these crude efforts maintained an atmosphere of moral panic about foreign infiltration. And in March 1917, when the United States began arresting radical Indian activists for violating America's neutrality laws, old fears about imperial vulnerability to immigrants were also reanimated. Those activists, mostly based on the West Coast, had taken German money to fund the running of

guns back into the British Empire, planning to trigger an armed rebellion. Apart from a brief uprising in Singapore in 1915, such efforts
were suppressed effectively by British and American counterintelligence agencies, which had collaborated in surveilling the diaspora
of radical anticolonialists. What became known as the "Hindu Conspiracy" trial—despite the fact that the majority of the players were
Sikh, not Hindu—was nevertheless a reminder of the old fears of a
global coalition against Anglo-American imperialism. It helped consolidate a fear of "Hindu" radicalism that justified new restrictions on
Indian immigration in 1917.[41]

Given the success with which these "spy" operations had been
shut down, given especially that they had posed no threat to
national-security information, there was no obvious need for a new
secrecy law. But under the pressure of war, a new culture of security consciousness had taken root, and the figure of the "spy" was no
longer simply a threat to military intelligence. Instead, fanned on
by fears of foreign subversion, counterespionage was expanding to
include a variety of projects aimed at increasing security.

The process could be seen most clearly, once again, in Britain. In
August 1914, in the first days of the war, British counterintelligence
officers had quickly and efficiently arrested a small and inept German
spy ring. (Only one of the twenty-one arrestees was ever brought to
trial, a sign of how little espionage they had actually conducted.)
But when the home secretary boasted of this intelligence coup to the
press, it made no dent in the cultural assumption that the nation was
infested with spies. Such easy success "does not square with what
we know of the German spy system," huffed the *Times*; after all,
the Germans were a "race of spies." Le Queux and Lord Northcliffe
continued to publish sensationalist, best-selling stories exposing the
threat. In 1918 one MP claimed he had come into possession of a
"black book" listing the 47,000 sexual perverts in the government
who were being blackmailed by German agents. The political pressure remained on the security branches.[42]

In fact, the definition of an espionage threat expanded. "Contra
Espionage goes far beyond the business of detecting foreign spies,"

explained Basil Thomson, who headed Scotland Yard's Special Branch and would soon become Britain's first director of intelligence. "Enemy intrigue ramifies in every direction."[43]

To begin with, Thomson explained, the counterintelligence officer needed to pay attention to "aliens." Fear of spies, as always intertwined with the fear of the foreigner, led to the wartime internment of 32,000 enemy aliens in Great Britain. (Along with many minor acts of discrimination. When one Austrian-born British citizen tried to register his pigeons, as required under the Defense of the Realm Act, the police came and killed them.) Counterespionage also required, Thomson asserted, paying attention to "revolutionary matters"—for political radicals threatened security and were often funded by foreign intelligence officers—and even to "labor unrest," which could be whipped on by foreign propaganda and which would undermine the war effort. Those new security bureaucracies that had emerged out of the spy scares of the prewar years spent the war surveilling aliens and labor activists and pacifists and anyone else who seemed to have politics out of line with their vision of the imperial interest. The line between counterintelligence and political policing, always blurry, had effectively dissolved.[44]

A similar process was at work in the United States, and it explained the desire to replace the Defense Secrets Act with a new espionage act. Robert Lansing, Wilson's secretary of state, called for "legislation covering foreign intrigues in our internal affairs such as conspiracies to blow up factories, to encourage strikes, to interfere with industrial operations, to gather information of this government's secrets, etc." In a 1916 speech to the National Security League that was reprinted in the *North American Review* and the *New York Times*, Democratic politician John B. Stanchfield took, like Thomson, a broad view of the "Peril of Espionage." The spy, Stanchfield argued, was no longer an "erratic adventurer setting forth in war to discover and ferret out the military moves and plans of the emperor." Instead, the work of the secret service agent had become "prosaic and intensely systematic," waged in peace and in war, aimed at all manner of disruptions to the national defense: "Besides preventing the discovery of data concerning military affairs and state secrets, we must prepare to meet the danger of the actual destruction by spies of the instrumentalities of our Government and of their positive interference with every kind of internal measure designed for our national protection."[45]

Every kind of internal measure designed for our national protection— that covered a lot. It meant the need to protect fortresses and battleships and railroads and telephone wires from sabotage. It meant protecting all plants, factories, mills, and mines that might play any role in a wartime economy, protecting them not only from "actual physical destruction" but "the maintenance of secrecy as to their processes and capacity [and] also the duty of securing them against paralysis produced by the fomenting of strikes." To try to organize a labor strike in any part of the economy, in this view, was a form of foreign subversion of the war effort. So was trying to glean any information about any part of the nation's defense economy.

Given this expansive vision of security, it was little wonder that Stanchfield considered the Defense Secrets Act deficient. He thought that three improvements were urgent: (1) "the adoption of a policy of greater secrecy"; (2) "the adoption and development of a system of counter-espionage, in other words, a secret service engaged in . . . the occupation of watching and spying on spies"; and (3) "punitive legislation"—i.e., a new espionage act.

Within the administration, such a law was being prepared by Assistant Attorney General Charles Warren, who had broad responsibilities for matters relating to neutrality and internal security. A patrician from New England, Warren had been one of the founders of the Immigration Restriction League, and he carried his antipathy to foreigners into his work on wartime security. He was an advocate of summarily arresting and interning enemy aliens and of barring the publication of all German-language newspapers. Later, once America had entered the war, Warren would push for new laws that would allow for the court-martial of civilians suspected of a broad array of subversive behavior. "One man shot after court martial," he said, "is worth a hundred arrests." That was so controversial that he was forced to resign from the administration in April 1918. (He failed up, going on to write a Pulitzer Prize–winning history of the Supreme Court that established him as the nation's leading legal historian.[46])

In 1916, when he was still in the administration's good graces, Warren prepared fourteen separate statutes aimed at securing the nation from his broad vision of foreign threats; in early 1917 they were consolidated into one omnibus espionage law. Espionage provided a synecdoche for a broad new vision of security. The Espionage Act gave the president new powers to regulate passports and the departure of private vessels, made it illegal to impersonate US officials or fraudulently use US seals, and allowed the president to ban the export of certain goods essential to the war effort.[47]

At the heart of the Espionage Act were unprecedented measures to control the US public sphere. One important section made it illegal to interfere with the draft; another provided the postmaster general with authority to regulate the mail. Both reflected the belief that some forms of speech needed to be censored in order to effectively wage the war.

Crucially, the first two sections of the act replaced the 1911 Defense Secrets Act and expanded the regulation of "information relating to the national defense." The new law had much harsher penalties—collecting such information, once punishable by a year in jail or a $1,000 fine, was now to be met with two years in jail or a $10,000 fine; transferring such information to a foreigner, once punishable by ten years in jail, could now be punished by twenty years in times of peace and by death in times of war. It also became illegal to obtain information from a wider variety of locations— whereas the 1911 act had named eleven types of places, the 1917 law added an additional thirteen: dockyards, submarine bases, mines, telegraph stations, and so forth. And Section 6 of the proposed new law gave the president authority to unilaterally declare other sorts of information as "relating to the national defense," a proviso that would allow these sections to expand, accordion-like, to cover ever-vaster areas.

When the Senate began considering the new law in February, it proved controversial. Particularly troubling to critics was Section 2(c), which gave the president the power to ban the publication or communication of any information "relating to the public defense." The phrase went undefined; it is not clear if its authors thought it meant something different from "information relating to the national defense." But that wasn't the major problem with the clause. For Section 2(c) was a general censorship law.

Perhaps no one was more offended by the Espionage Act than Senator Albert B. Cummins. On February 17 the elegant, aloof lawyer from Iowa took to the Senate floor to attack what he thought was a "monstrous" bill, one that sought to establish government powers "that the tyrants of the olden times never dared to exercise." "Whoever is responsible" for the law, Cummins thought, "does not understand American liberty at all, and has no sympathy with our institutions. He is imagining that we have returned to a time when the citizens of the country are to be kept in absolute ignorance of all public matters pertaining to the national defense." Cummins tried to introduce fourteen different amendments to the law to make it more palatable, but he had little success. When he began to realize that his colleagues supported the law as drafted, Cummins complained that they had "gone mad. We have forgotten that we live in a Republic. We are thinking only of German spies and English spies."[48]

Cummins wasn't a firebrand or a radical, and he wasn't given to performative martyrdom. He was not the kind of politician to champion "forlorn hopes to make a record for a cause," the *Nation* observed, but the "kind of public man who can always be relied upon to do the well-considered thing." Over the course of his career, his cautious pragmatism had produced a more progressive politician than those familiar with his personal conservatism might have predicted. He had made his name as a lawyer representing Populist farmers in their struggle against a barbed-wire monopoly. As governor of Iowa, he enacted a Progressive program to curtail the excesses of corporate consolidation and exploitation; as senator, he favored measures to expand the power of the federal government to protect the public welfare. Throughout, Cummins retained a key belief in democratic self-governance—he favored women's suffrage and the direct election of senators—and was deeply opposed to the consolidation of autonomous executive power and the rise of militarism.[49]

So the Espionage Act stuck in his craw. "If the Czar of Russia were to see this law," Cummins complained, "he would feel greatly offended to think that he could not put a similar one into effect." Section 2(c)'s censorship provision was particularly troubling because it meant that "the president can absolutely command silence in the U.S. upon every subject" he so desired. Cummins thought it was "an absolute suppression of free speech" and "an absolute overthrow of a free press."[50]

The champions of the bill did not dispute this interpretation of the scope of Section 2(c). Warren was asked by a congressional committee whether the clause was "broad enough . . . to permit the sealing up of everything." "Yes," he replied, "it is broad enough for the President to exercise the power to seal up everything." "I do not see why we should limit the power of the President," added Senator Lee Overman, who was steering the bill through the Senate. "We are giving a great deal of power to the President; and I think he ought to have it."[51]

This was typical of Overman's attitude to presidential authority. A close confidant of Wilson, Overman was a Democratic Party loyalist whose political rise had begun in the segregationist movement that "redeemed" North Carolina in the 1870s and culminated, thanks to the blessings of a seat made safe by Jim Crow, in leadership positions in key Senate committees. Now he warned darkly that the nation was being swarmed by a hundred thousand German spies, that constitutional rights were worth nothing if the government were to fall, that you would not have a constitution if you did not have a country. "If we cannot give such power" to the president, Overman thought, "then God help this country."[52]

Overman's alarmism seemed sufficient to carry the day. After four days, the Senate voted by a margin of sixty to ten to pass the law—including the controversial censorship Section 2(c). But the law never came up for debate in the House before the 64th Congress adjourned two weeks later.[53]

Before Congress could again take up the bill, the United States had entered the war. During the debate over Section 2(c), the Germans had resumed unrestricted submarine warfare in the Atlantic; the week after the Senate had passed the Espionage Act, the British had leaked to the United States the Zimmerman telegram, in which the Germans had sought an alliance with Mexico in exchange for the return of land in Arizona, Texas, and New Mexico that the United States had conquered in 1848.[54]

On April 2, Wilson called Congress into special session to ask for a declaration of war. Among his many reasons for the war were vague and exaggerated claims that Germany had "filled our unsuspecting communities and even our office of government with spies and set criminal intrigues everywhere afoot against our national unity." (Ironically, almost all of the German spy operations in the United States had by then ceased, having rolled up operations in January, when submarine warfare resumed.) Within days of the declaration of war on April 6, the Wilson administration was asking Congress to hurry up and pass the Espionage Act.[55]

By then, the newspaper industry had rallied against Section 2(c). Newspaper representatives met privately with the Justice Department to lobby against the section, their professional societies passed resolutions condemning it, and papers across the country attacked the law on their editorial pages. The *New York Times*, which ran no fewer than seven editorials opposing the clause, thought it was "Prussian," a "monstrous abuse of authority," and "an insidious assault upon the very foundations which underlie our free institutions."[56]

The press rightly feared that Section 2(c) would impinge directly on its freedom to publish news of the war and rushed to argue that such censorship would harm both democracy and the war effort. Much was made of the fact that the press's ability to uncover incompetence and corruption in the armed forces would be impaired by Section 2(c), which would have criminalized such important spurs to military reform as Lord Northcliffe's recent exposés of ammunition shortages at the British front or the revelation that US soldiers had been provided with low-quality, "embalmed" beef during the Spanish-American War in 1898.

The press onslaught—as well as a petition signed by 600,000 Americans—made its mark on the Hill. On May 12 many members crossed the floor as the Senate voted narrowly, 39–38, to cut Section 2(c) from the law. The week before, the House had voted by a larger margin to cut the section from its version of the law. The administration continued to push for it, Wilson going so far as to send a public letter to Congress declaring that Section 2(c) was "necessary for the protection of the nation." But it had lost the fight.[57]

On June 7 the Espionage Act, without the odious censorship clause, was passed through Congress.[58]

Superficially, this was a victory for American democracy. An effort to extend the power of the presidency to regulate the public sphere had been turned aside, and the Espionage Act would leave the media free to report on affairs relating to national defense. The contrast with Great Britain was edifying. There, the Official Secrets Act most definitely applied to the press, and the threat of prosecution hung so menacingly over the practice of journalism that it forced the news industry and the government to develop a workaround—the D-Notice committee, a secretive, voluntary arrangement in which the government gave the press private notice of ostensibly secret items that it could publish and of those that, for the honor and security of the empire, it should not.[59]

But if one dug a little deeper, the US story was murkier. The pressure to pass such a sweeping censorship bill and the hasty way in which amendments had been made had produced a poorly drawn, ambiguous law. The abolition of Section 2(c) seemed to exempt the press from prosecution, but other sections of the law seemed to leave the door open. For instance, Section 794(b), which made it illegal to communicate information to the enemy during war, explicitly listed "publishing" as one form of banned communication. That clause seemed designed to cover traditional espionage—a spy slipping a story into a German-owned paper, for instance—not the inadvertent communication to the enemy that might happen if a journalist published a story for the benefit of the public. But it wasn't clear, and the congressional debate, which focused more on Section 2(c), had not done anything to clarify it. Meanwhile, Section 793(d), which made it illegal to "willfully communicate" information relating to the national defense to those not authorized to receive it, seemed on its face like it *would* cover the press—but perhaps the absence of the word *publish* in this section was intended to exempt newspapers?

If you tried to answer such questions, you would quickly stumble on an even bigger problem. The various clauses of Section 793 all took the same form—they made it illegal to gather "information relating to the national defense" without authorization or to communicate such information to those unauthorized to receive it. But the law defined neither part of that formulation: it never said what it meant by "information relating to the national defense" or defined a process by which one was authorized to receive it. Both phrases had ended up in the law by default, having been copied from the Defense Secrets Act of 1911, which had been inspired by similar formulations in the British Official Secrets Act. They had never been really thought through. When Warren was writing the 1917 law, he had been dissatisfied with them but unable to come up with anything better.[60] The plan seems to have been to clarify their meaning by giving the authority to the president to define information as "relating to national defense," but in conference that section was cut from the bill as part of the broader reaction against presidential overreach that had seen the elimination of Section 2(c). It seems that

Congress didn't want to give the president unilateral authority to determine if something was "information relating to the national defense," although it never came out and explained exactly why it cut those sections.

The move introduced a foundational uncertainty into the Espionage Act, one that would haunt the law to the present day. "Information relating to the national defense" is a broad and nebulous phrase, made only more so by the fact that one section of the bill actually uses a different phrase: "information relating to the public defense." An early version of the House bill did make an effort to define "national defense," but it offered only a nondefinition: "any person, place, or thing in anywise having to do with the preparation for or the consideration or execution of any military or naval plans, expeditions, orders, supplies or warfare for the advantage, defense or security of the U.S." In any case, that clause had also been cut without a clear explanation. Whether members of Congress thought it simply commonsensical and hence unnecessary and superfluous, or objectionably broad, was unclear.[61]

The Espionage Act was on the books; what it meant was far from certain.

The first clash between state secrecy and America's commitment to civil liberties had produced, above all, confusion. New secrecy laws had been passed, motivated by exaggerated fears of foreign spies. The Wilson administration had sought such sweeping powers that it had forced Congress and the newspaper industry to draw a line in the sand. But the effort to protect civil liberties from government overreach had prevented any serious consideration of the meaning of the secrecy laws. Rushed revisions had left key provisions without clear meaning.

In the medium term, trying to make sense of these orphaned provisions would cause the emerging national-security state numerous headaches as it struggled to work out how to apply such a confusing law. Decades later, security hawks would come to find the law's ambiguity a blessing.

But in the short term, all eyes would be on other sections of the law, aimed at Americans with less institutional clout than the newspaper industry. During the war the state would use the Espionage Act not to protect secrets but to police the speech of dissidents.

Chapter 2

THE SPEECH CRIMES
OF EUGENE DEBS

Eugene V. Debs, mid-speech, sometime between 1912 and 1918. (Library of Congress, photograph by International News Photos)

E ARLY IN THE SECOND SUMMER OF THE WAR, EUGENE DEBS GAVE
the picnicking members of the Socialist Party of Ohio a hell of a
speech. He was sixty-three and not in the best of health, but he threw
himself into the performance, stretching out over the platform to com-
mune directly with the crowd in Nimisilla Park, reaching out with his
hands to emphasize his points. "It felt exactly," one of the members of
the audience said, "as if that forefinger was hitting you on the nose."

We have no recording of the speech. In fact, we have no recordings of any of the speeches that Debs gave over his long career as a
labor activist and perennial presidential candidate for the Socialist
Party. So it is hard to know why this gaunt man, dressed in the bow
tie and collar of a small-town professional, looking more than a little
like the dour farmer in Grant Wood's *American Gothic*, was such a
captivating orator. Yet Debs had a "voice that could do with a crowd
what it willed," according to novelist Ernest Poole, "not because of
the mind behind it, but because of the great warm heart which the
crowd felt speaking there." "Most of all," recalled another devotee, "I
remember his intensity and what seemed to me to be his quivering
sensitiveness to pain."[1]

Whatever the key to Debs's charisma, at least one man in the
crowd in Canton was unmoved on that June afternoon in 1918.
Clyde Miller was no Socialist. In fact, he thought that Socialists
were traitors who were undermining the war effort. And the war
effort was something that Miller took very seriously. Even before
the United States had entered World War I the previous year, Miller
had been up for the fight and tried to enlist in the Canadian Army,
only to be rejected for poor eyesight, a condition that had doomed
his multiple efforts to enlist in the US Army as well. He had done
his part instead on the home front. He had joined the American
Protective League, a patriotic organization that acted as an auxiliary
to the wartime security state, and he participated in raids on immigrant homes in Cleveland, looking for dissidents. In his day job—
he was a journalist at the *Cleveland Plain Dealer*—he had written
lurid front-page stories that whipped up fears of spies, saboteurs, and
slackers. And those guilty of the crime of sedition.[2]

Miller had come to watch Debs's speech to gather evidence that he could use against the most famous Socialist in America. He had cornered Debs earlier that day, trying to get the politician on record saying something that could be interpreted as opposing the war. But Debs had seen the trap and batted Miller's questions away. Debs was coy during his speech, too. "It is extremely dangerous to exercise the constitutional right of free speech in a country fighting to make democracy safe in the world," he had explained, to knowing laughter from the crowd, so "I must be exceedingly careful, prudent in what I say, and even more prudent as to how I say it. I may not be able to say all I think, but I am not going to say anything that I do not think."[3]

Still, given his politics, Debs could not avoid speaking out in solidarity with his Socialist comrades who had been persecuted for their criticism of the war. For instance, Rose Pastor Stokes had been sentenced to ten years in jail for declaring that she was for the people, not the profiteers who were running the government. "Stokes never uttered a word she did not have a legal, constitutional right to utter," Debs asserted. If she was "guilty of crime, so am I."[4]

Amid the slim pickings of what was otherwise a run-of-the-mill Socialist stump speech, this was about as close to sedition as Miller could find. In Miller's mind, Debs had been all but taunting the law. So when the pro-war journalist called his story into the editorial room, this was his main angle. "Debs Invites Arrest" was the headline the next day.[5]

Two weeks later, Debs was arrested in Cleveland on his way to address another Socialist meeting. For his speech in Nimisilla Park, he was charged with violating the Espionage Act, found guilty, and sentenced to ten years in jail. There had been no suggestion that Debs had committed anything close to "espionage" as we commonly understand the term. There was no suspicion that he was spying, no allegations that the midwesterner was in hock to a foreign power.

Rather, the Espionage Act had been used, as it was used more than two thousand times during the war, to punish radical antiwar speech. Today, this would be a remarkable violation of First Amendment rights. But at the time it was unsurprising. The First

Amendment did not yet have its modern luster; the speech rights of Americans could be restricted if they were seen to harm the common good. During the war, this meant that antiwar speech was beyond the pale—it was seen as an interference with the war, an aid to the enemy, little different from spying or sabotage. If a speech caused laborers to go on strike, disrupting war production, how was that any different in its effects from blowing the factory up? Both were, in the minds of the Wilson administration, a form of "espionage."

And in the censorious minds of people like Miller, it didn't take much to rise to the level of "antiwar speech," particularly when the speakers were political radicals like Debs. For decades, in fact, radical labor activists had struggled to defend their rights to free speech against both state censorship and violent suppression by self-appointed patriots like Miller.

Debs's arrest marked the crescendo of this much longer struggle over the meaning of free speech in a democracy roiled by class conflict. The story of the Espionage Act during World War I was not an episode in the history of intelligence and counterintelligence, but a turning point in the long and violent struggle between labor and the capitalist state in industrializing America.

1918 was not the first time Debs had served time for speech crimes. Twenty-four years earlier, in 1894, he had been sentenced to six months in Woodstock jail in Illinois for encouraging workers to strike against the Pullman Company. The strike had begun when George Pullman, who had made a fortune leasing luxury sleeping cars to rail lines, slashed wages during the depression of 1893 without reducing the cost of living in Pullman, his company town just south of Chicago. It had escalated when the American Railway Union, a national union that Debs had organized the previous year, refused to handle any trains featuring Pullman cars. And it had become a crisis when a coalition of rail companies vowed to fire any workers participating in the boycott. Within weeks, 125,000 workers were on strike. The nation's train system screeched to a halt.

On this national stage, the bosses had a trump. Richard Olney, the nation's attorney general, had made his career as a corporate attorney for the rail companies, and he still served on some of their boards. Olney now argued that the boycott threatened to interfere with the delivery of the mail, an issue of concern to the federal government. When rail companies cleverly began hitching Pullman cars to all mail cars, the boycotters were checkmated. The federal government won a court order that prevented labor leaders from organizing the boycott; any such efforts, the court ruled, constituted an interference with the mail and a violation of federal law.[6]

Then the government sent in federal troops to force delivery of the mail. The troops were under the command of Nelson Miles, a Civil War veteran who had made his name waging violent war against Native Americans in the West. He crushed the strike, his troops killing thirteen strikers and wounding fifty-seven others. "It was not the soldiers that ended the strike," Debs clarified; "it was simply the United States courts that ended the strike."[7]

Debs himself was arrested and found guilty of disobeying the court's injunction against the strikers. Technically, he was guilty. The injunction had been sweeping, rendering it illegal to make any effort to direct, incite, encourage, or persuade anyone to "refuse to perform the duties of their employment." The court had successfully made it illegal to say the sorts of things that one needed to say to organize a strike.[8]

The case reflected the central dynamics of free-speech law in the decades before World War I. Today, we think of the First Amendment as providing a general right for all speakers to articulate their views without fear of retribution from the state. The way we enforce that right is to go to the courts, which rule on the basis of abstract principle to make sure that as many voices as possible can be heard, regardless of how popular or unpopular they may be—even if the majority of the population may think those voices contribute little to public life, or may actually be a nuisance, or actively harmful. Think of the Westboro Baptist Church, whose homophobic, inflammatory protests at military funerals were recognized as having "special protection" under the First Amendment by the Supreme Court in 2011.[9]

That's not how the First Amendment worked during Debs's life. Although it was the case, even then, that the amendment read, "Congress shall make no law abridging the freedom of speech, or freedom of the press," everyone understood that the right to free speech had very clear limits.

In his influential 1833 *Commentaries on the Constitution of the United States*, Joseph Story had explained the common understanding of the First Amendment: "That this amendment was intended to secure to every citizen an absolute right to speak, or write, or print, whatever he might please, without any responsibility, public or private therefor, is a supposition too wild to be indulged by any rational man." When state constitutions provided for a right to free speech, they too clarified that citizens would be "responsible for the abuse of that right." In 1900 the Connecticut Supreme Court quite bluntly reasserted that "the liberty protected is not the right to perpetuate acts of licentiousness, or any act inconsistent with the peace or safety of the state."[10]

Throughout the nineteenth century, speech rights were therefore strictly curtailed when they were seen to undermine or abuse the public good. In practice, of course, the "public good" was defined by those in power. So in the antebellum South, abolitionist material was outlawed. Criticism of public officials could be met by criminal charges for libel. In the middle decades of the nineteenth century, material that was considered "obscene" was banned by state law and prohibited from the mail by federal law—meaning it was illegal to mail even basic information about birth control.[11]

To modern ears, all that censorship may seem to make a mockery of the very language of the First Amendment. If unpopular speech could be punished, what did the First Amendment actually protect? There are two answers to this question. The first is that even if the First Amendment did not protect you from being punished for your speech, it did protect your right to speak in the first place. This was not just jurisprudential sophistry—the First Amendment established a well-respected prohibition against prepublication censorship, what is known as "prior restraint." The right to publish without prior approval, without review by a board of censors, was an important right, not to be taken for granted. When members of Congress worried that the press-censorship provisions of the Espionage Act threatened press freedom, for instance, it was precisely because they feared it would establish just such a system of prior restraint, and for this reason they eliminated those sections of the bill.

The second answer is more abstract but perhaps more important. When we say that the First Amendment protects "freedom of speech," we don't mean that it protects every last speech act. Even today, when US laws protect the most expansive vision of free speech in world history, no one thinks twice when people are charged for insider trading, for conspiracy to commit a crime, for blackmail, for breaching patient or client confidentiality. All these crimes involve speaking, but none of them are considered violations of "freedom of speech." Like all legal terms, "freedom of speech" has borders— it covers some speech acts but not others. How those borders are defined change over time. What is considered "freedom of speech" worthy of protection and what is considered speech that falls outside of constitutional protection differ from one period to the next. They are the product of political struggle, of philosophical debate, and of legal recalibration. They are the product, in other words, of history.[12]

This is what was at stake in Debs's prosecution in the Pullman case. The words he used to organize the boycott were not seen as "freedom of speech" but as the abuse of that right, a criminal act, an effort to conspire to obstruct interstate commerce of the rail and the delivery of the mail. It was a problem that labor organizers faced time and again in the decades around 1900. In 1907 Samuel Gompers, a rival labor leader and head of the more conservative American Federation of Labor, tried to organize a consumer boycott in support of a strike at Buck's Stove and Range Corporation. But as was typical of the era, the corporation won an injunction banning the boycott, and Gompers was sentenced to jail for sending out a pamphlet adding the company to a "we don't patronize" list. When

Gompers tried to claim that such a court order violated his right to free speech, the Supreme Court scoffed at the suggestion. There was speech that was protected by the First Amendment, the justices suggested, and then there were "verbal acts . . . exceeding any possible right of speech which a single individual might have."

Or, as a spokesperson for the National Association of Manufacturers put it, there was no difference between "enjoin[ing] the use of [a man's] hands or his feet or his head to do some unlawful thing . . . [and getting] the injunction in connection with the use of the tongue."[13]

As part of their effort to organize the working class and thus remake American society, labor activists needed to expand the sorts of speech that were included in the "freedom of speech" protected by the First Amendment. Otherwise, they would find their every attempt to organize and advocate declared illegal. So the primary free-speech activists of Debs's era came from the ranks of radical labor. In the increasingly violent, bare-knuckle conflict over the economic order of Gilded Age America, more radical free-speech claims and more radical labor demands ratcheted up together.

Debs himself reflected the general trend. He had not originally been a radical. Born in a middle-class house to French immigrants in Terre Haute, Indiana, Eugene Victor Debs had always been a believer in populist republicanism. He was named for Eugene Sue and Victor Hugo; *Les Misérables* and the philosophy of Tom Paine were guiding lights.

Debs also had a lifelong romance with work on the railroad. He had dropped out of school to work as a paint scraper for a rail company—he kept his first tool his entire life—and then worked for a short time as a rail fireman (a dangerous job that involved not the putting out of fires but stoking the flames that powered the steam engines). When a close friend fell on the tracks and died, Debs returned to Terre Haute to work as a white-collar clerk. He was soon secretary for the Brotherhood of Firemen, one of the many fraternal societies that peppered the workforce in the era before unions and that operated as mutual-aid societies and hiring organizations. These were not militant organizations. Like the rest of their leadership, Debs still believed that harmonious relations between management and labor were both possible and desirable. He thought that the Great Rail Strike of 1877 was unnecessarily divisive.

As Debs approached middle age and took up a prominent position as the editor of the national *Firemen's Magazine*, the increasingly violent struggles between capital and labor began to radicalize him. The rail and steel barons of the Gilded Age were building ostentatious homes, reveling in untold wealth, even as they paid their employees a pittance for hard, dangerous work. At least 35,000 per year were dying in industrial accidents; hundreds of thousands more suffered brutal injuries at work; untold numbers were malnourished or exposed to industrial waste and died young.[14]

When workers tried to band together to win better wages and better work conditions, the elite called in the power of the state, violently securing the status quo. In 1892, when a mining strike in the Coeur d'Alene district of Idaho turned violent, martial law was declared. The strikers were arrested and held in temporary bullpens for months, until the strike was broken. In the same year, violence erupted in Homestead, Pennsylvania, when unionized workers were locked out of a Carnegie steel factory. When management tried to bring in replacements, the workers resisted. Both sides were armed; union negotiations devolved into an old-fashioned military siege— management had built an eleven-foot fence, topped with barbed wire, to protect their plant; efforts to bring scabs in by barge were met with efforts to set the river on fire. The governor sent in troops to restore order, and after many months, the strikers declared defeat. "If the year 1892 taught the workingmen any lesson worthy of heed," Debs wrote, "it was that the capitalist class, like a devilfish, had grasped them with its tentacles and was dragging them down to the fathomless depths of degradation. To escape the prehensile clutch of these monsters constitutes a standing challenge to organized labor for 1893."[15]

Hence Debs's role in the establishment of the American Railway Union, which sought to match the arms race with capital, to organize at sufficient scale that it would not be possible to isolate strikers and then suppress them. The defeat at Pullman, and his subsequent imprisonment, radicalized Debs yet further. He first read *Das Kapital* while serving his term in the Woodstock jail, which began the final stretch of his slow conversion to outright Socialism. "The issue is Socialism v Capitalism," he announced in a coming-out editorial on New Year's Day 1897. "I am for Socialism because I am for humanity."[16]

For the next two decades, as he continued to fuse radical labor politics with homespun republicanism and the rhetoric of Christian humanism, Debs became the most important advocate for Socialism in America. Unlike less radical labor leaders, he was committed to industrial unionism, and he helped found the Industrial Workers of the World (IWW), dedicated to organizing all workers in "One Big Union." And unlike some strands of the radical labor movement, he never abandoned his faith in political action or the power of the ballot. He helped found the Socialist Party of America and would be its presidential candidate in the first four elections of the twentieth century. In 1912 one in every seventeen voters, some nine hundred thousand people, chose Debs for the White House. By then, Debs was "the embodiment of the American proletarian movement," as one Oklahoma Socialist put it. "There are many socialists," explained another supporter, "but only one Debs."[17]

Throughout, Debs remained a keen advocate of the right to free speech. After an anarchist rally at Haymarket Square in Chicago turned violent in 1886, eight anarchists were sentenced to death—not because they could be shown to have thrown a bomb but on account of their radical speech, which was treated as evidence of a conspiracy to commit acts of violence. Debs condemned both anarchism and labor violence, but not as much as he condemned state repression of political dissent. The "twin glories of American government," he said, were free speech and the free press. If the Haymarket verdict stood, then "free speech is as dead in America as it is in Russia." When another comrade was sentenced to jail for sending "scurrilous, defamatory and threatening" literature in the mail two decades later, Debs led the protest movement, comparing the jailed Socialist to John Peter Zenger, the free-press martyr of colonial America. "Let the shibboleth of the American people ring from ocean to ocean and resound throughout the land," proclaimed Debs: "free speech, a free press, and a free people!"[18]

It was no surprise that Debs was so invested in the politics of expression. He was, above all, a public intellectual, a man who conducted politics by giving speeches and writing magazine articles. Given the still-nascent state of the American labor movement, he well understood that his political role was to "teach social consciousness." If the party ever managed to win political power, Debs acknowledged, it would need a different sort of leader, one more interested in backroom deals and policy than in public speaking. But for now, it needed a preacher and a performer and a polemicist. Debs, who had been drawn to early vaudeville as a child and who believed that the editor of the labor paper was the most important officer in a union, was designed for the role.[19]

Debs's commitments were not idiosyncratic. They were typical of the partisan politics of free expression in his time. Despite all the factional splits that roiled the radical Left in these years, a commitment to free speech was a central unifying principle, a prime means for producing solidarity, and a political tactic no different from, and in fact very much a part of, the boycott, the picket, and the strike.

The most remarkable examples of this fight for free speech came from the West, where the Industrial Workers of the World (known as the Wobblies, for reasons unclear) threw themselves into the fray with characteristic radicalism. Street speaking was central to the IWW's political strategy because public halls would rarely rent to radicals. Fiery orators such as the teenage Elizabeth Gurly Flynn traveled the country to win converts to the cause; organizers took to soapboxes on the street corners where migrant laborers sought work. In passionate speeches, they tried to awaken working-class consciousness before laborers signed rapacious contracts with employment agencies.[20]

As the "jawsmiths" of the IWW descended on Spokane, Missoula, Fresno, and San Diego in the years around 1910, local governments passed ordinances barring public meetings and public speaking in an effort to rid the streets of these nuisances to public order. The Wobblies seized upon the laws as an opportunity for civil disobedience, as a way to make a point about the corruption of capitalist justice. As soon as a speaker was arrested for taking to the soapbox, another would step up to be arrested, and then another, and another. They demanded individual trials in order to mock the criminal justice system, gum up the judicial works, and provide an opportunity for yet more speechifying from the stand.

At first, in places such as Fresno and Spokane, these tactics led the cities to back down from enforcing the speaking bans. But the toll on the Wobblies was intense, particularly when speakers were met with vigilante violence. Whipped on by an angry press, vigilantes seized Wobblies in San Diego in 1912 and took them to the edge of town to beat them. ("Hanging is none too good for [the Wobblies]," screeched an editorial in the *San Diego Tribune*. "They would be much better dead, for they are absolutely useless in the human economy; they are the waste material of creation and should be drained off into the sewer of oblivion there to rot in cold obstruction like any other excrement.") When Wobblies tried to organize the lumber town of Everett, Washington, in 1916, they were beaten and forcibly deported. When they tried to return, the police opened fire, killing at least five and injuring thirty-one. Shortly thereafter, the IWW abandoned its efforts to win the right to free speech through civil disobedience.[21]

In such ways was the fight for free speech deeply intertwined with the violent labor struggles that roiled the nation until the outbreak of World War I.

For Debs, the war was a disaster. As the European working classes rallied to their flags and then murdered each other by the hundreds of thousands in the muddy trenches of France, they seemed to make a mockery of the Socialist vision: whatever the workers of the world were up to, they were not uniting.

Debs nevertheless maintained the faith, arguing in a series of speeches in the first months of the war that the United States had to stay out of the conflict: "I have no country to fight for; my country is the earth and I am a citizen of the world." Americans should "have no fear of invasion . . . the enemy we need to prepare against is a domestic and not a foreign one." The class war was still all that mattered.[22]

By early 1915, Debs had staked out a clear position in the debates over preparedness and intervention that would dominate American politics until the US entry into the war in April 1917. But then his health gave out.

For decades, he had pushed his body beyond its limits. On the lecture circuit and campaign trail, he gave long, exhausting speeches night after night, week on week, covering the vast distances between appearances sleeping in uncomfortable upright train seats (he maintained a lifelong boycott of Pullman's sleeping cars). And when he ended his speeches, sweaty but high on the crowd, he could never resist socializing with his fellow Socialists, which of course meant drinking, for Debs loved a tipple. Throughout his life he had run himself ragged, periodically collapsing with illnesses that required weeks of recovery. As he turned sixty, it was all catching up to him. Just before the war, he had needed an operation on his throat. And the breakdowns were coming on more frequently. When he collapsed in the spring of 1915, it was his second such episode in two years. He was bedridden for six weeks, suffering torn leg muscles, congestion, and exhaustion so severe that he required "large doses of morphine" to keep him "from going frantic."[23]

After a lengthy stay at a sanatorium, Debs returned to Terre Haute in the fall of 1915, where he began tentatively speaking and writing on the politics of labor and the war. But he was much reduced as a public figure. In 1916, for the first time since the nineteenth century, he did not run for president (he campaigned instead for a congressional seat in Indiana, where he ran a distant second). Allen Benson was the Socialists' presidential candidate—he had won the nomination by virtue of his antiwar commitments, and his platform centered on a proposed constitutional amendment that would require a referendum before the United States could declare war, with those voting "yes" to be first in line for conscription. Benson did poorly in the election. He was no Debs, and Woodrow Wilson ate into the pacifist vote when he pledged to keep the US out of the war.[24]

Still, Benson's campaign revealed the emergence of an increasingly militant pacifism on the American left. New organizations such as the American Union Against Militarism and the Women's Peace Party had been formed in 1915. Unlike an earlier generation of peace organizations, which were mainly interested in securing the stability of the international financial order that so benefited their genteel, aristocratic membership—and which discreetly shelved their pacifism whenever a war broke out—these new organizations drew their members from reform movements. Composed of social workers, suffragists, and Socialists, they saw peace as a radical cause, requiring the reformation of the political and social order. Their antimilitarism was deeply influenced by feminism, particularly by the then-popular biological argument that, as Charlotte Perkins Gilman put it, "in warfare, *per se*, we find maleness in its absurdest extremes. Here is . . . the whole gamut of basic masculinity, from the initial instinct of combat, through every form of glorious ostentation with the loudest possible accompaniment of noise."[25]

After the US entered the war, the Socialist Party called a convention in St. Louis. Debs was ill again and did not attend the meeting, but his party maintained his pacifist line. "I am a socialist, a labor unionist, and a believer in the Prince of Peace first," declared Kate Richards O'Hare, "and an American second. If need be, I will give my life and the life of my mate to serve my class, but never with my consent will they be given to add to the profits and protect the stolen wealth of the bankers, food speculators and ammunition makers."

O'Hare helped write the convention's "Resolution on War and Militarism," which declared that the "mad orgy of death and destruction which is now convulsing unfortunate Europe was caused by the conflict of capitalist interests." It reaffirmed the Socialist Party's "allegiance to the principle of internationalism and working-class solidarity the world over" and pledged "continuous, active and public opposition to the war." It was a radical statement and caused some members of the party to quit in disgust. But it was endorsed by the overwhelming majority of delegates to the convention.

And it put the Socialist Party and its radical allies on a collision course with the Espionage Act, which was then being debated in Congress. The Socialists gathered in St. Louis pledged "vigorous resistance to all reactionary measures, such as censorship of press and mails, restriction of the rights of free speech, assemblage, and organization, or compulsory arbitration and limitation of the right to strike."[26]

In proposing the Espionage Act, the Wilson administration had defined *espionage* broadly, as anything that interfered with the war effort. In such a view, pacifist opposition to the war was a form of "espionage"—especially if one thought it was really motivated by pro-German sentiments. "German sympathizers are now working along lines that tend to cover the chances of detection," opined the *New York Times* in 1917. "Many of them have joined the Socialist Party, and are preaching sedition under the guise of socialist doctrine."[27] In the wake of the St. Louis convention, one congressman read the entire Socialist Party platform into the *Congressional Record* as proof that the Espionage Act was needed.[28]

In other words, the war had intensified the struggles over free speech that had been central to the labor strife of the previous years, providing conservatives with a new rationale for purging radical speech from the public sphere. Radical labor advocacy, previously treated by the state as speech that lay outside constitutional protections because of its dangers to property relations, commerce, and the social order, was now also being treated as a form of foreign subversion of the war effort.

Two provisions of the Espionage Act gave the government new capacities to censor the Left. The first granted the postmaster general the power to exclude from the mail "any matter advocating or urging treason, insurrection, or forcible resistance to any law of the United States." The second made it illegal to "make or convey false reports or false statements with intent to interfere with the operation or success of the military or the naval forces of the U.S. or to promote the success of its enemies." Violating this second provision would be met with a sentence of up to twenty years in jail.[29]

Both provisions had originally been even more draconian. The Justice Department's proposed legislation had allowed the exclusion of all "treasonable" or "anarchistic" material from the mail, as well as the punishment, with up to life terms, of all speech likely to cause "disaffection" with the war effort. Although neither section was as controversial as 2(c), the ultimately deleted press-censorship provision, both did attract criticism from radical pacifists who worried that these were vague clauses that threatened free speech. Enough members of Congress shared such concerns that they eliminated these more obviously sweeping sections of the bill. But it turned out to make little difference, for even the ostensibly restrained final language of the Espionage Act gave officials more than enough leeway to censor to their hearts' content.[30]

Postmaster General Albert Burleson, the vain Democratic Party loyalist who had segregated the post office in 1913, wasted no time in deploying the nonmailability provisions to censor radical critics of the war. In fact, he barred the *Hallettsville Rebel* from the mail six days before the Espionage Act was signed into law—its editor, Red Tom Hickey, had been involved in the Farmers and Laborers Protective Association in Burleson's native Texas. The day after the law was passed, Burleson sent a note to his network of local postmasters asking them to "keep a close watch" on the mail for violations of the law, which he interpreted to cover anything that might "embarrass or hamper the Government in conducting the War."

Within a month, fifteen publications had been excluded from the mail, including the *International Socialist Review*, the *Masses*, the *Milwaukee Leader*, the *Appeal to Reason*, *Watson's Jeffersonian Magazine*, and the *National Rip-Saw*, in which many of Debs's articles were published. By the end of the war, seventy-five papers had suffered Burleson's wrath; forty-five of them were Socialist, the remainder German or Gaelic.[31]

As with the postal provisions, so with the speech provisions. More than two thousand people were charged with speech crimes during the war. Many of the prosecutions targeted such mild forms of protest that they seem almost satirical, a deliberate send-up of the exquisite sensitivity of the censorial mind. Walter Matthey attended a meeting in Iowa in which he applauded some "disloyal" sentiments uttered from the stage, and then donated a quarter. He got a year in jail. In Lansing, Michigan, William Powell was pressured into buying a liberty bond and then complained about it to a relative: "I hope the government goes to hell so it will be of no value . . . this is a rich man's war and the US is simply fighting for money." He got twenty years. Robert Goldstein managed to get himself arrested for making a patriotic, pro-war movie about the American Revolution. His crime? Like all directors of war movies, he needed to show the villains doing villainous things—but in depicting British war crimes, he inadvertently portrayed an ally in the *current* war in a negative light. That was worth a sentence of ten years.[32]

In theory, the Espionage Act should not have covered such forms of expression; it had no general censorship provision. But the courts at the time embraced a line of legal reasoning that converted the act's prohibition on interfering with military recruitment into a much more sweeping prohibition on speech. It had four steps, which can be seen most plainly in the successful prosecution of Frank Shaffer, a wealthy farmer who had published a book in which he asserted that "the war itself is wrong. Its prosecution will be a crime. There is not a question raised, an issue involved, a cause at stake which is worth the life of one blue-jacket on the sea or one khaki-coat in the trenches."[33]

It was obvious, as even the court had to agree, that the text of the Espionage Act did not make it a crime to disapprove of the war. But, the court explained, that wasn't the question: "the question is whether the natural and probable tendency and effect of the words" was to interfere with the draft. Shifting the question was Step 1. Step 2 was to assert that it was obvious, as a matter of abstract logic, that recruitment or enlistment could be "obstructed by attacking the justice of the cause . . . and by undermining the spirit of loyalty."

Steps 3 and 4 were a little tricky, designed to offset clever lawyerly objections. Step 3 was to point out that the law did not require the prosecutor to show that recruitment had actually been obstructed— it was illegal to make statements that were *intended* to obstruct recruitment, regardless of their success. And Step 4 was the doozy, because it made it incredibly easy to prove such intent. How did the court know that Shaffer intended to interfere with military recruitment when he wrote those objectionable sentences? "He must be presumed to have intended the natural and probable consequences of what he knowingly did." If the court thought it probable that your criticism of the war could interfere with recruitment, you were presumed to be guilty of interfering with the war effort. The Espionage Act had become a censorship law.[34]

This sprawling interpretation of the law made it a useful tool for punishing Socialists, who were committed, after St. Louis, to pacifism. O'Hare, who had helped write the St. Louis manifesto, was indicted for an antiwar speech just a month after the Espionage Act passed. Anyone enlisting in the army, she had said, was going to be "used for fertilizer," and the women of the United States had become "nothing more or less than brood sows to raise children to get into the Army to be made into fertilizer." Victor Berger, who had been the first Socialist elected to Congress and was now editing an antiwar newspaper, was hit with twenty-six counts of violating the Espionage Act. At the time, he was running for one of Wisconsin's Senate seats with billboards that read "War is hell caused by capitalism. Socialists demand peace." He lost that race but was elected to the House of Representatives while his case was awaiting trial. Then he was sentenced to twenty years in jail, and the House refused to seat him. He would not take his seat until 1923, when his conviction was dropped on account of prejudicial statements the trial judge had made about Germans.[35]

Behind such punitive censorship was a broader culture of intolerance for dissent. The US public was deeply polarized by the war. On Capitol Hill, as Congress debated the war resolution, an argument between pro-war senator Henry Cabot Lodge and a group of pacifists devolved into a fistfight. The declaration of war itself was met with competing protests on the grounds of the Capitol and across the nation. A meeting of antiwar demonstrators in Baltimore was "smashed to bits" by a pro-war crowd of four thousand, led by professors from Johns Hopkins.[36]

With the coming of the war, the state threw its authority behind the angry, intolerant, pro-war crowd. Pro-war propaganda flooded the nation. "German agents are everywhere," warned one government ad: "Report the man who spreads pessimistic stories, . . . cries for peace or belittles our efforts to win the war." Attorney General Thomas Gregory asked local prosecutors to watch for treason and dissent, and he asked all US citizens to serve as "voluntary detectives" to report suspicious activity. Groups sprang up to police the speech of their fellow citizens, giving themselves hokey names that trivialized their quite serious purpose: the Boy Spies of America, the Sedition Slammers, the Terrible Threateners. A forty-two-year-old advertising man formed the American Protective League, which tasked itself with enforcing the draft laws and keeping a watchful eye on the public. It soon had 250,000 members; with self-issued badges declaring themselves to be members of the "Secret Service Division," they conducted three million "investigations" of their fellow citizens. Their newsletter was called the *Spy Glass*.[37]

The result was a climate of deep intolerance. Anything Germanic was an obvious target. German music and German composers and

German conductors, so fashionable before the war, were banned in many places. South Dakota banned speaking German in public; the University of Texas fired every German on its staff. In Debs's hometown of Terre Haute, vigilantes gathered German books from citizens and burned them in the street.[38]

It was a short step from there to mob violence. The citizens of Terre Haute lynched a Socialist coal miner for refusing to buy a liberty bond, one of seventy Americans lynched during the war. When murder was possible, so were other acts of crude intimidation. After pacifist preacher Herbert Bigelow gave an antiwar speech in Kentucky, he was seized by men in Klan robes, stripped, tied to a tree, and whipped—all in the name of the women and children of Belgium and France. A merchant charged with making disloyal remarks in St. Louis was dragged from his home in his pajamas and made to kiss each of the forty-eight stars on the flag. Elsewhere, suspected dissidents were tarred and feathered and whipped, had their heads forcibly shaved and painted red, were beaten and forced to cross the road wearing dog collars, and other acts that were equal parts puerile and horrific.[39]

If this was mob violence—and it was—it was organized by elite citizens in local communities and sanctioned by the powers that be. In Nevada, the crowd that tarred and feathered a citizen for "lukewarmness toward the cause of the U.S." was headed by the local sheriff; the governor thought even such rough tactics "all helped the cause." The former ambassador to Germany, James Gerard, blathered that "we should hog-tie every disloyal German-American, feed every pacifist raw meat and hang every traitor to a lamp post." From the comfort of their offices, the elite press talked just as tough. *Life* magazine ran a cartoon promising a "remedy for the soap-box traitor": a lynching. In Terre Haute the local paper called for all antiwar Socialists to be swept into a prisoner-of-war camp—or boiled in oil. The attorney general, who should have been responsible for cooling tensions, simply cheered the vigilantes on: "May God have mercy [on war dissenters,] for they need expect none from an outraged people and an avenging government."[40]

A. B. Walker, "A Remedy for the Soap-Box Traitor," *Life*, November 1, 1917. (Image provided by Mary Anne Trasciatti)

As always, the IWW got the worst of it. In the first months of the war, groups of vigilantes, many of them members of the military, raided IWW headquarters in Kansas City, Detroit, Seattle, and Duluth. "The first step in the whipping of Germany is to strangle the IWWs," declared the *Tulsa Daily World*. "Kill 'em, just as you would any other kind of a snake. Don't scotch 'em, kill 'em. And kill 'em dead. It is no time to waste money on trials and continuances and things like that. All that is necessary is the evidence and a firing squad." That night, seventeen Wobblies under arrest in Tulsa were seized by men in black robes and black masks. These self-declared "Knights of Liberty" took the Wobblies to the edge of town, whipped them with a cat-of-nine-tails, poured boiling tar on their open wounds, feathered them, and drove them out of town under a volley of gunfire.[41]

In July, strikes in the copper district of Arizona broke out after a fire killed 164 miners—most of whom had asphyxiated because the mine lacked the escape doors required by law. Interference with copper production had not been tolerated in peacetime; in wartime, when copper was used in the manufacture of cartridges, cannons, airplanes, and ships, it was anathema, an urgent threat to the nation.

At 6:30 on the morning of July 12, a group of vigilantes organized by leading citizens in the mining town of Bisbee began going door-to-door, asking all residents at gunpoint if they were ready to return to work. Those who refused to do so were seized and held for the day in the sun-scorched ballpark—it was July in Arizona, and temperatures reached 112 degrees—before 1,186 of them were loaded onto cow trains and deported to the desert in New Mexico. No one was ever held accountable.[42]

No one was ever charged with the lynching of Wobbly organizer Frank Little in Butte, Montana, later that month, either. Little was a veteran of the free-speech fights and numerous organizing drives. By the time he arrived in Butte, his slight frame bore the scars of a life of tough work and even tougher labor fights—he was missing an eye and in desperate need of surgery for a herniated disk. But he continued to give radical antiwar speeches in Butte—Wilson was a "lying tyrant"; soldiers were "scabs in uniform"—until he was seized from bed at 3:30 in the morning by six men, taken to the edge of town, dragged behind a car, and hanged from a bridge. The next morning, his body was found with a board bearing an inscription in red crayon: "others take notice, first and last warning. 3-7-77." Those

The forced march of the IWWs from Lowell (a part of Bisbee, Arizona) on July 12, 1917. (Library of Congress)

digits, whose origins and meaning are unclear, had been used as a signature by Montana vigilante groups since the nineteenth century. Today they adorn the crest of the Montana Highway Patrol.[43]

The political response to such violence against dissenters was, remarkably, to further criminalize speech. Mob violence was seen not as a by-product of state-sanctioned intolerance and persecution but as a result of insufficient government repression. Had Little been "arrested and put in jail for his seditious and incendiary talks," asserted Montana senator Henry Lee Myers, "he would not have been lynched." Government laxity was forcing concerned patriots to take matters into their own hands. "Unless more vigorous action is taken by the Federal officials in Montana," Myers warned, "I fear there will be other lynchings in that state."[44]

In August 1917, Myers therefore proposed a new law that would criminalize a broader swath of seditious speech. Before it could advance, the Wilson administration had decided that it could use the already existing provisions of the Espionage Act to squash the Wobblies. In September, federal agents raided IWW offices across the nation, gathering truckloads of Wobbly correspondence and publications that were combed for evidence of statements that could be interpreted as a conspiracy to interfere with the transport of war supplies, the draft, or the war effort generally. Based on such evidence, the leadership of the Wobblies were collectively charged with 17,022 violations of the Espionage Act and other statutes. Trial proceedings were begun against 101 of them and lasted for months. At the end of it, the jury took less than an hour to find all 101 guilty of all of the crimes with which they were charged. Myers's federal sedition law died in committee.[45]

Yet the idea of a tougher censorship law lived on in Montana. In early 1918, in a rare judicial stand against the sweep of the Espionage Act, Federal District Court judge George Bourquin acquitted Ves Hall of making false statements with the intent of interfering with the armed forces. Hall had complained loudly about the war at a picnic and in a hotel kitchen and in a "hot and furious saloon argument": he hoped Germany would "whip" the United States, and he thought Wilson was a "British tool [and] a servant of Wall Street millionaires." By its letter, Bourquin ruled, the Espionage Act made criminal such "disloyal utterances" only if they were intended to obstruct the armed forces. As there were no soldiers or sailors within hundreds of miles of Hall's sixty-person hometown, it wasn't plausible that Hall had really been attempting to interfere with the armed forces. It would be hard, Bourquin pointed out, to convict a man for attempted murder if he fired a small pistol three miles away from any intended target.[46]

The decision went down poorly. "Feeling is running high," reported Montana governor Sam V. Stewart. "I really expect some killing as a result of the construction of the law in the Hall case." He called a special legislative session to remedy the situation, and within a month, Montana had a new sedition act. It was based on the bill that Myers had introduced to the Senate after Little's lynching and made it a crime to "utter, print, write or publish any disloyal, profane, scurrilous, contemptuous or abusive language" about the government, constitution, flag, or soldiers and sailors of the United States. Curiously, the law explicitly forbade any criticism of their uniforms as well. It also became illegal to "urge, incite or advocate any curtailment of production" of any war materiel. A total of seventy-nine Montanans would be prosecuted under the act for such threatening talk as calling the wartime food regulations a "big joke." The traveling wine salesman guilty of that particular offense was sentenced to hard labor for between seven-and-a-half and twenty years.[47]

Just twelve weeks after Montana's sedition law went into effect, the US Congress added the same provisions into the Espionage Act. Myers, along with his fellow Montanan Senator Thomas J. Walsh, had successfully lobbied for the adoption of their state's law at the federal level. But they were pushing on an open door, for Justice Department officials were equally keen to toughen the Espionage Act. As early as February, Attorney General Gregory had asked his assistants Charles Warren and John Lord O'Brian to "consider amending the Espionage Act in some way adequate to get around Judge Bourquin's ruling in Montana."[48]

Gregory shared the concerns of other patriots that mob violence was a product of government laxity. In April he explained the need for new legislation to the American Bar Association, citing the recent lynching of Robert Prager as an example of the kind of lawlessness that was undermining the war effort. (Prager was a German American coal miner whose neighbors in Collinsville, Illinois, suspected him of spying for Germany. He was no spy—in fact, he had tried to join the US Navy but had been turned away because he had a glass eye. On the day the Senate began debating amendments to the Espionage Act, a large mob marched him out of town, stripped him, strung him up, and then dropped him by the neck three times, once each for the red, white, and blue.) Gregory thought that such violence was a product of "a condition of mind where people say: 'the government is giving us no protection; spies are blowing up our factories; they are giving information to Germany; our boys are being shot in the rear.'" And while the nation's top law-enforcement official couldn't come out and condone mob violence, he sympathized with such sentiments, for he agreed that the laws weren't giving adequate protection against espionage. The previous year, his department had tried to pass laws adequate to the war emergency, he explained, and "we secured the passage of the Espionage Act, but most of the teeth which we tried to put in were taken out." They had been taken out by Congress, which had amended and weakened the act, and they had been taken out by meddlesome judges like Bourquin, which had made the law "impossible . . . to enforce in some jurisdictions." It was therefore necessary to amend the Espionage Act to "make it much more drastic"—not to crack down on nationalistic lynchings but to do the work of the patriotic mob for them. After all, Gregory still maintained that the "greatest menace" to the country was the "insidious propaganda of the pacifist."[49]

In May Congress passed the amendments to the Espionage Act that became known as the Sedition Act. Advocates for the bill had whipped up fears of both mob violence (Senator Myers reminded

his colleagues what had happened to Frank Little) and foreign subversion (to vote against the bill, argued Senator Overman, was to
"throw a cloak of protection around every spy in this country and
every traitor and every Bolshevik and every IWW"). There were
a number of senators who understandably feared that the new law
would interfere with free speech, and they voted to add an amendment clarifying that people could not be found guilty of violating
the law if they said true things "with good motives and for justifiable ends." But the Justice Department worried that would make
the bill useless in combating "that dangerous form of propaganda
known as pacifism" because even Socialists said they were acting for
the undeniably good motive of promoting "human happiness." DOJ
pressure was sufficient to ensure that the free-speech amendment
was dropped from the bill in conference, and on May 4 the Senate passed the law by a 2-to-1 margin. Three days later the House
approved by a vote of 293 to 1. The lone vote against it came from
Meyer London, the only Socialist in Congress.[50]

Debs, increasingly despondent, watched the persecution of his comrades from his home—and frequently from his sickbed. In the late
summer of 1917 he suffered his third major collapse. For the rest of
the year he was under doctor's orders to "keep free from excitement."
Even so, in the spring of 1918 he was bedridden yet again. He continued to write articles defending radicals from the accusations of
the patriots and continued calling for the working class to rise up
against the Wall Street warmongers. But the magazines in which
he published were the very same ones that Postmaster Burleson was
busy repressing, and Debs was itching to return to the fray: "I cannot
be free while my comrades and fellow-workers are jailed for warning
people about this war."[51]

Finally, by the summer of 1918, Debs's health had improved to
the point that he could begin speaking in public again. In early June
he began speaking to audiences close to home, in Indiana, to avoid
too much strain on his body. Friends warned him to be careful, for

the government would be watching. "Of course," Debs said, "I'll take about two jumps and they'll nail me, but that's all right." He was soon venturing farther afield, to places such as Canton, Ohio.[52]

When Debs took the stage in Nimisilla Park, it was a long-overdue response to the excesses of wartime censorship. Debs condemned the deportation of the Bisbee miners and the lynching of Prager, and he paid homage to the leaders of the Ohio Socialist Party serving time in a nearby workhouse for interfering with the draft. He derided the exclusion of left-wing journals from the mail, the persecution of radical speakers, and the imprisonment of O'Hare for criticizing the war. "Think of sentencing a woman to the penitentiary simply for talking," he said. "The United States, under plutocratic rule, is the only country that would send a woman to prison for five years for exercising her constitutional right of free speech." It was a fitting cap to decades of conflict over the politics of free expression.[53]

But did the speech itself violate the Espionage Act? The pro-war journalist Miller, watching suspiciously from the crowd, had thought so, and the stories he sent out over the wire certainly made it seem like Debs had crossed the low bar that had been established for prosecution. And among the articles that ran on the day after the speech was a small story in which the federal prosecutor for the District of Northern Ohio, Edwin Wertz, promised to charge Debs under the Espionage Act. It had also been written by Miller, who was its author in a more fundamental sense as well. For as soon as Miller had got off the phone with his newsroom, he had made a second call to "Ed," his old friend in the prosecutor's office. Throughout the war, the journalist and the prosecutor had formed a happy team— favorable coverage exchanged for exclusive access to lurid stories of antiwar traitors, all in the name of producing a patriotic public culture. Now, Miller gave Wertz his version of the speech and asked the obvious question: "Are you going to let this fellow get away with it?" "No man is too big to violate the Espionage Act" was Wertz's response. "I will ask for his indictment." "And so," recalled Miller, "I phoned that in. It made a nice Page One box. The story was given a big play. The press services picked it up. It became Page One all over the country."[54]

But when Wertz actually got a transcript of the speech, he had second thoughts. The situation didn't look anywhere near as simple as Miller had made it sound. Wertz sent the transcript to the Justice Department for a second opinion. They confirmed that the case was "by no means a clear one." Debs's criticisms of the way the courts were applying the Espionage Act didn't rise to the level of interference with the war effort, nor were his "references to the St. Louis platform . . . sufficiently clear and definite." And although some of Debs's criticisms of the war—such as suggestions that his audience was fit for "more than cannon fodder"—were close to the line, and possibly over it, the Justice Department wrote that it "does not feel strongly convinced that a prosecution is advisable."[55]

Wertz pressed ahead anyway. Miller had boxed him in; he was on record promising a prosecution and had little interest in appearing to back down to help a radical Socialist. He charged Debs with ten violations of the Espionage Act, including some under the recent sedition amendments.[56]

Even given the weakness of the case, the prosecution went smoothly. As had been proven time and again during the war, the Espionage Act gave the prosecution a great deal of latitude. To establish that Debs was guilty of making statements that were intended to cause insubordination in the army or obstruct the draft, Wertz needed to prove three things. First, he needed to show that Debs had said things that could have that effect, which he accomplished by quoting selectively from the speech transcript. Second, Wertz needed to show that Debs intended to disrupt the war effort, accomplished with helpful testimony from a Naval Intelligence agent who had spied on a Socialist meeting and heard Debs criticize the war. Third, Wertz needed to show that the speech was heard by men of draft age—easily accomplished by finding Nimisilla picnickers of the right age and gender and putting them on the witness stand. There was no need to prove that the speech had actually caused disaffection or insubordination.

Debs's legal team did argue that if his speech was criminal, then the Espionage Act violated the Constitution. But their heart wasn't really in it; they knew that wasn't how the First Amendment was widely understood. One of Debs's attorneys, lacking any trial work to do, was tasked primarily with keeping Debs from slipping out to a nearby saloon during the testimony. Figuring he was bound for jail, Debs was trying to enjoy his last days of freedom.[57]

Just as they had been back in Pullman in 1894, the words that Debs spoke were treated only as an effort to cause a crime—and were thus themselves a criminal act. And the jury was hardly sympathetic. Cleveland in 1918 was a working-class, immigrant city; the year before, one-third of the electorate had voted for the Socialist candidate in the mayoral race. But at the time, the names for jury pools were provided by county judges, so the jury of Debs's "peers" was composed exclusively of members of the Yankee middle class; on average, they were older than seventy.[58] It took them less than six hours to return a guilty verdict.

Before sentencing, Debs gave one last speech, perhaps the finest of his career. "The Espionage Act," he said, was a "despotic enactment in flagrant conflict with democratic principles and the spirit of free institutions." But he asked for no mercy, for he "never so clearly comprehended as now the great struggle between the powers of greed and exploitation . . . [and] the rising hosts of industrial freedom and justice." The use of the Espionage Act during the war had clarified the battle lines that had so dominated his long life of labor struggle. Ever the optimist, even in the depths of the war, Debs could see the "dawn of the better day for humanity" just on the horizon; he thought that the "cross is bending, the midnight is passing, and joy cometh with the morning." But for now he was happy to take his lot, for he was "not one bit better than the meanest on earth." "While there is a lower class," he concluded, "I am in it, and while there is a criminal element, I am of it, and while there is a soul in prison, I am not free."[59]

The judge was happy to oblige. He sentenced Debs to ten years in prison. "Debs' voice is now stilled," crowed the *Cleveland Plain Dealer*, "as it should have been stilled long ago. Doctrines such as he has been pleased to preach are not to be tolerated. The question of free speech is in no wise involved. It is a question of national safety."[60]

Chapter 3

1919, YEAR OF
THE BOMBS

Attorney General A. Mitchell Palmer, star-
ing out of the bombed-out window of his
DC home on June 2, 1919. After the bombing he would champion a new politics of
national security, including a peacetime sedition act. (Library of Congress, photograph
by Harris & Ewing)

Tहे FIRST BOMB WAS SENT TO OLE HANSON, THE MAYOR OF SE-
attle, who had recently called out the troops to put down a general strike. The bomb arrived on April 28, 1919, but it was leaking
acid and easily identified before it went off. The second bomb was
sent to former Georgia senator Thomas Hardwick, who had recently
cosponsored a law to deport anarchists. This one was in better shape
when it was opened on April 29 by Hardwick's unsuspecting Black
maid, Ethel Williams, who lost her hands in the explosion.

The next thirty-two bombs were intercepted before they reached
their targets. A clerk in the New York City post office read about the
Hanson and Hardwick bombs in the paper and remembered that
he had seen a stack of similarly marked packages on his undeliver-
able shelf. He returned to the office, and, sure enough, there they
were, sixteen packages all marked with a Gimbel department store
label, all labeled "Novelty—a sample," and all lacking sufficient
postage for delivery. Over the next weeks, another sixteen bombs
were similarly discovered en route to their targets.

Their intended recipients had all, like Hardwick and Hanson,
crossed the anarchist movement in various ways. And many of them
had something else in common: they had used the Espionage Act
as a weapon against the Left. Postmaster General Albert Burleson,
who had so vigorously used the Espionage Act to censor the radical
press, was on the list. So was Senator Lee Overman, who had ushered the Espionage Act through Congress. So were Judge Kenesaw
Mountain Landis, who had overseen the Espionage Act trial of
the Wobblies in Chicago, and Frank Nebeker, who had prosecuted
the case.[1]

So were two other men whose dealings with the Espionage Act
were only just beginning. One of the bombs was addressed to Oliver Wendell Holmes Jr., the renowned Supreme Court justice. Just
months before, Holmes had written the opinion that had dismissed
the appeals by Eugene Debs, as well as several other radicals, of
their Espionage Act convictions. A. Mitchell Palmer, recently nominated as US attorney general, also had his name on a bomb. He had
inherited the Justice Department's wartime reputation, as well as its

sweeping powers: even five months after the November 1918 armistice, the Espionage and Sedition Acts were still on the books.[2]

Over the coming year, both Holmes and Palmer would grapple with the meaning of the law. They faced a simple question: what was the future of the Espionage Act in the postwar order? Palmer sought to perpetuate the censorship regime of the war. In 1919 and 1920 he positioned himself as a new type of national-security demagogue, calling for a permanent sedition act to secure the nation from threats of disorder and rebellion. Meanwhile, Holmes had to reckon with the place of such censorship in the constitutional order, seeking, in a series of influential decisions, to determine whether the Espionage Act was compatible with the First Amendment.

They did so at a combustible moment in world history. The war had collapsed empires and triggered uprisings. The recent Russian Revolution, which would shape the course of the twentieth century, was front of mind as Americans debated the future of the Espionage Act. But in 1919 there was also revolution in Ireland and Germany, ongoing revolutionary turmoil in Mexico, and massive protests in Egypt, Korea, and China. In the city of Amritsar, India, a peaceful protest against the extension of wartime security regulations had been violently put down by British security forces, which fired more than 1,500 rounds into a crowd of civilians.[3]

In the United States, too, the passions unleashed by the war were not easily tamed. In Cleveland on May Day, Socialists protesting Debs's conviction were assaulted by patriotic vigilantes. A riot broke out, the entire downtown a "seething mass of Socialists, police, civilians and soldiers, the latter riding down the rioters in army trucks and tanks." At least two died, and hundreds were wounded. In New York, World War I veterans raided Socialist headquarters, burning books and destroying furniture and forcing immigrants to sing "The Star-Spangled Banner." When a man in Washington, DC, refused to stand for the national anthem at an event a few days later, he was shot three times in the back by a sailor, who was cheered by the crowd.[4]

Meanwhile, there were racial pogroms across the country: in Washington, DC, where the theft of a white woman's umbrella led a mob of navy men to interrogate and beat Black men across the southwest quadrant of the city, producing such chaos that two thousand federal troops had to be deployed; in Elaine, Arkansas, where dozens if not hundreds of Black sharecroppers trying to organize a union were murdered by vigilante groups, their bodies thrown into the river; in Chicago, where a group of Black boys drifting to the wrong side of a segregated beach triggered days of violence. Many thought that the turmoil was a product of radical plots to encourage Black uprising. "Reds Try to Stir Negroes to Revolt" was a *New York Times* headline. James Byrnes, then a congressional delegate from South Carolina but later to be a secretary of state and a Supreme Court justice, thought that W. E. B. Du Bois should have been prosecuted under the Espionage Act for calling for civil rights for black veterans.[5]

In the background, the Spanish flu took 675,000 American lives, raising the political temperature, adding to the dread. "There is hardly a respectable citizen of my acquaintance," one West Virginian told Palmer in October, "who does not believe that we are on the verge of armed conflict in this country." It was a fertile atmosphere for paranoia and for the adoption of heavy-handed tools of censorship. "Silence the incendiary advocates of force," cried the *Washington Post*. "Bring the law's hand down upon the violent and the inciter of violence. Do it now."[6]

For a moment, it looked like the federal government would give in to such fears. Yet the nation ultimately retreated from a peacetime censorship regime. In the spring of 1919, in the first Supreme Court cases to consider the meaning of the First Amendment, Holmes wrote unanimous opinions upholding the constitutionality of the Espionage Act prosecutions during the war. Yet by the fall, when the court considered another wartime case, Holmes had changed his mind, issuing a famous dissent in the *Abrams* case that marked the beginning of the rise of the modern right to free speech. Meanwhile, although Palmer had shot to national prominence by deporting radical immigrants and building a new bureaucracy committed to political surveillance and censorship, his campaign for the White House, and his hopes for a permanent Sedition Act, collapsed when his paranoid predictions of revolution failed to materialize. To a surprising extent, the trajectories of these two men were influenced by the advocacy of a small cluster of civil libertarians, who had mobilized in response to the excess of wartime censorship and who now sought to protect the rights of Americans to dissent.

These clashes over the role of censorship in the heated politics of this revolutionary moment not only shaped the future of the Espionage Act. They also planted the seeds from which would sprout both the majesty of the modern First Amendment and the sprawling bureaucracy of the modern national-security state.

A month after he was sentenced to prison, Debs appealed his case to the Supreme Court.[7] It was one of three very similar Espionage Act cases that the court heard in early 1919. The issues in all were plain, their significance clear. Did the government have the power, as its lawyers argued, to imprison radical critics of the war? Or did the First Amendment protect the rights of dissidents to express their opinions? These were new questions: the Supreme Court had never really paused to consider the meaning of right to free speech. It had heard very few cases on the subject, each of which it had dealt with perfunctorily.

Radicals like Debs expected little sympathy from the courts. "The trial of a Socialist in a capitalist court is at best a farcical affair," Debs had declared in his speech at Nimisilla Park. Judges were appointed "through the influence and power of corporate capital . . . and when they go to the bench, they go, not to serve the people, but to serve the interests that place them and keep them where they are."[8]

The outcome of his appeal did nothing to change Debs's mind. The justices unanimously agreed to uphold his conviction, as they did in both the other Espionage Act cases they heard that spring. The job of writing up all three decisions was given to Holmes.

By virtue of his encounter with the Espionage Act in 1919, Holmes would enter the history books as the father of modern civil liberties. But as he prepared these first Espionage Act opinions, that outcome was far from inevitable. In fact, it was highly improbable. For Holmes was far from a liberal. His political and judicial philosophies were both much darker and much stranger than his contemporary reputation suggests.

On one level, Holmes remained a Boston Brahmin, the sort of American aristocrat who could calmly confess that "I loathe the thick-fingered clowns we call the people" and declare his politics, with lofty detachment, to be "an unconvinced conservatism." He had no sympathy for Socialists, no patience for all the fuss about economic inequality. He thought that "the crowd now has substantially all there is" and didn't believe that "cutting off the luxuries of the few would make an appreciable difference" to the poor—a convenient sentiment for a man who owned an oceanfront summer home on Boston's North Shore and who spent his downtime during the war buying art for his comfortable DC row home.[9]

But class prejudice was not the dominant trait in Holmes's philosophy. For the defining event in Holmes's life, even at the age of

Supreme Court Justice Oliver Wendell Holmes Jr. on a stroll in 1914. (Library of Congress, photograph by Harris & Ewing)

seventy-seven, was his experience of combat in the Civil War. Before the attack on Fort Sumter, Holmes had been an ardent abolitionist, and he had happily dropped out of Harvard to enlist in the Union Army. Holmes saw horrible things during the war. He lost friends, suffered from dysentery, and was badly wounded three times. Those three years, "soaked in a sea of death," as he put it, made a deep and lasting impression on the young man.[10]

"Every society," he came to believe, "rests on the death of men." Civilization was little more than a veneer; society had no way to resolve underlying conflict: "Force, mitigated so far as may be by good manners, is the *ultima ratio*, and between two groups that want to make inconsistent kinds of world I see no remedy except force." He concluded that "the logical result of a fundamental difference is for one side to kill the other—and that persecution has much to be said for it."[11]

Gone was the abolitionist belief in social progress. Gone, too, was any faith in human reason and betterment; Holmes saw "no reason for attributing to man a significance different in kind from that which belongs to a baboon or a grain of sand." Gone was even the belief in belief. "I don't believe much in anything that is," Holmes explained, "but I believe a damned sight less in anything that isn't."[12]

It was a remarkably bleak worldview. There were no transcendent truths. "Truth," Holmes said, "was the majority vote of the nation that can lick all others." Existence was without higher meaning. Life was, and would remain, nasty, brutish, and short. "I respect your respect for the human soul," he wrote to a close friend in 1919, "while still doubting whether to share it. The formula of life to great masses would be Feed-Foutre [Fuck] and Finish, and I am not so sure it won't remain so."[13]

On the bench, where Holmes spent five decades of his life, such nihilism manifested primarily as a resigned, condescending tolerance for the will of the majority of the population. The courts had to defer to the laws enacted by the politicians who won elections. Not believing in universal truths, Holmes was little inclined to insist on the defense of rights against the tyranny of the majority. Unlike his peers in the judiciary, who were keen to preserve the rights of property and free enterprise from what they saw as state interference with the free market, Holmes wrote dissenting opinions upholding the constitutionality of all sorts of economic reform: maximum-hour laws and minimum-wage laws, laws to ban child labor and laws to ban employers from interfering with union drives in their work-places. Holmes was even willing to concede that labor deserved to strike and picket and boycott. He thought it was natural that work-ers would seek to organize, that the strike was a "lawful instrument in the universal struggle of life."[14]

His opinions on these matters—particularly because they were almost always offered in dissent—made him look like an ally to the progressive and labor movements. He wasn't. Holmes thought their reform measures were silly and pointless, if not wrongheaded. At times, in fact, he happily supported the repression of labor: in 1904, when the Colorado governor had imposed martial law to repress a mining strike and had imprisoned a union leader for two-and-a-half months without trial, Holmes had ruled that it was no violation of due process because the state had the right to preserve itself. The un-derlying principle was simple: "My agreement or disagreement has nothing to do with the right of the majority to embody their opin-ions in law." Or as he put it more plainly to a friend, "If my fellow citizens want to go to Hell, I will help them."[15]

The flip side of this deference to majority rule was an antipa-thy to the rights of minorities. If the political majority believed in doing something for the public good, on what possible grounds could individuals resist? Holmes was therefore perfectly comfort-able upholding the constitutionality of segregationist laws in the Jim Crow South.[16]

And he was completely uninterested in protecting the right to free speech. Over the course of his career Holmes had ruled that one could not claim the right to speak in a public park if the govern-ment denied it to you, or the right to criticize a court decision if the court enjoined you, or the right to write editorials that encouraged nudity in violation of public-decency laws. In all these cases, the law represented the will of the majority, and if the law believed that the speech harmed the public good, well, that was the end of it. "We should deal with the act of speech," Holmes thought, "as we deal with any overt act that we don't like."[17]

That was particularly the case in times of war, which made plain that any talk of individual rights was just bunk: "The most fundamental of the supposed pre-existing rights—the right to life—is sacrificed without a scruple not only in war, but whenever the interests of society, that is, of the predominant power in the community, is thought to demand it." The state could ask you to die in service of the war effort; of course it could ask you to shut up.[18]

In any case, the cynical old soldier was disinclined to tolerate wartime dissent. "Damn a man," he had written to a friend when World War I broke out, "who ain't for his country, right or wrong."[19]

So when Holmes retreated to his study to write the first opinions on the constitutionality of the Espionage Act, he didn't have to do a lot of thinking. It didn't matter that this was the first time the Supreme Court had turned its attention to the First Amendment in a sustained fashion. These were easy ones.

Holmes began with the case of Charles Schenck, the general secretary of the Socialist Party of Philadelphia, who had been sentenced to jail for sending a pamphlet to men who had passed their draft-board physical exam. The pamphlet argued that conscription was unconstitutional and called on the men to assert their rights to protest—by such admittedly vanilla tactics as joining the Socialist Party and writing to their congressmen to ask for a repeal of the conscription law.

Did Schenck have a right to that kind of speech? "In ordinary times," Holmes conceded, he would. But the right to free speech was dependent on its circumstances, and wartime was different; the state had the right to protect the draft from obstruction. If words would create a "clear and present danger that they will bring about the substantive evils that Congress has a right to prevent," then Congress had to have the right to ban the words. To illuminate the point that speech had its limits, Holmes reached for a metaphor: "The most stringent protection of free speech would not protect a man in falsely shouting fire in a theatre and causing a panic."[20]

The metaphor has become such a familiar part of American political culture that it is easy to forget how strange it is. To limit the right to free speech, Holmes was comparing a pamphlet urging citizens to petition Congress to mischievously causing a stampede in a theater. The situations are really quite dissimilar—the harm in the theater is rather more "clear and present" than the harm from the pamphlet. (Particularly given that very few of the pamphlets seem to have actually found their way into the hands of enlisted men. Many were impounded by postal censors. Of those that reached their target, most were, in the time-honored tradition of political flyers, ignored.) And quite a lot turns on the fact that the cry of fire in the theater was "false" in Holmes's metaphor. You would create a "clear and present" danger of a stampede anytime you yelled fire in a theater, but if there actually was a fire, the risk would be worth it. In assuming that criticism of the war was the equivalent of a "false" shout of fire, Holmes had put his thumb on the scale, ruling out the possibility that Socialist critics of the war could have been identifying a real threat to the body politic.[21]

This unhelpful metaphor seems itself to have been a product of the violent labor struggles of the preceding decades. It had been introduced into the case history by Ohio prosecutor Edwin Wertz as a way of discrediting Eugene Debs's claims to a right to free speech— Debs was claiming, Wertz argued, the right to go into a "crowded theatre . . . and yell 'fire' when there was no fire and people [would be] trampled to death." Where Wertz got the metaphor from is unclear, but it seems likely he was thinking of a very similar sequence of events that had recently happened in Calumet, Michigan. During a protracted strike by immigrant copper miners in 1913, the Ladies Auxiliary of the Western Federation of Miners had organized a children's Christmas party on the second floor of the Italian Hall. During the party, someone yelled fire, and there was a crush to reach the only door at the bottom of the narrow stairs. Seventy-three died, fifty-six of them children under the age of sixteen, many still holding Christmas presents. The tragedy made the front page of the *New York Times* and papers around the country, and it had entered the political culture—Woody Guthrie's 1939 ballad "The 1913 Massacre" captured the widespread assumption by those on the Left that the fateful shout had come from an antiunion vigilante spotted at the hall. Introduced by Wertz in his effort to prosecute Debs, stripped of its political context, it was no surprise that the metaphor intrigued Holmes. For the justice was something of a firebug—he told friends they should wake him if there was a fire to look at—and turned repeatedly to fire metaphors in his writing.[22]

With the help of his misleading metaphor, it had taken Holmes only six short paragraphs to uphold Schenck's conviction and rule that the First Amendment posed no obstacle to the sweeping censorship regime established by the Espionage Act during the war. He dispatched just as easily with the other two Espionage Act appeals. In fact, they revealed just how deferential the court was to the right of the state to suppress dissent. Jacob Frohwerk, editor of a small German-language newspaper, had been convicted for a series of articles critical of the draft and the war. (The list included an article deploring recent draft riots but in a tone that "might be taken to convey an innuendo of a different sort.") It would have been easy to distinguish the case from *Schenck*. Frohwerk had been editing a newspaper; unlike Schenck's pamphlet, it was not obviously aimed at persuading enlisting men, and thus the danger of harming the war effort was even less "clear and present" than it had been in the earlier case. But Holmes was not interested in such distinctions. "It is impossible to say," he ruled, "that it might not have been found that the circulation of the paper was in quarters where a little breath would be enough to kindle a flame." With the help of another fire metaphor, that hypothetical line of reasoning endorsed the use of the Espionage Act as a general censorship bill during wartime. How could any newspaper guarantee that its contents might not circulate to an army camp?[23]

That left the *Debs* case. This would have been the easiest case for Holmes to treat differently. Debs had not written a pamphlet; he had not explicitly criticized the war. There was no obvious "clear and present danger"—a phrase that Holmes did not even use in his opinion—and the speech was very far removed from a false shout of fire in a theater. Most of it had concerned Socialism, which Holmes had to concede was legal (although he couldn't hide his condescension when summarizing it as "the usual contrasts between capitalists and laboring men, sneers at the advice to cultivate war gardens, attribution to plutocrats of the high price of coal, &c."). But if the jury had ruled that such speech had the "natural" or "probable" effect of interfering with recruitment, then, following *Schenck*, Holmes concluded that it was not protected by the First Amendment. Debs's conviction was upheld.[24]

The Supreme Court had resoundingly placed itself on the side of the patriots who sought to censor the radical Left. In any future war the path was open for the ongoing suppression of speech when the security of the state seemed to justify it. And Schenck, Frohwerk, and Debs remained in prison. Hence the wrath of the anarchists two months later.

"I suppose," Holmes wrote to a friend on May 1, "it was the Debs incident that secured me the honor of being among those destined to receive an explosive machine."[25]

A. Mitchell Palmer had, like Holmes, been destined to receive a bomb on May Day. And like Holmes, he had been spared for want of a postage stamp. But at a quarter past eleven on the night of June 2, the front of his house was torn open by a detonation. This bomb had been hand-delivered by an anarchist—no messing with postage this time—and it seems that the messenger slipped as he placed the device. The explosion killed the hapless radical and created a scene of grisly chaos in Palmer's tony Northwest DC neighborhood. Windows were shattered up and down the street; the trees were so "bespattered with blood and fragments of human flesh" that the fire department had to hose the block down. Parts of the bomber's body sailed into the homes of Senator Claude Swanson (two doors down from

Palmer) and the Norwegian envoy (three doors down). The bomber's scalp was found on the roof of the house opposite Palmer's, which happened to be the residence of Franklin and Eleanor Roosevelt.[26]

Pamphlets printed on pink paper fluttered down amid the gore, promising revolutionary class war. ("There will have to be bloodshed; we will not dodge; there will have to be murder; we will kill, because it is necessary; there will have to be destruction, we will destroy to rid the world of your tyrannical institutions.") Having learned the lessons of World War I, the pamphleteers took pains to assert that they were not Germans or paid agents of the Germans. But with the war over, imperial Germany was no longer the international bugaboo. A new menace haunted the minds of insecure Americans. The bombings, warned the *Washington Post*, were the "first sample of Soviet Government."[27]

On the same night, bombs went off in seven other cities.

What would become known as the "red scare" had begun in earnest. For Palmer, the June bombings set off a yearlong quest to establish himself as the guardian of the nation's security. He sought new laws to censor dissent, perfected new techniques to punish radicals, established new security bureaucracies, and ran for president on a militantly patriotic law-and-order platform. He failed to achieve much of what he hoped for. Even so, in the year after the bombing Palmer would lay the foundation for much of the security state we live with today.

Before 1919, during his career as an influential congressman and Democratic Party insider, Palmer was neither a hawk nor a reactionary. He was a progressive, a moderate reformist, and a pacifist. When Wilson offered him the position of secretary of war, Palmer declined, citing his beliefs as a Quaker. (The night of the June bombing, FDR later joked, Palmer had regressed into Quakerisms: "he was 'theeing' and 'thouing' me all over the place."[28])

Palmer served the war instead as the alien enemy property custodian—seizing hundreds of millions of dollars of German property for public administration or sale to Americans, enjoying the opportunities thus created for patronage and graft, and coming to a new appreciation of the powers that war provided to the executive branch. When Thomas Gregory stepped down as attorney general in the spring of 1919—Gregory missed making money in private practice—Palmer was nominated to replace him.[29]

At first, Palmer seemed to retreat from the excesses of his predecessor's vision of national security. He continued to distance the Justice Department from the vigilante groups, calling private espionage "entirely at variance with our theories of government." With the war over, he dropped hundreds of pending Espionage Act cases, advocated for clemency for one hundred individuals in jail on Espionage Act charges, and released ten thousand enemy aliens from detention.[30]

The June bombing ended this flirtation with liberalism. "The morning after my house was blown up," he recalled, "I stood in the middle of the wreckage of my library with Congressmen and Senators, and without a dissenting voice they called upon me in strong terms to exercise all the power that was possible . . . to run to earth the criminals who were behind that kind of outrage." The message was clear: "I was shouted at from every editorial sanctum in America from sea to sea. I was preached upon from every pulpit. I was urged—I could feel it dinned into my ears—throughout the country to do something and do it now, and do it quick, and do it in a way that would bring results to stop this sort of thing in the U.S." For an ambitious politician—and above all else, Palmer wanted power—it was an irresistible lure. Palmer moved quickly to seize the issue.[31]

Within weeks of the explosion, Palmer had recalibrated the Department of Justice to focus on the threat of radicalism. William J. Flynn, former head of the Secret Service and a man with a national reputation as an expert on policing anarchism, became the new head of the Bureau of Investigation. Flynn was soon telling people, on the basis of no evidence, that the June bombings had been orchestrated by men "connected with Russian bolshevism, aided by Hun money." (In reality, the bombings had been done by a small, unaffiliated group of Italian anarchists. An Italian-English dictionary, found amid the remains of the bomber, was dismissed as a "ruse.") Palmer and his aides went to Congress to seek, and receive, new funding to investigate the red menace. Plans were announced to deport radicals en masse. In August a new Radical Division was created in the Bureau of Investigation. To head it, Palmer appointed an ambitious, efficient twenty-four-year-old by the name of J. Edgar Hoover.[32]

Despite the flurry of institutional activity, Palmer was worried that he lacked the legal authority to really go after radicals. For months, Palmer had been asking for the passage of a peacetime sedition act to take the place of the Espionage Act, which was, strictly speaking, enforceable only in times of war and of no use after the armistice. Without such a law, Palmer was forced to scour the statutes for any viable means to prosecute advocates of revolution. Palmer went after the small El Ariete Society of anarchists in Buffalo by using a Civil War–era section of the criminal code intended to prevent insurrection. The case was thrown out of court; that statute didn't apply to mere propaganda, no matter how violently militant. The uncertainties of the law had boxed Palmer in, forcing on him an unnatural passivity.[33]

By October, pressure was mounting on the attorney general to show some spine. Republican senator Miles Poindexter, who had been a jingoistic patriot during the war and was now eyeing a run for the presidency, began attacking Palmer and the Wilson administration for being too soft on radicals. Poindexter thought there were "innumerable instances of government aid and sympathy for revolutionary anarchists," and he said that if the "government continues in that supine and indifferent attitude . . . there is real danger that the government will fall." Poindexter proposed a Senate resolution asking Palmer to explain himself and his inaction. What was being done to prosecute those who "preached anarchy and sedition"? It passed unanimously and won support from the press. The *New York Times* worried that Palmer wasn't tough enough on radical immigrants, that he was clinging to "antiquated opinions," that he suffered a "pre-Adamite sentimentality." It was particularly embarrassing, sniped the *Times*, coming from Palmer. After all, these "enthusiasts of destruction tried to kill Mr. Palmer himself. The sound of their bombs is still in our ears."[34]

Behind the scenes, Palmer's Justice Department (DOJ) had in fact been preparing the groundwork for a purge of radical aliens. Palmer still lacked a peacetime sedition act, but in 1918 Congress had amended the Immigration Act to make it easier to deport anarchists. At the time, the Labor Department was responsible for immigration policy, but the DOJ had the manpower and the funds, so a bureaucratic compromise was brokered: Justice would send the names of deportable individuals to Labor, which would issue arrest warrants, which would be executed by Justice, which would then turn over the arrested aliens to Labor to deport. On November 7, Bureau of Investigation agents swept out in eleven cities to arrest hundreds of radicals; some were "badly beaten" as they were taken into custody. What were known as the "Palmer raids" had begun.[35]

The next week, Palmer sent his response to the Poindexter resolution, showing that he *was* taking action. He cited the November 7 raids, as well as the vast surveillance work that Hoover's Radical Division had carried out to prepare for them: files opened on 60,000 "radically inclined individuals" and the monitoring of 471 publications. And Palmer reiterated the need for a stringent new peacetime sedition law. In fact, he sent over a draft statute that would have made it illegal to advocate interfering with any law of the United States, or to belong to any organization doing so, and that would allow the denaturalization and deportation of any immigrant who violated the statute.[36]

Palmer's proposed law was one of *seventy* different peacetime sedition bills that had been proposed in Congress over the previous months, and more were on their way. The year since the armistice had brought not a return to tolerance but a heightened clamor for the permanent continuation of the sorts of censorship that the Espionage Act had facilitated during the war. The proposed laws imagined giving the government the power to silence, deport, or even execute advocates of revolution. One suggested banning the German language from the mails, another to turn Guam into a penal colony for political extremists.[37]

Palmer had emerged as the key figure in this effort to make the wartime Espionage Act permanent. His political calculations were simple. In the short term, there was no easier way to build a firewall against critics, such as Poindexter, who were positioning themselves as nationalist demagogues; taking the patriotic high ground would cut their legs out, establishing his political legitimacy. And just over the horizon were even greater rewards. Even before Wilson suffered a debilitating stroke in early October, the president had been a distant figure, preoccupied by negotiations over the peace in Paris and then by the fight to ratify the League of Nations. By the time of the Palmer raids, with the sick Wilson sidelined, there was a power vacuum. The way was open for a member of the administration to seize the bully pulpit, to position himself for the presidential election in 1920.

Palmer planned to take it. Three days after the November 7 raids, the *Wall Street Journal* declared that Palmer was the most likely Democratic nominee for the next election. Seizing his moment, Palmer promised that there would be no "let-up" on the radicals. Palmer's Justice Department was just getting started.[38]

On the same day, the Supreme Court handed down a decision in yet another Espionage Act case. *Abrams v. U.S.* concerned not Socialist critics of the war but a small group of Jewish immigrants involved in the anarchist world of New York. Back in August 1918, they had prepared two leaflets, one in English and one in Yiddish, that criticized Wilson's deployment of US soldiers to Siberia, ostensibly to protect a Czech army that had been stranded there after the Bolshevik revolution. To leftists at the time, it understandably looked like a US effort to throw its weight behind the anti-Bolshevik forces in the Russian civil war.[39]

On August 23, 1918, the anarchists had thrown the pamphlets, which called for a general strike, from upper-story windows on the

Lower East Side in the hopes they would be read by workers heading to their morning shift. One of the anarchists was apprehended in the act and quickly turned in his colleagues, who were charged under the Sedition Act amendments with trying to disrupt the production of military materiel.

Their prosecution was quick and predictable, distinguished only by the prejudice that they experienced during each step of the criminal justice system. It is likely they were beaten during interrogation, and one man, Jacob Schwartz, died in the Tombs awaiting trial—pneumonia was the official cause of death, although his lawyer always maintained it was a result of poor treatment. The district attorney who drew up the prosecution was a veteran of the Spanish-American War, a defender of Jim Crow in his native Alabama, and on record as favoring the "extermination" of antiwar dissent. And the trial judge, former Alabama congressman Henry DeLamar Clayton Jr., was a man with deep prejudice against immigrants and radicals and pacifists. He had recently lost a brother in combat against the Germans and wore a black armband and his brother's gold star throughout a trial in which he sparred with the defendants, expressed his desire that they be deported, and took particular umbrage at the politics of the twenty-one-year-old Mollie Steimer, the youngest of the defendants, whom he questioned about such irrelevant matters as her attitudes to free love and marriage. (Ordinarily, the defendants might have expected a less antagonistic judge in New York, but the courts were so overwhelmed with war work that they had called in help from less busy districts.)[40]

It was not a surprise that the jury returned a guilty verdict after only sixty-six minutes or that Clayton gave an almost two-hour diatribe against Communism and German espionage as he handed down sentences of twenty years to the three male defendants and fifteen years to Steimer. Their lawyer appealed to the Supreme Court, complaining that the prosecution violated his clients' First Amendment rights.[41]

Given Holmes's opinions in the unanimous *Schenck*, *Frohwerk*, and *Debs* decisions only six months earlier, it wasn't a promising line of appeal. If anything, the case for prosecuting the Abrams defendants was stronger than it had been in those first Espionage Act cases. The Sedition Act made it illegal to interfere with wartime production: the threat that a general strike posed to production was more straightforward than the threat to recruitment at stake in those earlier cases. And the defendants had distributed their call directly to workers, arguably creating a more "clear and present" danger than the speeches and pamphlets and newspaper articles of the earlier cases, all of which had involved rather circuitous routes to servicemen and hadn't directly called for civil disobedience. Unsurprisingly, seven of the justices simply applied the *Schenck* precedent and upheld the convictions.

But then a surprising thing happened. Oliver Wendell Holmes dissented, deciding that the defendants in *Abrams* had exactly the right to free speech he had so recently denied to Debs, Frohwerk, and Schenck.

Holmes had spent the summer reflecting ruefully on his Espionage Act decisions in the spring, which had produced an unexpected and unwelcome wave of criticism. As early as April, he was already complaining to a friend that he was receiving "stupid letters of protest against a decision that Debs, a noted agitator, was rightly convicted of obstructing the recruiting service." Then an article was published in the *New Republic* by Ernst Freund, a progressive reformer and legal scholar with deep commitments to immigrant and worker rights, which argued that Holmes's decisions were bad and that his famous analogy to the false shout of fire was "manifestly inappropriate." The article stung because the magazine and the author were exactly the sort of progressives who had lionized Holmes for his decisions on economic-regulation cases. They had helped establish Holmes's reputation as a judicial giant, an experience that he had found quite agreeable. Now they had turned on him. In a defensive pique, Holmes drafted a reply to the magazine in which he complained that "I hated to have to write the Debs case and still more those of the other poor devils before us" but nevertheless maintained that he had applied the law correctly.[42]

Holmes never sent the letter to the magazine, but he did send it to one of his closest confidants: Harold J. Laski. Holmes and Laski were an odd pair. Laski was only twenty-four, five full decades younger than the judge. And the young British academic was very much a man of the Left, not normally a winning attribute for Holmes. But the two had been introduced to each other by another young progressive in the *New Republic* crowd, Felix Frankfurter, and had hit it off, drawn to each other by a mutual intellectual respect and perhaps some deeper psychological currents—the childless Holmes would sign his letters to Laski "my dear lad" and sometimes refer to him as "my son" or "my boy." In April, Laski had read the Freund article, enjoyed it, and sent it on to Holmes to see what the old man made of it. Holmes had sent his draft letter in reply, adding a cover note that he thought Freund's argument was "poor stuff."[43]

It turned out to be the opening salvo in a debate between the two friends about the meaning of free speech that would have major consequences for US history. Over the summer, Laski bombarded Holmes with reading material on the history and theory of free speech, which Holmes read closely and seriously. (Interspersed, to be fair, with less heady stuff, such as the most recent John Buchan spy thriller, which Holmes stayed up late to finish. "I got one leg on the fly paper and then I was caught," Holmes confessed.[44])

Through Laski, Holmes became exposed to the ideas of a new constellation of activists promoting the right to free speech. Its core had emerged out of the same radical labor and pacifist movements that had been persecuted under the Espionage Act. Crystal Eastman was one of its most important early members. She had cut her teeth studying the law and politics of the workplace accidents maiming so many workers and then helped organize both the Women's Peace Party and the American Union Against Militarism (AUAM). Even before the war had begun, Eastman and the AUAM had lobbied against the passage of the Espionage Act because of the threat it posed to civil liberties.[45]

After war broke out, Eastman thought that the AUAM was the "logical group to defend the other American liberties, free speech, free press, and free assembly." The AUAM's Conscientious Objectors Bureau was soon renamed the Civil Liberties Bureau, and Eastman was joined in the work by Roger Baldwin, a social worker who had been inspired by Emma Goldman to turn to radicalism. (Baldwin had come on board as a temporary replacement when Eastman needed time off during a complicated pregnancy.) Together, Eastman and Baldwin led the increasingly militant National Civil Liberties Bureau out of the AUAM. As an independent body, it supported the Wobblies during their Espionage Act trial in 1917.[46]

Inevitably, these advocates of civil liberties themselves became a target of suspicion and repression. A number of their pamphlets were denied mailing privileges by the postmaster general (as was the *Masses*, a magazine edited by Eastman's brother, Max). Roger Baldwin's phone was tapped, in the hopes of finding evidence of an Espionage Act violation. In August 1918, government investigators raided the Civil Liberties Bureau's offices and seized its records. Baldwin would ultimately serve jail time for conscientious objection. Eastman, too, was forced to take a backseat. Her pregnancy had led to kidney disease, which limited her capacity to work until her untimely death in 1928, at only forty-seven. But the Civil Liberties Bureau survived even as its parent, the AUAM, collapsed. In January 1920 the Civil Liberties Bureau would adopt the name by which it is still known: the American Civil Liberties Union. Baldwin would head it until 1950.[47]

By 1919, the vision of free speech first articulated by these radicals was beginning to gain support from within the progressive and liberal mainstream. With a little distance, the excesses of the war had served as an object lesson in the dangers of censorship, convincing a new constellation of journalists, intellectuals, and politicians that the right to free speech was an important check on the strong government they otherwise wished to encourage. Bringing these disparate visions of civil liberties together was no easy task. It would be the work of years and would require suppressing the origins of the movement in radical labor politics. But in 1919, when civil liberties were only beginning to emerge in their modern form, it was a surprisingly potent coalition. The harassed and marginalized advocates of free speech found that their new allies in the establishment had a direct line to the heart of US politics.

Laski was pulling many of the strings that threaded this loose network together. In late 1918 he had helped Zechariah Chafee Jr., a young law professor at Harvard who had begun studying the Espionage Act speech cases, to publish an early version of his findings in the *New Republic*. In the summer of 1919, when Chafee had published his research in a long *Harvard Law Review* piece, Laski sent it to Holmes and then arranged for Chafee and Holmes to meet over tea to discuss it. Chafee's article seemed calculated to convert Holmes to the side of free speech. It focused less on individual rights to speech than on the social benefit to be gained from allowing for free expression: a Darwinian argument for robust debate that would appeal to the relativistic old justice. And it creatively reread Holmes's three Espionage Act opinions in the spring to argue that *Schenck* and *Frohwerk* were correctly decided. Holmes's theory that speech that posed a "clear and present danger" could be censored was sensible, Chafee conceded. The only problem was that Holmes had applied his test incorrectly in deciding against Debs. If Holmes had stuck to his own brilliant logic, Chafee suggested, it would have led him to protect the speech rights of dissidents, like Debs, who couldn't really be said to pose a clear and present danger that would justify interfering in the free exchange of ideas.[48]

When Holmes wrote his dissent in the *Abrams* case in the fall, it was easy to see the imprint of his summertime crash course in the philosophy of free speech. He now interpreted his clear-and-present-danger test from the spring in a manner very similar to Chafee's, and he decided that the *Abrams* pamphleteers did not rise to the level—seven different times in his opinion he reiterated that the danger needed to be "imminent" or "immediate." And inspired by his reading of Chafee and John Stuart Mill, he hit upon a new understanding of the social benefit of the right of free speech. Yes, he began, it was easy to see why a majority might want to censor speech. "Persecution for the expression of opinion seems to me perfectly logical," he conceded, summing up what had been his position only six months earlier. "But when men have realized that time has upset many fighting faiths, they may come to believe even more than they believe the very foundations of their own conduct that the ultimate good desired is better reached by free trade in ideas—that the best test of truth is the power of the thought to get itself accepted in competition of the market." A new metaphor—the market, not the burning theater—now guided his thinking.[49]

That metaphor, the "marketplace of ideas," would guide the rise of the First Amendment in the twentieth century. It wasn't the metaphor that Laski or Chafee or Debs or Baldwin would have chosen, for they were critics of laissez-faire economics. The more conservative Holmes had filtered their calls for freedom into his own language— along with his free-speech reading, he had read a biography of Adam Smith in the summer of 1919. Indeed, the dissent hardly made Holmes their political ally in their broader projects of political and economic reform. Holmes retained his hostility to radicals; the only twentieth-century reform cause he was particularly drawn to was eugenics. Holmes upheld the speech rights of the *Abrams* defendants in part because he thought they were so insignificant that they posed no real threat. He called them "poor and puny anonymities" and thought that the "silly" leaflets advocated a "creed of ignorance and immaturity."[50]

At a key moment of history, however, Holmes had been willing to take a stand for the right to free speech. Holmes, one of the nation's most important theorists of judicial process, understood perfectly well that his decisions on the Supreme Court were political, interpretive acts, not the simple application of preexisting law. As he famously put it, "The life of the law is not logic but experience." And his experience of friendship with Laski was crucial in his change of heart in 1919. Laski had introduced him to the ideas that shifted his attitudes. Laski served as the messenger conveying the disapproval of the progressives whose respect Holmes had so relished. And Laski provided an object lesson of the threats that intolerance posed to American culture. For by the fall of 1919, Laski was himself suffering for speaking out in support of a controversial strike of Boston police officers. As Holmes was considering the *Abrams* case, Laski had written to Holmes to ask for help in surviving a campaign to have him fired from Harvard.[51]

Holmes's decision to stand with Abrams and Laski was a noteworthy act of dissent against the patriotic Right. There was real pressure on Holmes to decide the other way. Three days before the *Abrams* decision was handed down, on the night of Palmer's November 7 raids, three justices came to Holmes's house to try to convince him to withdraw his dissent. Given the turmoil in the streets of the nation, given the threat posed by anarchists and radicals, they asked Holmes to act like a soldier, to close ranks with them and put the safety of the country first. In the quiet of his study—which had been targeted for a bomb by anarchists only months before—Holmes's wife had agreed with them. But Holmes stuck to his guns, entering into the judicial record a powerful defense of the right to free speech. If life was struggle and conflict, you couldn't give one side the power to completely squash the opposition. You had to leave the door open to the possibility that the tables might turn in the future.[52]

Over the long term, Holmes's *Abrams* dissent would itself prove precisely this theory of political change. Beginning as a powerless protest against the decision of his peers, it ultimately proved its success in the marketplace of ideas. In a slow and contentious process over many decades of activism by civil libertarians of various political stripes, the sorts of speech that were protected by the First Amendment would be radically expanded, creating the liberal—and libertarian—public sphere of the early twenty-first century. Holmes's dissent in *Abrams* was the birth of the modern First Amendment.

Of course, that was cold comfort to the defendants in the case. When the Supreme Court upheld her conviction, Mollie Steimer was already in custody—she had been arrested for political advocacy yet again. So was Herman Lachowsky—he had been picked up in Palmer's raid on November 7 and was being detained on Ellis Island. Jacob Abrams and Samuel Lipman were still out on bail and tried to escape to Mexico, but were quickly captured. All four were sent to jail—the three men serving time in the same Atlanta federal penitentiary as Eugene Debs—before being deported to the Soviet Union in November 1921.[53]

In the months after the *Abrams* decision, Attorney General Palmer, with the eager help of Hoover, pressed on with his efforts to deport radicals. On December 21, 1919, 249 of the individuals seized in earlier raids were loaded onto an old troop transport from the Spanish-American War and deported to Russia. Alexander Berkman and Emma Goldman, who was a citizen but had been denaturalized, were the most famous of them. Most were anonymous; a number of men were permanently separated from their families. The press was delighted by what it dubbed the Soviet Ark. "It is to be hoped and expected," swooned the *Cleveland Plain Dealer*, "that other vessels, larger, more commodious, carrying similar cargoes, will follow in her wake."[54]

On New Year's Eve, 1920, Palmer promised the nation that his Justice Department would "keep up an unflinching, persistent, aggressive warfare" against radicalism. "The 'Red' movement," he clarified in a demagogic address, "does not mean an attitude of protest against alleged defects in our present political and economic organization of society. It does not represent the radicalism of progress. It represents a specific doctrine, namely, the introduction of dictatorship the world over by force and violence." Radicals, Palmer warned, threatened all who went to church or who owned farms, or their homes, or liberty bonds.[55]

Two days later, Bureau of Investigation agents swarmed out in cities across the nation, rounding up those whose names had made it onto Hoover's lists, and many more besides. In Seattle, one immigration inspector reported, the agents just "went to various pool rooms etc. in which foreigners congregated, and they simply sent up in trucks all of them that happened to be there." So chaotic and haphazard were the raids that the exact number of people arrested has never been clear, but it was thousands, possibly as many as 7,500. Hundreds were arrested because they had joined the Socialist Party for entirely innocent reasons—to go to a social, to sing in a choir—and then been automatically registered as members of the Communist Party when their local had affiliated with the newer organization. In Lynn, Massachusetts, twenty-nine men were arrested because they were trying to form a cooperative bakery. The conditions in which these individuals were held matched the slapdash cruelty of the methods used to arrest them. In Detroit eight hundred men were held in an improvised jail, with no food for the first twenty-four hours and only one toilet for all of them. Never mind all that, said the *Washington Post*: "There is no time to waste on hairsplitting over infringement of liberty."[56]

Palmer was flying high, promising the nation they would soon see "a second, third and fourth Soviet Ark." The press ate it up. The *New York Times* happily conceded it had been wrong about the attorney general: "If some or any of us, impatient for the swift confusion of the Reds, have ever questioned the alacrity, resolute will, and fruitful, intelligent vigor of the DOJ in hunting down those enemies of the US, the questioners and the doubters have now cause to approve and applaud."[57]

In March, Palmer announced he was a candidate for the presidency. He ran on a nationalist platform, aiming to "tear out the radical seeds that have entangled American ideas in their poisonous theories," hoping to stop "the blaze of revolution sweeping over every American institution of law and order." "Red agitators" who were spreading the "disease of evil thinking" needed to be purged: 90 percent of them weren't even American. In opposition to such foreign subversives—with their "sly and crafty eyes . . . [their] lopsided faces, sloping brows and misshapen features"—Palmer defended the true Americans. "I am myself an American," he told a crowd just before the Georgia primary, "and I love to preach my doctrine before undiluted one hundred percent Americans, because my platform is, in a word, undiluted Americanism and undying loyalty to the republic."[58]

Passing a peacetime sedition act remained one of his central goals. As he stated, "This is the kind of measure the Department of Justice must have if it is going to stamp out this grave menace of sedition," and "it has been hailed generally by red-blooded Americans as a measure 'with teeth in it.'" Just days after the January raid, Congress had consolidated the seventy proposed sedition laws into one bill. It was so extreme that even Palmer conceded that it "makes me shudder a little": it punished some forms of sedition with the death penalty, gave the postmaster general ongoing powers to keep seditious material out of the mail, and threatened to define all labor agitation as sedition. Palmer succeeded in having a "milder" bill substituted, one that still promised up to twenty years in prison for any speech that was intended to cause the overthrow of the government or interfere with the execution of any law, or that threatened any act of force, hate, revenge, or injury against any US person or property. The fact that Palmer could appear the voice of centrist reason suggests just how powerful were the currents of nationalism sweeping the political class.[59]

The Senate did pass one version of the law, but the House kept it in committee for further work. It was simply too controversial. Organized labor had spoken out against it. So had the American Newspaper Publishers Association, which had helped kill Section 2(c) of the Espionage Act in 1917; the press was particularly worried about the power the new law would give the postmaster general to exclude newspapers from the mail. Sailing into such headwinds, the bill's passage slowed. It did not pass during the feverish period of the Palmer raids, when the national mood was running hot and angry and intolerant. The delay was crucial.[60]

Over the spring and early summer, a backlash to the nationalist extremes of Palmer's Justice Department kicked in. It was orchestrated by the same coalition of civil libertarians that had pushed back against the Espionage Act during the war and that had influenced Oliver Wendell Holmes when he changed his mind about the meaning of the First Amendment the previous summer. Now, they lobbied against Palmer's sedition bill and took on the excesses of his deportation program.

In January, Francis Fisher Kane had resigned as US Attorney in Pennsylvania in protest of the Palmer raids and then testified against any "new espionage legislation" because "there is too much repression in this country of free speech and of the freedom of the press, that we do not need any legislation on the subject, that the public has gone much too far." In May, Kane was one of twelve lawyers to sign the seventy-five-page *Report upon the Illegal Practices of the United States Department of Justice*, which documented the abuses of the January raids. Much of the information in the report had been provided by Baldwin and Eastman's National Civil Liberties Bureau; among Kane's cosigners were Ernst Freund, Felix Frankfurter, and Zechariah Chafee Jr. (who had also testified against the peacetime sedition law).[61]

By then, Palmer's star had faded; the report was the final blow that killed his national reputation. Louis F. Post, a left-leaning official in the Department of Labor, had reviewed the deportation orders that had come out of the January raids, concluded that most were bunk, and begun canceling all those based on illegally seized evidence or wrongful arrest—some 2,700 of them. Palmer had counterattacked, accusing Post of "habitually tender solicitude for social revolution and perverted sympathy for the criminal anarchists of the country." Impeachment hearings against Post were begun in late April.[62]

But in his efforts to capitalize on the fear of radicals, Palmer had overplayed his hand. His accusations that a rail strike in April was part of an international Communist conspiracy to overthrow the government, establish a dictatorship of the proletariat, and "transport to this country the exact chaotic condition that exists in Russia" did little but convince even conservative labor leaders that Palmer was their enemy.[63]

And then Palmer predicted that on May 1 there would be a general strike and a national wave of assassinations intended to overthrow the government. The nation went on high alert. The entire New York City police force, eleven thousand strong, was put on active duty from midnight on April 30 until 8 a.m. on May 2. In Boston, cops were placed on guard at strategic locations around the city and were provided with seven automobiles mounted with machine guns to be deployed as needed to put down unrest.[64]

May Day came, nothing happened, and Palmer was a laughingstock. A cartoon in the *Chicago Tribune* the next weekend depicted Palmer on a stroll, every man, woman, child, and baby on the street appearing to him to wear the beard of a European radical. Post came out of the impeachment hearings looking like a hero for keeping his head and maintaining the rule of law; Palmer seemed a victim of his own paranoid fantasies. Congress would later conduct hearings to work out what had gone wrong under Palmer's watch.[65]

Palmer's presidential campaign sputtered to a halt. Despite primary defeats, which he sought to blame on "alien reds," Palmer was still the favored candidate of the party insiders when he arrived at the San Francisco convention in June. The city was bedecked with posters of the attorney general holding a law book and admonishing the public with a stern finger. "The Fighting Quaker" was one slogan; "Laying Down the Law" another. He received a thirty-six-minute ovation when nominated, and he polled second, with 256 votes, on the first ballot.[66]

But it was over. He had lost his air of legitimacy and didn't look like a winner. On the twelfth ballot his support began to trickle away, and he was a distant third by the twenty-second. After a brief rally on the thirty-sixth ballot, his candidacy collapsed. It took forty-four ballots for a deeply divided party to nominate James Cox of Ohio, with Franklin Roosevelt as his young running mate.[67]

Amid the backlash against the Palmer raids and the implosion of Palmer's reputation, the proposed peacetime sedition law slipped into oblivion. It never reemerged from committee; it had come to seem a step too far, a dangerous and unnecessary interference with civil liberties. During the election that fall, Cox distanced himself from Palmer and lost anyway, to Warren Harding, who promised a return to normalcy.

Normalcy meant, among other things, closing the book on the Espionage Act. During the campaign, pressure had mounted to commute the sentences of the victims of Espionage Act censorship, most of whom still sat in prison. Releasing them wasn't simply a symbolic issue, for the years they spent in jail for speech crimes were tough. There was the usual violence in jail and the difficulties created by separation from families, especially the inability to provide for dependents. The Wobblies frequently ran afoul of the harsh prison discipline of the period, landing in isolation or on restricted diets for failing to break enough rock, for laziness, for wasting food, for telling wardens to fuck themselves. Some had mental breakdowns and were transferred to insane asylums; others had their health permanently broken, often from tuberculosis. Ricardo Flores Magón, an exiled Mexican anarchist who was sentenced to twenty-one years for publishing an antiwar editorial, was denied proper medical care in Leavenworth and died in prison in 1922.[68]

Debs was the cause célèbre, particularly once he received, for the fifth time, the Socialist Party's 1920 nomination for the presidency. But the Wilson administration would not budge, and Debs campaigned from his cell, winning 913,000 votes. Only at the end of 1921 would Debs walk free, having been offered clemency by Harding along with two dozen other political prisoners. His fellow inmates gave him an ovation as he left the penitentiary. The *New York Times*, which had argued that Debs should serve the entire term, complained that a "shallow, howling minority has had its way."[69]

A loose network of labor and civil-liberties activists continued to push for the release of the remaining political prisoners. In April 1922, Kate Richards O'Hare, who had been released from her own Espionage Act imprisonment early, led a march of the children and wives of the still imprisoned. They camped outside the White House, holding signs that read "Debs is free—why not my daddy?" Over the course of 1923 the remaining victims of the Espionage Act had their sentences commuted. FDR offered them amnesty in 1933.[70] It was a belated acknowledgment of just how wrongheaded their prosecution had been in the first place.

The eighteen months immediately following World War I were an important turning point in the history of the Espionage Act. During the war, the law had been used to develop a sweeping censorship apparatus. In the panicky, twitchy months after the war, amid fears of revolution and radicals and bombs, the United States had flirted with consolidating that censorial regime. But then, thanks in large part to the lobbying of a small network of left-leaning civil-liberties activists, the US had recoiled from this vision of a public sphere regimented and disciplined by antiradical patriotism.

The United States was not, by any means, done with the politics of censorship or the lure of national-security demagoguery—in Wisconsin, Joe McCarthy had just turned thirteen years old when Debs was released from prison. Nevertheless, a moment of danger had passed. In March 1921, in one sign of its desire to distance itself from the hysteria of the war years, Congress quietly removed the Sedition Act amendments to the Espionage Act.[71]

However, the rest of the Espionage Act remained on the books, including those vague and confusing clauses intended to protect the secrecy of "information relating to the national defense."

And a nascent national-security bureaucracy was beginning to emerge, with its own interests in securing the secrecy of its records and operations. During the red scare, Palmer had elevated Hoover to a new perch. The young bureaucrat made his name by cultivating files of confidential information on those he considered radicals. Hoover would soon rise even further. As head of the FBI for five decades, he would prove a stern guardian of both the nation and his secrets.

This was a new form of national-security politics. It was not focused on censoring radical critics of American policy. Rather, it sought to act in secret, to shield its efforts to secure the nation not just from foreign spies but also, unavoidably, from the gaze of the public.

Yet if an effective secrecy regime was to be established, it would be necessary to make sense of the Espionage Act and to untangle the difficulties created by its hasty passage in early 1917. That task would be taken up at a time when Palmer was a distant memory, during the presidency of his neighbor on the night of the June bombing: Franklin Delano Roosevelt.

Chapter 4

THE CREEPING SCOPE
OF THE SECRECY LAWS

Stanley Reed holds a press conference shortly after being nominated to the Supreme Court in 1938. On the bench, Reed would write the opinion declaring that the information provisions of the Espionage Act were constitutional. (Library of Congress, photograph by Harris & Ewing)

T HE LEGAL CASE THAT FORCED THE SUPREME COURT TO CON-
sider the Espionage Act's secrecy clauses began with an absent-
minded trip to the dry cleaner. Mikhail Gorin was a Soviet citizen
who had moved to Los Angeles in 1936 to take up work organizing
American tours of the USSR for Amtorg, the Soviet trading company. He was also a spy, receiving information on Japanese activity on the West Coast from a contact in the San Pedro branch of
US Naval Intelligence. In September 1938 he accidentally left in
his pocket a paper containing some of the intelligence he received
when he dropped his suit off to be laundered. The dry cleaner took
the suspicious sheet of notes to the Hollywood police station, which
promptly informed the FBI.[1]

The documents led the feds straight to Hafis Salich, who had been
born in Russia in 1905 and then migrated to the United States via
Manchuria and Japan in the early 1920s. After becoming a citizen,
he worked as a cop in Berkeley for five years, and then, in 1936, he
had taken up his current job: Naval Intelligence, San Pedro.

Confronted by the FBI, Salich confessed. Gorin had approached
him in 1937, he said, seeking only information about Japan's activities, not any intelligence on the US. Salich had reported the
overture to his boss at Naval Intelligence, although the two remembered that conversation differently. Salich said he had the OK
to share some low-level intelligence with Gorin, especially if he
could barter it for Soviet intel. Salich's boss said that was nonsense,
that he had told Salich to break contact with the Soviet agent. But
there was no way to know for sure because the Office of Naval
Intelligence had lost Salich's file, including the memo recording
the conversation.[2]

However it happened, Salich ultimately provided Gorin with
summaries of about fifty Naval Intelligence reports. In exchange,
Gorin gave Salich $1,700. Salich was having marital trouble and was
hard up for cash. He was thankful for the "loan."[3]

It seemed an open-and-shut violation of the Espionage Act. Both
men were charged with gathering information relating to the national defense (Section 793) and with transferring it to a foreign

power (Section 794). In March 1939 a jury found them guilty. Salich was given four years in prison, Gorin six. Were it wartime, added the judge, he would have imposed the death penalty.[4]

But there was an important wrinkle. Salich contended that the information he had given to Gorin couldn't possibly constitute espionage. It was far too innocuous, simply documenting the movements of Japanese American fishing vessels and citizens, along with some rumors about their political affiliations. The only thing close to technical military information was a report on the use of acid to erode a ship's hull, and that had subsequently been published. In any case, it wasn't as if the Soviet Union and the United States were at war. FDR's administration had recognized the USSR in 1933, and at the time Salich had given information to Gorin, relations between the two nations were about as good as they would ever be; the Hitler-Stalin pact wasn't signed until five months after the 1939 trial had ended. As Salich and Gorin both pointed out, this was a sharing of information between allies about a common foe: Japan, which was a rising Pacific power, beginning to flex its muscles in Manchuria and China.

Yes, Salich conceded, what he had done was "highly unethical." But it wasn't "inimical to the best interests of the U.S.," which was surely the bar for being found guilty of spying. And if the sharing of such information fell within the prohibitions of the Espionage Act, his lawyers argued, then the Espionage Act would threaten to render illegal all manner of discussion of defense matters and thus violate the First Amendment's guarantee of the right to free speech. They appealed his case all the way to the Supreme Court.[5]

Gorin asked the Supreme Court to clarify the relationship between the twin legacies of 1919, each of which had flourished in the interwar years. First Amendment rights, championed now not only by radical activists but increasingly by the powerful newspaper industry, had begun to erect a firewall against government censorship. But at the same time, a slowly expanding national-security bureaucracy was claiming the need for new powers to keep its secrets in the geopolitical gloom. Whether these competing pressures could be reconciled with the vague language of the Espionage Act was an open question.

When World War I came to its formal, legal end at the belated date of 1921, the sections of the Espionage Act that had regulated speech and mailing privileges were sunsetted. They would not return to force until the outbreak of World War II. When there was no war, as in the 1920s and 1930s, the censorship powers of the Espionage Act lay dormant.

There was no war, that is, in a technical sense. There were plenty of military interventions in the "interwar" years, plenty of occupations, a good deal of violence. From 1920 to 1932 the United States deployed troops in foreign nations twenty times, in such places as Panama, Cuba, Honduras, and China (the last on seven separate occasions). The US occupied the Dominican Republic from 1916 to 1924, Nicaragua from 1926 to 1933, and Haiti for nearly twenty years, from 1915 to 1934. But none of these were "wars." They were police actions of various sorts, interventions aimed at maintaining order and financial stability, at protecting Americans—and US property—from anticolonial insurgencies. These occupying forces often imposed censorship regimes, of course, as did the colonial governments. In the Philippines, still a US colony twenty years after the initial occupation, punitive sedition laws led to the successful prosecution of hundreds of leaders of the local Communist Party.[6]

But such laws did not apply within the continental United States. There was nothing to stop someone like James Weldon Johnson traveling to Haiti on a fact-finding mission and then returning to the US to publish a series of exposés on the brutal use of forced labor to build roads, or the uncomfortable fact that the reserves of the Haitian National Bank had been transferred to Wall Street, where they were being kept safe by a commercial US bank that would later evolve into Citibank. Evidence that some marines had raped children, that they had opened fire on an anti-occupation protest at Aux Cayes, killing at least twenty-five, circulated among Black activists in the

United States and ultimately led to congressional hearings. To the extent that most Americans remained ignorant of their imperial adventures in the interwar years, neither censorship nor secrecy could be blamed.[7]

Back in the United States, although there was no federal law to regulate criticism of particular wars or occupations, the Left still found its rights to free speech curtailed. By 1921, thirty-five states and two territories had laws on the books that made it illegal to advocate the overthrow of the government, clauses that were interpreted broadly to include a great deal of Communist political activity. To underscore their antiradical intent, thirty-two states also had laws that banned the flying of the red flags of international Communism.[8] It was a continuation, at the local level, of the censorial politics of the wartime Espionage Act and the postwar Palmer raids.

The fact that these were state laws, not federal laws, raised an interesting legal problem. Since the passage of the First Amendment, the assumption had been that it applied only to the federal government. James Madison had in fact tried to add an additional clause to the Bill of Rights in 1791 that would have protected speech rights from the states, but although he thought it "the most valuable amendment in the whole list," it was rejected by the Senate. "While we deny that Congress have a right to control the freedom of the press," Thomas Jefferson explained, "we have ever asserted the right of the states, and their exclusive right to do so."[9]

That attitude continued to hold in the early 1920s, particularly given that there was no great judicial tolerance for radical speech in the wake of the Supreme Court's Espionage Act decisions of 1919. But throughout the decade, as the American Civil Liberties Union (ACLU) continued advocating for the right to free speech and began to win converts to its liberal philosophy, the tension between the First Amendment and all this state censorship became harder to ignore.

The Supreme Court, its membership beginning to shift with the natural turnover of justices, slowly began to rule that the First Amendment did apply to the states and shortly thereafter began protecting the rights of radicals. In 1927 the Supreme Court

overturned the conviction of one member of what was left of the
IWW under a Kansas criminal-conspiracy law. By the late 1930s,
a court now helmed by Chief Justice Charles Evans Hughes was
upholding the rights of Communists in Oregon to meet, and the
rights of Angelo Herndon, a Black Communist, to recruit party
members in Georgia. These were narrow, tentative victories: Herndon had spent twenty-six months in a chain gang while his appeal
worked its way through the courts, and the Supreme Court had
ruled in his favor by the narrowest of margins, 5–4. Nevertheless,
they were indicative of the ways that censorship of even radical
speech was beginning to fall out of favor.[10]

The First Amendment's power was growing because it had also
come to have some more respectable champions than the radical
labor movement. One of the era's most important court cases, *Near
v. Minnesota*, stemmed from the decision of a local government to
censor an anti-Semitic right-wing gossip rag run by Jay Near. Using
a public-nuisance law, the government had won a court injunction
that prevented Near's paper from continuing to publish. The ACLU,
holding its nose for the sake of principle, had protested the decision
but was then squeezed out of the case by the right-wing publisher of
the *Chicago Tribune*, Robert McCormick, who was heading a new
Freedom of Press Committee for the American Newspaper Publishers Association. With the backing of the newspaper industry, Near
won his case in the Supreme Court, setting a powerful precedent
that it was almost impossible to restrain the press from publishing.[11]

Even as it granted the press its victory, the Supreme Court did
suggest that prior restraints might be acceptable in some extreme
instances, such as to prevent the "publication of the sailing dates of
transports or the number and location of troops." As the right to
free speech expanded, the court was carving out a small category
of information that could be held secret in the interests of national
security. The boundaries of that category, only impressionistically
sketched in the 1930s, would come to be very important.[12]

Nevertheless, it was remarkable how far the nation had come
since 1918. By the mid-1930s, the Espionage Act's speech provisions

had been dormant for more than fifteen years, the Supreme Court was upholding the speech rights of even radical dissidents, and a powerful lobby was forming behind the First Amendment. When former marine Smedley Butler, a decorated veteran of so many of the era's military occupations, published a memoir complaining that he was a "racketeer for capitalism" who had "helped in the raping of half a dozen Central American republics for the benefit of Wall Street," he was met with some criticism but no legal sanction. Less than two decades before, hundreds of Socialists had gone to jail for saying less.[13]

It was the publication of the memoirs of another veteran of America's clandestine security branches that revealed the inadequacy of even those sections of the Espionage Act that remained in force in peacetime. In 1931 Herbert Yardley, the former head of America's code-breaking unit, had published a best-selling memoir that described the hitherto secretive world of signals intelligence. In 1933 he sought to publish a sequel.

Yardley was a fortunate son of the American Midwest, the kind of charmed teenager who performed equally well on the football field, at exam time, and in the storm and stress of high school social life: lots of dates, lots of friends, lots of successfully executed pranks. He was also a mean poker player. Like high school heroes ever since, he had been taught that the world would bend to meet his desires. Although he learned his father's business—telegraphy—he hankered for more than small-town Indiana life. In 1912, at the age of twenty-three, he set off to Washington for an entry-level position as a clerk in the State Department's code room.[14]

It was boring, menial work, but he was close enough to the action to smell it. He soaked up workplace banter about all the mischief that his senior colleagues had got up to in Latin America and became intrigued by their uses of encryption. He read books about cryptography at the Library of Congress and began practicing his new skills on the encoded messages in the office. In 1916 he decoded correspondence between Woodrow Wilson and presidential adviser Edward M. House, who was in Europe trying to engineer a peace settlement.

Yardley was amazed at how bad US codes were, how easily hacked. He began work on what would turn out to be a one-hundred-page report on the inadequacy of American communications security. He gave it to his boss a year later, as America was entering the war.[15]

Yardley was always a charmer, and he was soon put in charge of a new military intelligence division responsible for codes and ciphers. It had been organized by Ralph Van Deman, apostle of American counterintelligence, who had reorganized military intelligence at the same time that he advocated for passage of the Espionage Act. Copying the British, Van Deman's divisions were numbered. Yardley's group was MI-8. During the war, it decrypted almost eleven thousand messages.[16]

Code breaking had proved its worth, and Yardley had proved himself an able administrator. After the war, a decision was made to set up a permanent Cipher Bureau, jointly funded by the War Department and the State Department. State Department funds couldn't be used in Washington, so the bureau was based in New York, operating out of an office building registered to a company selling code to businesses that wanted to conduct their telegraphic correspondence in confidence. Yardley's true work was highly secret. The few in the know began referring to his organization as "America's Black Chamber"—named for the formidable cryptographic unit of the French monarchy in the 1600s, the *Cabinet Noir*.[17]

For a time, Yardley's proto–National Security Agency went swimmingly. Yardley worked his charms on executives at the main telegraph companies, who agreed to bend US law to secretly provide the Black Chamber with copies of the encoded messages flying back and forth across their wires. Yardley's team cracked them, passing along the information they learned to their bosses in the State and War Departments. His greatest success came in the Washington Naval Conference of 1922, an interwar effort at arms control in which the great powers sought to defuse the race for supremacy in the Pacific that had obsessed naval advocates—such as the anti-Japanese fear-monger Richmond Hobson—since the turn of the century. The British and Americans agreed to reduce the size of their fleets and make them equal; lesser powers agreed to cap their fleets at a percentage of the British and American maximum. Negotiations with the Japanese dragged out over the size of that percentage—the Japanese wanted a fleet 70 percent the size of their Anglo-American rivals; the Americans insisted it had to be 60 percent. US negotiators were aided by the fact that Yardley had cracked Japanese code, which meant they could read the instructions being sent to the Japanese delegation. The Americans knew the Japanese would be willing to settle for 60 percent. "Stud poker," Yardley crowed, "is not a very difficult game after you see your opponent's hole card."[18]

But then Yardley's luck turned. As the emergency practices of the war faded, as normalcy resumed, the wire companies became increasingly nervous about illegally turning cables over to the Black Chamber. When the flow of cables dried up, so did the Black Chamber's ability to crack their codes, which meant that Yardley was providing less and less intelligence to his bosses. The budget shrank; staff were let go; the intel became yet more paltry. Yardley was, in the words of a colleague, nevertheless living the "life of Reilly"—enjoying time in the speakeasies of Prohibition-era New York, running a real estate business on the side, perfecting his impressive golf game. By the mid-1920s, he was apparently working his government job for only an hour a day. The Black Chamber had become irrelevant. It shed no light on the key foreign-relations crises of the late 1920s.[19]

In 1929, when Henry Stimson, the new secretary of state, learned of the chamber's existence, he was appalled. "Gentlemen," he said, "do not read each other's mail." The sentiment, a reflection of Stimson's stern morality, didn't represent a naive faith that the world was on the cusp of an era of peace. Yardley's unit wasn't offering nearly enough benefit to counterbalance the reputational hit that Stimson's State Department would take if knowledge of its existence became public. If there was a need for cryptography, better it be housed exclusively in the army, giving American diplomats at State distance and deniability. On Thursday, October 31, 1929, the Black Chamber was shut down.[20]

Yardley was put out of work at the worst possible time. Two days earlier, on Black Tuesday, the bottom had fallen out of the stock market, taking Yardley's real estate business along with it. The Great Depression had begun, and the always profligate Yardley had nothing stashed away. Desperate for money, he decided to sell his story. He contacted a high-powered literary agent and started writing.

At first, publishers were anxious about putting Yardley's book out, seeking legal advice about any potential jeopardy they faced for spilling secrets. The lawyers struggled to make sense of the confusing laws. Given the "highly unusual nature of the facts," one legal firm was "unable to find any authority squarely in point" but advised against publication out of fear that government could either claim a property right in the material or could enjoin publication for interfering with government functions—it was telling that the Espionage Act was not even considered in the analysis. Another firm, faced with the same lack of certainty, came to the opposite conclusion. Deciding that no statutes "defining treason, sedition, or espionage were being infringed," it recommended publication. The lawyers also went over the text with a fine-tooth comb, looking especially for any risk of libel, and they asked for a number of revisions. But they ultimately gave it a green light.[21]

America's Black Chamber was published, and it was a hit. Previous cryptography books had been dry and technical; Yardley had written a page-turner. The *Saturday Evening Post* ran excerpts in installments. The book got front-page headlines and showed that there was a market for spooky memoirs that spilled the inside scoop on the recent past. It was soon on its third printing and sold well overseas too, particularly in Japan.

Yardley had played fast and loose with the truth, exaggerating key stories and making others up entirely. There was a "lot of junk" in the book, Yardley confessed privately, but "if I didn't dramatize . . .

the reader would go to sleep." The public, equally titillated and out-raged, thought they were reading a confessional. The book, com-plained the *New York Evening Post*, "betrays government secrets with a detail and clarity of writing that makes one gasp."[22]

Within the government, among the patriots, Yardley's actions were an outrage. The *Boston Globe* accused him of treason and called for the stripping of his Distinguished Service Medal.[23]

But the government found itself powerless to act. Were Yardley still an officer, he could be court-martialed. But he had been fired, and before the book came out, he had resigned from the reserves, too, just to be sure. "There is no law known to this office," admitted the judge advocate general, "which would render this individual li-able to any prosecution or penalty."[24] Whatever the vague clauses of the Espionage Act meant, they didn't seem to cover a disclosure like Yardley's. He was free to enjoy his literary success.

Yardley burned through his book royalties with typical haste and went looking for other get-rich-quick schemes. He dabbled as a Hollywood consultant, sold little coding puzzles ("Yardleygrams") to a magazine, partnered with ghostwriters to churn out pulpy spy stories, started an invisible-ink business. None of it succeeded. Ex-perimenting with his ink formula, he sliced his hand on a glass plate and ended up losing a finger to infection. Inevitably, he was drawn back to the well, contracting a ghostwriter to produce a sequel to *America's Black Chamber*, one that would document in greater detail his glory years in the early 1920s. A few months later, he had a man-uscript in hand. *Japanese Diplomatic Secrets, 1921–1923* ran to almost a thousand pages. A far cry from his first book, it was a turgid com-pendium of decoded cables. His publisher passed on it.

The Justice Department then got word that Yardley was going to try to place the book with Macmillan, a troubling development not only because Yardley was establishing a precedent that a person could legally profit from selling secrets but also because publication would risk further straining relations with Japan; US nonrecognition of Ja-pan's recent occupation of Manchuria was already causing problems enough. Luckily for the government, Macmillan's president, George

Platt Brett Jr., had been a member of military intelligence during the war. Brett was in the habit of checking with his old friends in the military before publishing anything that might embarrass them, so he was all ears when an ambitious young federal prosecutor—future presidential candidate Thomas Dewey—called him up and asked him to turn Yardley's manuscript in for review. The Justice Department seized the seven manila folders containing the bloated book, declared it all classified, and impounded it. *Japanese Diplomatic Secrets* wouldn't again see the light of day until journalist James Bamford got it declassified while writing his pathbreaking history of the National Security Agency in 1979.[25]

It looked, for a moment, like that would be the end of it. No book publishers were overly concerned about the loss of an unpublishable manuscript. And Dewey also worked his contacts in the newspaper industry to keep the story of censorship on the down-low.

But the government didn't just want to stop Yardley. It wanted to make sure that there would be no more Yardleys in the future. The problem was that there didn't seem to be a law that could effectively do so; no one thought that the Espionage Act was up to the task. It would have to be supplemented with additional legislation.

In the midst of FDR's first hundred days in office, as the new administration was frantically passing laws to try to kick-start the nation's economy, the administration introduced a bill to the House "for the protection of government records." Congressional sponsors warned darkly that the bill was urgent, that there was a pressing need to stop "leaks from confidential official records and communications." "The special circumstances under which the bill comes up here," one of them intoned, "are such that I would not care to take the responsibility for disclosing them." It passed the House after the briefest of debates.[26]

Then the press got wind of it. It turned out the bill was incredibly loosely drawn, that it would make illegal the publication of almost any information gleaned from any government document. The proposed law, cried newspaper trade journal *Editor and Publisher*, "serves notice upon journalism, and readers who feel like freemen, that their constitutional liberties hang by slim threads." The law "dragged the free press by the heels deliberately, mercilessly, in the very spirit of a Hitler, Mussolini or a Stalin."[27]

The response of the government was swift. Secretary of State Cordell Hull "urged that any provisions that could possibly be construed . . . [to affect] freedom of the press be stricken out."[28] The bill was narrowed to cover only information gleaned from diplomatic code. It applied only to government employees. "By no stretch of the imagination," *Editor and Publisher* exhaled, "can the measure now be construed as an attempt to muzzle the press in any way." In its new form, it was easily enacted. It is still on the books today.[29]

In all, the Yardley affair revealed the central dynamics that drove the evolution of the Espionage Act in the twentieth century. Time and again, security-minded politicians would try to use the Espionage Act to control the public sphere. This raised obvious concerns about freedoms of speech and press. We often think of these two parts of the First Amendment as synonymous, but in the early twentieth century they were in fact championed by very different interest groups. The press clause was championed by the powerful newspaper industry, plump on advertising dollars and willing to throw its political weight around. When it opposed the Espionage Act as a violation of its freedoms, it had great success in checking the breadth of the law. This had happened in 1917, when the press forced revisions to the Espionage Act, and it happened again in 1933. By contrast, the right to free speech was often claimed not by the newspaper industry but by individual speakers, particularly by radicals. As revealed during World War I and in the Supreme Court's Espionage Act cases in 1919, these were claims that were easily brushed aside in the interests of national security.

In the Yardley affair, we can see the first signs of the uneasy détente between the Espionage Act and the First Amendment that would emerge out of these political clashes. Efforts to secure secrets by censoring the mainstream press were nonstarters. When the press mobilized the First Amendment, it was too powerful a shield to be overcome. But the desire to secure secrets persisted. When one path was blocked, that desire for control flowed, like water, toward easier targets. The state left the press alone and focused its energies on preventing information from leaking out in the first place.

Senator Hiram Johnson, who had opposed the censorship provisions of the Espionage Act back in 1917, saw what was happening as his colleagues passed the new law aimed at Yardley's book: "The members of the press set up the usual howl of the press about the freedom of the press and how this sort of statute would interfere with them. The result was that, of course, everybody ran to cover and the bill was amended in the twinkling of an eye in order that the press should not be interfered with and the freedom of the press at all hazards should be preserved." Fair enough, Johnson conceded, but why was no one concerned about the rights of the ex-official who wanted to inform the press? What about the right of such a "humble individual to express himself freely?"[30]

As the press slipped out of reach, censorship began to coil more tightly around the government employee.

If the Yardley affair began to foreshadow the future of the Espionage Act, it also revealed how uncertain its meaning was in the interwar years. The Espionage Act was known, in its early years, for censoring radicals who had criticized World War I. Its role in policing the nation's secrets was as yet far from clear.

The simple fact was that the sections of the Espionage Act aimed at regulating the disclosure of information were not being used. For all the anxieties about spies that had accompanied the passage of the Defense Secrets Act and the Espionage Act, no one was prosecuted for spying for eighteen years after the end of World War I. Only in 1936 was the first peacetime spy prosecuted in the United States, when Harry Thompson was arrested for passing naval information to the Japanese. The next year brought a second case, that of John Farnsworth, a former naval aviator who was also passing information to the Japanese. Both men were motivated by basic greed, selling secrets for cash. These were open-and-shut cases that did little to clarify the meaning of the law.[31]

The constitutionality of the information-disclosure sections of the Espionage Act was thus untested at the time of Gorin and Salich's prosecution. To their lawyers, focusing on the ambiguity of the law seemed like a plausible strategy. They made a novel effort to suggest that "information relating to the national defense" wasn't a vague and sprawling phrase but a precise and narrow one. It was defined, they suggested, by the first clause of the act, Section 793(a), which banned the gathering of information from any of a list of twenty-four specific places: navy yards, forts, arsenals, etc. When later clauses of the act used the phrase, this was all they meant. And because the information Salich had given to Gorin hadn't come from any of those named places, the Espionage Act didn't apply.

It was a clever idea, but there was nothing in the language of the act or the legislative history to suggest that 793(a) was intended to define terms for the rest of the law. The court easily brushed the argument aside.

But if "information relating to the national defense" was not limited by the list of places in Section 793(a), what *were* its limits? The trial judge had said that this was something for the jury to decide, instructing them that "the term 'national defense' includes all matters directly and reasonably connected with the defense of our nation against its enemies." The jurors would have to determine if there was a "reasonable and direct" connection between the information at question in the case and the "national defense."[32]

The problem, as Salich's lawyer (and former New Deal official) Donald Richberg pointed out, was that an awful lot of things could be connected to national defense by the early 1940s. "Is there any function of the government today which is not connected with national defense?" he asked the court.[33]

Once upon a time, it had been easy to imagine that war and defense were discrete, limited domains. Battlefields were bounded places, far away from the cities and farms of everyday life. Armies were mustered up for a period of time, then demobilized, soldiers becoming citizens once more. Wartime was exceptional. During peace, institutions concerned with national defense would be relatively small and easily identified.

Total mobilization for World War I, followed by the strife of the interwar period and the rise of airpower, had made a mockery of such neat distinctions. A nation's entire economy, every aspect of its civilian life, became relevant to war mobilization—there was, in fact, a home front. The interwar dictatorships had learned that lesson particularly well, regimenting their societies during the peace in preparation for future conflict. That meant their rivals had to do the same. Wartime and peacetime began to blur, as did the distinction between civil and military.[34]

In the intelligence branches of the navy and the army, in academic think tanks established to study the new problem of "geopolitics," those responsible for guarding US interests groped for a way to express the expanding stakes of their work. To make sense of the new conditions, they felt the need for a new term. They stopped thinking of themselves as advocates of "national defense" and started thinking of themselves as guardians of "national security."[35]

Until now, the phrase had been uncommon. Presidents had invoked "national security" just a handful of times, often as mere rhetoric, frequently in connection not with issues of foreign relations but with calls for greater economic security. The first time that FDR used the phrase "national security" was in his second fireside chat in 1933, when he outlined the measures his new administration was taking to help Americans buffeted by the Great Depression. From 1938 to 1941, FDR would use the phrase more times than all previous presidents combined. But by then the concept of "national security" had switched tracks. It now belonged firmly to the realm of foreign relations and geopolitics.[36]

For its advocates, the term seemed to indicate a new philosophy of politics, a new way of thinking about the world. "Security is a broad concept; as distinguished from mere defense," explained the entrepreneurial academic Edward Mead Earle in 1941. Earle did more than anyone to define the term *national security* and bring it into vogue, particularly via an important research seminar he organized at Princeton in the years on either side of the *Gorin* case.[37] James Forrestal, who would soon become navy secretary, was one of many who attended Earle's conversations. As his influence grew, as he became one of the architects of the postwar national-security state, Forrestal would preach the new gospel. "I am using the word security here consistently and continuously rather than 'defense,'" Forrestal would take pains to emphasize. "It has been a fetish of mine that the question of *national security* is not merely a question of the Army and Navy. We have to take into account our whole potential for war, our mines, industry, manpower, research, and all the activities that go into normal civilian life."[38]

In truth, it wasn't obvious that "national defense" had been such a limited category before this time. The architects of the Espionage Act back in the Wilson administration had also taken a broad approach to the problem of security and had been comfortable reading an expansive program of policing speech and production and the border into the term *national defense*. Nevertheless, in the late 1930s the term *national security* came into vogue on the assumption that it covered a wider terrain. It would prove to be a powerfully elastic discourse, a hungry concept, always seeing new threats over the horizon and under the bed. One could always have just a bit more security.

When the *Gorin* case asked the Supreme Court to weigh in on just what "information relating to national defense" actually meant, it was therefore asking the court to participate in this broader debate. Was "national defense" a narrower concept than "national security"? Could the vague clauses of the Espionage Act be stretched to cover all the domains of life that related to the national security? Or would the effort to do so render the Espionage Act unconstitutional?

The court brushed the problem aside. As Justice Stanley Reed wrote for a unanimous court, the "use of the words 'national defense' has given them" a "well understood connotation." That meant they weren't too vague. But what did they mean? Here the court borrowed from the government's brief to provide what came close to a nondefinition. *National defense* was "a generic concept of broad connotations, referring to the military and naval establishments and related activities of national preparedness."[39]

The court had not fully embraced the new concept of "national security." In fact, it had made some effort to distance itself from the calls for a new philosophy that sought to blur foreign and domestic politics, announcing that "the traditional concept of war as a struggle between nations is not changed." But in a context in which people *were* expanding their understanding of the elements that were "related" to "national preparedness," there was plenty of space within the court's (non-) definition of the key terms to pour the new logic of national security into the Espionage Act's empty vessel of "national defense."[40]

The court wasn't too troubled by the vague way it had defined "relating to the national defense" because it didn't think the key check on the sprawl of the Espionage Act lay in limiting the sort of information it covered. "The obvious delimiting words in the statute," it thought, were the clauses requiring those prosecuted to "have acted in bad faith."[41]

When the Wilson administration had first proposed the Espionage Act to Congress, its prohibitions on sharing information relating to the national defense were absolute. They were what is known as strict liability: they made it illegal to gather or communicate such information regardless of why you did it. Such blanket prohibitions risked criminalizing all sorts of innocent acts, such as casual conversation about the nation's military or newspaper commentary on defense policy. So in 1917 critics of the bill, such as Albert Cummins, pushed for the addition of some standard of intent to make sure that the law exempted innocent behavior.

At first, the Wilson administration had resisted these reforms—a broad law was fine, it thought, because you could trust that prosecutors wouldn't bring cases against the innocent. But then, in a conference hearing during which no records seem to have been kept, the administration acceded to the demand. We don't know exactly why it did so, and we don't know what it thought its revisions meant. That's a shame because the intent requirements that were added to the four clauses regulating defense information are confusing. The broadest of the clauses, which made it illegal to communicate such information, required simply that you did so "willfully." The other three clauses, including the clause that Gorin and Salich had violated, seem to have a much higher standard. They say you are guilty only if you gather or communicate information with "intent or reason to believe that the information to be obtained is to be used to the injury of the United States or to the advantage of any foreign nation."[42]

Gorin and Salich were arguing that they hadn't acted with such an intent. By sharing information about a common foe, they certainly hadn't intended to injure the United States. The US and the USSR "had a common cause," Salich said, "and by helping them I would also be indirectly helping our own cause."[43]

Whether or not one sympathizes with the defendants, the issue they raised was important. The intent requirements were seen as the key limitation on these sprawling clauses. The government claimed that the reason that the Espionage Act wouldn't threaten a journalist communicating defense information to his or her readers was that the journalist wouldn't have the requisite intent. But the government brief didn't explain what the intent requirements meant or how they worked—it just asserted that journalists would be "automatically excluded" from prosecution. How the court interpreted these requirements would shape the scope of the Espionage Act ever after.[44]

The Supreme Court ruled that Gorin and Salich did have the necessary intent, which was probably fair enough, given the facts of the case. But the way the ruling defined these crucial intent requirements radically lowered the bar for prosecutions under the Espionage Act. There were two problems with the intent requirements in the law, and the court's ruling in *Gorin* amplified both of them.

The first problem was the idea that it was criminal not only to injure the United States but also to "advantage a foreign nation." That meant, as the court explained, that the government did not need to show any actual harm to the US resulting from the disclosure. It needed only to show that a foreign nation would benefit, which was a low standard. Who doesn't benefit from receiving more information? Even if the information is bunk, that itself is valuable knowledge. The thinking of the court reflected, unconsciously, the zero-sum vision of geopolitics then coming into fashion. International politics was a Hobbesian war of all against all. According to the philosophy of the Espionage Act, as the court put it, "no distinction is made between friend or enemy." If today's friend may become tomorrow's enemy, the only way to secure the nation is to keep defense information away from all foreign eyes.[45]

The second problem with the intent requirements was the blurriness created by the phrase "intent or reason to believe." To prove intent, absent a confession, is difficult. One can always claim naive surprise at the outcome of one's actions; this is what Salich was trying to do. But once the law offers the prosecutors the lower standard—"reason to believe"—it moves away from subjective guilt and back toward strict liability. Particularly if, as the jury instructions in this case put it, this means asking not if the particular defendant had "reasons to believe" that harm would ensue but only if they "reasonably should have concluded" that harm would ensue. Under such a standard, if there was a social consensus emerging around the need for heightened secrecy, that would be sufficient to prove anyone guilty of espionage even if they shared defense information not with the intent to harm the United States but with the intent of informing the public about military policy. It was similar to the dynamics that had turned the speech provisions of the World War I Espionage Act into a general censorship tool.[46]

Gorin and Salich also raised a final challenge to the law, one that would have a long afterlife. It was up to the jury to determine whether information was related to the national defense and whether the defendants should have concluded that sharing it would advantage another nation. That meant that the information at question in the trial had to be shared with the jury. But if the government was willing to share it with the jury, didn't that prove there was no great need to keep it secret in the first place? Gorin and Salich thought it proved the information was not important, that its disclosure did not harm the United States or help any other nation. The courts didn't agree with Gorin and Salich, although they did recognize the problems that this need to disclose secrets created. "Such procedure was a necessity in order to try the case," explained the appeals court. "Whether it is sound, we think is a question for the determination of Congress."[47] It would be decades before Congress took up that challenge. Until then, governments seeking to prosecute the disclosure of secrets would need to risk further publicizing those secrets to win a conviction. It would prove a powerful check on the government's ability to make use of the Espionage Act.

Taken as a whole, the Supreme Court's ruling in *Gorin* stretched the vague provisions of the Espionage Act into a new and troubling shape, which did not go unrecognized at the time. "The Opinion in the [*Gorin*] Case Gives Espionage Act Far Wider Scope" was one *Los Angeles Times* headline. Although the *Illinois Law Review* generally applauded the "soundness" of Reed's decision, it also worried that it had given the Espionage Act an "elasticity" that might prove troublesome in the future. Would the act cover the circulation of information about the productive capacity of factories, or the morale of Americans, or the political opinions of subversive organizations? These fell within a "twilight zone" that might be related to "national defense" even though a democracy needed the right to discuss them freely. *Gorin* seemed such a significant step beyond the way the law had previously been understood that the author of this article thought that the court had basically taken on the role of "judicial-legislators by construing a 23-year-old statute so as to make it conform to present day problems." It would be better, he thought, if Congress passed new legislation to clarify the meaning of the Espionage Act.[48]

A new espionage law never came, and the problems of national defense were about to intensify. *Gorin* was decided on the cusp of a new era of secrecy. The modern classification system had not yet come into existence. Before World War II, recalled the influential Washington journalists Joe and Stewart Alsop, "There was hardly such a thing, as yet, as a classification stamp in all of Washington."[49]

But within the army and the navy, the engines of secrecy were beginning to whir. Late in 1917 the US Army had for the first time adopted a system of classifying information as "confidential," "secret," or "for official circulation only." It had been borrowed from the British and French, and it lived on after the war. In 1932 the Office of Naval Intelligence had begun suggesting that information should be classified not only if its disclosure would harm the "national defense" but also if it might threaten the "national security." In 1936 the army quietly revised its classification rules in precisely such a fashion. Two years later the navy did the same. In a 1940 executive order, FDR conferred presidential recognition on the classification system that the armed forces had been slowly developing since 1917. It wouldn't be the last time a president had something to say about the need for classification.[50]

It is unclear whether the Supreme Court justices in 1941 would have agreed that anything stamped secret by today's classification system would have fallen within their notion of "national defense information." But by ruling that national defense information was a "generic concept of broad connotations," they created space in the law into which our modern secrecy practices could grow.

And although the court was relying on the intent requirements to delimit the scope of the act, the broadest of the information-disclosure provisions—Section 793(d)—required only that the accused communicated or kept unauthorized defense information "willfully." Neither Gorin nor Salich was charged under 793(d), so the court didn't need to grapple with this problem in 1941. But as the classification system expanded in later years, the lack of meaningful intent requirements for 793(d) would make it a powerful tool for prosecutors.

The Supreme Court has never since ruled on the constitutionality of the Espionage Act. *Gorin*, decided at a very different moment, still guides the law today.

Eleven months after the *Gorin* decision, in early December 1941, the United States decoded some troubling Japanese messages. Stimson's decision to close Yardley's Black Chamber twelve years earlier hadn't really ended the practice of US code breaking. What looked like a death sentence was actually a bureaucratic reshuffle—cryptography continued, quietly, in the army and the navy.

By the end of 1941, Japan's diplomatic code had once again been broken, although its naval code remained unreadable. On the weekend of December 6, messages were decoded that revealed the Japanese were about to break diplomatic relations with the United States. It was obvious that an attack was coming, although its location was unclear—those details were on Japanese naval channels.

For all the technical skill of US code breakers, efforts to get word of their discovery to America's Pacific Headquarters were hamstrung by the cumbersome bureaucracy that circulated signals intelligence within the administration. In part, these processes had developed in reaction to the bickering between army and navy units, which both wanted the credit for intelligence breakthroughs and had required the sorts of Solomonic routines favored by parents of squabbling kids—for a time, the army had received intercepts for decryption on even days of the week, the navy on odd days. There was also the more sensible desire to keep secret the fact that Japanese code had been broken, which meant a delay as messages were sent out on secure channels.

The result was that the warnings of an impending attack reached Pearl Harbor fifteen-and-a-half hours after they were intercepted. It was about 3 p.m. local time on December 7. The Japanese attack had finished six hours earlier. The US and the Espionage Act were once again going to war.[51]

Chapter 5

THE NAZI SPY WHO WASN'T

The thirty-three convicted members of the Duquesne spy ring, arrested by the FBI in 1941. Edmund Carl Heine is in the second row from the top, second from the right. (Library of Congress)

FIVE DAYS AFTER PEARL HARBOR, EDMUND CARL HEINE WAS convicted of spying for the Nazis. He had been arrested just months after the *Gorin* decision, along with thirty-two other members of a Nazi spy ring. It was the largest espionage case in US history, and by fanning fears of Axis spies and saboteurs in the weeks before America entered the war, it helped encourage a new fixation on national security. During the war, a range of new security practices were created, aimed to hasten American victory and guard against prying foreign eyes. Many of these "wartime" measures would linger into the Cold War.

Yet three months after the atomic bombs fell on Japan and brought the war to a close, Heine successfully appealed his conviction. After spending the war in jail for violating the Espionage Act, the fifty-four-year-old former automobile executive was released. He had been guilty of spying until he wasn't.

The reversal revealed the ramshackle nature of the wartime security state. The war led to experimentation with a patchwork of methods: some new forms of classification, some prosecution of dissident speech, the inculcation of a broader culture of caution and deference to state security. Unlike the situation during World War I, all these methods had to accommodate the rising respect for First Amendment rights. There would be no return to mass censorship. But the federal government had not yet worked out how to use the vague provisions of the Espionage Act to protect a secretive bureaucracy.

The little-known Heine case thus captured the secrecy regime at a moment of transition. By the time that Heine appealed his conviction, security-conscious hawks in the administration had grown dissatisfied. When he walked free in 1945, it helped convince them that the World War II secrecy system was a failure and that new measures would be needed in the postwar world.

Heine was born in eastern Germany in 1891, but his life was shaped by the global currents of the twentieth century. At the age of twenty-three, just weeks before the outbreak of World War I, he migrated to the United States, taking advantage of the last years of the open border to flee a forced marriage—he had impregnated a barmaid while traveling as a hardware salesman. Friends he made on the boat to America helped him find work in a hardware store in Detroit. After a brief interlude working on a farm, he took a job with the Ford Tractor Company in Dearborn.[1]

For a time, the smooth-talking Heine rode the crest of the internationally expanding automobile industry. He was quickly promoted from laborer to product demonstrator to foreign sales representative in the Caribbean and Latin America. In 1920 he became a US citizen. In Rio de Janeiro in 1922, he married a German-born woman then working as a Ford secretary. In 1929 he was promoted to manage and oversee the building of a new Ford plant in Cologne.

Six years later, Heine's fortunate life hit an unexpected roadblock: Ford fired him. Exactly why he was fired never became clear, although the incident became the subject of dispute when Heine was charged with espionage six years later. Heine's version of the story emphasized his patriotism and cast himself as a victim of Ford's efforts to appease the Nazi government. He claimed that Ford wanted to place a German citizen at the head of its German operations and had ordered him to abandon his US citizenship if he wanted to keep his job. He also asserted that the Nazis were boycotting any dealings with him because of a rumor that he had built American munitions during World War I. Ford executives disputed this account, suggesting that Heine was "not clicking with the German authorities" because of an illegal exchange of foreign currency with the manager of Ford in Holland and because he had become an unbearable and slightly slimy self-aggrandizer when placed in a position of authority. However it happened, Heine was out of work.

And amid the geopolitical turmoil of the 1930s, he could not reestablish his career. In 1935 he went to Spain to oversee the construction of an assembly plant for a Chrysler distributor. But upon the outbreak of the Spanish Civil War, he fled to Antwerp on a US battle cruiser. A subsequent assignment to North Africa was undermined by political upheaval and the collapsing international market for cars. In 1938 Chrysler fired him. Heine, along with his wife and three children, retreated to a family home in Bavaria, where they lived on his considerable savings through the last days of the peace.

In late 1939, after the Nazi invasion of Poland triggered World War II, the US consulate in Munich contacted Heine to inform him that he risked becoming stranded in Europe if he did not return to the United States to renew his passport. Heine began planning to cross the Atlantic once more. In March 1940, as he was making his arrangements, Heine met with Volkswagen executives, who asked him to do some work for them while he was in the US. He was to recover some deposits paid to US companies—the contracts had been broken amid the outbreak of hostilities—and gather information about the American aviation industry. Volkswagen, with its close connection to the Nazi war machine, wanted to know the types and quantities of planes that American companies were producing, the location and capacity of airplane factories, whether stainless steel or aluminum was the preferred material, how the planes were welded. They wanted, as Heine put it, a "fairly complete portrayal of the aeroplane situation in the U.S."[2]

And upon his arrival in the United States in the early summer of 1940, Heine set out to give them one. But he did so by entirely innocuous methods. He leafed through magazines, books, and newspapers. He read technical manuals and industry journals. For five dollars, he bought photographs of fifty planes from Thorell's Aircraft Photo Service, which was run out of the Bridgeport, Connecticut, home of an aerial photographer in the army. He went to the World's Fair in New York to look at aircraft exhibits and chat with attendants. He placed an ad in *Popular Aviation* magazine asking for basic instruction about planes. Boyd Aldrich, a ground instructor and aircraft mechanic, answered the ad and gave Heine a tour of Washington airports, during which he happily answered Heine's many questions. (Heine claimed that he wanted to bond with his plane-mad son in Germany; he was so cluelessly adrift, he told Aldrich in a moment of faux self-pity, that he couldn't even talk to the boy about a model airplane he had recently given him.) On July 22 he wrote to the Consolidated Aircraft Corporation, asking if the company would be so kind as to settle a bet he had with a friend after reading a recent boastful advertisement in a trade journal: was the plane that Consolidated had built in only nine months, by chance, a B-24? Three days later, a public-relations assistant at Consolidated wrote back: yes, yes it was.[3]

Heine took all of this readily available information, curated and consolidated it, and wrote it up in reports that he signed "Heinrich." And then he sent them to one of two addresses he had been given by Volkswagen. The first was in Lima, Peru. The second was on East 54th Street in New York. It was the address of Lilly Stein, a Vienna-born model who was working as a courier for a network of Nazi spies.

"Nazi spy ring" has an undeniably ominous tone. But in general, Nazi intelligence efforts in the United States were comically inept, more Colonel Klink than supervillain. Establishing a robust network of spies within the US was never a priority for the German regime. No one wanted to repeat the mistakes of World War I, when efforts to spy on the Americans had only antagonized them and brought them into the war. Combined with the usual tensions between competing branches of the Nazi state, support for spies remained ambivalent for much of the decade. As a result, Nazi operations were small-scale sideshows for most of the 1930s. By the end of the decade, when the war ramped up and caution could be abandoned, it was too late to cultivate agents with sufficiently deep cover. Nazi intelligence therefore relied on a haphazard crew of amateur agents, none of whom were really up to the task.[4]

Take Guenther Rumrich, an alcoholic dishwasher who had twice joined the US Army and twice gone AWOL—the second time after embezzling money. In 1936 Rumrich read a memoir by the chief of German intelligence during World War I. Inspired, he wrote a letter to a Nazi newspaper, lying about his military rank and offering his services to the Third Reich. If you want me, he said, put a personal ad in the *New York Times* for Theodore Kerner. Four days in a row in April, the ad ran, and Rumrich was in.[5]

But Rumrich couldn't do much. He read the newspapers and public reports on the US military and sent his notes to an address in Dundee, Scotland. Pretending to be a major in the medical corps, he made a phone call to learn about the rates of venereal disease in US armed forces. He made some crude and quickly abandoned plans to lure the commanding officer of a coastal artillery unit to a hotel in Washington for a fictitious meeting, where an accomplice would jump out of a closet and steal his documents. Pretending to work for the State Department, he tried to order blank passports from the Passport Division: the Nazis wanted to run agents into the USSR disguised as Americans.

Rumrich was easily caught. The Passport Division quickly twigged that the strange passport order was a hoax and alerted the New York Alien Squad. Meanwhile, British intelligence was monitoring all mail going to that address in Dundee, which belonged to a Scottish-German hairdresser with a penchant for spy novels, whose "feeble" efforts at spy craft had been quickly identified. When MI5 read about Rumrich's plans for the hotel smash and grab, it quietly alerted the United States.[6]

After he was arrested, Rumrich snitched quickly, naming a series of equally underwhelming spies. For instance, Johanna Hofmann served as a courier taking documents across the Atlantic on German shipping lines. When FBI agents arrested Hofmann as her ship came into port in 1938, they found in her luggage both encoded letters and the key to the code. She had been supposed to learn the key by heart and then destroy it but had never gotten around to doing so.

The spy ring in which Heine was intertwined had similar flaws. The twenty-four-year-old Lilly Stein had migrated to New York with a passport provided by Nazi military intelligence and a visa provided by a lover in the State Department. As she was using her feminine charms to try to develop her own informants, she was also forwarding information sent to her by an odd assortment of self-selected spies. Alex Wheeler-Hill, a notorious Nazi sympathizer and brother of the leader of the American Bund, volunteered to radio secret messages to Hamburg, only to realize he didn't know how to set up the radio. He eventually had a friend build him one, but the friend—another flamboyant Nazi—went about it so conspicuously that the radio-parts salesman reported him to the FBI. The aging Fritz Duquesne, a self-aggrandizing soldier of fortune who had been writing his own legend since fighting the British in the Boer War (he had spied for Germany in World War I, escaped from multiple jails, advised Teddy Roosevelt on big-game hunting, claimed to have guided the U-boat that killed Lord Kitchener, and pretended to be an Australian war hero on the New York lecture circuit), helped out by gathering "intelligence" on US gas masks from stories in the *New York Times*.[7]

Because the Germans failed to compartmentalize their network, all of these spies were soon connected by one man at the center of the ring: William Sebold, a German-born American citizen who had been blackmailed into working for Nazi intelligence when visiting his mother in Mülheim in 1939. Just before the trip, Sebold had quit his job as a mechanic at the Consolidated Aircraft Company, but the position was still listed on his immigration card, which drew the attention of the Gestapo. If he wouldn't spy for the Nazis, Sebold was told, they would tell the Americans that he had failed to disclose a youthful smuggling conviction when he had migrated to the United States, a violation that would jeopardize his American citizenship.

It was a desperate tactic to recruit an intelligence agent, and it backfired. Sebold agreed to participate, was quickly trained in rudimentary spy craft, and returned to New York, where he established a dummy business corporation ("Diesel Research") to coordinate US efforts and communicate with Nazi officials via shortwave radio. But Sebold had been allowed to visit the US Consulate in Cologne before his departure and had promptly informed it about his dilemma, so from the jump, he was working as a double agent. With help from the FBI, Sebold leased an office for his dummy corporation in room 627 in the Knickerbocker Building on Times Square. FBI

agents in rooms 626 and 628 secretly filmed his clandestine meetings with Nazi spies. Meanwhile, the FBI oversaw all Sebold's radio
communications—they read incoming messages, edited outgoing
messages, and added a stream of false intelligence to the mix for
good measure.

By the middle of 1941, the FBI had what they needed. On June
27, 250 FBI agents swept out to arrest the 33 members of the ring.
The largest espionage arrests in the nation's history were a media
sensation. Despite Duquesne's marginal involvement, the elderly
glory hound got the headlines. News of what became known as the
Duquesne spy ring was on front pages across the country. Only if
readers followed the jump and read to the end of the article might
they learn that an automobile executive named Edmund Heine was
one of those arrested. The *New York Times* carried pictures of 27
members of the ring. The boringly bourgeois Heine, whose spying
evoked little of the literary thriller, was not one of them.[8]

What had this motley crew of spies accomplished? Not a great
deal. They hadn't even attempted to cultivate sources of political intelligence; their efforts were focused on industrial espionage. Like
Heine, they sought details about the latest US production methods.
And like Heine, they focused most of their activities on gathering
such information from publicly available sources. Because geopolitical conflict had disrupted international networks, it was faster
and cheaper for a spy to read the *New York Times* and radio a summary back to Hamburg than it was for a German to subscribe to the
paper—those papers would take four weeks to arrive, and buying
them ate into valuable foreign-exchange reserves. There were benefits to gathering information in this way, but it was hardly cloak-and-
dagger stuff.[9]

Meanwhile, efforts to pilfer secret production techniques had little consequence even when they were successful. Hermann Lang
scored the Nazi spies' greatest triumph when he stole blueprints for
the Norden bombsight, whose accuracy made it a tightly guarded
military secret: anyone handling the bombsight had to swear to secrecy and sign an acknowledgment that they were familiar with the

Espionage Act. Until 1943, US fliers covered the bombsight with tarpaulin when carrying it to planes so that prying eyes could not even glimpse the device. Lang was an inspector at the Norden factory on Lafayette Street in Manhattan, and he was sometimes responsible for securing the blueprints of the bombsight at the end of the day. A Nazi true believer who had participated in the Munich Putsch before migrating to the United States in 1927, Lang took the blueprints home in the evening and traced a partial copy. In 1937 the oversized prints were rolled into an umbrella and couriered back to Germany by a Nazi spy who pretended to rely on the umbrella to help with a limp. The Luftwaffe reconstructed a model of the bombsight and praised its "interesting technical solutions," which were seen to be superior to their own sight, the Lotfe. But the benefits did not outweigh the difficulties posed by manufacturing and deploying a new sight at massive scale: the Lotfe was already in production and was familiar to German bombardiers. So although the US continued to guard its "secret" bombsight closely for another five years, the Luftwaffe never did anything with it. In any case, it was not the precision of US bombing that mattered to the outcome of the war but its capacity for mass devastation, as the tragedies of Dresden and Tokyo and Hiroshima soon revealed.[10]

And in the 1930s, most industrial "secrets" weren't guarded nearly as much as the Norden bombsight was. When it came to transmitting industrial details abroad, the work of a handful of spies paled in comparison to the prewar actions of US firms that brazenly shared the details of the devices they were building for the US military with international partners. Brazil was building destroyers using US plans, undermining any efforts to secure those plans at US factories. Others continued to share patents and models with foreign companies. BMW and German aviation companies bought planes and engines and propellers from the United States. As late as 1938, Standard Oil gave German chemical giant I.G. Farben complete details about how to manufacture synthetic rubber, precious information in light of later, and entirely predictable, rubber shortages during the war. "The fact is," concluded the *New York Times* in 1938, "that the

peacetime spy in America has scant 'pickings.' There are few real secrets, military or otherwise, here or elsewhere." Given the global sale
of US technology, "The spy's role is limited. Much of his time, as the
Rumrich testimony has shown, is spent in a desperate search for the
obvious."[11]

The FBI begged to differ, inflating the importance and skill of the
Nazi spy rings in order to inflate its own successes in breaking them.
J. Edgar Hoover gave press conference after press conference ex-
plaining the dangers that Nazi spies and saboteurs posed to the
United States. "Never in our history," he warned in 1940, "has our
national security been menaced as it is today."[12]

The media ate up the FBI's version of events. The desultory Rumrich affair was presented as a "spy thriller—in real life," as one *New
York Times* headline put it. John Turrou, the FBI agent responsible for the arrest of Rumrich, sold his story to the *New York Post*.
Within a week the *Post* was running ads warning that the United
States had been "stripped of every important naval and military secret it possessed." It promised that its upcoming series would reveal
the "swirling, gigantic, insidious maze of plots and counterplots in
the maddest and most vicious and insane spy syndicate in modern
history."[13]

Turrou resigned from the FBI to seek profit as a celebrity spy
catcher, an effort that enraged Hoover, who carefully controlled
the Bureau's image in the press. Hoover didn't want agents profit-
ing from their work or stealing his limelight. Beginning in 1935,
after Hoover's onetime golden boy Melvin Purvis had sought fame
for his role in killing John Dillinger, the director made all agents
sign a confidentiality agreement. Now the FBI flirted with charging
Turrou under the Espionage Act for breaking that agreement and
illegally sharing national-security information. But the espionage
laws were unclear, and the Bureau settled on another strategy to
control the narrative: the DOJ applied for a court injunction to prevent the *Post* from publishing Turrou's story. For a brief moment, as

the *Post* was temporarily enjoined while the court considered the application, it looked like a major constitutional case would break out. J. David Stern, the liberal publisher of the *Post*, complained that this was an "unprecedented attempt to erase freedom of the press from the constitution" and promised to fight for his right to print. But under pressure from FDR—who questioned Stern's "patriotism and ethics"—the publisher quietly agreed to hold publication until the criminal trial of the Rumrich ring had concluded. Because Stern backed down, the courts would not consider whether newspapers could be enjoined from publishing national-security information until the Pentagon Papers case, three decades later.[14]

Despite the public spat between Hoover and Turrou—each attacked the other in angry magazine articles—the two were selling the same bill of goods. Both built up the spy menace, and both trumped up the FBI's counterespionage bona fides; the only difference was how much credit Turrou himself could claim. So when the ex-agent's story was finally serialized in the *Post*, when it was published in book form as *Nazi Spies in America*, and when he went on the lecture circuit to call for tougher espionage laws, Turrou worked to embellish Hoover's narrative that only the watchful eye of the FBI was keeping the country safe.

In that narrative, fact and fantasy blurred; Americans were besieged with images of devious, villainous spies. Pulp fiction and comic books burst at the seams with menacing Nazi masterminds. The year 1941 saw the creation of Captain America, a patriotic superhero who combated spies and saboteurs on the home front. In 1939 Warner Bros. got in on the act when it released *Confessions of a Nazi Spy*. Turrou had been hired to consult on the film, which deployed documentary techniques to enhance its verisimilitude. The *Chicago Tribune* praised it as a "brilliantly revealing exposé of the spy system of the Third Reich." Hollywood, ever keen to jump on a bandwagon, was soon churning out spy films. In 1942 it released seventy films about spies, saboteurs, and subversives. A government agency complained that these movies were so exaggerated that they were misleading the public.[15]

Never mind that the actual story was far less exciting. The spies had not stolen much. And it had hardly taken a genius to catch them; the spies kept turning themselves in. Sebold had simply walked into the US consulate in Cologne one day. Carl Reuper, a mechanic in a New Jersey airplane factory, flat-out told a fellow employee that he was a German spy and asked where he could find technical drawings—the colleague went straight to the FBI. Meanwhile, the FBI made embarrassing mistakes that let most of the Rumrich ring slip out of their fingers and back across the Atlantic. The heroes and villains of the spy stories that Americans were consuming in their media bore only a loose resemblance to the flawed characters and petty events of reality.[16]

But amid the frightening descent into war, the threat of espionage seemed very real. In the mid-1930s the FBI received only about 35 tips about suspected espionage per year; in 1939 it received 1,615. By August 1940, almost one in two Americans believed their communities had been infiltrated. Earlier that summer, a Michigan man murdered a neighbor he believed to be a foreign spy.[17]

The federal government began to assume new powers to guard against these foreign spies and subversives. In 1938 the Foreign Agent Registration Act was passed, requiring individuals working on behalf of foreign governments to register with the State Department—some 7,600 did so. The next year, FDR centralized counterintelligence operations and then gave the FBI primary responsibility over them. Privately, the president gave the FBI authorization to tap people's phones. And Hoover began drawing up a list of individuals who might need to be locked up during a war. By 1954, there were 26,000 names on it.[18]

When the trial of the Duquesne spy ring began in Brooklyn in September 1941, the country was therefore unlikely to consider the case coolly. Nineteen of the thirty-three indicted spies pled guilty. Heine was one of the fourteen who maintained his innocence, arguing that the information he had sent to the Nazis was so innocuous and easily accessible that it could not possibly rise to the level of espionage. In fact, Heine asserted, he had been asked to gather information of a "confidential nature" by Volkswagen but had deliberately avoided doing so.[19]

It wasn't a successful argument. The trial judge specifically instructed the jury that the Espionage Act was "not restricted to information derived from secret or confidential government sources." And as the fourteen-week trial entered its final days, Japan bombed Pearl Harbor. On December 12, one day after Hitler had declared war on the United States, the jury retired to consider the charges. Only eight hours later, they returned to the courtroom; one of the defense lawyers "could see the hatred in the jury's eyes." All of the defendants were found guilty. Heine was sentenced to two years in jail for failing to register as an agent of a foreign power and eighteen years for espionage. Along with Duquesne and Lang, who had stolen the Norden bombsight, Heine received the longest sentence of the spy ring.[20]

While Heine sat in his cell in Atlanta, his lawyer, George Gordon Battle, who had worked with the National Civil Liberties Bureau during World War I, prepared to appeal the decision.[21] Battle planned to argue, once more, that the Espionage Act could not apply to the facts of Heine's case. For if it applied to even publicly available information, then it threatened to interfere with the freedom of Americans to debate and discuss the war economy.

By the time that Heine was sent to jail, the US government was already struggling to secure the nation's secrets from enemy eyes and to do so without interfering with the civil liberties of its citizens. The manner in which it chose to regulate information during the war would have important implications for both the outcome of Heine's appeal and the trajectory of the Espionage Act.

On the same day that the jury found Heine guilty, FDR announced the creation of the new Office of Censorship (OC). "Americans abhor censorship," explained the president, "[but] some degree of censorship is necessary in war time, and we are at war." The OC was soon given powers to censor messages sent internationally by mail and cable. But out of deference to the First Amendment, it was not given any legal authority to censor the press. Instead, the nation's press was asked to "abstain voluntarily from the dissemination of detailed information of certain kinds." Staffed by a team of nine journalists, the OC prepared a five-page Code of Wartime Practices for the media, which listed the sorts of information the press should not publish if it wished to aid in the war effort: troop movements, casualty lists, diplomatic missions, war contracts, supplies of strategic materials, and so forth. Tens of thousands of copies were sent to the newsrooms of the nation.[22]

In short, the OC asked the press to censor itself. "Don't look on this office as something giving you a permit to print," explained the instructor of a class that the OC ran for forty editors in 1942. "Look on yourself as allies or associate members of the OC and make up your own mind what you think should be properly published in wartime in this country." Again and again, the OC asked the press to act responsibly to protect the nation's interests. "There isn't any story in the world that is good enough to justify risking the life of a single American soldier," journalists were repeatedly reminded. "Ask yourself, 'is this information I would like to have if I were the enemy?' then let your conscience and your patriotism guide your decision."[23]

The press quickly fell into line. By 1944, Byron Price, the former Associated Press managing editor who now served as the director of censorship, was boasting that "literally thousands of items are eliminated every hour on a voluntary basis." If anything, Price was worried that a "dangerous psychology of over-censorship" was being created.[24]

Most of the Office of Censorship's time was therefore spent answering thousands of queries from anxious editors who wanted to know whether or not they should run a particular story. The OC never formally "approved" or "disapproved" particular stories; it never killed a story or insisted on deletions or changes. And it had no authority to prosecute or punish the occasional violations of the code it uncovered. But it could make recommendations, offer assurances, ask for clarification. The press was more than happy to participate in the process. "Tell us what should not be printed," pleaded the managing editor of the *Los Angeles Times*; "we will play ball."[25]

A typical request came in to the OC from the *Knoxville News-Sentinel* on December 11, 1943. At 12:24 in the afternoon, an interesting story had come over the wire: the Associated Press (AP) was reporting a press conference in which Tennessee's Selective Service director had explained that a weapon was being made in Oak Ridge that would end the war. At 1:23 the editor at Knoxville put in a call to the OC: Was this the kind of thing that the patriotic *News-Sentinel* should avoid printing? One imagines a sharp intake of breath on the other end of the line. Six months earlier, the OC had met with officials involved in the Manhattan Project and issued a memo asking the press to avoid publishing any information about "the production or utilization of atom smashing, atomic energy, atomic fission, atomic splitting." The OC wanted so few references to atomic energy in the press that it would "lead the enemy to believe we never think about such a thing"—it was even asking the publisher of *Superman* comics to remove vague references to cyclotrons and atom smashing. (Ironically, these extreme efforts were themselves a tell. In early 1942, when scientific journals suddenly stopped publishing theoretical work on fission, international observers knew what was up. "A seal of silence has been imposed," one Soviet scientist wrote to Stalin, "and this is the best proof of the vigorous work now going on abroad."[26])

Within thirty minutes of the call from the *News-Sentinel*, the OC had conferred with the AP, which sent out a bulletin at 2 p.m. asking its members not to publish the story. Afternoon editions including the offending story were already being printed, but the presses were stopped, and changes were made. For the OC, it was an example of the system working at its finest. Voluntary self-censorship helped preserve the most important secret of the war.[27]

If this was censorship, it was a far cry from the heavy-handed re-pression of World War I. In part, as the patriotic cooperation of the press revealed, there was less dissent in World War II than there had been three decades earlier. Following the attack on Pearl Har-bor, the nation had rallied to the flag, with pacifism and isolationism sidelined. And two decades since the closing of the border, there were fewer Americans who identified primarily as immigrants—the foreign-language press, so troubling to World War I censors, had already entered a period of sharp decline and was easily monitored.

But the difference in censorship between the two wars was also a product of the rising respect for the First Amendment in US culture. According to the letter of the law, the state still had the same restric-tive powers that it had during World War I. When the US entered the war, the old Espionage Act prohibitions on causing disloyalty in the armed forces or interfering with recruitment came back into force. And in 1940 the president had signed an alien registration act. Known as the Smith Act, it required all aliens to be fingerprinted and made it illegal to "advocate, abet, advise, or teach the duty, ne-cessity, desirability or propriety of overthrowing or destroying any government in the U.S. by force or violence" or to "print, publish, edit, issue, circulate, sell, distribute, or publicly display any written or printed matter" that did so. By an overwhelming margin, Con-gress had adopted a sweeping peacetime sedition bill of the sort that Attorney General Palmer had sought in 1920—only four members of the House voted against it.[28]

The crucial difference was in the ways that these laws were en-forced and adjudicated. This time, committed civil libertarians occu-pied key positions in the wartime administration and on the bench. Francis Biddle, the attorney general, had clerked under Oliver Wen-dell Holmes and was a member of the ACLU. Weeks before US entry into the war, he had given a speech promising that the US "will not again fall into the disgraceful hysteria of witch hunts . . . which were such a dark chapter in our record of the last war." Local prosecutors would not be given a free hand to bring speech charges on their own initiative; they would need approval from Biddle's office. Shortly after Pearl Harbor, Biddle dismissed Espionage Act charges brought against speakers in Los Angeles who praised Hitler or suggested that Japan had more right to Hawaii than the United States did.[29]

During the war, only a small handful of figures on the margins of US politics were punished for their political speech. The Espionage Act was used to imprison about twenty Black nationalists who cheered on the Japanese Empire, as well as a small number of explicit fascists, such as William Dudley Pelley, who had modeled his small movement of "Silver Shirts" on Hitler's SS and blamed FDR's war policy on a Zionist conspiracy. An effort was also made to prosecute a motley array of American fascist leaders on both Espionage Act and Smith Act charges. It was a media circus of a trial, full of histrionic speechifying and endless delays. Two years after indictments were issued, a seven-month trial ended in 1944, when the judge passed away just before the jury was about to reach a decision. The Justice Department soon dropped the charges and washed its hands of the entire spectacle.[30]

The only other effort to use the sweeping provisions of the Smith Act had come in June 1941, when twenty-nine Trotskyists in a Minneapolis teamsters local were charged with advocating the overthrow of the government. Despite the radicalism and marginality of the defendants—infamously, even the Communist Party supported the prosecution of its anti-Stalinist rivals—the prosecution was controversial. Justice Department lawyers were unsure if the prosecution was justified; Biddle came to regret it. (FDR had wanted it in part because the teamsters president, a political ally who was seeking to purge radical challengers from his union, had telegrammed the White House to ask for help.) Only eighteen of the defendants were found guilty, and they were sentenced to relatively lenient terms of between twelve and sixteen months. Even so, civil libertarians protested the outcome, and three Supreme Court justices tried in vain to hear an appeal. The case foreshadowed the uses to which the Smith Act would be put in the Cold War, but the story during World War II was one of restraint.[31]

Indeed, one of the rare successful wartime Espionage Act prosecutions ultimately proved a death knell for the law's use as a censorship tool. O. M. Hartzel had been sent to jail for mailing leaflets to the troops that denounced the war as a Zionist-British plot and called for the foreign occupation of the United States rather than a war between white nations. Hartzel favored a war of white Americans against the "yellow races." It was a more vicious piece of political propaganda than those of the Socialist pamphleteers who had been convicted of Espionage Act violations in the last war. Yet when the Supreme Court heard Hartzel's appeal in 1944, it overruled his conviction, finding that he had the right to such speech. It was neither the first nor last time that right-wing propagandists would receive more First Amendment protections than left-wing agitators, and it was a narrow, technical decision: 5–4. But it indicated how far the right to speech had advanced in the quarter century since Holmes had ruled on *Debs* and *Schenck*. And it narrowed the applicability of the censorship clauses of the Espionage Act moving forward.[32]

As the state was losing both the capacity and the will to censor speech, however, it was becoming increasingly interested in controlling information. This trade-off was given its plainest articulation when secret war plans had been leaked to the press just days before Pearl Harbor. The War Plans Division had spent the fall of 1941 drafting a detailed "Victory Program": a secret assessment of the military strategy, manpower requirements, and industrial output that would be required to win a war against the Nazis. On December 4, its details were published in the *Chicago Tribune*. "FDR's War Plans!," trumpeted the angry *Tribune* headline, would cost $150 billion and require ten million Americans in uniform. In a nation still divided about involvement in the war, it was a potentially scandalous leak.[33]

In the brief window before Pearl Harbor rendered the whole matter irrelevant, the administration must have been tempted to lash out at the *Tribune*. The newspaper, and its archconservative publisher, Robert McCormick, had been a thorn in the side of the Roosevelt administration since the Democrats had come into office. McCormick, who thought that FDR was on a "campaign to destroy the constitution," had repeatedly attacked the New Deal and used his newspaper to try to unseat the president. On election night in 1936, pro-Roosevelt crowds had celebrated their victory by egging the *Tribune* building and setting fire to a *Tribune* delivery truck. And then McCormick had emerged as one of the nation's most vociferous critics of FDR's foreign policy. Henry Luce called McCormick one of the "Three Furies of Isolation"—the other two were McCormick's cousins, Cissy and Joseph Patterson, each of whom also published a newspaper. FDR referred to them as the "McCormick-Patterson Axis." At a cabinet meeting on December 6, even Francis Biddle floated the possibility of prosecuting McCormick under the Espionage Act for publishing the victory plan.[34]

Yet when FDR's press secretary, Stephen Early, addressed the nation's press about the leaked defense plans, he took pains to clarify that the *Tribune* had broken no law. "Your right to print the news is, I think, unchallenged and unquestioned," he assured the gathered reporters; in publishing the plans, the *Tribune* was simply "operating as a free press." (Early nevertheless took an understandable jab at the sensationalist spin the *Tribune* had put on things. "Had any other element of the press obtained the story," he complained, "it probably would have been more factually presented.") Rather than attacking McCormick or *Tribune* journalist Chesly Manly for publishing the leaked information, Early placed blame on the informant who had leaked the plans to the press. So did Secretary of War Henry Stimson, who said that the leaker, whoever it was, was "wanting in loyalty and patriotism." But the FBI investigation was lackluster, and as the number of potential suspects multiplied, the Justice Department abandoned the case, leading to persistent rumors that FDR had been playing three-dimensional chess and was not displeased for the plans to leak, perhaps as a way to discredit the *Tribune* or to boost British morale. Later, it became clear that the story had been passed to

Manly by isolationist senator Burton Wheeler, who had received it from an unnamed colonel.[35]

The principle that Early outlined was significant. The First Amendment suggested that the press should be free to publish whatever it could get its hands on. If the press had the right to publish state secrets, then it was the government's responsibility to keep that information from leaking.

To be sure, the principle was tested during the war. Seven months later, the front page of the *Tribune* carried yet another exclusive based on ostensibly secret government information. In its coverage of the Battle of the Midway, the *Tribune* included information that had come from a secret naval dispatch, which was itself based on the finally cracked Japanese naval code. (After Pearl Harbor, resources had flowed to the code breakers: a staff of 331 in 1941 had ballooned to 10,000 by war's end. Ironically, the secretary of war responsible for opening the funding spigot was Henry Stimson, the very same man who had shut down Yardley's Black Chamber in 1929.[36])

When the *Tribune* announced that "Navy Had Word of Jap Plan to Strike at Sea" and described in precise detail the location of enemy boats, it also revealed that the United States had broken the Japanese code. The story had been written by Stanley Johnston, a war correspondent who had been rescued from a sinking aircraft carrier in the Battle of the Coral Sea by a naval transport ship. While traveling back to the US, he had access to navy radio messages coming into the transport, including the secret dispatch about Midway, and he had promptly written them up for publication. FDR and Navy Secretary Frank Knox were outraged and wanted both Johnston and the *Tribune* prosecuted under the Espionage Act.

But it remained entirely unclear whether the act applied to the press. Seeking some legal clarity, Attorney General Biddle turned to the Office of Legal Counsel (OLC), which determined that Johnston's actions fell within the scope of the law's information-handling provisions. He was guilty of taking information related to the national defense and also, by publishing, of providing it to people not entitled to receive it.

But to find him guilty, the OLC thought it was necessary to show that Johnston had done so with the "intent or reason to believe" that the information would harm the United States or advantage another nation. Assistant Solicitor General Oscar Cox believed that it was "doubtful" that he had such an intent. (In fact, the FBI was simultaneously conducting background checks to see if the Australian-born Johnston was traitorous, although these turned up little.) Nevertheless, Cox concluded that it was "fairly apparent" that there was "reason to believe" that harm would be caused. Moreover, he thought Johnston's actions were "characterized by real turpitude and disregard of his obligations as a citizen. It is hard to believe that any jury or judge would take a sympathetic view of his case . . . he thoroughly deserves punishment." Cox even imagined that Johnston's editor and Robert McCormick, the publisher, might be successfully charged. And win or lose, a prosecution would send a message: "The indictment alone would have a salutary effect in preventing disclosures so dangerous to our war effort."[37]

Others within the administration were less certain. Former attorney general William D. Mitchell, who was prosecuting the case for the Department of Justice, concluded regretfully that there were "serious doubts as to the prospects of conviction . . . because of defects in the statute." It would be hard to prove that Johnston had reason to think that the information he found lying on the table was secret. Moreover, Johnston claimed that he had not intended to publish the material—instead, he had asked his editor to ascertain whether it could be published. Meanwhile, his editor claimed that he thought that the information had come from overheard conversations and that the prohibition on disclosing information to those not entitled to receive it covered only information in "a document, writing . . . or note." Assistant Attorney General Wendell Berge, who thought Johnston's behavior had been "despicable," therefore recommended that the prosecution be dropped.[38]

Biddle knew he had at best a weak case, but he nevertheless ordered the opening of a grand jury in Chicago; there was too much political pressure for him to back down. Yet after the hearings had already begun, the navy decided that it did not want to provide evidence that the Japanese code had been broken—it seemed that the Japanese had not drawn that conclusion from Johnston's story, so the trial risked producing the very harm it was meant to punish. With no evidence that a crime had been committed, the case collapsed. "In letting me go to Chicago . . . and then stopping the disclosure at that stage," complained the prosecutor Mitchell, the navy "sort of sold me down the river and the Department of Justice as well."[39]

There was never again such a serious effort to use the Espionage Act to prosecute a journalist. But although the *Chicago Tribune* rushed to claim a great victory for freedom of the press, the outcome reflected the problems of the law more than a deep commitment to First Amendment rights.

The lesson for the government was twofold. First, it was not clear that the Espionage Act could be easily applied to the press. Second, using the Espionage Act to punish the leak of secrets was tricky, for a trial risked further publicizing the disclosure. Both lessons reinforced the philosophy that Early had outlined when the *Tribune* leaked defense plans: best for the government to tighten up control of its secrets and thus avoid the problem in the first place.

The wartime government was indeed taking steps to hold information close to the vest, experimenting with a variety of methods, both old and new, to keep its secrets safe.

In 1940 FDR had issued an executive order that for the first time conferred presidential recognition on the classification systems that the armed forces had developed in the interwar period. In 1942 the Office of War Information extended these secrecy practices to civilian agencies for the duration of the war. In March 1944 a "Top Secret" classification was introduced to make British and US classification regimes parallel.[40]

Meanwhile, military censors assiduously screened dispatches from the front. And Leslie Groves carefully compartmentalized information in the Manhattan Project to help keep the details of the atomic bomb from spilling out. At Oak Ridge, one washerwoman was given the job of holding up uniforms to a machine that might click. Only later would she learn what she had not "needed" to know: the machine was a Geiger counter, and the frequent clicks signaled exposure to radiation.

Given the uncertain reach of the Espionage Act, ad hoc procedures were developed to ensure that personnel would not disclose their secrets. All employees in the Manhattan Project had to sign an oath clarifying that the information they were receiving was protected by the Espionage Act. Those working on bacteriological weapons were asked to sign the Espionage Act itself to show they understood the need for secrecy. Bureaucrats were still working out patches to make sure that the troublesome old phrase "information relating to the national defense" applied to the secrets they wanted to keep.[41]

And the state did not yet believe that it could truly trust its secrecy practices. It was worried that information was leaking out anyway. In fact, the simple existence of the Office of Censorship revealed the need for a safety net, for a second chance to catch and suppress secrets that had spilled to the press. It was an understandable anxiety because there were deep flaws in the World War II secrecy regime.

To begin with, federal employees could not yet be trusted to follow what were new and unfamiliar secrecy practices. In May 1943 the Office of War Information created a new government organization to improve security across the federal bureaucracy. As the staff of this Security Advisory Board—all of them armed-services officers—began to survey the task in front of them, they were dismayed. Federal employees were leaving classified information unlocked in buildings that made no effort to screen visitors. They were reading classified information on streetcars, proofreading classified information aloud in common areas, and taking classified information to unapproved commercial printing firms for reproduction.[42]

So the Security Advisory Board tried to develop a new culture. Best practices were outlined in memoranda: henceforth, classified material was to be pulped, not shredded, before being discarded.

Training sessions were run across the bureaucracy. (In one, a military officer lectured new employees on the Axis propensity for espionage: "My mental picture of a Jap is a little fellow with buck teeth and thick glasses taking a picture of something.") But it was an uphill battle.[43]

Lax security protocols were one thing; the legal status of classification raised deeper problems. Remarkably, there were no clear legal penalties for disclosing information simply because it was marked secret. In 1942 three federal employees had stolen information from Civil Service Records to sell it to a marketing firm. But the Justice Department's efforts to prosecute them had collapsed when it became clear that although it was illegal to conceal, mutilate, or destroy government documents, there were no clear prohibitions on stealing the information within them. In order to "plug the loophole," the administration had introduced a bill to Congress that would have punished the communication of "confidential" government information with a $5,000 fine and two years in jail. But because it had been drafted to cover both government employees and defense contractors, it was written broadly and would have barred journalists from communicating confidential information. Under protest from the news media—trade journal *Editor and Publisher* called it "one of the most iniquitous stabs at freedom of press and speech that had ever come before an American legislature"—the bill died quickly in committee. That left only the vague prohibitions of the Espionage Act. But did the simple act of classification turn something into information "relating to the national defense"?[44]

By the end of the war, security-conscious officials in the executive branch had grown dissatisfied with the entire jerry-rigged apparatus. Government officials did not know how to keep information secret; many were tempted to leak classified information to the press for personal or political gain. If they did, it was not clear that they could be punished. Meanwhile, if the press got hold of such information, the Midway case suggested the Espionage Act was of uncertain use. And although the Office of Censorship had encouraged the press to self-regulate during the war, there were no guarantees that this safety net would continue to work once the emergency conditions were over.

So in May 1944 the Security Advisory Board began exploring possibilities for reforming the laws of secrecy. In consultation with the Department of Justice, it produced a memo documenting the laws relating to information security and concluded, regretfully, that there was "at present no statute which prohibits the disclosure of general information obtained by government employees in the course of their employment." Although "there is an apparent need for a statute of this type," the lawyers warned, it would be difficult to draft, for it would have to be "very carefully drawn in order to make it sufficiently definite and certain and in order to escape the possible contention that it would curtail freedom of the press." At the time, both the War Production Board and the War Department were attempting to draft such a law. Nothing ever came of it.[45]

The war ended before any solution could be found. When the Office of War Information was abolished in August 1945, the Security Advisory Board was the only survivor. Transferred into a new State-War-Navy Coordinating Committee, it would continue its efforts to secure the nation's secrets in the postwar period.[46]

It was in this context that Heine's appeal was finally heard by three judges of the Second Circuit Court of Appeals. Their decision, issued in November 1945, was written by Learned Hand, who in 1919 had been part of the small circle of civil libertarians who had converted Oliver Wendell Holmes to the cause of free speech. In the years since, Hand had become a judicial titan, the most important US judge never to sit on the Supreme Court. In the course of his fifty-two years on the federal bench, he wrote some four thousand opinions, many of which are widely admired today.[47]

Heine's appeal wasn't Hand's first encounter with the Espionage Act. In fact, three decades earlier, Hand had been the first judge to grapple with the Espionage Act's ambiguities. Back in World War I, the first magazine to be barred from the mail had been the *Masses*, a monthly "revolutionary" journal. The magazine went to federal court to protest the ban, and in July 1917 the matter fell to Hand to adjudicate.[48]

Two years before the Supreme Court considered the Espionage Act in *Schenck*, *Frohwerk*, and *Debs*, Hand had to decide whether the *Masses* could be denied access to the mail. It was a sensitive matter, made more so by the fact that Hand was under consideration for promotion to a circuit court of appeals. In a letter to his wife, he explained his predicament. If he delayed or if his decision went against the government, "then whoop-la, your little man is in the mud." But, he continued, "there are times, when the old bunk about an independent and fearless judiciary means a good deal. This is one of them."

So Hand ruled against the government. Yes, he said, the *Masses* had criticized the government and the draft. But it had not expressly advocated any violation of the law. And as Hand understood Congress's intent in drafting the Espionage Act, it had meant to bar only explicit incitement of illegality. If the kinds of opinions expressed by the *Masses* were illegal, then the Espionage Act would sanction so much censorship that it would undermine freedom of debate. Congress could not have intended that, so the government could not ban the magazine from the mail.

It was a brave and brilliant decision, one that expressed the hallmarks of Hand's broader approach to the law. Hand was an advocate, and practitioner, of judicial restraint—like so many progressives, he thought the legislature had to be free to legislate. Angered by judicial disruption of economic regulations during the Gilded Age, he was leery of court-enforced minority rights, and he worried about the vagaries of judicial improvisation. But he was nevertheless a believer in free speech. In *Masses* he found a way to limit government interference in the free exchange of ideas: not by citing the Constitution but by rereading the statute in order to establish a clear standard by which judges could enforce the wishes of the legislature. If the speech "directly advocated resistance to the draft," then it was illegal; anything short of that was legal. This was much more protective of speech than the "clear and present danger" test that Holmes would articulate in 1919 and that drove the liberalization of speech rights for decades. And most importantly for Hand, it avoided asking judges to make hazy assessments about how "clear" or "present" the "danger" was. As he explained to Zechariah Chafee Jr., "I own I should prefer a qualitative formula, hard, conventional, difficult to evade."[49]

Hand wanted to avoid entangling judges in difficult calculations about the likely impact of the speech or in contemplation of the intent of the speaker. That way lay discretion, and subjectivity, and political pressure, and bias. Instead, judgment should be based on the objective facts of the speech itself: the words were either an express incitement or they were not. It was very close to the test that today governs criminal-advocacy cases and that the Supreme Court adopted only in 1969.

But in 1917, Hand's decision was widely condemned and quickly overruled. Unable to distribute through the mail, the *Masses* went out of business by the end of the year. And Hand, as he had predicted, was passed over for promotion. "Undoubtedly," his wife wrote in consolation, "it was the *Masses* decision which had hurt you but dear, I feel just as you do about it. You couldn't have done it differently and it was a fine thing to do."[50]

Now, three decades later, his reputation more than fully recovered, Hand was being asked to once again consider the Espionage Act's impact on civil liberties and national security. And he again sought to protect free speech without overstepping the narrow role of the judge, deferential to the wishes of the legislature.

Unlike the *Masses* case in 1917, when he had been the first judge to consider the law, Hand was now bound by the precedent of the *Gorin* decision. After all, Heine's argument was similar to the one that Gorin and Salich had made four years before: if the publicly available information he had sent to Germany was "information relating to the national defense," then the Espionage Act spilled out to threaten free speech. In *Gorin* a unanimous Supreme Court had ruled that "information relating to the national defense" was an expansive term but that the statute was satisfactorily limited by the requirement that the person sharing the information intended to injure the United States or advantage another nation. Arguably, Hand could simply have applied this test and rejected Heine's appeal. Information about airplane production fell within the "broad connotations" of national defense, and there was no doubt that in sending the information to Germany, Heine was advantaging another nation. In fact, Hand was quick to uphold Heine's conviction for failing to register as the agent of a foreign power. "Nobody but a simpleton," he said, could fail to conclude that Heine was working for the Nazis.

But in light of the experiences of the war, and of his broader judicial philosophy, Hand thought that simply applying the *Gorin* test in this manner was unsatisfying. The mobilization of the war economy had revealed just how expansive a category "information relating to the national defense" actually was. "It seems plain," Hand observed, that the phrase could not be intended to "cover information about all those activities which become tributary to the 'national defense' in time of war; for in modern war there are none which do not." And trying to limit the sprawl of the law by relying on the intent requirement was no real limitation at all—sending information even to an ally would always "advantage another nation." The *Gorin* test, in short, would make it "criminal to send to a subject of Britain or to a citizen of France a railway map, a list of merchant ships, a description of automobile assembly technique, an account of the latest discoveries in antisepsis, or in plant or animal breeding, or even a work upon modern physics."[51]

In fact, during the war the way that the Espionage Act was understood had threatened to disrupt just this sort of information sharing. In 1942 defense contractors sending Lend-Lease material abroad had refused to share manufacturing techniques and maintenance manuals for fear that this might violate the Espionage Act. Attorney General Biddle was forced to write a special opinion stipulating that the *Gorin* decision did not apply to this sort of sharing among allies. (Although Lend-Lease did involve sharing secret information and thus did technically advantage foreign nations, he clarified, this was but a "means to an end" of advantaging the US itself.)[52] The only way to definitely avoid running afoul of the Espionage Act, Hand implied, was to send no information overseas whatsoever, but "such an assertion of national isolationism is certainly not to be imputed to Congress."

Rather than risk such "extravagant and absurd consequences," rather than impose such a "drastic repression of the free exchange of information," Hand decided to subtly rearrange *Gorin's* interpretation of the Espionage Act. In the *Gorin* decision the Supreme Court had mentioned secrecy as a factor to be considered when assessing the intent of the person distributing national defense information. Because publicly available information was still "information relating to the national defense," it fell within the scope of the Espionage Act, but if it was not secret, then there could "in all likelihood be no reasonable intent to give advantage to a foreign government" by sharing it. This was intended to contain the scope of the act. But it was a weak check—just one factor to be considered in determining intent. Leaving so much to the discretion of the judge was hardly Hand's preferred way of interpreting statutes.[53]

Hand moved the role of secrecy in the test. Rather than using it as a factor to assess the intent of the person conveying the information, he used it to define the parameters of "information relating to the national defense." If information had been made public by the armed forces, he argued, it had to be lawful to transmit it. Only if information was kept secret, Hand ruled, could it be considered "information relating to the national defense." Because the information that Heine had shared had not been kept secret, it was not covered by the Espionage Act. Heine's conviction was reversed.

It was a classic example of Hand's jurisprudence. Though claiming to be simply applying the *Gorin* precedent, he had in fact cleverly reworked it. Though claiming to be simply interpreting statutory language in light of congressional intent—he buttressed his decision with a quick gloss on the admittedly inconclusive debate surrounding the passage of the bill in 1917—he did so with reference to constitutional considerations about the "free exchange of information."

And by elevating the role of secrecy in determining the scope of the act, he sought to put the law on crisper, more objective foundations. As in the *Masses* case three decades earlier, Hand didn't want judges considering intent and consequences. He wanted a law based on the objective character of the information: either it was secret or it wasn't.

Although the decision served in the present case to limit the Espionage Act, it did risk creating another problem: opening the door to a new level of deference to governmental secrecy. If the government began declaring more information "secret," then the meaning of "information relating to the national defense" would again expand. Hand was not ignorant of the risk. "Secrets," he observed, "is an equivocal word whose definition might prove treacherous." Still, he maintained that "the [armed] services must be trusted to determine what information may be published without prejudice to the 'national defense.'"

With the benefit of hindsight, with knowledge of the abuses of secrecy that would soon begin to accrue, this appears to be a stunningly naive assumption. But it was understandable at the time. Better to create some burden on the state to declare information "related to the national defense" than to rely on the vague, quotidian definition provided by the *Gorin* decision, which hardly limited the uses that the state could make of the Espionage Act. And if someone had to make political decisions about what information fell into what categories, it was in keeping with Hand's broader philosophy that these decisions should be made not by judges but by the executive branch. His philosophy had been forged in the Progressive Era; he did not yet see how important it would be for judges to question national-security claims in the Cold War.

At first, in fact, the executive branch itself did not grasp the implications of Hand's decision. The Department of Justice had lost the case and was angered by the outcome. The decision "seriously impairs the usefulness of the statute," complained an assistant attorney general. "It can hardly be said that Congress, in enacting a statute against spies, meant to permit a spy to roam about the United States and collect and transmit to his foreign employer for its advantage information connected with our national defense, which, while in the public domain, manifestly ought not be given passage beyond our shores."[54]

The Justice Department appealed to the Supreme Court, arguing that if the decision was allowed to stand, the DOJ would have no choice but to massively escalate its control over information. Hand's decision, the DOJ protested, "may well operate as an invitation to those in charge of national security to withhold and restrict the circulation of national defense information to a far greater extent than has heretofore been deemed necessary." To keep information away from a spy like Heine, "responsible security officers" would be forced to keep so many secrets that it would prevent the US public from making "innocent use of information, directly or indirectly related to national defense, for scientific and educational purposes." These were prophetic threats. But the Supreme Court declined to hear the appeal. Hand's decision stood.[55]

For Heine, that was the end of the matter. He went free and, having played his role in the drama of the war, retreated from public view. Apart from a halfhearted and quickly abandoned attempt to make him register under the Internal Security Act in 1950, he left no further traces on the historical record.[56]

The arc of Heine's case had broader implications. It revealed the patchwork nature of the secrecy regime, the still-unsettled jurisprudence of the Espionage Act. And Hand's effort to make sense of the law reflected a foundational shift in the philosophy of censorship since World War I. In 1918 the state had been perfectly comfortable censoring speech to secure the war effort. During World War II, as a result of two decades of civil-liberties activism, such censorship was no longer acceptable. But the desire to secure secrets persisted, and the new rejection of censorship came with an important exemption. "Free speech," explained Director of Censorship Byron Price, "does not mean and never has meant the right to play fast and loose with information, as distinguished from opinion." "Freedom of the press," he continued, "was freedom to express your opinion, criticize, advocate and complain, but not freedom to disclose information."[57]

As censorship coiled more tightly around information than around speech, as the effort to keep secrets from foreign spies inevitably also kept them from the American public, a new problem arose. University of Chicago president Robert Hutchins, who led a 1944 inquiry into the state of US press freedom, explained the change well. In 1918 censorship had taken place in the public sphere, so "the interference with publication was itself public and could be criticized and attacked." But "in this war, you never could find out why certain information could not be published." The politics of censorship were becoming harder to see. Even as the right to free speech was expanding, the quest for secrecy was hollowing it out.[58]

The irony was that America's enemies had conducted astonishingly little espionage during the war. After the dismantling of the Duquesne spy ring, the Nazis managed to land just two small teams of saboteurs on US soil over the course of the war. Neither group accomplished any sabotage before disaffected members turned themselves in to the FBI. Once arrested, they were secretly tried in newly created presidential commissions that quickly returned guilty verdicts: six of the accused were executed within eight weeks of their arrival in the United States. Setting a precedent that would matter a great deal after 9/11, the Supreme Court ruled that the entire improvised process was constitutional.[59]

On the West Coast, meanwhile, wholly imaginary fears of Japanese spies led to an even greater travesty: the expulsion of 120,000 Japanese Americans from the West Coast and their internment in harsh concentration camps in the nation's interior. When it came time for the Supreme Court to consider whether *this* was constitutional, the War Department simply lied, making up hundreds of instances of subversive activities to justify internment as a "military necessity." The court concluded that it had no reason to question the "judgement of the military commander that the danger of espionage and sabotage to our military resources was imminent."[60]

By 1945, Americans had proven themselves willing to twist their constitutional order out of shape to address a nonexistent threat of Axis espionage. And it would soon become clear that there *had* been spies operating in the US during the war. They had been working not for the Axis but for an ally: the Soviet Union.

Chapter 6

RED HERRINGS, OR, THE COLD WAR SPY SCARE

Ethel and Julius Rosenberg as they leave the US Court House in New York City, having been found guilty of espionage in 1951. (Library of Congress, photograph by Roger Higgins, New York World-Telegram)

THE 1948 PULITZER PRIZE FOR JOURNALISM WENT TO NAT FIN-
ney of the *Minneapolis Tribune* "for his stories on the plan of the
Truman administration to impose secrecy about the ordinary affairs
of federal civil agencies in peacetime."[1]

The previous October, Finney had received a leaked copy of a plan
to create a new classification scheme across the entire federal government. During World War II the Office of War Information's efforts to classify information had been understood to be a temporary
measure. Now the same Security Advisory Board that had policed
secret information during the war was trying to establish a classification system on a permanent basis.

It was a controversial proposal, not least because the draft rules
would have allowed the government to classify anything that "although not endangering the national security, would be prejudicial
to the interests or prestige of the nation, or any governmental activity . . . or would cause administrative embarrassment or difficulty."
Amid congressional hearings and protests from newspapers, which
complained fairly that this "censorship-at-the-source" plan would
criminalize all sorts of journalism and cover up government incompetence and malfeasance, the Truman administration distanced itself from the proposed rules. The chair of the board that had written
them was dismissed, Finney got his Pulitzer, and it seemed that the
threat of a new secrecy regime had been averted.[2]

Yet only four years later, in 1951, Truman issued an executive
order that created precisely such a peacetime classification system.
This time, the press and the nation accepted it. In fact, Truman's
classification system is still with us today.

The 1951 order was the capstone of an astonishing flurry of new
secrecy laws and practices that were rushed into existence in the early
Cold War. Amid a panic about Soviet spies, many thought the still-
murky provisions of the Espionage Act insufficient to protect the
nation's secrets. Under Truman's watch came a concentrated effort
to rectify the uncertainties created by the passage of the bill under
Woodrow Wilson: new laws to preserve atomic and cryptographic
secrets; reforms to toughen the Espionage Act; the creation of a

classification system and a loyalty program that finally plugged the holes of the 1917 law, granting the president powers to define "information relating to the national defense" as well as the procedures for accessing it.

Where Wilson failed, Truman now succeeded. Ever after, the executive branch would have astonishing powers to declare information secret.

Truman's role as father of the modern secrecy regime was far from preordained. A failed haberdasher, a lackluster farmer, a product of the Kansas City political machine, Truman was the very definition of the accidental president. Unlike Woodrow Wilson, a Princeton professor with a PhD in political science, Truman had no abstract theories about the office. (In fact, he was the last occupant of the White House who did not have a college degree.) To the extent that his Senate career had exposed him to the problems of state secrecy, he had been a champion of Congress's right to know what the executive branch was up to—he made his name heading a congressional investigation of the World War II defense sector. On the coattails of his work ferreting out government waste, he emerged as a compromise candidate for the vice-presidential nomination in 1944—favored by neither the party's Jim Crow southern bloc nor its progressive northeasterners, but acceptable enough to both. When FDR won the election, Truman was an ailing heartbeat away from the presidency.[3]

On April 12, 1945, Truman was pouring himself an evening bourbon when he got the news that FDR had died. In the eighty-two days since the inauguration, Truman and the secretive president had spoken in private only twice. It seemed hard for anyone to come to grips with the fact that little Harry Truman now occupied the most powerful office in the world: he looked, one DC socialite said, more like a dentist. At FDR's funeral, the crowd stood to attention to welcome Eleanor; they forgot to rise when their new president entered the room. Truman himself seemed in shock. "Boys," he said to some reporters on his first day in office, "if you ever pray, pray for me now. I don't know whether you fellas ever had a load of hay fall on you, but when they told me yesterday what happened, I felt like the moon, the stars, and all the planets had fallen on me. I've got the most terribly responsible job a man ever had."[4]

The responsibilities *were* overwhelming. There was the war to end, the postwar peace to negotiate. There was no time to come up to speed. Three weeks after taking office, Truman had to pick up ongoing negotiations with the Soviets, the wartime alliance already fraught and fraying. Like inexperienced, insecure men in so many lesser walks of life, Truman puffed out his chest and tried to look tough, lecturing Foreign Minister Molotov about what Truman took to be Soviet obligations. "I have never been talked to like that in my life," complained Molotov. "Carry out your agreements and you won't get talked to like that again," blustered Truman. That night, Truman boasted that "I gave it to him straight. I let him have it. It was straight one-two to the jaw." But the bravado couldn't fully cover his uncertainty. After the meeting with Molotov, Truman had turned to an aide, a man with more diplomatic experience, and asked, "I want to know what you think: did I do right?"[5]

There was something similarly brittle about the swagger with which the United States was carrying itself as a global superpower. It was clear that the US—spared the devastation of battle, its economy humming, its military capacity unrivaled—was going to dominate the postwar world. But with great responsibility came great anxiety, a worry that such heights of success and power could not last. "We have about 50% of the world's wealth, but only 6.3% of its population," observed a secret State Department policy document. "Our real task in the coming period is to devise a pattern of relationships which will permit us to maintain this position of disparity without positive detriment to our national security."[6]

The imperial conflicts at the turn of the twentieth century had produced the first great anxiety about spies, as well as the first flourishing of secrecy laws and security bureaucracies. Now a new era of superpower conflict was producing a new politics of national security.

These were the cascading pressures thrust on Harry Truman when he ascended to the White House. There was the need to secure America's global dominance from foreign rivals. There was the need to shore up the New Deal and the governing majority of the Democratic Party, both under attack by Republicans eager to seize on any weakness in order to return to power. And there was the need to solidify his own position in the White House, to establish himself as his own man.

News that the United States had secretly developed a new atomic bomb helped on all three fronts at once. In the summer of 1945, while attending diplomatic negotiations in bombed-out Potsdam, Truman was told that the bomb had been successfully tested in New Mexico. "The President was tremendously pepped up," recalled Henry Stimson, the secretary of war. "He said it gave him an entirely new feeling of confidence." When Truman was informed that Hiroshima had been bombed, he was momentarily giddy, proclaiming "this is the greatest thing in history." He wanted to redesign the presidential seal, replacing the arrows clutched in the eagle's talons with lightning bolts to better represent the elemental powers the new president now had in his grasp.[7]

That sense of security was too good to last. Less than a month later, a disgruntled twenty-six-year-old cipher clerk in the Soviet embassy in Ottawa was told he was being recalled to the USSR. Igor Gouzenko decided to defect. He gathered up a pile of secret papers that documented the existence of a Soviet espionage ring that had penetrated the US and Canadian governments, including the top-secret Manhattan Project, and took them to a local newspaper, which couldn't understand what he was talking about and turned him away. He went next to the local office of the Mounties to seek asylum and was turned away again. Then the Soviets broke into his apartment building, seeking their missing documents. At that point, Gouzenko was quickly brought in from the cold, the Canadian prime minister was briefed, and the US government was duly informed. In the interests of investigating further, and to avoid upsetting the delicate postwar negotiations with Stalin, it was decided to keep news of the spy ring quiet, at least for now.[8]

The next month, another defector walked into FBI offices in New York: Elizabeth Bentley, a Vassar graduate who had joined the Communist Party in the 1930s and helped her lover, Louis Golos, run spy rings in the government. Bentley was a troubled soul, a woman who battled alcoholism and loneliness throughout her life and who struck many as an untrustworthy fabulist. At first she was turned away, just as she had been turned away in a previous effort to contact the FBI in New Haven. But in November she tried for a third time to alert the FBI about Soviet spies. This time, they listened, writing up a 107-page report, which named 150 suspected spies.[9]

Thus began a sordid, angry, and sad period in US history. The fear of Soviet spies would sour Americans' relationships with one another and with their government. So deep were the ructions and recriminations of the Cold War spy scare that the truth of Bentley's allegations remained controversial for decades. To anticommunist Cold Warriors, she and her fellow informants were brave truth tellers, the front lines of liberal democracy's defense against totalitarian incursion. To leftists and liberals, those who felt the sharp edge of the period's anticommunism, spying allegations were either paranoid fantasies or cynical efforts to purge the Left from American life. The argument raged with particular fury because, in the key early years of the Cold War, there was remarkably little firm evidence; what you believed had to turn on whom you trusted.

Half a century later, new evidence finally came to light. It turned out that a small group of American code breakers working in a converted schoolhouse in northern Virginia had been able to crack the Soviet code in the late 1940s, just as many of them had cracked Japanese code a few years earlier. Throughout the war, the formidable signals-intelligence apparatus had habitually collected coded Soviet messages, even though none of them could be read. Then the

Soviets made an encryption mistake. The security of their system depended on the use of "one-time" numerical codes; under the press of war, the Soviets had started reusing the code pads, which meant that patterns began to emerge, making it possible, if still devilishly difficult, to break the code. By early 1952, what was known as the Venona Project had decoded almost three thousand encrypted messages sent from 1942 to 1944. The decrypted messages revealed that some 350 Americans were spying for the Soviets. None of this was public knowledge until 1995. To preserve operational security, it was kept highly classified; not even Truman seems to have been informed. (Ironically, the fact that the US was decoding old cables wasn't a secret to the Soviets. There was a mole in Venona, and the Americans had also briefed the head of British counterintelligence, Kim Philby, a double agent who promptly informed his handlers in Moscow.)[10]

After the Cold War, the declassification of Venona, combined with a brief window of access to KGB archives in post-Soviet Russia, revealed that there were, in fact, Soviet spies in the US during World War II. This was not the home-run vindication of the anti-communists that it is often assumed to be. The evidence, frequently cryptic and partial, is often less decisive than one might think; historians continue to litigate the cases of particular individuals, an effort that has become even more challenging given the loss of access to KGB archives in Putin's Russia. Still, there is no doubt that there was an espionage effort aimed at the United States. The problem is that the existence of spy networks was not, of itself, sufficient to explain the moral panic that swept US politics in the early Cold War.[11]

For the espionage operations were often much less exciting or troubling than they appeared at the time. Since the early 1930s, it was true, the Soviets had run a serious industrial-espionage program, seeking to learn the best US production techniques to help Stalin's crash modernization of the Soviet economy. Albert Brothman, an industrial engineer, provided Bentley with blueprints he had drawn up for aviation fuel, synthetic rubber, food processing, and soap making. Another spy procured for the Soviets details of the film technology used by 20th Century Fox. No doubt, some of this material had important political consequences. One of the technologies that the Soviets stole was the miniature recorder, so essential to wiretapping; the symbol of Eastern Bloc surveillance was in fact an American export. But the stolen information paled in comparison to the free transfer of technology both in the 1930s, when the Soviet Union was the largest purchaser of US industrial machinery, and during World War II, when the US transferred $11 billion worth of Lend-Lease aid to the Soviets, including technical manuals and 100,000 patents.[12]

Meanwhile, the stealing of political information frequently turned out to be equally mundane. Most of what passed for "political intelligence" was just a form of gossip, the sort of scuttlebutt that politicians will pass to a colleague over a drink, that a source will pass on to a handler over the next round. Or it was a form of low-circulation journalism, the passing of documents outlining policies and proposals in more detail than was publicly available. In the clubby world of elite politics, particularly in the heady days of the New Deal and World War II, when liberal Washington was small, and Democratic, and confident, there was nothing too unusual in this blurring of official and unofficial circuits of information. And there has never been anything unusual about spies, desperate to impress their bosses, gussying up their reports on the patently obvious with a smattering of rumor and then boasting about their intelligence scoops and their invaluable sources on the inside. Sometimes, of course, such intelligence gathering bears fruit. Often it doesn't. One of Bentley's most scandalous revelations was that she worked as courier for the Silvermaster Group, a network of federal employees in wartime agencies who passed on information about such matters as US military production. But Soviet handlers in Moscow complained that they weren't getting anything useful from the ring, just "an incidental motley collection of information."[13]

Even the stealing of atomic secrets turns out, on closer examination, to be a rather ambiguous accomplishment. A small number of Soviet spies and agents—perhaps a dozen or so—did gain access to the Manhattan Project, and they did pass details about bomb construction back to Moscow. The real question is how significant those pilfered details were to the Soviets' successful testing of a bomb in 1949. In part because of the big deal made about the secrecy of the Manhattan Project during the war, many Americans seem to have thought, as Vannevar Bush, who had overseen America's scientific war, put it, "that there was a secret, written perhaps on a single sheet of paper, some sort of magic formula . . . [that] if we guard this, we alone would have the atom bomb indefinitely."[14]

In fact, as all the scientists involved in the Manhattan Project knew, there was no real secret. The fundamental science was widely understood. The challenges were a series of logistical and engineering problems related to the sourcing of uranium at scale and the production of efficient triggers. After Hiroshima showed that it was possible to solve those problems, it was inevitable that the Soviets would do whatever it took to match the Americans. Truman boasted that the Soviets would "never" get the bomb; most scientists in 1945 expected it would take them no more than three to five years. In that sense, the Soviet bomb arrived right on schedule. Would it have if not for the spying? That's the kind of counterfactual question that historians are normally loath to answer. But even those most confident that espionage sped up the Soviet bomb think that it did so by at most one to two years.[15]

Regardless of how damaging Soviet espionage actually was, the simple fact was that the US had sufficient laws on the books to police it. The Espionage Act made it illegal to pass information relating to the national defense to foreign governments. It provided the government with more than enough power to prosecute Soviet spies, as the case of the Rosenbergs revealed.

The FBI had been set on the trail of the Rosenbergs by Venona's decoded messages, which had named Klaus Fuchs, a German-born British physicist deeply involved in the Manhattan Project, as a spy for the Soviets. Fuchs confessed when confronted by British counterintelligence, and he also offered up the name of Harry Gold, who had been running industrial secrets, such as varnish and lacquer formulas, to the Soviets since the 1930s. Gold was not a member of the Communist Party but a left-leaning Jew, raised in a household of Debs supporters. His faith in the USSR hinged on his belief that it was less anti-Semitic than a mid-century Philadelphia in which he had been subject to crude discrimination. Gold also confessed, adding that he had another source in the Manhattan Project.[16]

This was David Greenglass, a machinist from New York, who named his brother-in-law, Julius Rosenberg, as another spy. Julius had also been named in the Venona transcripts as the center of a yet larger ring of industrial spies. But then the string of confessions came to a halt. Julius would not confess, and he would not name additional names. The desire to keep the Venona transcripts secret meant that this key evidence against him could not be introduced in a trial. So the prosecutors had to get creative. "The only thing that will break this man Rosenberg," explained one of the DOJ lawyers in a confidential session, "is the prospect of a death penalty or getting the chair, plus that if we can convict his wife, too . . . that combination may serve to make this fellow disgorge." There was only one problem, the lawyer confessed: "The case is not too strong against Mrs. Rosenberg."[17]

Pressure was put on Greenglass to implicate his sister; in exchange, Greenglass's wife would not be charged. Greenglass did the deal, selling out his sister to save his wife. Coached up by the prosecutors—including a young Roy Cohn, the slick lawyer later to serve as wingman to Joe McCarthy and later still as adviser to Donald Trump—Greenglass and his wife spun a story in which Ethel pressured them into spying and then typed up their intelligence reports. In truth, the Greenglasses were true believers, the sort of people who signed letters to each other "with all the love of Marx and all the humanity of Lenin."[18]

The Rosenbergs still wouldn't crack. The trial was a public spectacle, the Rosenbergs accused of sharing the very secret of the bomb. (In reality, Greenglass, who had only a high school education, provided quite crude drawings of the bomb to the Soviets and incorrectly reported the number of lenses it contained. Leslie Groves, who had run the Manhattan Project, later said the information was "of minor value.") Cowed by the charges, the Rosenbergs' underqualified lawyers offered poor defenses—Ethel was represented by a real estate lawyer, who got the job only because he was the father of Julius's lawyer. After fourteen days, Julius and Ethel were found guilty of violating the Espionage Act on the flimsy confessions of their relatives. Judge Irving Kaufman blamed the pair for the outbreak of the Korean war and sentenced them to death, the maximum penalty allowed for spying in wartime. It was the first and only time that those clauses of the Espionage Act had been used. Kaufman went out of his way to advocate adding the death penalty to even peacetime prosecutions.[19]

Even if Ethel had been guilty, she was being sentenced to death for typing up some low-value information. David Greenglass got fifteen years for his crimes and was out in ten. Klaus Fuchs, whose information was more valuable to the Soviets, received a fourteen-year sentence in the United Kingdom. Released after nine, he lived out his later years in East Germany.[20]

On June 19, 1953, Ethel and Julius were executed at Sing Sing. In a final cruelty, Ethel did not die from the first electric shock or the second, but only after the fifth agonizing jolt. She left behind two boys, aged ten and six.[21]

The Espionage Act clearly had sufficient teeth to prosecute Soviet spies. To the extent that the authorities had difficulty winning convictions, the problems were entirely of their own making.

In 1945, for instance, an intelligence official noticed that an article on postwar Thai diplomacy that had been published in the left-wing *Amerasia* magazine was remarkably similar to a classified paper he had written. He reported it, and government investigators illegally broke into *Amerasia*'s offices six times, as well as the homes of a number of journalists and government employees. They found lots of documents, many classified, and thought they had discovered an espionage ring. In truth, they had found evidence of garden-variety politics-by-leaking. Within the government there were deep divisions over the nation's Asia policy, about whether it made sense to support Chiang Kai-shek's nationalists exclusively or whether overtures to Mao's Communists needed to be made as well. Those who favored the latter policy were leaking to *Amerasia* to help make their case.

FBI wiretaps found no evidence that the documents, whose military or diplomatic value was unclear, had been transferred to a foreign power. But Truman wanted to pursue a prosecution anyway because he was worried that disgruntled, left-leaning holdovers from the FDR administration might undermine his foreign policy. He wanted "to use this case as an example to other persons in government service who may be divulging confidential information." So six individuals—three journalists and three government employees—were charged with violating the Espionage Act. But the evidence was flimsy, and the grand jury voted to indict only three of the six. Then one of the accused, surprised at how easily FBI agents had found documents in his house on the day of his arrest, learned from his landlord about the illegal break-ins. The prosecution quickly cut a plea deal with the two remaining suspects before the entire case fell apart.[22]

In the highly partisan atmosphere, this mangled outcome was subject to competing interpretations. Some thought that the government's success in getting a plea deal was a sign of the troubling power of the Espionage Act. Two-thirds of journalists worried that the *Amerasia* affair revealed a new threat to press freedom, an effort to criminalize stories based on policy leaks, particularly when the acting secretary of state announced, erroneously, that this was but the start of a new crackdown on leaks. By contrast, J. Edgar Hoover thought that the collapsing case revealed the inadequate policing of espionage. He leaked information about the case to a right-wing congressman who called for hearings into the Democratic "cover-up." In 1946 the scandal failed to catch fire. But it would be revived after the "loss" of China in 1949, becoming for right-wing anticommunists a totemic example of the lax liberal attitude to spies.[23]

Government misconduct fouled another spy investigation, too. In 1949 decoded Venona transcripts revealed that Judith Coplon, who worked in the Justice Department, was spying for the Soviets. Because the FBI still hoped to keep Venona secret, it needed to improvise to gain the evidence needed for a conviction. Agents set up illegal wiretaps in Coplon's house and started a sting operation in which they fed Coplon dummy documents and tracked her from DC to New York, where she was supposed to pass them to her Soviet handler. The sting operation was a bit of a bust—she never did pass over the documents—but there was no real doubt about her guilt. The FBI won Espionage Act convictions in both New York (for conspiring to transfer documents to a foreign power) and DC (for taking documents without authorization).

The problem was that during one of the trials, the judge had asked to see the FBI files that Coplon was accused of stealing. These made plain how much wiretapping the FBI was doing and led not only to a public-relations scandal for the Bureau but also to an appeal from Coplon that her prosecution was illegal. In New York, the appeal was heard by Learned Hand. In his third great clash with the Espionage Act, Hand reversed Coplon's conviction and called for a retrial. By this point, Hoover was frantic to prevent the revelation of any further FBI practices. There was no retrial. Coplon's case would linger in limbo until it was finally dismissed in 1967.

Hoover's penchant for secrecy had ruined a perfectly straightforward Espionage Act prosecution. Yet the lesson he took from the Coplon affair was that there had been too much transparency, that FBI files should never be seen in court. The FBI began keeping information from illegal wiretaps in separate, secret files, easier to keep from prying eyes.[24]

However, the main reason there were so few successful espionage prosecutions during the postwar spy scare was that the threat of

Soviet espionage had largely passed. In November 1945, when the FBI went looking for the hundred government employees that Bentley had named as possible Soviet spies, it found that seventy-three had already left government service. The extensive loyalty program that Truman established in 1947 would go on to screen five million federal workers over the next decade and subject twenty-five thousand to "full-field investigations." It turned up not a single spy.[25]

It isn't hard to understand why there were so few spies in the US government. In the late 1930s and the early years of the war, it had been briefly possible to imagine that sharing information with Communist comrades was a form of progressive politics. It was a product of romantic misconceptions about the Bolshevik experiment, of radical discontent with the inequities of Depression-era America, of the moral urgency of the fight against fascism and the moral expediency of the alliance with Stalin. Until the World War II ramp-up, the federal government's lax information-security practices also made it easier both to take documents and to convince oneself that there was nothing terribly wrong in doing so.

By the late 1940s, all of that had changed. Heightened US counterintelligence practices made the risks of spying more apparent. The window of easy solidarity with the Soviet Union had been closed by revelations about show trials, by the red army's brutal advance, by the emerging Cold War. Meanwhile, the Soviet state was seeking to exert new control over the ramshackle networks of sympathizers and informants that had been feeding it information throughout the war. But replacing the amateur spy runners of the Communist underground with a new breed of professional, calculating intelligence officers meant disrupting relationships of trust. It was deeply alienating for those involved. For instance, Bentley feared and despised her new handlers, which led her to defect. As the defections mounted, Soviet intelligence doubled down on their new logic of control. In the wake of Bentley's visit to the FBI in late 1945, the KGB recalled several agents and put a number of programs on ice.[26]

For all these reasons, the threat of espionage had largely passed by the time that the spy scare really heated up. Although there would be the occasional Soviet spy in later years—the CIA's Aldrich Ames or the FBI's Robert Hanssen—they were motivated not by radical ideology but by simple greed.[27]

The second red scare was powered instead by politics. In early 1947 an effort to bring criminal charges against the spies named by Bentley collapsed for lack of evidence: it was her word against those of the accused. But then Bentley sold her story to the press. At first, she did so anonymously; Bentley, a perfectly pleasant-looking forty-year-old brunette, was written up as a "beautiful young blonde." The sorts of espionage the "svelte and striking" spy had conducted were similarly gussied up in the purple prose of pulp fiction. And then someone— most likely Hoover—gave Bentley's name to conservatives on Capitol Hill. As she testified in front of politicians keen to flay the Truman administration for its weakness on Communism, her allegations would grow yet more exaggerated.[28]

In the 1940s a significant phalanx of politicians made anticommunism a central cause. For Republicans, eager to return to power after four terms in the political wilderness, the allure of the issue was obvious. The New Deal had radically expanded the federal

Elizabeth Bentley, the "blonde spy queen," circa 1948. (Library of Congress, photograph by C. M. Stieglitz, New York World-Telegram)

bureaucracy, and given that bureaucracy's political leanings, it wasn't that hard to find employees who could be tied to liberal or progressive causes. In the 1946 midterms—an election that one GOP candidate had declared a choice "basically between communism and republicanism"—many Republicans had red-baited their opponents on the way to retaking Congress. One of them was a young Richard Nixon, who had accused his opponent of adopting the "Moscow" line and then devoted his maiden speech in Congress to attacking the "political and espionage activities" of the Communist Party.[29]

But within the strange coalition that was the mid-century Democratic Party, the red baiters had many allies. Most of them came from the Jim Crow South, but their most important member, Pat McCarran, hailed from Nevada, where he had made a name as a lawyer in what was still small-town Reno, handling the state's most important export business: no-fault divorce. In 1932 he got elected to the Senate, where he was soon in charge of the all-powerful Judiciary Committee. He hated the New Deal, hated Communists, hated the UN (a "haven for spies and communists"). Above all, he hated immigrants and spent a career pressing for legislation to bar "undesirables from abroad." The postwar spy scare combined all his hatreds under one banner. By the early 1950s, he found himself head of a new Senate Internal Security subcommittee.[30]

These politicians were the heirs to the nativist moral panic cultivated by Richmond Hobson in 1911 and the politics of national-security demagoguery pioneered by Attorney General Palmer in the similarly panicky years after World War I. But now they were aided by a well-established national-security bureaucracy that could funnel them useful information from its confidential files and add to their allegations a veneer of technocratic rationality, of objective expertise. The most important of the bureaucrats was Hoover. Fighting radicalism had been his path to power back in the days of the Palmer raids, and he reacted to the return of the "red menace" in the 1930s and 1940s by warning all who would listen that Communists were "masters of deceit" who needed to be purged from the body politic. There was also a network of less famous figures, including hawkish bureaucrats in such obscure offices as the Visa Division and the Passport Office. The latter, for instance, had been headed since 1927 by Ruth Shipley. She was one of the most powerful figures in Washington and part of a family steeped in the national-security bureaucracy: one brother had preceded Hoover as the head of a precursor to the FBI; the other was the intelligence agent who had investigated the *Amerasia* leak; a sister worked in military intelligence. Shipley had the ability to unilaterally deny American citizens a passport, and hence the right to leave the country, if she thought their travel not in the best interests of the United States. "One of the things I believe in," boasted Shipley, "is refusing passports to Communists."[31]

The heart of this anticommunist political project was not a fear of spies but a broader desire to expunge radicalism from the body politic. In the late 1930s, when there actually had been some Soviet espionage in the United States, the House Un-American Activities Committee (HUAC) had been largely uninterested in it, preferring to focus its energies instead on exposing "subversive" propaganda. In the 1940s the culture war continued with infamous hearings on radicals in Hollywood, during which the young president of the Screen Actors Guild, Ronald Reagan, named names and began his decades-long evolution from milquetoast New Dealer to avatar of the American Right. Congress didn't have to legislate to purify the film industry. Drawing up a blacklist of radicals who would be denied work, the industry censored itself.[32]

Yet the state also worked to censor Communists, both real and alleged. The Espionage Act, constrained by the *Hartzel* case of World War II, was no longer a particularly useful censorship tool, although creative officials in the Justice Department read obscure provisions of its old mailing regulations to give the post office the power to eliminate foreign propaganda from the mail. Foreign magazines and research materials requested by universities and students and political activists stopped arriving because customs officials were destroying them at the border. In St. Paul, Minnesota, the official in charge spoke no Russian and was identifying material for destruction with only the help of a dictionary.[33]

More effective was the Smith Act, the peacetime sedition bill that had been passed in 1940 and made it illegal to advocate the overthrow of the US government. In 1948 the Justice Department indicted eleven leaders of the Communist Party under the act, not for advocating any imminent coup but for "conspiring to advocate." After a controversial trial, they were found guilty. In 1951 the Supreme Court upheld their convictions. By 1956, a hundred more people would be found guilty of violating the act.[34]

Once again, the right to free speech had very clear limits. But despite the chilling effect this censorship cast across the nation's politics, the scale of the repression did not match what had come in World War I, where ten times as many dissenters had gone to jail in less than two years. The civil-liberties gains of the interwar years were not completely rolled back.

And it was telling that the censorship of the second red scare generally took a different form than the first. It was more bureaucratic in mode, more technocratic in delivery, focused on narrower bands of activity, less associated with the crude repression of mob violence. The Passport Division denied passports to hundreds of Americans whose travel Ruth Shipley deemed "not in the best interests of the United States": such luminaries as Linus Pauling, W. E. B. Du Bois, and Paul Robeson. Until the mid-1950s, those denied the right to leave the country had no right to protest the decision or even to learn the basis on which their application had been denied.[35]

Government loyalty boards likewise screened employees, looking for "security risks." Twenty-seven hundred people lost their jobs in the loyalty hearings, twelve thousand more resigned, and many others learned to censor themselves, to retreat from political life. The purges were a major factor in the development of modern American politics. The left wing of the Democratic Party was cowed, with consequences for public policy for decades. Gays and lesbians were also a particular target of the loyalty purges, ostensibly because their sexuality made them vulnerable to blackmail and hence a security risk. In the Truman years, twice as many people were fired from the State Department on charges of homosexuality as on grounds of subversion. Frank Kameny, a government astronomer fired in the late 1950s, would in response become a leader of the modern gay-rights movement.[36]

More than a serious reaction to espionage, the cultural war on Communism was a political struggle about the future of the country as well as a way of waging war on the New Deal state. But accusations of spying kept resurfacing. They were essential to the anticommunist case. Of the 250,000 Americans who had passed through the Communist Party in the previous decades, of the many more who had been involved in various groups now considered suspicious, only about 350 people had actually engaged in espionage, and not all of them were federal employees. But that was enough to prove that Communists were not simply a minor political party but an active threat, a foreign conspiracy. The spy charges gave the entire enterprise crucial legitimacy.[37]

The most famous spy (melo)drama of the period, the Hiss-Chambers case, captured the broader dynamics. In the summer of 1948, Whittaker Chambers, a former Communist, told HUAC that Alger Hiss had been a comrade in the 1930s. His testimony was a media event—the first congressional hearings ever televised—and Richard Nixon milked the occasion for all it was worth. For Hiss was a caricature of the New Deal insider: he had gone to Harvard, clerked for Oliver Wendell Holmes, been at Yalta, and served as the secretary-general of the San Francisco conference that created the United Nations. He was an ideal figure to be used to tear down the Democrats, particularly when the much hated secretary of state Dean Acheson rallied to defend him. (Acheson really got up the noses of the Republicans. "I watch [Acheson's] smart aleck manner, and his British clothes and that New Dealism, that everlasting New Dealism in everything he says and does," complained Hugh Butler, senator from Nebraska, "and I want to shout, Get out! Get Out! You stand for everything that has been wrong in the United States for years."[38])

This was, at first, the substance of the Hiss-Chambers affair: a case of he-said, he-said, and mostly a matter of political warfare. Hiss, by all accounts, won the first round when he deftly answered HUAC's interrogation, protesting vigorously that he had never even met Chambers. But then he challenged Chambers to repeat the allegations without the legal immunity offered to congressional testimony. In late August 1948, Chambers went on *Meet the Press* and accused Hiss, once again, of being a Communist. Hiss sued for slander.[39]

For a moment, it seemed the air was going out of the spy scare. The Justice Department was close to shutting down its investigation into Hiss. In his underdog 1948 reelection campaign, Harry Truman was dismissing the espionage allegations as a "red herring," complaining that HUAC was spreading "wild and false accusations" that were helping the Communists, promising that if he won the election he would abolish the committee. To everyone's surprise, Truman was returned to the White House. But he would have less success ending the second red scare.[40]

For Chambers, backed into a corner by Hiss's libel suit, now made a new charge: Hiss wasn't just a secret Communist, seeking to influence government policy, as Chambers had been saying for years; Hiss and Chambers had also worked together to spy for the Soviets in the mid-1930s. And Chambers had proof—when he had defected from the Communist Party in 1938, he had stashed a set of stolen documents with a relative as a "life preserver," evidence that he could threaten to disclose if the Communist Party sought retribution for his apostasy. In the fall of 1948, more than ten years later, he turned over copies of State Department documents, some produced on Hiss's typewriter, some in Hiss's hand, as well as three rolls of microfilmed documents—the latter dramatically unveiled from a short-term hiding place in a carved-out pumpkin on Chambers's Maryland farm.

As with most of the spying cases of the period, the Pumpkin Papers were not about ongoing activities but about matters so old that the Espionage Act's statute of limitations had expired. Yet Hiss had testified to Congress that he had never met Chambers or given him any documents. He was tried for perjury and found guilty. On January 25, 1950, Hiss was sentenced to five years in jail.

The spy scare was rekindled. Two weeks later, the junior senator from Wisconsin, until then an irrelevancy, told a small gathering of Republicans in Wheeling, West Virginia, that he knew of 205 Communists still working in the State Department. Joe McCarthy had finally found his political cause.[41]

Amerasia, Bentley, Coplon, Hiss-Chambers, the Rosenbergs—the spy scares of the early Cold War hit with a cultural weight that was far greater than the sum of their individual parts. A giant moral panic was whipped up, creating the impression that espionage was a major problem, that the nation's secrets, and hence its security, were at risk. "The atmosphere," complained Nat Finney's *Minneapolis Tribune*, "is woven out of the propaganda of fear—fear of an external enemy, fear of economic collapse, lack of confidence in and respect for the democratic free enterprise system." Added historian Robert Heilbroner, "It is, I think, the fear of losing our place in the sun, of finding ourselves at bay, that motivated a great deal of the anti-communism."[42]

Simply citing the existence of the Espionage Act was no way to assuage such elemental emotions, particularly given the cloud of uncertainty that still hung around the law. During the second red scare, the Espionage Act would be reformed and extended, bringing into existence what the *Minneapolis Tribune* called "an enormous secrecy blanket, of a character to which the American people have never heretofore submitted."[43]

One strategy was to patch the Espionage Act by passing new legislation to ensure the secrecy of particular classes of information that seemed to slip into the cracks of the existing law. Out of concern that atomic information was not "information relating to the national defense," the Atomic Energy Act was enacted—the bill's authors thought it would be easier to pass a new law than to amend the Espionage Act itself. The draconian new law made it illegal to circulate any "restricted data" about atomic energy: not just information produced by the state, but any information about atomic energy that fell within the law's definition, regardless of where it came from. For a time, there were proposals to pass a similar law to regulate information about radar technology. And in 1950 Congress added a new section to the Espionage Act that made it illegal to communicate information about signals intelligence—it was concerned that the 1933 law it had passed in the wake of the Yardley affair wasn't strong enough. Like the Atomic Energy Act, this new section—798—did not stop at regulating government employees but also barred the publication of classified communications intelligence. And both laws were strict liability, requiring no intent to harm the nation. In such ways did the perceived inadequacies of the Espionage Act produce a new layer of secrecy law.[44]

Meanwhile, at the urging of the security bureaucracy, the Espionage Act itself was made more severe in 1950. Penalties for conspiring to violate the law were increased, the statute of limitations extended from three years to ten. (The *Hiss* case was on many minds, although John Rankin wanted to settle an older score. "There are plenty of Japs in this country, and especially in Hawaii, today who participated in the perpetration of the Pearl Harbor disaster," he fumed. "I do not care how long it has been. I do not care if it has been fifty years, when one them is caught . . . he ought to be hanged by the neck until he is dead."[45])

Congress also made another change to the law in 1950, one that has caused confusion to this day. Section 793(d) was already one of the shaggiest provisions of the original 1917 law. It made it illegal to communicate documents relating to the national defense without authorization or to retain them if you were ordered to give them up. Unlike the other sections of the law, it had no intent requirement: you were guilty of these things if you did so "willfully." Congress now sought to strengthen these already sweeping provisions by extending them to cover the communication of oral information—as opposed to only physical documents—and by making it illegal to retain documents even if you were not asked to return them.

The result of these highly technical changes was a law that directly threatened the press. If a source sent a journalist a document, anything short of turning it in would constitute "willful retention" and a violation of the law. If the journalist published, they would also be "willfully communicating" it without authorization. West Virginia senator Harley Kilgore complained that the new law "might make practically every newspaper in the U.S. and all the publishers, editors and reporters into criminals."[46]

Whether or not this was intentional was unclear. At a congressional hearing on the law, the intelligence branches claimed that the new clauses explicitly criminalized publication of information relating to the national defense. Attorney General Tom Clark told the same hearing that "we do not intend to prosecute papers." When the Legal Research Service of the Library of Congress weighed in, it seemed to misread the text of the new law, explaining that newspapers would be prosecuted only if they retained or published information with intent to harm the United States or benefit another nation. But although those intent requirements guided much of the rest of the act, they applied only to one clause of the proposed revisions: those concerning the oral communication of information. The clauses that Kilgore was concerned about required only that retention or publication was done "willfully."[47]

If the experts were confused by the increasingly convoluted intricacies of the Espionage Act's intent requirements, congressional advocates of the bill were blithely unconcerned. "I am not worried about the meaning of anybody's intent," said Tennessee Republican John Jennings airily. "Every lawyer knows what intent means. . . . There is nothing highly technical about this. . . . Just let it be said once and for all that this is a law for the protection of the United States of America and it is aimed at a man who wants to betray this country."[48]

There was little serious attention paid to these amendments to the Espionage Act because they were passed as part of the omnibus 1950 Internal Security Act. Prepared by McCarran and Shipley, based on a bill first proposed in 1947 by Richard Nixon and other Republican anticommunists, the Internal Security Act was one of the most odious pieces of legislation ever enacted by Congress. It required members of organizations judged a part of the Communist movement to register with a Subversive Activities Control Board and barred Communists from even applying for passports. In times of war or emergency, it gave the president the power to round up anyone he believed might participate in "espionage or sabotage" and hold them in concentration camps.

Given its contents, Truman tried to veto the law, only to be overridden by Congress. The Supreme Court later held large parts of it unconstitutional.[49] Civil libertarians had bigger fish to fry than these seemingly technocratic tinkerings with the Espionage Act. Yet the Espionage Act reforms—the last ever enacted—were significant. The scope of the law had been expanded, pulling a vast array of press activity under the threatening cloud of prosecution.

Then, in September 1951, Truman made the most significant change to the nation's secrecy regime since the passage of the Espionage Act in 1917. He did so not by an amendment to the statute but by a unilateral executive order that did exactly what had been threatened in Finney's 1947 Pulitzer Prize–winning stories. For the first time, Truman established a permanent classification system for the entire federal government.

It turned out that Finney's story hadn't killed the classification plans, just delayed them. Only eight months after he published, the National Security Council reiterated the need for a new classification order that would standardize and secure information across the federal government, and the Interdepartmental Committee on Internal Security began working on it. The White House watched this work carefully to ensure that there would be no repeat of the embarrassment of 1947. When early drafts of the order sought to secure information whose disclosure would harm the "prestige" of the United States, Truman's staff deleted all such language and added a clause clarifying that only security information could be classified.[50]

The new system defined four classes of information—Top Secret, Secret, Confidential, and Restricted—that needed to be kept secret "in the interest of national security." It created standardized procedures for handling that information. Most significantly, the order explicitly invoked the Espionage Act. When classified information circulated outside the executive branch, it needed to be stamped with a notation that made clear that the classification meant "this material contains information affecting the national defense of the United States within the meaning of the espionage laws, Title 18, U.S.C. secs 793 and 794, the transmission or revelation of which in any manner to an unauthorized person is prohibited by law."

In essence, the classification system was a plug-in to the Espionage Act, an effort to finally bring clarity to those confusing clauses that had been orphaned by Congress in 1917. But nowhere did it come out and say that the classification system was defining "information relating to the national defense." This was because the order was not intended to limit the reach of the Espionage Act; it was not supposed to undermine any of the previous patches, such as the Atomic Energy Act, which had been created to define that confusing legal category. It was an expansion of the law more than a clarification. Anything classified fell within the Espionage Act, but the Espionage Act could still apply even if something was not classified.[51]

"Information relating to national defense" now included anything that a member of the executive branch determined might harm the "national security." Thirty years before, Congress had declined to give President Wilson authority to determine which information should be kept secret. Truman now took that power by executive order.

He did so by basing his order not on any specific statutory authority but simply "by virtue of the authority vested in me by the Constitution and statutes, and as President of the United States." A decade earlier, when FDR had first recognized and extended the classification systems of the armed forces in the run-up to World War II, his executive order doing so was based on powers granted by a 1938 statute making it illegal to photograph or sketch military or naval installations. It was a bit of a stretch to turn that law into a general order for classification—FDR did so by defining all "information" as a type of equipment—but the effort testified to the fact that the president needed to get the authority from somewhere. In 1950, when Truman updated FDR's order to cover the new category of "Top Secret" information—the first time that a president used the phrase—he did so by citing the same 1938 statute. But now, one year later, Truman was done with the pretense. He, and every president after him, would claim a constitutional right to classify.[52]

Precisely where this authority comes from is far from clear. Nothing in the Constitution explicitly gives the president power to keep secrets; the only reference to secrecy in the text of the Constitution gives Congress the power to keep *its* proceedings secret if it sees fit. But the Constitution is remarkably vague on the subject of presidential powers. It just vests the "executive power" in the office; gives the president the power, in conjunction with the Senate, to make treaties and appoint ambassadors; and declares that the president shall be commander in chief in times of war. How the framers intended these deliberately separated powers to work in practice was not clear; divided about such things in the first place, they gave them little time at the Constitutional Convention, focusing instead on matters like representation and federalism. Much remained unresolved: Was "commander in chief" a role that came into existence only during wars that Congress had declared? Or was it a permanent role, one that also existed in peacetime? In either case, what were the rules in the quasi-peace of the Cold War? How did control over foreign policy, confusingly divided between the presidency and the Senate, intersect with Congress's right to declare war? Could the president sign agreements or act so brusquely that it forced the nation into war? What limits could Congress place on the president's ability to negotiate foreign policy without overstepping its mark?[53]

At the time that Truman issued his classification order, all of these questions were being answered in the president's favor. Wilson had blazed a trail for executive power during World War I; during the descent into World War II, FDR had taken it further. In the early Cold War, when many worried that democratic government lacked the brutal efficiency of totalitarian enemies, the deck was stacked for giving the president the unilateral authority to keep the nation safe. "Yielding some democratic control of foreign affairs," argued a diplomatic historian in 1948, "is the price we may have to pay for greater physical security."[54]

The new classification system came at a time when Truman's constitutional authority was at its highest tide. Only the year before, Truman had committed US troops to fight in the Korean war without asking for congressional approval. Congress didn't complain and meekly appropriated the necessary money to fight the war. Apart from a bill introduced by a small cluster of conservative senators, which went precisely nowhere, there was likewise no political effort to challenge the constitutionality of the new classification system.[55]

Nor was the order challenged in court. In fact, the Supreme Court has never ruled directly on the constitutionality of the classification system. The most explicit discussion of the issue would not come until 1988, when the court announced that the power to classify "flows primarily from this constitutional investment of power in the president and exists quite apart from any explicit congressional grant." But that was just dicta—it was not part of a binding precedent.[56]

And although it is true that the courts have been more highly deferential to the president on matters of foreign policy than on domestic policy, it is a bit too simple to say that classification is simply a tool of foreign affairs: it reaches into domestic political and economic and intellectual life as well. In 1952, the year after Truman created the modern secrecy regime, the Supreme Court overruled his attempt to seize steel mills during a strike, a form of domestic coercion that he had attempted to justify in the interests of national security. One could imagine a similar argument being made in the field of information. But in 1951, no one really tried.[57]

There was a second reason that Truman's order was seen as legitimate: the press did not fight it either. When creating the new classification system, the Truman administration made it a priority to bring the press on board. White House staffers met with representatives of the newspaper industry to clear an early draft of the rules. The plan was to tell the press that classification would not apply to them, only to government employees. The new order had "nothing to do with this information getting into newspapers," as Truman's press secretary, Joe Short, explained to a group of journalists; "it had to do with the way they were being handled in individual offices."[58]

But as so frequently happened, Truman didn't stay on message. During the press conference explaining the new system, Truman started listing examples of secret information that he claimed had been published in the press: aerial maps of US cities, the location of atomic energy plants in *Fortune* magazine, a mysterious study done at Yale that suggested, implausibly, that 95 percent of all US secrets were being published in the papers. This created the impression that Truman was mainly worried about regulating the press, an impression that only deepened when Truman began an improvised lecture to the correspondents about their obligations to self-censor to protect the national security. *New York Times* columnist Arthur Krock called it a "tongue-lashing."[59]

This wasn't the point of the order at all, and Short tried to cut his boss off with "gestures and a couple of agonizing whispers." But Truman seemed not to understand the central issues involved. "Joe wants me to make it perfectly clear that this order only applies to officials of the U.S. government," Truman said at one point, which was exactly the party line. But in the next breath he added, "My comments, though, apply to everybody who gives away state secrets." Short was forced to issue a follow-up statement clarifying that "the recent executive order on classified information does not in any way alter the right of citizens to publish anything."[60]

What followed was a brief controversy as some members of the press worried that Truman wanted to censor them. But it soon died down. "The President didn't aim this at the press," explained Anthony Leviero of the *New York Times*. "This order is directed at espionage and we have to accept it as such." The new order, added the DC correspondent for the *Miami Daily News*, wouldn't affect him "one whit." Their freedom to publish guaranteed, the press made its peace with a new secrecy regime. It had come to accept, in the words of Leviero, that an order aimed at "preserving military secrets" was "not censorship."[61]

In 1953 Eisenhower overwrote Truman's order with his own classification order, which made only superficial changes (the bottom category of "Restricted" was abolished, for instance, leaving in place the tripartite classification system we know today). Eisenhower's order would stay in place until the early 1970s. Since then, six other presidents have replaced the order with their own, and although there have been differences among them—particularly around things like declassification rules—they have not changed the underlying architecture of the secrecy regime.[62]

It soon became apparent that the system produced massive overclassification. In 1956 the Defense Department surveyed the secrecy regime and concluded that 90 percent of items that were being classified should not have been. In coming decades a remarkable chorus of experts agreed: a 1970 scientific task force; former Supreme Court justice Arthur Goldberg; Rodney B. McDaniel, the executive secretary of Ronald Reagan's National Security Council; and Thomas Kean, who was chair of the 9/11 Commission. In 1971 one retired security classification official told Congress that 99.5 percent of the classified documents he had seen could have been released without harming defense interests.[63]

Such overclassification is a product of simple, bureaucratic logics. Presidents have routinely warned against overclassification; even Truman's 1951 executive order instructed employees to "avoid over-classification" by assigning information the "lowest security classification consistent with its proper protection." The problem is that such instructions have always been the merest lip service to transparency. They have never been meaningfully enforced. A 1972 congressional subcommittee found 2,500 cases in which executive employees had been punished for improperly releasing information. They discovered not a single case in which someone had been punished for overclassification.[64]

To prevent overclassification, it was not enough to offer, as Truman did, a generic condemnation or to call for respecting the public's right to know. Nor was it enough to ask the classifier to offer a reason for classification. When such a system was finally introduced under the Clinton presidency, all the classifier had to do was cite a relevant generic category of classifiable information, a mindless task that was soon turned into a drop-down menu on computers across the government.[65]

The obvious solution would have been to create a meaningful counterweight to the incentives to classify. As Truman was rolling out his order, there had been proposals for just such a system. A small group of journalists, including one of the future advocates for the Freedom of Information Act, argued that the problem was not with the act of classification per se. It was with the inadequate safeguards to prevent abuse and error. Their idea, pushed also by Senator William Benton and the ACLU, was to appoint a civilian to the National Security Council who could act as a "people's advocate" or an "anti-censor." If such an individual, aided by a sufficiently large staff, could hear appeals and complaints, if they could conduct spot audits and punish instances of overclassification, then it might go a long way to keeping the classification system in check. The Defense Department and the Justice Department were apparently happy to create such an office, but State was opposed: it didn't want to cede agency autonomy to a central committee. The proposal went nowhere, replaced instead by an interdepartmental committee that would "advise" agencies on how to implement classification. It had no police power. Press Secretary Short told journalists not to worry, that they could bring complaints to him, and he would advocate for greater transparency. But such informal pressure was no match for the engines of classification.[66]

Put yourself in the position of the government employee, trying to decide what stamp to put on a document at the end of a tiring day in the office. The entire logic of the national-security state is built on risk aversion, on a desire to protect against horrific, worst-case events, however unlikely. Who would want to be responsible for disclosing information that might create such a risk? The pressure is all on the side of classifying, even when the executive order explicitly instructs you to err in the direction of underclassification when in doubt, as was the case during the Carter, Clinton, and Obama presidencies. (In between them, the Reagan and Bush executive orders quite conspicuously removed this instruction—Reagan in fact urged overclassification when in doubt—one sign of the way that classification rules slide around at the whim of the administration in power.)[67] Even assuming good faith on behalf of classifiers, the system is geared to produce overclassification.

And there are other reasons to classify documents, too. The cynical might classify a document to prevent scrutiny, or embarrassment, or scandal. You aren't supposed to classify for such reasons, but it is an obvious temptation. In 1947 the draft classification orders killed by Finney's scoop had explicitly allowed for keeping embarrassing information secret; in 1951 Truman had to reprimand the Office of Price Stabilization when it proposed suppressing information that "might prove embarrassing." No one said the quiet part out loud after that, but the line between "harmful to national security" and "embarrassing to this administration or agency" is blurry—particularly in an era of ideological warfare, when one could say, in all earnestness, that revealing American hypocrisy or racism or incompetence was no way to win hearts and minds in the global struggle with Communist propaganda. "It quickly becomes apparent to any person who has considerable experience with classified material," reflected Erwin Griswold, some years after he had served as Richard Nixon's solicitor general, that "the principal concern of the classifiers is not with national security, but rather with governmental embarrassment of one sort or another."[68]

Overclassification also feeds on itself, incentivizing yet more overclassification. In a federal bureaucracy swimming in classified information, the best way to make your information stand out is to label it highly classified. Since the 1950s, superiors trying to quickly sift through mountains of paper have relied on classification stamps to sort the good stuff from the dreck. To unilaterally disarm in such an environment, to send unclassified memos up the chain, is to risk being ignored. Today, when classified and unclassified emails are sent on separate systems, it is to risk your message being lost amid endless notifications about parking-lot closings and lunchtime events.[69]

For all these reasons, it soon became apparent that absurd items were being classified. A congressman inquired about the plush furnishings inside military transport planes—the photos were stamped as secret, as was his letter of request. The United States Information Agency classified the name of a propaganda movie it had made, apparently because it was an embarrassing flop. The Department of Labor was classifying the amount of peanut butter the armed services were buying so that no one could use it to deduce the size of the armed forces, even though that figure was being published monthly by the Defense Department. If such material was being classified, so too were matters of clear public interest: the names of people traveling on Defense Department junkets, air force accident reports, information on imports arriving at ports on the Great Lakes (though not the ports of the East or West Coast).[70]

Regardless, the courts have been highly deferential to the act of classification. They have preferred not to adjudicate whether the executive branch classified information correctly, for to question whether information really needed to be kept secret would have involved a court in political questions beyond its ken. "It would be intolerable," proclaimed the Supreme Court, "that courts, without the relevant information, should review and perhaps nullify actions of the Executive taken on information properly held secret." In such ways, secrecy produced its own legitimacy.[71]

In the interwar years, the sprawl of the Espionage Act had been limited by the ambiguity of the mental-intent requirements and uncertainty about the scope of "information relating to national defense." In the *Gorin* and *Heine* decisions, the courts had relied on narrow(ish) definitions of these two concepts to uphold the constitutionality of the Espionage Act. But in the early Cold War, Truman expanded the sorts of information that were covered, and Congress lowered the intent requirements. The existence of the classification order then made it easier to meet those intent requirements; if something had been stamped as secret, both prosecutors and judges began saying, that proved that there was reason to believe its disclosure would harm the United States.[72]

After 1951, the Espionage Act had more power than ever before.

The new laws and the new classification scheme helped usher in a profound new era of secrecy. Government agencies now operated in a "general climate of secrecy," observed one journalist in 1957, where it was assumed that "if an item wasn't marked secret, there must have been a mistake." By the mid-1950s, one survey found federal agencies had created some thirty categories of "non-security" information they were trying to hold close "for official distribution" or "official use only." In the mid-1950s, the Commerce and Defense Departments briefly tried to limit the release of even unclassified information that might be of "possible use" to hostile nations. Like an inkblot, the secrecy stamps bled out, covering ever-greater parts of the government.[73]

The new culture of secrecy was not merely broad. It had depths, too, sunken parts of the state far removed from public oversight. Code breaking had proved its worth many times over during World War II, but efforts to put it on a more permanent footing afterward kept running aground on the old interservice rivalries. After years of ineffective bureaucratic experimentation, Harry Truman issued a top-secret order in his last days in office that created a new centralized organization: the National Security Agency (NSA). By 1960, it had a workforce of twelve thousand, aided by a further sixty thousand cryptologists in various other agencies who were operating a global network of intercept positions. At the center of the web, the NSA was classifying so much paper that it was forced to experiment with wholesale pulping efforts and then build a massive, as well as massively faulty, incinerator on its vast complex in Fort Meade, Maryland. Its capacities to monitor communications would remain highly secret for years. NSA, ran an inside joke, stood for No Such Agency.[74]

And then there was the CIA. The United States had been a relative laggard in forming a centralized intelligence agency—it wasn't the kind of thing that it was easy for a liberal democracy to admit it wanted. In the interwar period the US had made do by patching together an intelligence program from competing bureaucracies: military and naval intelligence gathered intel; State did some lackluster analysis; the marines took care of counterinsurgency in the colonies; the FBI handled counterintelligence and built a little fiefdom in Latin America called the Special Intelligence Service. But such a jerry-rigged system couldn't survive the geopolitical pressures of World War II, and in 1941 FDR established a new office, the Coordinator of Information, which soon evolved into the Office of Strategic Services (OSS).

During the war the OSS had been controversial. "In a global and totalitarian war," its millionaire chief, William "Wild Bill" Donovan, had declared, "intelligence must be global and totalitarian." The OSS soon earned a reputation for risk taking, its ambitions frequently outrunning its competence. (In a famed intelligence operation that it was running in Istanbul, nearly one in eight informants was a Nazi double agent.) When Truman received a report on its scattershot record, he quickly abolished the OSS.[75]

Yet the desire for political intelligence remained. Three months later, Truman established an informal Central Intelligence Group, which was intended at first to operate as something like an internal news desk, producing a centralized flow of information in the White House. In 1947 an obscure section of the National Security Act renamed the group the Central Intelligence Agency and gave it the broadest mandate possible: to "perform such other functions and duties related to intelligence activities as the National Security Council may from time to time direct." Another clause charged the CIA with "protecting intelligence sources and methods from unauthorized disclosure"—one more vote of no confidence in the Espionage Act's capacity to keep secrets, one more patch to the secrecy regime. In 1949, without any debate, Congress passed another law, the CIA Act, which freed the organization from revealing its budget, its practices, its administrative setup. "When you are in the spy business," declared one of the bill's advocates, "you can't go shouting about it from the house-tops."[76]

Intelligence is a difficult business, and it is easy to play Monday-morning quarterback. Even so, the CIA wasn't much of an intelligence agency. It struggled to establish sources in the Communist Bloc. In 1948 it had only thirty-eight analysts working on Eastern Europe—only nine of whom had spent any time there, and only twelve of whom spoke any Russian. In Seoul in 1952, not a single one of its two hundred officers spoke Korean. The CIA was surprised by the Berlin blockade and the first Soviet nuclear tests, guaranteed that the Chinese would not invade during the Korean war, and had no idea that the Hungarian uprising was about to break out (and then advised, once it did, that Khrushchev might fall within days). "At no time," concluded a secret CIA history of its operations in Hungary, "did we have anything that could or should have been mistaken for an intelligence operation."[77]

There was a simple explanation for the CIA's lackluster record. Its real passion was political warfare. In the late 1940s it began massive propaganda campaigns designed to roll back Communism, to rally hearts and minds to the free world. It dropped millions of leaflets behind the Iron Curtain, secretly funneled money into cultural organizations and anticommunist political parties, established radio stations to broadcast the good word of liberal capitalism. By then, it had begun covert operations, too, arming expatriates and parachuting them into Albania, Poland, Russia, Ukraine, North Korea, and Tibet in the hopes of triggering nationalist uprisings and civil war. They were suicide missions, "not only ineffective," in the words of an internal CIA history, but "probably morally reprehensible in the number of lives lost." What was discreetly known as the Office of Policy Coordination expanded its clandestine activities anyway. By

1952, the CIA was devoting 60 percent of its personnel and 74 percent of its budget to covert ops.[78]

The main arenas for action were Asia, Africa, Latin America, and the Middle East, where the superpowers struggled for influence and control over nations seeking to chart a path to independence. The CIA had succeeded in establishing client regimes in America's semicolonial periphery when it orchestrated coups in Iran (in 1953) and Guatemala (in 1954). In both cases, reformist governments had sought to establish national control over key industries long dominated by foreign powers. But when the Mossadegh government sought to nationalize Iran's oil, when the Arbenz government sought to buy back fallow land held by the United Fruit Company, these developments struck US officials as a dangerous show of independence and a possible flirtation with Communism. Eisenhower's CIA director, Allen Dulles, a corporate lawyer who had been an OSS operative during World War II—and a man who had had business ties to the United Fruit Company—approved plans for regime change.

In truth, both coups were haphazard, crude affairs that nearly fell apart multiple times. In Guatemala one CIA officer left plans in his hotel room, where they were discovered by the government. In Iran the CIA's preferred head of state, the shah, had been bullied into participating in the plot by his more assertive sister and got cold feet partway through the coup. He fled to Rome, where he awkwardly ran into a vacationing Dulles in the hotel lobby and had to be coaxed back to Tehran to take power.[79]

But unsettling a government wasn't rocket science. Bribe enough thugs to create chaos on the streets, blow some things up, broadcast to the public that an invasion may be coming, fly a few threatening planes overhead—it was relatively easy to panic the public and delegitimize the government, particularly in polities that were, like all polities, internally divided. Reestablishing a legitimate government would turn out to be another thing entirely. Guatemala descended into four decades of dictatorship and violence, in which two hundred thousand were murdered in brutal pogroms. In Iran the shah clung to power by relying on US-trained security forces—the notorious

SAVAK—to suppress dissent. It worked until the Iranian revolution of 1979. (The CIA, of course, was relying on SAVAK for intelligence and had not a clue that that revolution was coming.[80])

The details of these 1950s coups were technically secret. They were surrounded by a fog of plausible deniability. But through a network of friends in the media, the CIA was also leaking favorable stories about its work, building a legend as a geopolitical puppet master. "A helping hand in the rescue of one country such as Guatemala or Iran from Communism," concluded one fawning article in the *Saturday Evening Post*, "is worth the CIA's annual budget many times over." Over the coming years, believing its own propaganda about Iran and Guatemala—the latter's code name, tellingly, was PBSUCCESS—the CIA ramped up clandestine activities. Eisenhower ran 170 covert operations in his two terms in office; in only three years, Kennedy nearly matched him. When things went wrong in places such as the Congo, Indonesia, Laos, Syria, and Vietnam, those stories didn't make the papers. Only when things went really, spectacularly wrong in the Bay of Pigs were there second thoughts about what the CIA was actually up to.[81]

Other things, horror-show things, were kept quiet, too. In 1950 the CIA began psychological experiments. During the Korean war a number of US prisoners of war had "confessed" to conducting biological war, and several chose to remain in North Korea rather than being repatriated to the United States at war's end. Americans were convinced this was evidence of Communist "brain-washing," and the race was on to emulate it. In the privacy of the Panama Canal Zone and on a military base in Japan, the CIA began injecting suspected double agents with drugs and subjecting them to brutal interrogation. LSD was one of the "truth-serums" that were tested. Within a few years, a more ambitious program had evolved: MK-ULTRA. Hundreds of Americans were fed drugs, many of them without giving consent. One mental patient in Kentucky was dosed with LSD continuously for 174 days. At least two people died as a result; one of them was a civilian scientist attached to the program, Frank Olson, who was given LSD without his consent and later fell to his death from a hotel window. Like democracies, minds were proving much easier for the CIA to break than to rebuild. And it was all kept secret. "Precautions must be taken," said the CIA inspector general in 1957, "not only to protect operations from exposure to enemy forces but also to conceal these activities from the American public in general."[82]

As early as 1954, Senator Mike Mansfield began calling for more congressional oversight. "Secrecy now beclouds everything about the CIA," he complained, "its cost, its efficiency, its success, and its failures." But proposed bills went down to defeat. Congress didn't want to know what was being done in its name. Meanwhile, an Eisenhower-ordered review committee gave the CIA its blessing: "It is now clear that we are facing an implacable enemy whose avowed objective is world domination by whatever means and at whatever cost. There are no rules in such a game. Hitherto acceptable norms of human conduct do not apply."[83]

Yet for all the efforts to protect the nation's secrets, for all the anti-communist laws and policies, a feeling of security remained elusive. If anything, the more secretive the government was, the more paranoid the nation's politics became.

The career of Joe McCarthy was the clearest example of the feedback loops that the second spy scare created. McCarthy, for whom we now name the period, was actually late to the politics of anticommunism. He was a symptom, not a cause. His breakthrough speech in Wheeling, West Virginia, wasn't given until February 1950—years after Nixon and Hoover and McCarran had first sounded the alarm about red spies. The speech itself was a retread of familiar themes, largely plagiarized from Richard Nixon and the conservative press. What made McCarthy distinctive was simply the shamelessness with which he would claim to have secret documents in his possession that proved Communist infiltration—in Wheeling there were 205 names on the sheet of paper he angrily waved; the next day there were 57; two weeks later there were 81.[84]

For four years, McCarthy would fling accusations at an ever-shifting lineup of government agencies, seeing hints of subversion and cover-up everywhere he looked. The existence of Truman's loyalty program, intended to inoculate his government from charges of subversion, had actually added fuel to the conspiracist fires by creating obscure new bureaucracies conducting classified investigations. It came to an end only when McCarthy took on the army, an institution whose patriotic bona fides were hard to challenge. Not long after, the conspiracist fever mutated yet again, giving birth to the John Birch Society, whose founders believed that Dwight Eisenhower and the Dulles brothers were secret Soviet agents.[85]

There has long been a conspiratorial strain in American politics. Throughout the nineteenth century there were repeated anxieties that the world was being run by a secret cabal of Freemasons, or Catholics, or Jewish bankers. But the postwar years ushered in a new epoch. As the government constituted itself as a sort of secret society—with its rituals of classification and loyalty, with its elaborate hierarchies of insiders and outsiders—it was the US government that became the prime object of conspiracy theorizing.

For the rest of the century, the most widespread conspiracy theories would focus on sites of actual government secrecy. The Moon landing was a hoax, John F. Kennedy's assassination an inside job. Area 51, the secret air base at which the CIA test-flew spy planes, actually housed UFOs and aliens. Over time, as new secrets came to light, they would be incorporated into ever-more-elaborate patterns. Rumors of the CIA's psychological experiments proved particularly potent; every conspiracy theory could be improved with an allegation of mind control. And the sheer insanity of some of the secret state's plots and programs, themselves stranger than fiction, gave even outlandish folk theories a patina of plausibility. Like primitive life at the bottom of ocean trenches, nourished by the subterranean power leaking through cracks in the Earth's crust, conspiracy theories feasted on their glimpses of America's secret state and grew baroque and strange in the dark.[86]

There was no psychological comfort for those in the highest branches of the security state, either. Frank Wisner was the freewheeling architect of the CIA's political warfare in the 1940s. With frenzied confidence, he managed a global propaganda program that he called the "mighty Wurlitzer," dreamed of placing toilet paper emblazoned with the face of the Hungarian dictator in the bathroom of trains running into Budapest, and parachuted hundreds of Albanian nationalists to their deaths in an infiltration project he called Operation Fiend. Fiend was a disaster because it had a leak. James Jesus Angleton, one of the CIA's most influential figures, a man who ran its first operations in Italy and then headed counterintelligence, was sharing Fiend's details with his equally urbane equivalent in British intelligence: Kim Philby, the Soviet double agent, who shared the landing schedule with the Albanian government.[87]

No mind is built to handle the guilt and pressure of such work. By the mid-1950s, both Wisner and Angleton were cracking under the strain. The chain-smoking Angleton's eccentricities became ever more pronounced—cloistered in his office, tending to his rare orchids, he saw double agents everywhere. His paranoia derailed the careers of dozens of employees without cause and gummed up the works of US intelligence. Meanwhile, Wisner's manic energy curdled. He started experiencing erratic mood swings, which he thought were the product of Soviet mind control. He suspected that former associates working for the nation's newspapers were Soviet agents and spent frantic hours on the phone trying to convince them to delete minor details from their stories. In 1958, spiraling, he was finally convinced to enter a mental hospital, where he was treated, in the custom of the time, with electroshock therapy. It didn't help. Wisner died by suicide in 1965.[88]

The fall of James Forrestal was even more precipitous. Forrestal had been one of the most ebullient advocates of US supremacy after the war. "As long as we can outproduce the world, can control the sea and can strike inland with the atomic bomb," he confessed to his diary in 1947, "we can assume certain risks otherwise unacceptable." He was an early champion of an expansive vision of America's national security, and he was a key architect of Cold War policy. It had been Forrestal who had come up with an important scheme to funnel Marshall Plan money via back channels to the CIA in order to give it a slush fund for political warfare, and Forrestal who, as navy secretary, had won the turf wars created by the unification of America's armed services under a new Department of Defense. A workaholic, a master bureaucratic politician, he was rewarded with the title of America's first defense secretary. It was a poisoned chalice. When guiding the creation of the Defense Department, Forrestal had fought hard to preserve the relative autonomy of the services. Now he found himself unable to corral them.[89]

In his many bureaucratic battles he had made many enemies who sniped at him in the press, who criticized his politics, who sought his replacement. In 1948 Forrestal made a fatal error—he met with Truman's opponent in the election, Thomas Dewey, in the apparent hopes of maintaining his perch regardless of who won the White House. In early 1949 Truman forced him out.

Forrestal's marriage had long been unhappy, and the strain of managing America's fractious defense policy had worn him to a nub. Suffering from insomnia, he had become indecisive and erratic, developing the disconcerting tic of repeatedly dipping his fingers into his drink and slowly tracing his lips. Losing his job was the final straw. Not long after, a friend found him at home with the blinds drawn, whispering about a Communist-Zionist conspiracy running through the White House that had James Forrestal in its crosshairs. An air force plane was chartered to fly him to Florida for R&R, but even while walking on the beach he was convinced that the umbrella stands were wiretapped, that the Kremlin had him marked for assassination, that a Communist invasion of the US was imminent, if not already under way. He was transferred to the Bethesda Naval Hospital, where he continued to imagine he was being spied upon. One night, he was copying a poem by Sophocles by hand and stopped midway through the word *nightingale.* "Nightingale" had been the code name of a secret CIA program that he had approved back when he was on the National Security Council. It had sent Ukrainian

refugees, including many ex-Nazis who had participated in the Ho-
locaust, behind the Iron Curtain to foment civil war. Forrestal tied
one end of his dressing-gown sash to the radiator, the other to his
neck, and threw himself out of the window.[90]

The secretive national-security state that Forrestal had helped to
build lived on. So did the vast defense economy that he had helped
to create and the fractious rivalries between the armed services that
he had struggled to control. Out of those conflicts would emerge
the first major test of the Espionage Act's newly burnished power to
control leaked secrets during the Cold War.

Chapter 7

MISSILE GAPS

During a 1957 television address from the White House, Dwight Eisenhower inspects the nose cone of a missile recently returned from space. During his presidency, a secretive military-industrial complex would grow up around new military technologies like the missile. (Library of Congress, photograph by Warren K. Leffler)

J ust after Thanksgiving, 1956, Colonel John C. Nickerson sent a document containing classified information about ballistic missile development to a small network of politicians, journalists, and industrialists. It didn't seem a particularly risky act. A little aggressive perhaps, chafing at the limits of propriety, but also a part of Nickerson's job, which was to lobby on behalf of the army ballistic missile program. And his missiles were newly endangered because the defense secretary had recently decided to support a rival missile program being run by the air force. Nickerson had sent out his anonymous document in one last effort to protest the decision and preserve his funding.

It took only a few weeks to trace the source. It had been pretty obvious that the document had come from someone in the army missile program based at the Redstone Arsenal in Huntsville, Alabama. And the typewriter used to prepare it was distinctive, which led directly to a machine used by Nickerson's secretary. On the morning of January 2, Nickerson was interviewed by an inspector general. Nickerson bluffed his way through the interrogation and then rushed home to try to burn the papers tying him to the document before the military police arrived. He wasn't fast enough. MPs found some classified papers in his desk drawer and some unsecured papers in his briefcase.[1]

What came next was a surprise. Nickerson was not only charged with fifteen violations of security regulations and with making false statements to the inspector general; he was also charged with violating the Espionage Act. "How could that possibly be true?" he asked. The 1917 law had never been used in such a case. It wasn't even on Nickerson's radar.[2]

Nickerson was a graduate of West Point, a decorated artillery officer in World War II, a patriot. At only forty-one, he was a full colonel and a rising star of the rockets branch. Now, for the apparently innocuous act of sharing classified information with journalists and politicians—the sort of thing that went on *all the time* in 1950s Washington—he faced forty-six years in jail. "I can't believe," he said, "all this is happening to a man whose only crime is loving the army too much."[3]

Nickerson's case has been almost entirely forgotten. He is never mentioned in the same breath as famous leakers prosecuted under the Espionage Act: Daniel Ellsberg, Chelsea Manning, Edward Snowden. In fact, most people think that Daniel Ellsberg was the first leaker so charged. But fourteen years before Ellsberg's case came Nickerson's, which established the template for the modern leak prosecution and revealed many of its ongoing pathologies.[4]

Nickerson's trial for leaking also revealed a great deal about the role of secrecy in the military-industrial complex as it emerged in the 1950s. For Nickerson's missile program was at the center of the controversial politics of weapons development in the Eisenhower years. Missile development was seen as the key to competition with the Soviets, not only in the Strangelovian quest for nuclear supremacy but also in the race to the stars. "There are occasions," observed one journalist in 1957, "when in a single human drama all the conflicts of an era are concentrated. The Nickerson trial seems likely to be one of those."[5]

The Truman administration had projected a $13 billion defense budget for 1951. Thanks to the Korean war, it ended up spending $58 billion that year and $70 billion the next. This was the dawn of a vast, permanent defense economy, for even when adjusted for inflation, military spending would never return to pre-Korea levels: the average post-Korea defense budget was two-and-a-half times the size of the average budget of the late 1940s.[6] Government contracts sustained massive industries; research grants subsidized astonishing new technologies. The open spigot didn't just reshape America's economy, its military, and its diplomacy. It also reorganized the very geography of the nation itself, as money flowed away from the old industrial core of the Midwest and into booming states of the South and West. The land was cheaper there, the unions weaker, the weather better suited to things like flight testing.

This was a political economy with the emphasis on *political*. There was no better form of constituent service than the provision of steady jobs and federal investment. Cozy relations soon developed between military contractors and Cold War congressmen. Mendel Rivers brought to his district in South Carolina an air force base, a navy base, a missile center, and a naval hospital. By the end of his quarter century in the House, much of it as chair of the Armed Services Committee, the federal payroll in the district ran to three billion dollars per annum. "Rivers Delivers" was his perennial, and perennially successful, campaign slogan. Henry "Scoop" Jackson likewise brought so many aviation contracts to Washington state that he became known as the "Senator for Boeing." Out of such politics emerged a new gun belt of local economies growing fat on defense dollars.[7]

Huntsville was one of them. A faded cotton town, losing population as its mills closed in the Depression and the descendants of its enslaved laborers migrated north, it was a beneficiary of federal largesse three times over. Thanks to the New Deal, it fell within the power range of the Tennessee Valley Authority. That made it a feasible site for an ordnance and chemical plant during World War II. And because no one wanted to buy those plants when they were shuttered after the war, they were still available when the army went looking for a home for its rocket-development program.

When that program moved to Huntsville in 1950, it brought with it 120 German rocket experts. These were men who had worked on the ur-missile of the missile age, Hitler's V-2, which had been developed in a secretive underground factory built by their own enslaved laborers. After the war, a secret US government project had hoovered them up, seeking to annex Nazi knowledge to the American Century. They were brought first to Fort Bliss on short-term contracts, then carefully shepherded through denazification and immigration bureaucracies to become permanent US citizens at the heart of the Cold War economy. When they arrived in Huntsville, the town had only 16,500 residents. On the backs of their work at

Redstone Arsenal, Huntsville would take off, growing by 850 percent over the next two decades.[8]

In early 1956, John Nickerson added to the population boom
when he transferred from a Pentagon job to help run the new Army
Ballistic Missile Agency at Redstone.[9] By then, the army had come
to see the development of new missiles as something close to an ex-
istential issue. It desperately needed a new weapon to compete with
its greatest rival. That wasn't the Soviet Union. It was the air force.

In the late 1940s, in an effort to avoid paralyzing and wasteful rivalries, the armed services had been unified under a centralized Defense Department. But the unification had been only halfhearted,
and its main effect was to exacerbate tensions between the services,
now forced into competition at close quarters for the favor of a defense secretary who had enough power to incentivize lobbying but
not enough power to keep it in check.

By the Eisenhower years, the air force was clearly the favored
child. The army had expended its political capital in the early Cold
War fruitlessly lobbying for universal military service. The air force
had established a monopoly on the atomic bomb, the weapon of the
future. After Korea, when the budget-conscious Eisenhower sought
to bring some fiscal discipline to the Pentagon without weakening
America's geopolitical position, he did so by going all in on the air
force and its nuclear arsenal. Massive retaliation was the keystone
of his so-called New Look. The threat of apocalyptic nuclear war
would keep the Soviets at bay; during Ike's two terms in office, the
nuclear stockpile increased from one thousand warheads to eighteen
thousand. And nukes promised security on the relative cheap. Given
such awesome force, it was simply wasteful to maintain a large army,
for land wars between superpowers seemed a thing of the past. (The
tricksy conflicts of the decolonizing world were another matter, but
such brushfire wars, it was assumed, could be handled discreetly by
the CIA, whose budget was a black box.) In 1954 three-quarters of
the budget cuts Eisenhower imposed on the defense sector were ab-
sorbed by the army.[10]

Missiles seemed to offer a way back into the game. The United States had flirted with long-range missile development since World War II. Some 114 different projects had been started, but the vast majority of them had been abandoned. As late as 1949, Vannevar Bush, dean of US military research and development (R&D), dismissed long-range guided missiles as a fantasy. At that point, the air force, with the smug complacency of dominant companies in every industry, was spending $3 billion on airplane development and only $39 million on missiles. When the air force did begin focusing on missile development, in the mid-1950s, it was at first focused on super-long-range missiles, what are now known as intercontinental ballistic missiles (ICBMs).[11]

Nickerson and his Army Ballistic Missile Agency, by contrast, were focused on intermediate-range ballistic missiles (IRBMs). If they could develop such a weapon before the air force developed its ICBM, they could stake a claim to also control the deployment of the missiles. Unifying discrete branches of the armed services had required dividing the labor over particular military technologies to avoid wasteful duplication. It had been a difficult process of bureaucratic negotiation, but it had been done: the army, for instance, was barred from having any planes with wing loads of more than five thousand pounds, which meant that it relied on the air force for air support and transport.[12]

The development of a new technology like the IRBM would disrupt the old status quo, forcing a new clarification of the division of labor. What sort of weapon was a missile? The air force said it was like a pilotless plane and should belong under air force control. The army responded that it was really just a long-range piece of artillery, and thus fell within its jurisdiction. Whoever built it first would strengthen the claim for definition and control. Army strategists began imagining science-fictional battlefields in which they would hurl tactical atomic weapons across the horizon. The best way to reduce casualties in any future war, Nickerson explained, was to "destroy enemy forces with atomic ballistic missiles at long ranges before these enemy forces can close with our own troops."[13]

The army also saw another potential benefit to innovating in the missile field. The German scientists at Redstone had long dreamed of spaceflight. The rockets they were making were getting agonizingly close. Give us $100,000 more, pleaded Wernher von Braun, their intellectual leader, and we will put a satellite into orbit before any rival nation. "It would be a blow to U.S. prestige," he said in 1954, "if we did not do it first."[14]

Yet in the summer of 1955, the US government authorized a rival satellite program being developed by a scientific research bureau attached to the navy, even though it was relatively far behind the Redstone group. Technical considerations seem to have been outweighed by optics. It would look a lot better if the first American satellite went into space on a scientific rocket rather than a missile made by ex-Nazis.[15]

The army's IRBM program thus provided a way to keep one foot in the door of the space race while also waging competition with the air force for control of missiles. In 1955 the Defense Department decided to develop an IRBM as soon as possible, fearing that the United States was falling behind the Soviets and that the wait for the ICBM would be too long. In November it instructed both the army and the air force to begin working on IRBMs with a range of 1,500 miles. The army's missile was soon known as the Jupiter. Weapons being the deities of the age, the air force called its missile the Thor.[16]

What followed was a year of frenetic competition between the rival services. There are many ways that setting up a competition can be a spur to technological development. But none of them were at play in the Thor-Jupiter controversy. Competition in a market can force rivals to keep costs down, but this was not a factor here, where the incentives were to spend government money quickly. In fact, the air force spent extravagantly, sinking money into production facilities even before it had a workable concept, on the hopes that sunk capital would make it harder to later cut off funding. And although controlled competition can be a way to produce an optimal technical product, this requires centralized oversight, disciplined experimentation, and the sharing of information—not the secretive, suspicious competition of the rival rocket groups.[17]

So the main result of this year of chaotic competition was an intensification of lobbying and a deeper politicization of weapons development. Both the army and the air force were incentivized to leak information to politicians and the press, to wage a propaganda war to win the contract for their program. This was Nickerson's role. He was, as he put it, "one of a new breed of missilemen-politicians, engaged in a lone-wolf operation to sell new weapons projects to the government."[18]

Nickerson threw himself into the work. According to one of his oldest friends, he was a man without hobbies and had only two interests: his family and the army. After World War II, understanding the high-tech future of warfare, he had sought out a position as a liaison officer to the Jet Propulsion Lab at Cal Tech. While posted to the university, he took an aeronautics degree on his own dime to better understand the new weapons being developed. When he moved to the Pentagon, and then to Huntsville, he brought with him an unusual combination of technical, bureaucratic, and combat expertise.[19]

During the war, his colleagues remembered, Nickerson had been a "most aggressive" commander, keen to take the battle to the enemy. He brought the same drive to his lobbying for the missile program. Nickerson "was a man of great energy, almost indefatigable in energy with a singleness of purpose," recalled his friend. "Once he takes an objective he goes straight forward and he is not too much concerned with outside things. He gets the major objective and he goes for it as hard as he can." In 1956 and 1957 he worked himself to the bone, constantly on the phone with potential allies in the defense industry, schmoozing with local politicians at every opportunity, briefing officials at the Pentagon, spending so many weekends on the road to build his network that he was a noticeable absence at parties in the small and close-knit community in Huntsville. He was a natural "free wheeler and operator," and he loved being known as the "Secretary of State" of the missile team, as its "vice-president . . . in

Colonel John C. Nickerson
Jr. (University of Alabama–
Huntsville Archives and Special Collections, photograph
by US Army)

charge of corporate sales," as the man who could "grease the skids" of defense contracting.[20]

Yet however hard he worked, it didn't seem to be enough. For the clash between the army and the air force was more than a competition between two different types of missiles or even two branches of the armed forces. It was also a competition between two different political economies of weapons development. Nickerson and the Redstone Arsenal were still developing weapons in the traditional fashion. They were doing much of the design work in house, contracting with outside firms only for particular parts, which they then assembled and tested themselves. The air force, by contrast, had pioneered a new system built around outsourcing not just for particular components but for entire products. Air force missile programs were being worked on by seventeen contractors and some two hundred subcontractors, including some of the biggest companies in the nation. This gave them a powerful lobby; seven of the top ten defense contractors in the nation were aviation companies. The army's missile program, on the other hand, had just the one major contractor

in its stable: Chrysler, which was hardly dependent on defense contracts in the same fashion as the aviation companies. Nickerson was
the army's only champion.[21]

The missile team at Huntsville, having worked together since the
Nazi years, was pulling ahead of its less experienced rivals in the air
force. In September 1956 it launched an experimental Jupiter missile that went three thousand miles, more than double the required
range for the IRBM. (It might have gone farther too; the army had
made sure to weight its nose with sandbags so that von Braun wasn't
tempted to "accidentally" launch a satellite during testing.)[22]

It was a propaganda coup, the sort of thing the air force would
have broadcast to the world. But the army classified it. The team at
Huntsville grew increasingly agitated. They were coming to realize
that missile contracting was not a meritocracy. For every dollar that
the air force received for a contract, von Braun complained, it put
half into public relations. Air force contractors were running lavish
ads in the papers, many of them containing information that the
army would have declared classified in the interests of national security. "To the average citizen and to the average congressman on the
Hill," grumbled Nickerson, "it looked like the Air Force was doing
it all, where it was damn near true it was the other way round."[23] He
worked his network harder than ever, trying to convince anyone who
would listen that the army missile was the only way to go.

After a year of vicious lobbying, of endless rumor and speculation,
Defense Secretary Charlie Wilson finally inched toward a decision.
Eisenhower himself had weighed in on the controversy, accusing
the army of mission creep. So in November 1956, Wilson issued a
memo clarifying that the air force would have control over IRBMs.
(In effect, they were planes, not artillery.) The army would retain
control over missiles with a range of up to two hundred miles. Both
rocket-development projects continued for now, but the writing was
on the wall for the Jupiter team at Redstone. It was only a matter of
time before the rocket scientists were denied army funds—why pay
for a weapon for the envied air force?—or cannibalized by job offers from the private sector. Local businessmen in Huntsville began

rethinking their plans for expansion. The economic future of the town was in doubt.[24]

Nickerson wasn't going down without a fight. He knew that in 1949 a similar Defense Department ruling on an aircraft-carrier contract had been reversed when the navy had circulated an anonymous document to protest the decision. When Wilson's decision was handed down, Nickerson began preparing a similar document. He called it "Considerations on the Wilson Memorandum."[25]

"Considerations" leveled a barrage of charges. Citing the successful September test of the Jupiter, it argued that the army team was well ahead of the air force team, which had not yet begun testing. The claim turned out to be more correct than Nickerson could have known. Thor's early tests, which took place at the start of 1957, were disasters. The first flew six inches before exploding, the second lasted twenty seconds, and the third caught fire six minutes before launch.[26]

Given the obvious superiority of Jupiter, Nickerson suggested, one had to look elsewhere to explain Wilson's decision. To politics, for instance, where Nickerson spied an ongoing air force conspiracy against the army. Or to corporate corruption. One component in the Thor missile, Nickerson explained, was designed by AC Spark Plug, a subsidiary of General Motors, Charlie Wilson's old firm. Another was designed by Bell Systems, one of whose senior executives, Donald Quarles, was now serving as air force secretary and had written memos favoring Thor. Aviation companies such as Douglas Aircraft wanted to get government units like Redstone out of the field of missile development entirely so that it would remain the preserve of private contractors like them. Moreover, Nickerson added in a McCarthyite flourish, wouldn't it be safer to spread military development contracts around the United States, especially to inland sites like Huntsville, rather than have them clustered in coastal areas like southern California that were susceptible to enemy spies and saboteurs?[27]

In its twelve pages, "Considerations" hadn't disclosed all that much classified information. The most significant secret in the document was the fact that the September test had gone so well, but although this had never been officially confirmed, *Life* magazine had run a story to that effect earlier that month. "Considerations" also included some future dates for testing. And to support his claims, Nickerson had gotten copies of some of the internal memoranda from a friend in the Pentagon that outlined how Wilson had come to his decision. Nickerson had his secretary combine "Considerations" and the copies of the memos, and then, without stamping any of them as classified, he had the printing center at Huntsville run off three dozen copies in the first weeks of December.[28]

Nickerson's plan was to distribute them to people who could use the information to pressure Wilson to change his mind and award the IRBM contract to the Jupiter team. His boss, John Medaris, was in damage control in the wake of the memorandum, telling everyone at Huntsville that they should not protest the decision but keep on producing the best missile possible in the hopes that the air force would agree to purchase it. Nickerson dismissed that as a pose for public consumption. He and Medaris had come to a tacit understanding about how to handle the "ticklish political problem" of lobbying. Nickerson would take care of that on his own initiative so that Medaris would be insulated from any blowback and could maintain plausible deniability. "It was my job," Nickerson explained, "to short-cut channels to help change the [Defense] Secretary's mind."[29]

Most of what he did next was standard operating procedure. He met with Alabama's congressional delegates and gave them copies of "Considerations." No legal problems here because congressional representatives had the right to see classified documents. No political problems, either, for the representatives were eager to bring contracts to Alabama and keen to help. Nickerson then sent two copies of his documents to defense industry lobbyists at RCA and Reynolds Metals, contractors working with the army that might help push back against the powerful air force lobby. There was some legal jeopardy in doing so: although these men had security clearances, they had no "need to know" what was included in Nickerson's memorandum. But they knew how the game was played, so there was no real risk of political repercussions. Had Nickerson left it at that, it would have been a garden-variety case of lobbying, and no one would ever have thought twice about it.[30]

But Nickerson was fired up, and keen to push the envelope. Over the years, his personnel evaluations in the army had repeatedly noted he had a tendency to "impulsiveness and intuitive action"—he was so sure of himself, so convinced of the righteousness of his cause, that he could easily take things too far. "I am the kind of a guy," he later admitted, "that takes a direct approach." "This time," he confessed, "I cut too short."[31]

His first mistake was encouraging a member of his team to reach out to Drew Pearson, one of the leading muckraking journalists of Cold War Washington. Exactly what Nickerson intended to tell Pearson was never entirely clear. Nickerson claimed he wanted to give Pearson an off-the-record briefing of unclassified material, to try to get a story in the press that would raise questions about the missile decision. His employee, who had traveled to DC to share copies of "Considerations" with contacts on the Hill, thought he had been given instructions to send Pearson a copy of the memorandum. Either way, the confusion was a product of the slapdash, wink-wink nature of Nickerson's lobbying enterprise. He later took full blame for the fact that a copy of the memo ended up in Pearson's mailbox.[32]

Pearson was a man with vast files of rumor and gossip, and a widely read column—"Washington Merry-Go-Round"—that traded in inside scoops. "Considerations" was catnip, but although Pearson was thrilled to publish corruption allegations, he was concerned that the document also revealed classified test results and future test dates. Pearson, like many other Cold War journalists, had continued to abide by an even more informal version of the voluntary censorship code that had been in place during World War II, taking leaked documents to officials to see if they could be published without harming national security. So he took his copy of "Considerations" to the air force press-relations chief to seek guidance about which bits of the report he could use and which he should suppress. The press secretary seized the entire report and sent it up the chain, where it was stamped "Secret." An investigation into the leak was opened.[33]

The investigators soon discovered a second leak to the press. Nickerson had sent a copy of "Considerations" to the editor of *Missiles and Rockets*, the trade industry journal, in the hopes of getting a favorable story. This was an even bigger mistake because he had added three more documents containing technical information about Jupiter. Although almost all of the information in them was publicly available and none contained any revelations that would realistically help the Soviets, each was technically classified, so Nickerson put them in an envelope he marked "Secret." At *Missiles and Rockets* the editorial team, which lacked clearances, took one look at the "Secret" stamp and anxiously returned the items to the sender.[34]

That was enough to land Nickerson in hot water. The investigation triggered by Pearson's visit to the air force ended up producing eighteen charges against Nickerson. Fifteen of them were security violations. Nickerson had failed to classify "Considerations," had distributed it outside normal channels, and had been caught at home with classified documents. (This sounded ominous, but his home was on the Redstone base, and most of the documents were in his briefcase, from which he was separated on the morning of his arrest. "I want to avoid the impression," he said, "that my children were making paper-dolls out of secret documents.") He was also facing two charges of lying to the inspector general under oath, although the investigating officer thought those charges could be dismissed as a product of shock and confusion in the first flush of interrogation, as Nickerson had subsequently been a cooperative witness.[35]

That left the surprising charge of espionage. The investigating officer believed that this should also be dropped. This suggestion was overruled by the acting judge advocate general, who thought the investigator was perhaps overly swayed by the colloquial meaning of "espionage." In fact, he now clarified, the relevant clause (793) covered "knowingly delivering defense information with 'reason to believe' that it could be used to injure the U.S." The disagreement revealed ongoing confusion about the meaning of the intent requirements of the Espionage Act. Neither of the military lawyers seemed all that sure what the still-ambiguous clauses of the act meant; neither, in fact, even made it clear which subclause under Section 793 they believed that Nickerson had violated. But the charge stuck, to the shock and disappointment of Nickerson's defense counsel, who thought the unprecedented use of the law "patently absurd."[36]

To some extent, Nickerson was a victim of poor timing. Interservice rivalry had become a plague on the Eisenhower administration, with the endless leaks and rumors and accusations offering endless opportunities for the Democrats to score political points. The previous summer, Wilson had established a committee to explore the best ways to stanch the flow of leaks. Its final report, recommending more vigorous investigations and prosecutions of leakers, was handed down just three weeks before Nickerson started writing "Considerations." If Wilson wanted a test case, Nickerson had given him one on a platter.[37]

Nickerson had also accused Wilson, by name, of compromising national security in the interests of corporate profit. Nickerson's lawyers thought it pretty obvious what had happened: "It's the old tactic, familiar in military justice circles, of over-charging a defendant if the big boss is after him." Seeing clearly that they were in the midst of a deeply political case, they began writing to Congress to see if pressure could be brought to bear to drop the Espionage Act charges.[38]

John Sparkman, the Alabama senator who was close to Nickerson and had received a copy of "Considerations," was doing the same. "One of our greatest handicaps," he complained, "lies in the fact that the army feels it necessary to lean over backwards in order to convince the Defense Department of its good faith." In the endless wrestling match between the army and the Defense Department, Nickerson had gifted Secretary Wilson a new pressure point. The army would be forced to turn on one of their own.[39]

In late June, seventy-five journalists descended on Huntsville to cover what they expected to be a sensational court-martial. The company town had rallied behind their martyred champion. "It is kinda embarrassing," said Nickerson. "The merchants just don't want to take my money." He was being represented by high-powered lawyers: Ray Jenkins, who had been counsel for the Senate committee during the recently televised Army-McCarthy hearings, and Robert Bell, Senator Sparkman's former law partner. Journalists hoped they would see a knock-down, drag-out clash between the army and the Defense Department, learn about the future of warfare, and perhaps even receive the "first authoritative glimpse of the wonderland of space travel."[40]

There was little concern from the press about the unprecedented use of the Espionage Act or worry that it would interfere with the First Amendment. In some sense, this was surprising. Civil liberties were beginning to emerge from the deep freeze of the McCarthy era. The week before Nickerson's trial, on Monday, June 17, the Supreme Court had handed down four decisions that rolled back the excesses of the second red scare. One reversed a loyalty firing; two reversed the convictions of leftists who had refused to answer questions in front of anticommunist investigators and been convicted of contempt. And the fourth decision, perhaps the most important of them, overturned the Smith Act conviction of fourteen California Communists. It was a reversal of the court's anticommunist decisions of the early 1950s and the beginning of a long period in which speech rights would expand. Aghast at the court's liberal turn, right-wing critics dubbed it "Red Monday."[41]

Yet no one argued that Nickerson's speech rights had been violated. The obvious reason was that he was a military officer, and it had long been understood that speech rights had to be limited in the army. The Uniform Code of Military Justice prohibited all sorts of speech acts—dissent, political criticism, insubordination—that would raise First Amendment concerns if uttered by civilians. The courts had understandably upheld them on the grounds that military discipline ran on different principles than the liberal public sphere.

In the 1920s, for instance, Billy Mitchell had been found guilty of insubordinate and disrespectful speech when he had railed, prophetically, against the army's uninterest in developing airpower. His claims to be exercising his freedom of speech had been dismissed. Many were now comparing Nickerson to Mitchell; there was no reason to expect this modern-day martyr for military progress to fare any differently if he raised free-speech claims.[42]

Importantly for the history of the Espionage Act, the army was but an extreme example of a broader principle: government has much greater power to censor its employees than it does to censor civilians. At the time of Nickerson's trial, the presumption was that this power was close to absolute, that good governance required that the government, in its role as an employer, have the ability to police the sorts of speech in which its employees engaged. The reason that the state could ban employees from speaking out publicly on politics, that it could bar them from disclosing information they learned on their jobs, that it could even, during the heights of the second red scare, dismiss them for their political beliefs or associations was that the courts treated public employment as a privilege, not a right. As the granter of that privilege, the government could attach conditions to it. Oliver Wendell Holmes had expressed the principle most crisply in the 1890s when he ruled that a cop fired for violating rules against political activity had no right to appeal. "The petitioner may have a constitutional right to talk politics," Holmes explained, "but he has no constitutional right to be a policeman."[43]

It was only later, in the 1960s, that the courts realized that the public might also have an interest in receiving information from government employees. A 1968 Supreme Court decision began to recognize a First Amendment right of employees to speak out on matters of "public concern" and to balance the public's right to learn about government activity with their right to an effective and efficient government of well-regulated civil servants. That obviously opened up a whole tricky terrain of judicial discretion, and in 2006 a divided Supreme Court would tilt the balance strongly back toward the rights of the government to police its employees. But even in the relatively open window of the late twentieth century, there was no serious effort to argue that the employee's right to disclose classified information was a matter of "public concern" that should be protected by the First Amendment. And courts were highly dismissive of the few attempts that were made. By the time that courts were considering what sorts of practices constituted a "public concern," there was a well-settled assumption that the government had a right to enforce its classification system.[44]

Nickerson's case, coming just six years after the creation of the modern classification scheme, might have provided an opportunity to more seriously examine the presumption that national security and good governance prevented any disclosures of classified information. It would not have been necessary to question the right of the government to keep some secrets. To claim a First Amendment right to spill any and all classified information would be to make government secrecy an impossibility and to deny democratically elected governments any capacity to secure information should any one employee decide to leak it.

But the argument for a First Amendment interest in Nickerson's case could have been more modest. It would have been to question the presumption that the simple act of classification was sufficient to trump the public's right to know. It would have been to ask whether a single bureaucrat putting a stamp on a document was sufficient to establish that its secrecy was crucial to protecting the national security. It would have been to wonder whether the nation's security might sometimes be protected by public debate about, say, how its defense budget was being spent and whether it was being frittered away on corporate boondoggles.

Asking such questions would have required deciding whether the particular information at issue deserved to be classified in the first place. Army rocket scientists, for instance, testified at Nickerson's court-martial that 90 percent of the information that had been disclosed should not have been classified, that most of it would not have been classified by the air force, that even if the Soviets had read it, their reaction would have been "So what?"[45]

Beyond the questions of waste and corruption that Nickerson raised, there were other reasons to fear classification of such a vast section of the nation's economy. The defense industry was, of course, an industry, with a huge workforce toiling away on weapons of destruction. All the usual regulatory workplace problems arose there, too: labor disputes and discrimination and accidents. But the rise of secrecy gave the state a way to cover up such problems, as the famous *Reynolds* case had revealed just a few years before Nickerson's court-martial.

In 1948 a B-29 had crashed during a test flight in Georgia, killing nine of the crew, including three civilian defense contractors working on a secret missile-guidance system for the plane. Their widows sued the air force for damages, but the government refused to turn over the accident report because, it claimed, doing so would reveal military secrets. In 1953 the Supreme Court agreed with the government, inventing a new "State secrets privilege" that allowed the government to refuse to turn over evidence to a court if doing so would harm national security. The widows reached a settlement shortly thereafter, but a powerful precedent had been set.

At first, the government was cautious in its deployment of its new privilege, using it only five times in the next quarter century. But then it mushroomed: from 1977 to 2000, the state secrets privilege would be used sixty-two times. By 2000, ironically, the original B-29 accident report had been routinely declassified and posted online. One of the victim's daughters, who had been seven weeks old when she lost her father, found it. The report revealed no military secrets whatsoever. The secret missile-guidance system wasn't being tested on the day of the crash. It wasn't even on the plane. But neither was a heat shield, left off by simple sloppiness. Its absence had caused the accident. The state-secrets privilege was born of a desire to cover up old-fashioned negligence.[46]

Nickerson's case could have provided an opportunity to rethink the tendency to drape the defense sector in a veil of secrecy. For such an argument to have been politically effective, it would have required a more powerful champion than Nickerson. The jurisprudence of the time was stacked against him, as were the cultural presumptions about military discipline and respect for the chain of command.

A more likely advocate for the public's right to know would have been the press, always the Espionage Act's most effective nemesis. The press's interests in the case were straightforward. Nickerson had leaked to two journalists. In the culture of Cold War Washington, the press had come to rely on leaks and disclosures and background briefings. If leaks could be effectively plugged, the flow of information to the press would stop.

Yet the press did not rally to Nickerson's cause. It was distracted by a more direct threat to its liberties. The weekend before Nickerson's trial began, the Eisenhower-created Commission on Government Security released an eight-hundred-page report examining every aspect of the nation's security apparatus. Its security-minded members were dismayed to find classified information in "airplane journals, scientific periodicals and even the daily newspaper." The problem, they concluded, was that the laws against leaking punished only government employees. Yet "in many instances the chief culprits responsible" were "quite removed from government service." In many instances, in fact, they were journalists. Among its many recommendations for tightening security, the commission called for a new law against publishing classified information. It was yet another effort by security hawks to overcome the ambiguities of the Espionage Act by adding new, explicit provisions to ensure that the press would be covered. And yet again the press rallied to denounce the proposed bill as undemocratic, as a violation of the First Amendment.[47]

Given the press reaction, the bill was dead on arrival. But the controversy over the proposal drowned out the Nickerson trial. The week that Nickerson's trial began, Loyd Wright, the chair of the commission, gave an angry press conference denouncing press irresponsibility in publishing state secrets and named Pearson as a repeat offender. Pearson returned fire, citing as evidence of his responsibility his recent delivery of the Nickerson memo to the Defense Department. The exchange got alarmed front-page coverage in *Editor and Publisher*, the trade journal that served as a bellwether of the newspaper industry.

Apart from a three-sentence notice, buried on page 70, when Nicker-son's court-martial had been scheduled back in March, it was the only time that *Editor and Publisher* ever mentioned Nickerson's case.[48]

The events of late June 1957 revealed the uneasy truce that had been brokered between the secrecy regime and the First Amend-ment in the four decades since Woodrow Wilson had signed the Es-pionage Act into law. The Wright Commission's suggestion that the Espionage Act be extended to prosecute the press had become po-litically unthinkable. But Nickerson's prosecution for leaking raised few press concerns. The state's right to protect classified information by prosecuting leakers had come to seem legitimate. It was com-pletely compatible with the freedom of the newspaper industry, the most vociferous and powerful champion of the First Amendment.

As it turned out, the Nickerson trial was also an anticlimax. The day the trial began, Nickerson took a deal. He pleaded guilty to the fifteen security charges; in exchange, the Espionage Act and false-swearing charges were dropped. Why the government offered the deal, and why only at this late stage, is unclear. It seems most likely that the appetite for a big trial went away once it became ap-parent that Nickerson's lawyers were going to insist on putting Wil-son's defense policy on trial: they kept petitioning for the right to introduce classified information as evidence. A quieter settlement no doubt seemed a preferable exit from the whole embarrassing affair.[49]

Nickerson had wanted the deal from the start, offering it only two weeks after his arrest. He was "deeply hurt" by the charge of espio-nage, upset by the "disgrace" it brought on the army and his family. He wanted to distance himself from the odious associations of spy-ing and treason. His lawyers thought they had an "air-tight" defense against the Espionage Act charges but were happy to take the deal. It was what their client wanted, as well as the only sensible course of action, given the potentially severe penalties contained in the 1917 law. As a result, an early opportunity to make sense of what Section 793 meant in a leaking case slipped away.[50]

Over the next four days, as the gathered journalists made do with a shorter hearing to determine Nickerson's sentence, the Jupiter team did get a chance to complain about the air force and the Wilson memorandum. Some privately observed that the army was having its cake and eating it too—making a big show of frowning on Nickerson's leak while relishing the opportunity to air Nickerson's grievances out in front of the press. The air force grumbled that it was all a "propaganda stunt," one that it didn't "want to dignify with a reply."[51]

Nickerson had hoped he would get away with a slap on the wrist, something like a $500 fine, and then be back to selling missiles. But on the last day of the trial, General Medaris, his boss, threw him under the bus. Taking full advantage of the plausible deniability that their arrangement offered, Medaris testified that Nickerson had no "future potential value to the service." Medaris would not even be willing to work with his former "Secretary of State" again.[52]

Nickerson was suspended from rank for a year and fined $1,200. The fine was no problem: the same Huntsville elites who had paid for his fancy lawyers covered it. But for a man as wedded to his career as Nickerson, it was a deep blow to be told that he had "so destroyed confidence in your integrity and judgement as to render you unfit for many assignments." Nickerson was exiled to the mid-century army's version of Siberia: he was soon inspecting construction work in Panama. A few years later, he and his wife were killed in a car accident in New Mexico, not far from the site of the first atomic bomb explosion.[53]

Three months after the end of Nickerson's trial, the Soviets put the world's first satellite into orbit. Wilson's troubled time as defense secretary was coming to an end, and as luck would have it, the man who would soon replace him, Neil McElroy, was visiting Huntsville on the night that Sputnik first circled the Earth. Pressure was now on the United States to launch a satellite of its own. In the stunned silence at Huntsville as Sputnik tweeted its signal from the heavens, von Braun told McElroy that Redstone could have a satellite in space in sixty days.[54]

The first shot still belonged to the Navy's satellite program, whose time line for launch was accelerated. Amid much fanfare, a Vanguard missile was sent skyward on December 6. It flew about four feet, then crashed, a fiery anticlimax and a deep embarrassment. "Kaputnik," the press called it. Von Braun finally got his green light. On January 31, 1958, a Jupiter took America's first satellite into orbit. The good citizens of Huntsville rushed to the streets to celebrate. Remembering the Nickerson affair, they burned Charlie Wilson in effigy.[55]

Jupiter would leave a famous legacy in space. In 1960 von Braun and his team moved to the newly created National Aeronautics and Space Administration, where they built the rockets, based on the Jupiter, that took men to the moon. Before the arrival of the German missile scientists, Huntsville had been trying, a little desperately, to rebrand itself as "the watercress capital of America." Now it was "Rocket City, U.S.A." It would remain a booming hub of aerospace defense contracting. To arrive in the Huntsville airport today is to be greeted by the same advertisements for weapons systems— drones, helicopters, missiles—that also grace the Metro stop at the Pentagon.[56]

Less glory attached to the Jupiter as a weapon. Thor and Jupiter had both been designed as stopgaps, intended to buy some time before long-range ICBMs were operational. Given their limited range, they had to be based in Europe if they were to act as an anti-Soviet deterrent. Very few European nations were willing to accept them— apart from the dangers of making a country a target of any Soviet offensive, there were considerable political costs to letting the Americans park their nukes on your soil. So only seven squadrons were ever deployed: four Thor squadrons in the United Kingdom, two Jupiter squads in Turkey, and one in Italy. As anticipated, the development of ICBMs rendered them obsolete within a few years. For the rest of the century America's nuclear deterrence would rely on Polaris missiles housed in mobile submarines and Minutemen missiles hidden in the soil of nineteen US states. When Khrushchev

moved his own intermediate-range missiles into Cuba in the early
1960s, Kennedy quietly promised to retire the now pointless Jupiters
in order to defuse the ensuing Cuban Missile Crisis. Within five
years of Nickerson's court-martial, his missile had run its course and
been sent to the scrap heap.[57]

The most important consequence of the missile-development controversies of the 1950s lay in domestic politics. The embarrassment
of Sputnik led to a flurry of reform to ensure that the United States
would never fall behind the Soviets again. Money flowed into research and development; by 1960, three-quarters of national university research expenditures came from the federal government.
To avoid a repeat of the Thor-Jupiter controversy, another Defense
Reorganization Act was passed to give the defense secretary further
powers to minimize interservice rivalry. (The problems persisted,
leading to yet another Defense Reorganization Act in 1986.)[58]

To handle cutting-edge military development without the wasteful duplication that had plagued the development of missiles,
the highly secretive Advanced Research Projects Administration
(ARPA) was also established. Hidden from public oversight, its scientists had free range to explore ideas that seemed inspired by sci-fi
pulps: jet-packs, telekinesis, particle beams, an egg-shaped inter-
planetary spaceship the size of a twenty-story building and powered
by two hundred nuclear explosions. Much of the early work was
devoted to imagining defense systems to protect the United States
from Soviet missiles. Some of its projects were important boons to
research, as money poured into seismology to detect underground
testing. Others were crazed fever dreams, such as Project Argus,
which secretly tested nuclear explosions in the lower atmosphere
in the hopes of eventually detonating thousands of bombs per year
to build a radioactive force field. And some of its plans changed
the world. In the early 1960s an ARPA employee who had worked
on the computer systems designed to track Soviet bombers began
imagining that they could be linked together in a network. Others,

too, were excited by the possibility that networked communications systems would reduce American vulnerability to a nuclear attack. Before it evolved into the internet, the network they developed was called the ARPANET. Its first computers talked to each other in 1969.[59]

In the short term, such reforms in military research weren't enough to calm the political anxieties that Sputnik produced. In November 1957, just days after the Soviets had launched a second satellite, a secret committee assessing America's nuclear security called for a ramp-up of defense spending. The report quickly leaked, and Democrats eyeing the White House in 1960 spied an opening to the right of Eisenhower on issues of national security. The old man had been asleep at the wheel, they claimed. A "missile gap" had opened up. As soon as 1960, warned Joseph Alsop in his influential column, the Soviets would have five hundred ICBMs and the United States would have only thirty. John F. Kennedy, a pugnacious Cold Warrior and an Alsop favorite, was soon making much of the issue.[60]

By the time of the election, Eisenhower knew that such fears were false. Far from a senescent Luddite, he had overseen a massive expansion in high-tech intelligence gathering. CIA spy planes flew high above Soviet airspace snapping photographs of Soviet capacities. In 1960 the United States launched the world's first spy satellite to take even more photos. These confirmed that the Soviets didn't have five hundred ICBMs; they had but a bare handful of test rockets, none of which were ready to be launched.[61]

Yet Eisenhower could not go public with proof that the balance of arms favored the United States because all this intelligence, gathered illegally in violation of Soviet airspace, was secret. Secret, that is, from the US public. The Soviets could see the U2 planes on their radars, and in May 1960 they finally succeeded in shooting one down. The Eisenhower administration tried to play it off as a rogue weather plane, until Khrushchev triumphantly produced not only the wrecked plane but also its pilot. A planned superpower summit was canceled in the diplomatic fallout; CIA recklessness had scuttled an early opportunity for détente.[62]

At the polls in the fall, Kennedy won by the narrowest of margins, beating Ike's vice president, a characteristically surly and self-sorry Richard Nixon. In his farewell address, Eisenhower warned the nation of the dangers of a "military-industrial complex."[63]

Under Kennedy, defense budgets went up anyway, and contracting out was the preferred way to spend. Nickerson's Redstone had been close to the last hurrah for the old arsenal system; moving forward, America's weapons would be planned and built by the private sector. R&D money flowed through the economy. Demand for the silicon chips used to guide America's long-range missiles, bombers, and space rockets subsidized a nascent industry in northern California. (The price of the chips fell from $1,000 each in 1959 to $25 in 1963, at which point commercial users could afford them.) By 1962, a federal agency was warning that any move to disarmament could trigger a recession: twenty-two states in the nation were highly dependent on military spending. The profits flowed, as always, to the top. By 1968, half of Fortune's top fifty companies were in the defense sector.[64]

Efforts *were* made to promote economic efficiency and rationality in defense contracting. No one wanted to repeat the problems that had plagued missile development under Eisenhower. But no amount of technocratic tinkering could overcome the idiosyncrasies of the weapons market. There was only one buyer in this market. Because the products had become so staggeringly expensive and complex, only a few companies could realistically claim the expertise and capacity to deliver them. This meant that troublingly cozy relationships developed between buyers and sellers. One of the things that Nickerson complained about during his trial was how many Pentagon officials were retiring to cushy jobs with aviation companies. A 1960 congressional investigation found more than 750 high-ranking former military officers working for the nation's top 100 military contractors.[65]

The time scales involved in contracting for the weapons of the future produced further problems. Once a firm won a contract, it could essentially hold the military hostage. No one else was building a rival system, so were the military to cancel the contract, it would be depriving itself of the weapon, as well as losing all the capital already spent. There was therefore every incentive to massively underbid to win a contract and then use your leverage to ratchet up the costs later. During the Thor-Jupiter spat, von Braun had complained of what he called the "foot in the door policy" of the air force: a tendency to overpromise "because they felt once they have the contract, and so much money has been invested, then it is almost impossible for anybody to pull out of the thing." A 1962 study of twelve major weapons systems found they had cost on average 220 percent more than their original estimate. The burden was borne by the taxpayer, the money diverted from other causes.[66]

In theory, Congress was supposed to watch out for waste of the public dollar. Some politicians, of course, happily turned a blind eye when the money was flowing into their district. But even those who wanted to hold the defense sector accountable faced great difficulty in getting an accurate sense of what was really going on in the industry. The informational asymmetries in this marketplace were profound. As the Nickerson affair had demonstrated, it was very difficult to openly assess defense contracts when so much of the information was classified.

The problems in the sector could be seen most plainly in the troubled development of the C-5A transport plane. The C-5A was a mammoth thing, three-quarters the length of a football field, its engines sufficient to power a town of fifty thousand people. First mooted in 1962, first put under contract in 1964, it was designed to allow the rapid deployment of US military forces wherever trouble arose, to ferry in its cavernous belly large numbers of troops and all their equipment. Lockheed won the contract, promising to build 115 planes for $3 billion. Development was plagued by problems: wings that cracked from the heavy load, a defective landing gear. By 1971, costs had blown out to $5 billion. And that was to deliver only 81 planes, each of which could carry only half the load that had been initially promised. It was a staggering sum of money—developing the plane cost twice as much as all the federal money going to schools, three times as much as all federal poverty programs. But when Congress tried to take a look at what was going on, information about program costs was declared classified. When Ernest Fitzgerald, an auditor in the Defense Department, testified to Congress about the overruns in 1968, he was accused of disclosing classified information, reassigned to busywork, and then fired.[67]

There were many in Congress who were happy to keep writing the checks that Lockheed wanted: Lockheed faced bankruptcy if the contract was canceled, and there were subcontractors working on the C-5A in forty-one states. Those who were skeptical were finding it very hard to learn enough to challenge the project. "The great evil," explained one of them, Congressman Otis Pike of New York, "is not the military-industrial complex, but secrecy. Nobody—including Congress—knows what's going on. It's all classified . . . the military have no difficulty leaking classified documents to Congress and the press to support their views, but people who are opposed to them simply can't get their hands on anything."[68]

Fitzgerald, whose firing helped lead to the passage of whistle-blowing laws, is normally cited as the first whistleblower from the defense sector, the first to disclose classified information about bloat in the military-industrial complex. But the forgotten Nickerson has a good case for the title.

Including Nickerson in the genealogy of whistleblowers is a useful reminder of the difficulty of assessing what motivates someone to speak out. We want to adjudicate whether unauthorized disclosures "help" our national security or "hurt" it. In all their garbled glory, the intent requirements of the Espionage Act can at least be said to reflect this impulse. But this presumes that "national security" can be tested objectively, that it stands outside of politics.

During his trial, Nickerson was asked whether he had acted in the interests of national security or in his own professional interests. Nickerson knew that that was a false dichotomy. "It is obvious to me," he replied, "that the two things dove-tailed here." He thought that the air force missile program was inferior to his army program; he thought that the New Look policy undervalued the army; he thought that Wilson was making the wrong decisions for the wrong reasons and undermining the nation's security. The case is a reminder that national-security politics is still, at the end of the day, politics. It is a structure of conflict, something about which citizens in a democracy will disagree. The rise of secrecy meant control over access to information was in the hands of only one faction: the faction in power.[69]

The dynamics of Nickerson's case also reveal something very important about the power of the Espionage Act. It has a potency out of all proportion with the crimes it covers. A case like Nickerson's is of a very different order from formal espionage. Yet the law collapses the difference, bringing the stigma—and the penalties—associated with spying to a host of lesser activities, some of which may deserve to be criminal and some of which do not. The threat of an Espionage Act prosecution offers a leaker little incentive to fight the charges on their merits and gives prosecutors a powerful piece of leverage to win convictions on plea deals.

This legal dynamic helps explain one of the great mysteries of the Espionage Act's history. Leaks like Nickerson's were far from unusual in the 1950s. They remained ubiquitous ever after. In the mid-1980s, one study found that 42 percent of government employees had leaked information, a figure that it understandably concluded to be an understatement. Given the rise of classification and secrecy, a central part of the work of the foreign-policy journalist has long been the cultivation of sources who would leak information. This was how Pearson made his career. It was also the key to the success of the "Georgetown Set": the elite tribe of foreign-policy journalists, like Joseph and Stewart Alsop, who shared inside tips with their friends in the foreign service and the CIA over lavish Sunday-night suppers. From 1949 to 1969, something like 2 percent of the front-page stories in the *New York Times* were based on leaked information.[70]

In theory, anytime these leaks contained "information relating to the national defense," they were violations of the Espionage Act. If leaks are an everyday occurrence, then espionage prosecutions should be as well. Yet after Nickerson's case, there wouldn't be another prosecution for almost fifteen years, and it would be another fifteen years after that before there was a third. In part, as we will see, uncertainty about the meaning of the law as well as concerns about the First Amendment stayed the hand of the state in other cases. And the Espionage Act is not the only tool that the government has to punish leaks; it also has laws to prevent theft of government property and misuse of work computers, as well as a raft of administrative sanctions. But even if these sanctions are invoked with greater frequency than the Espionage Act, they still apply only to a small proportion of the leaks that take place.[71] The state has much more power to police leaks than it exercises.

The best explanation for this curious case of underenforcement comes from legal scholar David Pozen, who has argued that governments have no interest in strictly applying their leak laws for the simple reason that it serves the government interest to conduct politics by leaking. Leaked information, a Cold War journalist once observed, was the "coin" of the realm in politics. Politicians could use it to float a trial balloon, to prepare the way for a policy, to discredit a rival. Journalists relied on inside scoops to build their careers. The power dynamics inevitably bent the politics of the press toward those of the policy makers; the journalist dependent on the inside tip is unlikely to bite the hand that feeds. Over time, such exchanges helped to produce a Cold War consensus that stifled mid-century foreign-policy debates. There was little incentive for anyone to disrupt this cozy state of affairs by criminalizing it.[72]

But in the context of factional fights about Cold War policy, you would occasionally get someone like Nickerson, who would seek to leak information to challenge the assumptions of his superiors. Then the heavy hand of the state could descend. "The charges against me," Nickerson explained to a supporter in 1957, "arise from a situation wherein the Defense Department is using a security cloak to prevent disclosure of information that should be made public in the national interest." The real problem, he complained, was that disclosures that truly misled the public were "leaked at high levels." But those leakers would never be prosecuted. Or, as one observer of Nickerson's case put it, "Whether or not there is a 'leak' depends more on *who* leaks it than on the character of the information—and most often, I suspect, the largest leaks are at the top."[73]

If Nickerson was thus punished for his attempt to dissent from the defense policy of his superiors, we shouldn't lose sight of how limited his critique of the status quo was. He was an exuberant Cold Warrior, a militarist, an architect of the military-industrial complex. He just wanted to be the one to build the missiles, to belong to the service that got the glory of firing the atomic weapons when the war with the Soviets came. That he was the first target of the Espionage Act in the new era of Cold War secrecy is a sign of just how narrowed the political discourse had become in Eisenhower's America.

But soon, amid the turmoil of Vietnam, a more radical leaker would emerge from another sector of the nation's sprawling defense sector. The Espionage Act was lying in wait.

Chapter 8

PAPERS FROM THE PENTAGON

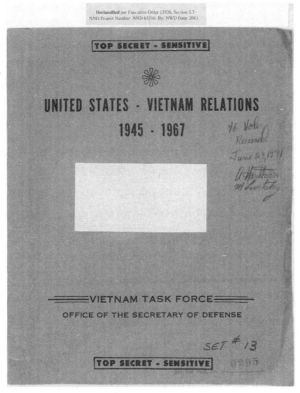

Front cover of the Pentagon Papers, an internal study of
the history of the Vietnam War that was kept secret until
leaked by Daniel Ellsberg in 1971. (National Archives and
Records Administration)

THE SECURITY GUARDS IN THE LOBBY OF RAND's LOS ANGELES offices paid Daniel Ellsberg no particular attention as he left the building on the night of October 1, 1969. Ellsberg often worked late, poring over classified documents at his desk before securing them in his safe and leaving for the day. But tonight, unbeknownst to the guards who waved him a friendly "good night," Ellsberg had stuffed his briefcase with sections of a classified study of the Vietnam War. It was a history of US policy dating back to the Truman years, one that revealed the decades of lies that had led the United States to wage a disastrous, futile war in Southeast Asia. Ellsberg had helped produce the policy and then participated in the war. But, increasingly influenced by the antiwar movement, he had come to believe the war was immoral and decided to share the classified study with the public.

Ellsberg took the documents to the office of a small advertising agency run by Lynda Sinay, the girlfriend of Tony Russo, a friend and former RAND employee. They spent the night slowly copying the study on an early Xerox machine, one page at a time, trying to cover the "Top Secret—Sensitive" stamp on each page. The next morning, Ellsberg stopped at a diner for an early breakfast, took a short nap, and then returned the documents to the office. That night he took another briefcase full of papers to the ad agency. He would repeat the routine for months—sometimes helped by Russo and Sinay, on one occasion helped by his children. There was work to go around. After all, the study that was soon known as the Pentagon Papers was seven thousand pages long.[1]

To describe Vietnam as a tragedy has become something of an American cliché, but all of the war movies, the endless historical studies, and the pat civics lessons can numb us to the colossal folly and extravagant brutality of American efforts to create and preserve an autonomous South Vietnam. By 1968, the United States had dropped twice as many tons of bombs on the small country as were dropped on Germany and Japan in World War II. The war killed

12–13 percent of the population of Vietnam—had the US lost the same proportion of its population, every man, woman, and child living in Arizona, California, and Michigan at the time would have died. Another 400,000 died in Laos, 700,000 more in Cambodia. And such bland statistics mask the suffering: the rape and the torture and the starvation, the flesh burned by napalm or stripped to the bone by white phosphorous or embedded with fiberglass fragments of cluster bombs, designed to be invisible to X-ray and thus much harder to surgically remove.[2]

Moreover, the war's consequences rippled out for decades. The destabilization of Cambodia led to the killing fields of Pol Pot; the spraying of Agent Orange led to cancers and nervous disorders and birth defects. Partisan clashes over the memory of the war further exacerbated the curdling of US political culture, and the immense cost of the war created inflationary pressures that helped break the postwar financial order, ending the golden age of capitalism. And all for naught. In 1975, after decades of foreign efforts designed to avoid just such an outcome, Vietnam was unified under Communist rule.

The policy that caused all of that misery had been forged in secret. Working behind the veil of classification, a small network of government officials had committed the United States to war and then lied to the public to make that war seem legitimate. Without public oversight, there was no course correction: the insiders continued to convince themselves that they were doing what was right, and no one else had access to the information that might convince them otherwise. Vietnam provides a case study of the policy distortions produced by excessive secrecy and the dangers that secrecy poses to democracy, to peace, and to human life.

Ellsberg had been one of the insiders responsible for the war; the Pentagon Papers documented his handiwork as well as the work of his colleagues and superiors. So as Ellsberg began removing the secret history from the RAND offices that October night, he was trying to build a bridge between the cloistered, classified world of the national-security bureaucracy and an antiwar movement seeking to rein in American militarism. And he was himself moving from the inside to the outside.

When the *New York Times* began publishing from the Pentagon Papers in June 1971, it triggered a constitutional crisis. Could the government prevent the press from publishing classified documents? Could leakers like Ellsberg be punished? The Pentagon Papers should have produced a jurisprudential reckoning with the patchwork secrecy regime that had been constructed after World War II. It should have been the moment when the nation came to terms with the institutions of Cold War secrecy.

Because of the worst excesses of the Nixon administration, it turned out to be a much stranger case than that.

The first decades of Ellsberg's life were spectacularly successful. His ascension took place at the heart of the new Cold War establishment, his unusual accomplishments reflecting entirely conventional convictions. The teenage Ellsberg wholeheartedly embraced Truman's foreign policy, and his hatred of Communism was locked in when the Soviets overthrew the Czech government during his final year in high school. He supported the intervention in Korea but missed the war while studying at Harvard (on a scholarship) and Cambridge (on a fellowship). By the time the war was over, he had graduated—third in his class—and also completed a good chunk of the coursework required for a PhD in economics.

He paused his studies to serve as an officer in the marines and then briefly extended his two-year term so he could deploy with his troops to the Mediterranean during the Suez Crisis. That extension had required deferring a position in the prestigious Harvard Society of Fellows, a unique blend of finishing school and research establishment. Once back at Harvard, he finished his PhD and immersed himself in the blossoming field of decision theory, seeking to understand how actors made decisions in conditions of uncertainty. In 1958 he joined the RAND Corporation.[3]

The **Research And Development** Corporation was the dominant think tank of the US defense establishment. Formed in 1945 to handle scientific and technical planning for the air force, it had become the leading edge of the outsourced defense economy. Within two years, it employed two hundred intellectuals from math, engineering, aerodynamics, physics, chemistry, economics, and psychology, all working to prepare for war and to manage the geopolitical order. It was RAND that wrote crucial early studies calling for the deployment of satellites, RAND that helped promote the idea of a missile gap. It became a seedbed for game theory, a close relation of the decision theory that so interested Ellsberg.[4]

By the time Ellsberg showed up for work, the RAND offices, located just a block from Santa Monica's beaches, were thrumming with efforts to understand the nuclear standoff. After Sputnik, the money was flowing in. Ellsberg spent his late twenties studying the bureaucratic hierarchies that governed the deployment of nuclear weapons.

It was intoxicating work for a Cold War liberal. Ellsberg was revealing the shocking inadequacies of the patchwork bureaucracy of the Eisenhower administration. With his fellow intellectuals at RAND, he was perfecting knowledge systems that were intended to simultaneously secure American hegemony and prevent nuclear war. We "shared a feeling," he later recalled, "that we were in the most literal sense working to save the world." RAND of the late 1950s was, Ellsberg thought, a kind of "secular priesthood"—replete with its sacred, secret knowledge.[5]

It was also ideal preparation for work in the Kennedy administration. An ex-marine with an economics degree from Harvard, Ellsberg personified the action intellectual most prized by the knights of America's Camelot. By the age of thirty, Ellsberg had been loaned out to help draft the war-strategy sections of the Defense Department's Basic National Security Policy. During the Cuban Missile Crisis he would join working groups trying to game out strategy for the White House.

In the fall of 1961, as part of a Pentagon task force seeking to assess policy in cases of limited—i.e., nonnuclear—war, Ellsberg went to Vietnam for the first time.

By then, the United States was already deeply involved in what was plainly an imperial war, even if no one was exactly talking about it as such. During World War II, Vietnam had been occupied by the Japanese; when that empire fell at the end of the war, Ho Chi Minh had declared independence. But the great powers had already decided that they would accept the surrender of the Japanese themselves. In failing to recognize Ho's declaration—the culmination of decades of anti-imperial advocacy—the Allies sowed the seeds for decades of strife.

In September 1945, British and French troops began to repress Vietnamese nationalists; by October, US merchant marine vessels were transporting French soldiers to Saigon. As World War II bled into a different war, US intelligence officer Peter Dewey was killed—the first American casualty of the Vietnam War. His final report, written just hours before his death, had concluded that "Cochinchina [southern Vietnam] is burning, the French and British are finished here, and we ought to clear out of Southeast Asia."[6]

It wasn't to be. As the French waged grinding, futile war against the Viet Minh, US support flooded in. By the end of the Truman presidency, the United States had supplied the French with 139,000 metric tons of materiel: hundreds of planes, 2,500 pieces of artillery, 100,000 guns, napalm.[7]

In theory, the Geneva Accords of 1954 should have provided the United States with an easy off-ramp. A cease-fire was signed with France, and Vietnam was temporarily divided into two regions, North and South, pending free elections to determine the future of the country in 1956. But as the Geneva Accords were being negotiated, John Foster Dulles informed congressional leaders that the United States would assume responsibility for the defense of South Vietnam from Communism. And neither the US nor the South Vietnamese government considered themselves bound to the pledge for free elections, the US on the spurious technicality that the elections would be monitored not by the UN but by an international control commission.[8]

US aid thus continued to flow, now to the corrupt and autocratic government of Ngo Dinh Diem rather than to the French. Fearful that the elections promised at Geneva would lead to Communist victory—"almost any type of election," observed the State Department in 1955, "would . . . give the communists a very significant if not decisive advantage"—Diem simply refused to hold them. Instead, he orchestrated a referendum establishing South Vietnam as a republic, with himself at its head. Diem received 98.2 percent of the vote; a Saigon electorate of 450,000 cast 605,000 votes in his favor. In the US he was hailed as a "Miracle Man," as "Vietnam's Man of Steel," as "the mandarin in a sharkskin suit who's upsetting the Reds' timetable."[9]

By 1956, the US was giving more aid to Diem's regime than to any other nation apart from Korea and Laos. The majority of it went to the military, which was being "trained" by a US military-assistance advisory group.[10] The heavy hand of the Diem government continued to alienate both peasants in the countryside and dissenting religious and political groups, such as the Buddhists, in the cities.

This was the Vietnam problem that John F. Kennedy inherited. In 1961 he sent advisers General Maxwell Taylor and Walt Rostow on a fact-finding mission to work out what to do in the nettlesome region. Their final report called for the introduction of six to eight thousand US combat troops, disguised as flood-relief workers, to help secure the Diem regime.[11]

Ellsberg's own fact-finding mission to Vietnam had ended just weeks before. Frank conversations with American military advisers on the ground left him less optimistic. Concluding that no glory could come from working on the region, he vowed to steer clear of Vietnam policy.

Meanwhile, Kennedy wasn't yet ready to deploy combat troops. Instead, he authorized the deployment of two fully armed helicopter companies as well as an expansion of advisers—by 1963, there were almost seventeen thousand of them, up from eight hundred when he had taken office.[12]

And there were other, even more slippery ways of shoring up Diem. Kennedy was a fan of covert ops; Ian Fleming was one of his favorite novelists. Even as the Bay of Pigs fiasco was unfolding in early 1961, Kennedy had given the ARPA, supposedly a research organization, the green light to begin "testing" new weapons to suppress the insurgency in South Vietnam. In November he approved its first big idea: chemical defoliation. "Operation Ranch Hand" had begun; it would spray four million acres of Vietnam with herbicide over the next eight years. ARPA soon contracted with RAND to help perfect the science of counterinsurgency, bringing veterans of the British war in Malaya, the French in Algeria, and US operations in the Philippines together in Washington to exchange notes.[13]

The United States's escalating involvement in Vietnam would have shocked the public, both domestically and internationally, so it was all conducted in secret. The first helicopters to deliver herbicides were painted to look like they belonged to the South Vietnamese army.[14]

None of it, of course, helped make the Diem government more legitimate. Just weeks before Kennedy was assassinated in Dallas, he sent word to a cabal of Vietnamese generals that the United States would not oppose a coup in Vietnam. On November 2, 1963, Diem was assassinated. South Vietnam would have eight different governments in the next eighteen months.[15]

Since his brief trip to the country in 1961, Ellsberg had stuck to his vow to avoid working on Vietnam. But Vietnam had developed a gravitational pull within the administration. In 1964 John T. McNaughton, assistant secretary of defense for international security, realized that he was spending something like 70 percent of his time on it, and he wanted a special assistant to help work through the mountain of paper he was receiving. McNaughton offered the gig to Ellsberg, whom he had known for several years through Harvard networks.[16]

It was a hard offer to refuse. Ellsberg would have access to information about decision making during an unfolding political crisis: real-world experience to add to his theoretical and historical studies. It can't have hurt that the position brought with it the highest civil service "supergrade"—GS-18—with pay and status equivalent to a deputy assistant secretary of state. On August 3, 1964, Ellsberg drove to the Pentagon to begin his first day at work.[17]

The previous night, the USS *Maddox* had come under North Vietnamese fire in the Gulf of Tonkin. The *Maddox* was conducting secret intelligence operations close to the coast, in support of covert attacks on the country that had been jointly planned by the Defense Department and the State Department. The fight lasted less than twenty minutes. Three North Vietnamese boats were badly damaged. The *Maddox* was barely grazed by a bullet.

Two nights later, on August 4, when the *Maddox* and another destroyer, the *Turner Joy*, returned to Vietnamese waters, their crew were anxious, their trigger fingers itchy. When their sonar men detected incoming torpedoes, they opened fire, pouring ammunition into what was, in fact, a dark and stormy night—an appropriately clichéd setting for the spinning of tales. The destroyers reported taking down two or perhaps three enemy ships. But when a US pilot flew over the scene, he could see "no boats, no boat wakes, no ricochets off boats, no boat impacts, no torpedo wakes—nothing but the black sea and American firepower." The *Maddox* sent a new cable: "Review of action makes many reported contacts and torpedoes fired appear very doubtful . . . freak weather effects and overeager sonar men may have accounted for many reports. No actual sightings by *Maddox*. Suggest complete evaluation before any further action."[18]

Back in Washington, the administration had already ordered "retaliatory" air strikes. Then a resolution, prepared two months earlier, was introduced to Congress. It gave the president open-ended authority to "take all necessary measures" to defend South Vietnam and prevent aggression against the US armed forces. Cables documenting the attacks were selectively leaked to the press, creating lurid accounts of North Vietnamese aggression against innocent US vessels. Members of the administration told Congress that there had been two attacks—no doubt about it—and that both were entirely unprovoked. After only ten hours of Senate debate, the resolution was passed by 88 votes to 2; it passed the House 416–0. Just three days after the fictitious second attack in the Gulf of Tonkin, just five days since the first, Congress had given the president the authority to wage war in Vietnam. "Like Grandma's Nightshirt," new president Lyndon Baines Johnson boasted, the Gulf of Tonkin resolution "covered everything."[19]

The Tonkin incident revealed something very important about the role of secrecy in the Vietnam War. Covert raids on North Vietnam weren't being kept secret to prevent the enemy from learning about them. The North Vietnamese were perfectly aware that there were US boats off their coastline, that they were being attacked and bombed. In fact, the entire purpose of missions like those of the *Maddox* was to communicate US resolve and military capacity to the North Vietnamese; they were seen as weapons of psychological war as much as anything else. The US response to the Tonkin incident was also designed to send very clear signals to the Communist bloc: both the legalese of the resolution and the level of bombing were calibrated to discipline Hanoi without bringing China or the USSR into the war.[20]

Rather, the purpose of secrecy during the Tonkin incident, as it was during the broader war, was to preserve the autonomy and legitimacy of American policy makers. Information was not being shielded from enemy eyes but from the American public and its representatives in Congress. In a January 1962 press conference, Kennedy was asked point-blank whether Americans were in combat in Vietnam. No, he said, even though the first US "adviser" had died a combat death just three weeks earlier. One month later, the administration issued an order stressing that the war was a South Vietnamese affair and reminding all those in the field that it was not in the US interest to depict or discuss Americans leading combat missions—classification duly ramped up. In March 1963, Scotty Reston, perhaps the most influential foreign-policy journalist in the country, told Congress that "we are engaged in quite a war in Vietnam, and this country hasn't the vaguest idea that it is in a war." As late as 1964, two-thirds of the public confessed to having given little or no thought to Vietnam.[21]

In the absence of public oversight, the bureaucrats had a free hand. Guided only by their own assumptions, they led the United States ever deeper into the war. In his new office in the Pentagon, Ellsberg was at the heart of the process. Each day he would sit at his desk overlooking the tidal basin and move through a stack of briefings; twelve feet of paper greeted him on his first day. Flanked by a burn bag on one side, and two four-drawer top-secret filing cabinets on the other, he quickly learned that only the most classified information was worth reviewing. It had to be marked "Top Secret" at least. Even better if it was stamped with one of the yet higher levels of classification that had come into being—"Eyes Only" or "No Distribution" or the more improvised efforts to tighten things even further, such as "literally eyes only of the secretary."[22]

Access to all that secret information did predictable things to policy makers. It "was exciting," Ellsberg recalled. "The incredible pace and the inside dope made you feel important, fully engaged, on an adrenaline high much of the time. Clearly it was addictive." And the more one's sense of self was tied up with being on the inside, the further removed one felt from those on the outside. Ellsberg came to share what he called the "universal ethos of the executive branch": "That for the Congress, the press, and the public to know much about what the president was doing for them, with our help, was at best unnecessary and irrelevant. At worst, it was an encouragement to uninformed (uncleared), short-sighted and parochial individuals and institutions to intervene in matters that were too complicated for them to understand and to muck it up."[23]

Worse still, the more the administration lied to the public, the larger the gap between them grew. It was a dangerously self-reinforcing cycle. "Once I was inside the government," Ellsberg said, "my awareness of how easily and pervasively Congress, the public, and journalists were fooled and misled contributed to a lack of respect for them and their potential contribution to better policy. That in turn made it easier to accept, to participate in, to keep quiet about practices of secrecy and deception that fooled them further."[24]

The simple truth was that for all the careful game-theoretic calibrations, for all the quantification and the fancy charts, Vietnam policy boiled down to some very basic assumptions. Communists wanted to expand; they needed to be shown resolve. Democrats could not afford, politically, to be seen as weak: "losing" Vietnam would do to their hopes for the 1960s what "losing" China had done to them in the early 1950s. Behind their veil of secrecy, the national-security bureaucrats shared not a hidden font of valuable information but a culture forged from a common set of simple moral references. Negotiating meant Munich meant appeasement, and was to be avoided. McCarthyite attacks were a powerful tool of the Right, and to be feared.

When the policy was expressed behind closed doors, in the inner chamber of secrecy, it was remarkably crude. "We don't have a prayer of staying in Vietnam," Kennedy told a confidant, "but I can't give up a piece of territory like that to the communists and then get the people to reelect me." In 1964 McNaughton sought to quantify US aims in supporting South Vietnam for Defense Secretary Robert McNamara, who wanted stats for everything. His conclusions were revealing: "70% to avoid a humiliating U.S. defeat. 20% to keep South Vietnamese territory from Chinese hands. 10% to permit the people of South Vietnam to enjoy a better, freer way of life."[25]

Vietnam, in short, was about the pride, toughness, and reputation of the policy makers. This meant that it was also about their manhood. LBJ feared losing Vietnam and being called "a coward. An unmanly man. A man without a spine." To explain containment he turned to a revealing metaphor: "If you let a bully come into your yard one day, the next day he'll be up on your porch, and the day after that he'll rape your wife in your own bed." There were easy ways to hold such fears at bay. "I didn't just screw Ho Chi Minh," LBJ crowed after bombs had rained down in "retaliation" for the Gulf of Tonkin. "I cut his pecker off."[26]

All the secrecy reinforced this culture of masculine bravery, of toughness, of resolve. Lower-level bureaucrats never questioned the underlying assumptions of the war—assigned policy problems, they went to work on them, assuming that the higher-ups had set the policy for good reason. When evidence came from the field to suggest that the Viet Cong were stronger than expected, the South Vietnamese army weaker, the government less legitimate, it was massaged away as political, defeatist, and weak. Those in the bureaucracy who nursed doubts about the policy kept them very quiet, hiding in pockets of anonymity created by overclassification, lest they be moved to the margins. In the fall of 1964, McNaughton asked Ellsberg to explore policy scenarios if South Vietnam did, in fact, collapse—the sort of thing one might expect the Department of Defense (DoD) to have explored before committing troops in order to preserve it. But McNaughton warned Ellsberg not to share his work with anyone because "you could be signing the death warrant to your career by having anything to do with calculations and decisions like these. A lot of people were ruined for less." In such ways did secrecy, and an unwillingness to stick out, create bureaucratic momentum behind the war.[27]

At a high enough level, one could speak more frankly, relying on secrecy to protect your reputation and the reputations of those above you. In October 1964, Undersecretary of State George Ball wrote a single-spaced, sixty-seven-page briefing that outlined why the war could not be won and should not be waged, and that advocated for a political settlement. He showed it to only the secretary of state, the defense secretary, and the national security advisor, which meant his doubts never received a proper airing. Ball's challenges to the basic assumptions of the war were never discussed in Congress, or the press, or even broadly in the bureaucracy. Ellsberg was largely unaware of this internal dissent—he caught a glimpse of it only late one night, when he snuck a peek at classified files in McNaughton's office that he wasn't authorized to read. The public knew nothing about it.[28]

As the war deepened, insiders like Ellsberg looked on as the public were fed half-truths and lies. LBJ ran for a second term in 1964 as a man opposed to expanding the war—that was the kind of reckless militarism he attributed to his archconservative rival, Barry Goldwater. "We are not about to send American boys 9 or 10,000 miles away from home to do what Asian boys ought to be doing for themselves," LBJ proclaimed. But he had already begun secretly bombing Laos, and by October there was a consensus in the White House that North Vietnam would also need to be bombed. On the day that Americans went to the polls to vote, LBJ established an interagency working group in the State Department to plan for expanding the war. One of its members was Daniel Ellsberg.[29]

Ellsberg remained close to the center of it during the crucial months of escalation after Johnson's landslide election. In February 1965, after a US helicopter base in Pleiku was attacked, Ellsberg helped gather information about Viet Cong assaults on the US forces. Such evidence built the case for the start of systematic bombing, code-named Rolling Thunder, that began in March. In July, when LBJ approved the sending of one hundred thousand additional combat troops to Vietnam, Ellsberg helped draft the speech that would announce the policy. He was surprised when LBJ told a televised audience that only fifty thousand more troops were being sent and even more surprised when LBJ insisted that the expansion did not "imply a change of policy." Privately, in fact, it was well-known that this was a full US commitment to fighting the war: LBJ had been briefed that even with four hundred thousand troops the chances of success were slim.[30] But the public deception was in perfect keeping with a policy that troop buildups being announced in a "piecemeal" fashion would "mitigate somewhat the crisis atmosphere." "This low-key treatment will not obviate [all] political and psychological problems," explained one internal memo, "but will allow us to handle them undramatically."[31]

Ellsberg did not flinch in the face of such duplicity. In 1965 he volunteered to go to Vietnam: he had been reassigned at work, he was recently divorced, and he seemed to be searching for meaning. He spent almost two years there, working on various pacification campaigns.[32]

The experience only reinforced his awareness of the vast gap between what was happening on the ground and what was being told to the American people. In late 1966 he accompanied Robert McNamara on one of the defense secretary's frequent visits to Vietnam. As they flew back, McNamara argued with aides that the United States was losing the war, that it was in a worse position now than it had been a year earlier. Ellsberg backed him up. But when they landed at Andrews Air Force Base, Ellsberg watched McNamara proclaim to the press, "I've just come back from Vietnam, and I'm glad to be able to tell you that we're showing great progress in every dimension. . . ."[33]

Back in the United States, vast sections of the public were becoming disillusioned by such lies. In their morning papers, they read pundits dissecting what had become known as LBJ's "credibility gap." And they were being presented with alternative interpretations by an ever-growing antiwar movement. The first teach-in had been held at the University of Michigan two weeks after the first marines landed at Da Nang in early 1965; that spring, twenty-five thousand people attended an antiwar protest at the White House organized by Students for a Democratic Society (SDS). As early as July 1965, civil-rights activists in tiny McComb had declared that "no Mississippi Negroes should be fighting in Vietnam for the White Man's freedom, until all the Negro people are free in Mississippi."[34]

In March, seventy-nine-year-old German immigrant Alice Herz set herself on fire in downtown Detroit to protest the escalation of bombing. Herz was a committed peace activist and a member of

Women's Strike for Peace, which had started as an antinuclear organization in the 1950s and was now increasingly involved in antiwar work. (That summer, they would organize a meeting between American and Vietnamese women in Indonesia in order to exchange more accurate information about the war. It was illegal for US citizens to travel to North Vietnam.) Herz was one of three Americans to die by self-immolation in 1965.[35]

McNamara had looked on with horror as one of them, Norman Morrison, a thirty-two-year-old pacifist, self-immolated outside the Pentagon later that year. McNamara knew that his own wife and children "shared many of Morrison's feelings about the war, as did the wives and children of several of my cabinet colleagues. And I believed I understood and shared some of his thoughts." But he responded by "bottling up my emotions and avoiding talking about them with anyone."[36]

Like all repressed emotions, McNamara's sought an out. After a visit to the Kennedy School of Government at Harvard in November 1966, McNamara began flirting with the idea of commissioning an internal study of Vietnam policy. In June 1967 he asked two staffers working under McNaughton—Morton Halperin and Leslie Gelb—to oversee the writing of a history of the decision-making process that brought the United States into the war.[37]

Rather than turning to the DoD's staff historians to prepare it, Halperin and Gelb were told to assemble in the International Security Office a small team to be kept secret from the other branches of the government. Exactly why McNamara chose this secretive path has never become entirely clear. He claimed it was to produce a record for future scholars; others claimed, not very convincingly, that he was preparing material to help Bobby Kennedy challenge LBJ for the Democratic nomination in the 1968 election. But it seems likely that McNamara was seeking, however unconsciously, to come to terms with his role in the unfolding tragedy. By 1967, this famously self-controlled man was struggling to maintain his grip: he was seen to burst spontaneously into tears, and the DC rumor mill was speculating that he was on the cusp of a breakdown. A systems man to the last, he sought inner peace not by going to confession or therapy but by commissioning one more study of bureaucratic process.[38]

Ellsberg, who had contracted a severe case of hepatitis in Vietnam and recently returned to both the US and RAND, was soon approached by Halperin and Gelb—both Harvard alums—to help write the history. Like the other thirty-five bureaucrats who helped write what would become the Pentagon Papers, he had free access to documents from the State and Defense Departments.[39]

What he read further hardened his sense that the war was a failure, that it was based on lies and needed to be opposed. In March, inspired by a leak of the true level of a recent troop request, he leaked classified cables to Neil Sheehan at the *New York Times* that showed that the United States had undervalued North Vietnamese troop strength. His goal was to communicate to the administration, via the press, that it could no longer lie with impunity. If the administration decided to further escalate the war, Ellsberg hoped to suggest, it would have to do so publicly or else risk the information leaking out.[40]

But Ellsberg was still committed to challenging the war from within the bureaucracy, as one powerful insider speaking truth to another. He had had, as yet, no real contact with the antiwar movement. Ellsberg had attended some early teach-ins—to argue the pro-war position for the government. And he had been in attendance at the first SDS antiwar protest in March 1965, but only because he was courting Patricia Marx, a public-radio host who had insisted that the protest should be their first date. They had continued to date while Ellsberg was in Vietnam—he proposed to her in the Ganges River, while on leave—but had then fallen out over the ethics of the war. Ellsberg, whatever his growing doubts, was at the time still an active participant in the conflict.[41]

But in 1968 and 1969, Ellsberg came into closer contact with the antiwar movement for the first time, an experience that would profoundly change his politics. In April 1968, Ellsberg attended a conference at Princeton University on "America in a Revolutionary World." Ellsberg was there as a professional counterrevolutionary, but the conference was being held just two days after LBJ had declared he would not seek the 1968 presidential nomination so that he could halt the bombing and prepare peace talks. Leftists at the conference believed that they had toppled a president and ended the war. Ellsberg was impressed. He sat at a table with American Friends Service Committee members who had protested nuclear testing in the 1950s—always a pet cause for Ellsberg—and delivered medicine to Vietnam. And at lunch, he began talking to Gandhian activist Janaki Natarjan, who explained to him the principles of nonviolent resistance. She told him about Martin Luther King Jr.'s powerful antiwar speech at the Riverside Church in 1967: Ellsberg had somehow missed King declaring, at considerable personal cost, that the United States was the "greatest purveyor of violence in the world today." It all seems to have blown Ellsberg's mind. He had built a career analyzing bargaining and conflict between geopolitical rivals; Natarjan was now explaining to him why the concept of "enemy" made no sense. An important, lasting friendship was born. (It probably didn't hurt Natarjan's message that Ellsberg found her beautiful.)[42]

Over the next year, Natarjan provided Ellsberg with book recommendations—Martin Luther King Jr., Barbara Deming, Henry David Thoreau's On Civil Disobedience, Howard Zinn, Noam Chomsky. A constellation of dissenters replaced all those Kennedy men as his North Star. But he still remained an insider: when Nixon took the Oval Office that fall, Ellsberg was asked to prepare a memo on Vietnam policy for Henry Kissinger. It can't have been easy to maintain these two sides of his political life. In late 1968, Ellsberg started going to psychoanalysis four days per week.[43]

Matters came to a head in the summer of 1969. Natarjan invited Ellsberg to attend the conference of War Resisters International, a pacifist organization that had been formed after World War I. At the conference, held at Haverford College, he fell into deep conversations with committed antiwar activists, including Bob Eaton, who was about to go to prison for draft resistance. To his own surprise, Ellsberg found himself agreeing to protest Eaton's sentence with other activists. Feeling "naked and raw," as well as "ridiculous," Ellsberg began handing out leaflets in downtown Philadelphia. It was his first public action against the war, and an experience he found liberating.

And then, on the last day of the conference, Randy Kehler, who was also soon to go to jail for draft resistance, spoke about his commitments to antiwar activism. The speech had a profound effect on Ellsberg. He began crying, went to the bathroom to gather himself, but "began to sob convulsively, uncontrollably." It was a breakdown, a reckoning with his role in history, and a symbolic rebirth: "It was as though an ax had split my head, and my heart broke open. But what had really happened was that my life had split in two."[44]

From Haverford, Ellsberg traveled to Washington to stop by the RAND offices before flying back to Los Angeles. He wanted to pick up the remaining volumes of the Pentagon Papers, which had been completed earlier in the year. All told, the study had ended up being seven thousand pages long, bound in forty-seven volumes. Four thousand pages were reproduced historical memos and reports and briefings, interspersed with three thousand pages of what is often called historical analysis but was really just a summary of the documents. The writers of the histories didn't have access to all the internal documents, such as those in the White House, or seek to embed the internal, bureaucratic history in any broader political or geopolitical context.

Still, the report provided a remarkable history of the inner policy process of the secretive national-security state. And, as such, it was itself classified. Following the classification policy of the time, because some documents in the study were stamped "Top Secret," each one of the seven thousand pages was stamped "Top Secret"—including reproductions of presidential speeches and New York Times articles. It was a typical instance of the habitual overclassification of the executive branch; even Nixon's defense secretary would later concede that 95 percent of the papers did not need to be classified. But for good measure, Gelb stamped the entire document "Top Secret—Sensitive." "Sensitive" had no legal significance, but it was an internal Pentagon stamp to indicate that the document might cause bureaucratic or political embarrassment. This was an understatement. Upon reading it, McNamara said that people could be hanged on the basis of what the Pentagon Papers revealed. But it contained no particular bombshells, no new facts, no particular smoking gun. Rather, in its totality, it revealed how flawed Vietnam policy had been.[45]

Only fifteen copies of the report were ever printed—five were sent to Defense Secretary Laird and one to Henry Kissinger; the remaining nine went to former LBJ and JFK staffers. Gelb and Halperin decided to store their copies in the RAND DC offices, but they were concerned that efforts might be made to destroy all copies of the report, so they decided not to enter the papers into RAND's control system for cataloging secret documents. Instead, they managed access to the hidden papers themselves.[46]

In March 1969 they decided to give Daniel Ellsberg access, apparently so that he could use them to prepare a RAND study on the "Lessons of Vietnam Policy." After personally couriering papers covering the latter years of the study back to Los Angeles, Ellsberg had spent the spring and early summer reading them. Now, in the wake of his call to action at Haverford, he was picking up the first half of the study.

As he read the earliest history of American involvement in Vietnam, back in the Truman and Eisenhower years, Ellsberg came to realize just how long the insiders had been lying to the public. Increasingly militant, he sought ways to more actively protest the war. In September he joined with five other RAND employees in writing an open letter to the *New York Times* and *Washington Post* that called for unilateral withdrawal. It got a little media play but had no broader effect—other than earning the animosity of the majority of RAND employees, who feared that the letter would threaten their access to defense contracts and the ears of the powerful. That reaction from colleagues he had earlier thought of as brave intellectuals, combined with the sorry story of insider duplicity contained in the Pentagon Papers, finally ended Ellsberg's lifelong desire to effect political change from the inside. He now believed that "inside consulting and advice" only undermined the possibility for democratic self-governance. The only way to change executive policy was to bring pressure "from outside, from Congress and the public."[47]

Ellsberg decided he needed to get the secret history into the public eye.

For help, he turned to Tony Russo, a former RAND colleague he had befriended in Vietnam. At the time, Russo had been interviewing North Vietnamese defectors and POWs for a RAND study of enemy morale and psychology, and he had come to the conclusion that the United States was on the wrong side of the war. He subsequently prepared studies documenting the impact of the herbicide program and the torture of prisoners in South Vietnam; RAND fired him. But he and Ellsberg had stayed close, meeting to talk about the war between dips at the beach. Let's copy and release the papers, Ellsberg now said. Russo agreed. Even better, he knew someone with a copy machine.

Ellsberg was late to the cause, but he was now fully committed. He spent the next months copying the papers in the evening, sometimes helped by Marx, with whom he had reunited in mid-1970.

Even so, it would take another eighteen months before Ellsberg shared the Pentagon Papers with the press. At first, he sought to make the documents public via political institutions that would offer him more political and legal protection. In the fall of 1969, Ellsberg offered the papers to Senator J. William Fulbright, the powerful chair of the Foreign Relations Committee, who had emerged as a leading critic of the war. But Fulbright was worried that publicizing the documents would harm the Senate's reputation as a trustworthy upholder of executive branch secrecy and risk cutting Senate committees off from access to classified material. Fulbright spent fruitless months asking the DoD to declassify the documents before ultimately declining to publicize them. So did George Mc-Govern, who feared that publicizing secret information would hurt his presidential run. An effort to introduce the papers as evidence in a criminal trial also failed. Ellsberg had arranged to be called as a witness in the trial of the Minnesota 8, who had tried to burn draft records—the idea was that he would testify that the war was based on lies and, upon being asked to provide evidence for such a serious allegation, would produce the papers. The judge was having none of it. Any effort to comment on war policy, he ruled, would constitute contempt of court.[48]

So in the spring of 1971, Ellsberg at last turned to the press. By this point, he had left RAND and taken up a position as a researcher at MIT. He once again reached out to *New York Times* reporter Neil Sheehan, who had made a name for himself as a critic of the war. The pair spent a long night in Washington discussing the war, and then Ellsberg invited Sheehan to look at copies of the papers, which he was storing at his brother-in-law's apartment.

There followed about a month of careful back-and-forth, as Sheehan asked to take possession of a copy and Ellsberg tried to maintain leverage by holding on to the papers himself—he was worried the *Times* would bury the papers or publish them in a piecemeal way that would blunt their impact. For a time, he gave Sheehan a key to the apartment storing the papers so that the journalist could read them and make notes. In April, Ellsberg turned forty-three of the forty-seven volumes of the study over to Sheehan; he always kept secret four volumes of the study that documented diplomatic negotiations. Ellsberg didn't know that the *Times* already had a small team cloistered away in the New York Hilton, carefully going through a copy of the papers that Sheehan and his wife had secretly made when the Ellsbergs were out of town.[49]

At the *Times*, possession of the papers led to a series of tense debates. Were they worth publishing? The editorial side thought they revealed a history of government duplicity and were an important scoop. Some in management worried they were of purely historical relevance and that publishing classified material would be a violation of the paper's responsibilities to national security.

And then there was the question of legal liability. For counsel, the paper turned, as always, to the blue-chip firm Lord, Day and Lord, which advised that publication risked violating both the Espionage Act and the executive order governing classification (Herbert Brownell, Eisenhower's attorney general and the author of that order, was senior partner at the firm). But the newspaper's general counsel, James C. Goodale, argued that the Espionage Act would be vague and unconstitutional if it applied to this historical material—such information, he thought, could not be said to "relate to the national defense." As for the executive order—well, that applied only to members of the executive branch, not the press. Even so, Goodale thought the Nixon administration would seek to enjoin the paper from publishing and might have some temporary success in doing so. He therefore urged that the paper publish all the material on one day, before legal challenges kicked in. For weeks, debate continued. All word of what was known internally as Project X was kept secret lest either the government or a rival paper learn that the *Times* was sitting on the study.[50]

In the end, publisher Arthur Sulzberger split the difference. He approved publication, in a series of articles over multiple days, but required that each article be carefully preapproved to ensure it did not include anything that could endanger national security. None of the original documents would be published in full; the stories would be framed as coverage of the internal study. On the front cover of June 13, 1971, next to a picture of Tricia Nixon's wedding, the *Times* finally ran its first stories based on the papers. They were broad pieces that outlined the nature of the study and promised more stories to come. On its inside pages, the paper ran stories on the deceptions surrounding the Gulf of Tonkin. Scotty Reston's column that day was on "The McNamara Papers," which "prove once more," the veteran correspondent concluded, "that truth is the first casualty of war and that war corrupts good men."[51]

For the briefest of moments that Sunday, it seemed that the Nixon administration would not react. Richard Nixon, always angling for a partisan weapon, thought that the historical documents could be used to discredit the Democrats. But then Henry Kissinger got involved, warning that leaks would make Nixon look weak and untrustworthy amid secret negotiations that were preparing the way for him to go to China. Meanwhile, on Monday morning, Assistant Attorney General Robert Mardian asked the Office of Legal Counsel (OLC) to explore the possibility of blocking the *Times* from further publication. Mardian was a staunch conservative who had made his name in Barry Goldwater's insurgent presidential campaign before prosecuting antiwar activists as head of the Internal Security Division of the Justice Department. Now, faced with an antiwar leaker, he received a welcome opinion from the OLC. Dicta in the *Near v. Minnesota* case of 1931 suggested that prior restraint of the press might be justifiable if publication would harm national security. The OLC opinion was written by a forty-five-year-old William Rehnquist, who would be appointed to the Supreme Court six months later.[52]

That night, Attorney General John Mitchell sent a telegram to *Times* publisher Sulzberger, warning that information in the Pentagon Papers was "information relating to the national defense and bear[ing] a Top Secret classification. As such, publication of this information is directly prohibited by the provisions of the Espionage law."[53] Mitchell asked the paper to cease further publication and to return the documents to the government.

The *Times* refused. A crowd of employees cheered as Tuesday's edition went to print featuring a third installment of stories from the classified study, as well as a front-page story on the administration's attempt to silence the paper. The next morning, the US government filed an injunction against the *Times*. The Pentagon Papers were going to court.[54]

Ellsberg was closely watching these events from his home in Cambridge. On Tuesday the government won a temporary restraining order to stop the *Times* from further publication until the case could be heard. When the Wednesday morning edition of the *Times* complied with that order, Ellsberg decided to share the papers with the *Washington Post* and reached out to journalist Bob Bagdikian, who had previously worked at RAND. Bagdikian gave assurances that the *Post* would run the papers if it could get them—Ben Bradlee, its editor, was desperate to compete with the *Times*—and was given an address in Cambridge where he could pick them up. As Bagdikian flew back from Boston to Washington—a carton of classified paper strapped into the passenger seat beside him—Ellsberg was named as the source of the documents by a *New York Times* journalist being interviewed on television.[55]

The *Times* had spent three months deciding whether or not to publish the Pentagon Papers; the *Post* spent fourteen hours. After an intense debate—counsel again warning against publication, management concerned that a criminal trial would foul the sale of company stock, which had begun trading publicly just two days earlier—the editors won the day. On Friday morning, the *Post* ran a front-page story documenting the role of the United States in delaying elections in South Vietnam in 1956. In its right-hand column, the front page also featured a picture of Ellsberg, who had gone underground upon being named as the suspected leaker and was now being hunted by the FBI. That afternoon, the US government, claiming that the *Post* was now also in violation of the Espionage Act, filed a second suit for injunction.[56]

For the next ten days, as the legal cases unfolded with astonishing speed, Ellsberg and Marx stayed on the move seeking to avoid arrest. They were sheltered by a small network of antiwar activists who hid the pair in their apartments, checked them into motels under fake names, delivered groceries and food to them. The identities of these activists are still largely unknown—Ellsberg always referred to them as the Lavender Hill mob, after the 1951 heist flick. But Natarjan was one of them, and in 2018 historian Gar Alperovitz came out as another. Alperovitz had been a congressional staffer during the Gulf of Tonkin debate and had tried to amend the resolution; he subsequently published an important revisionist account of America's decision to drop the atomic bombs and became active in the antiwar movement in Boston. He had met Ellsberg at a dinner party and now played a central role in helping Ellsberg ensure that injunctions against the *Times* and *Post* would not kill the story. Using the pseudonym "Mr. Boston," Alperovitz made contact with journalists at other newspapers and coordinated a small team of antiwar students who couriered sections of the Pentagon Papers to them. As the *Post* and *Times* tussled with the government in court, nineteen other papers published portions of the secret study.[57]

The legal cases were going poorly for the government. Influenced by the hawkish Mardian, the government adopted an extreme posture in its briefs. The decision to seek an injunction was, of itself, a heavy lift—prior restraint was rightly understood to be a particularly odious and heavy-handed form of censorship. To justify it, the government originally argued that the simple fact of classification settled the matter: the courts should defer to the expertise of the executive branch about which material had to be kept secret in the national interest. At first, it even insisted that no portion of the study could be declassified, including documents that were already in the public domain.[58]

When that strategy failed, it began trying to specify particular pieces of information that would cause particular harms to the national security. But its arguments were weak. Often, it tried to make the case in the broadest terms. Failure to keep secrets, it suggested, would reduce the trustworthiness of the government to foreign officials, harming diplomacy. (Never mind that that logic would render democratic oversight of diplomacy impossible.) Officials would not speak candidly about policy if they thought internal discussions would be leaked. (Never mind that all that secrecy about Vietnam had produced a toxic form of groupthink, not a free exchange of ideas.) Even when they sought to get down to details, they named diplomatic incidents that were already in the public domain, relied on cases that were in the four diplomatic volumes that Ellsberg had very intentionally not provided to the press, or suggested tortuous chains of hypotheticals: revealing the secret use of Thai air bases to bomb Vietnam *might* cause political problems abroad that *might* reduce the willingness of allies to help, which *might* slow the withdrawal of US troops.[59]

So the government failed to win its injunctions. In New York it couldn't even convince Judge Murray Gurfein, who was both a veteran of Army Intelligence *and* a recent Nixon appointee—he had been sworn in just days before, and this was his first case. It had no more success in front of liberal judge Gerhard Gesell in Washington. On appeal, the government won a retrial in New York—the court, unusually, was giving the government a do-over to show evidence of harm—but it lost again in DC. Given the confusion, both the *New York Times*—restrained from publication until the retrial—and the government appealed to the Supreme Court, which agreed to hear the case on Saturday, June 26. The case had run the judicial gamut, normally grindingly slow, in just thirteen days.[60]

On Wednesday, June 30, the court ruled 6–3 that the newspapers had the right to publish. Because of the speed of their deliberations, the justices issued a confusing spray of nine separate opinions—there was no time to consult, consolidate, and redraft. But the decision made clear that it was almost impossible for the government to justify prior restraint of the press. Rereading the same sections of *Near v. Minnesota* that the OLC had thought justified the injunction against the *Times* just two weeks earlier, Justice Brennan now asserted that "publication must inevitably, directly, and immediately cause the occurrence of an event kindred to imperiling the safety of a transport already at sea" if prior restraint was to be constitutional. The Pentagon Papers fell short of such a threat, as did almost everything else. On only one occasion since has the government even tried to enjoin the publication of national-security information: a brief and quickly abandoned effort to stop *Progressive* magazine from publishing an article on the science of the H-bomb in 1979.[61]

The headline outcome was a great victory for the freedom of the press, but the details buried in those nine opinions revealed far more ambiguity about the scope of the Espionage Act. Great cases make bad law, Oliver Wendell Holmes once observed; when it came to the security of classified information, the Pentagon Papers decision made almost no law. Yes, the decision had ended the threat of prior restraint, but everyone conceded that no portion of the Espionage Act sanctioned that, and it had been surprising that the government had even tried that strategy. The difficult question was what Section 793 of the Espionage Act meant, what powers it provided to the state to regulate the circulation of information that had been classified.[62]

The Pentagon Papers case should have provided an opportunity to resolve the uncertainty that had haunted this section of the law since 1917. One amicus brief filed by the National Emergency Civil Liberties Committee (NECLC)—which had split from the ACLU in the 1950s in order to defend the rights of alleged Communists— in fact tried to make the case that the Espionage Act was unconstitutional. Representing radical scholars such as Noam Chomsky, Howard Zinn, and Carl Schorske, NECLC argued that Section 793(e) of the Espionage Act was "unconstitutionally vague and void for overbreadth." The brief pointed to two familiar problems. First, no law established how access to national defense information was to be authorized apart from Executive Order 10501, whose terms were themselves vague, letting the executive branch decide for itself what information the public could and could not learn about its foreign policy. Second, the classified documents in the Pentagon Papers were "not battle plans, technical devices, war secrets or any other similar material, the disclosure of which might affect some current strategy of the armed forces of the United States." To say that these historical, political documents constituted "information relating to the national defense" revealed that this whole concept was "equally broad and vague." In short, the breadth of the Espionage Act was "so extraordinary that it cannot possibly stand consistent with established law," especially when it impinged on the First Amendment rights of the public to discuss weighty matters such as the wisdom of an ongoing war. These were compelling arguments.[63]

But because the government had pursued the outrageously puni-tive strategy of prior censorship, lawyers for the papers did not need to take on the secrecy laws to win the case for their clients. Rather, Yale law professor Alexander Bickel, who represented the *Times*, was willing to concede that classification and even some forms of prior restraint were constitutional, but he focused primarily on the lack of statutory authority to justify prior restraint in the matter at hand, and only secondarily on the particular threat that prior restraint posed to the First Amendment rights of the press to publish. (This was a more limited First Amendment right, it is worth noting, than the public right to know that was claimed in the NECLC brief.)[64]

So judges in the case did not need to grapple directly with the meaning of the Espionage Act. Yet many did so anyway, making comments that further muddied the jurisprudence of these confus-ing clauses. No fewer than five justices, in fact, suggested in dicta that even if prior restraint was unconstitutional, the Espionage Act would sanction criminal prosecutions against the press for publish-ing classified documents. "Failure by the government to justify prior restraints does not measure its constitutional entitlement to a convic-tion for criminal publication," explained Byron White, in a sentence that won praise from a number of other judges. "That the govern-ment mistakenly chose to proceed by injunction does not mean that it could not successfully proceed in another way." Even liberal justice William Douglas, normally a First Amendment absolutist, threw in a footnote stating blandly that "these documents contain data con-cerning the communications system of the United States publication of which is a crime. But the criminal sanction is not urged by the United States." Whether they drew on Section 798 of the Espio-nage Act (as did Douglas) or on 793 (as did White), a majority of the judges who had freed the press to publish the Pentagon Papers seemed to be practically inviting the government to now prosecute that act.[65]

In the end, of course, no prosecution of the press ever came. To do so after the horse had so clearly bolted the barn must have seemed unwise—particularly with an election coming, in which Nixon would seek, successfully, the endorsement of the nation's press. The indeterminacy of the law had its value, too. In April 1972, Deputy Assistant Attorney General for Internal Security Kevin Maroney warned a meeting of newspaper editors that the administration would bring Espionage Act prosecutions against any paper that published classified materials. Whether Section 793 applied to newspapers remained unclear, but the long shadow of the law continued to loom over the nation's press.[66]

For Ellsberg and Russo, the Espionage Act posed a more immediate danger. On June 28, with a decision pending in the Supreme Court case, Ellsberg turned himself in. He was charged with stealing government property and violating the Espionage Act, and he faced up to ten years in jail.[67]

Prosecuting Ellsberg seemed a much more promising avenue than prosecuting the press. "Hell, I wouldn't prosecute the *Times*," said Nixon. "My view is to prosecute the goddamn pricks that gave it to 'em."[68] But prosecuting the pricks went poorly, too. Russo was offered complete immunity to testify against Ellsberg, but refused. In fact, he refused to cooperate with the trial at all and was jailed for contempt of court. He then refused to cut his hair and was moved to solitary. He still wouldn't budge. The trial stalled.[69]

The Nixon administration—impatient, angry, increasingly paranoid—did not want to wait. The day after the Pentagon Papers decision, J. Edgar Hoover told Nixon that "we ought to be awful careful what we do in this case of this man Ellsberg" lest the press "make a martyr out of him." "Hoover is not going after this case as strong as I would like," the president complained. (He thought it was because Ellsberg's father-in-law, a wealthy toy manufacturer, was an official friend of the FBI and a frequent contributor to FBI charity drives.) Nixon had been deeply concerned about leaks since he took office and feared that Ellsberg could continue to leak if not put away in prison. He worried, too, about copycat leakers. "If we can't get anyone in this damn government to do something about the problem that may be the most serious one we have, then, by god, we'll do it ourselves," he complained to his staff. "I want you to set up a little group right here in the White House. Have them get off their tails and find out what's going on."[70]

In July a small unit was formed in the White House to "plug leaks of vital national security information." Headed by Egil Krogh, a young White House lawyer, and David Young, a National Security Council staffer, its key men were E. Howard Hunt, a former CIA officer, and G. Gordon Liddy, a former FBI agent. When Young told his mother-in-law that he was part of a small team fixing leaks in the White House, she said it was nice to have a plumber in the family. The Plumbers, soon to be infamous for the Watergate break-in, had been created.[71]

On September 3 the Plumbers committed their first act—they broke into the offices of Ellsberg's psychiatrist. They ransacked the files, seeking material to smear and blackmail Ellsberg and Russo. Nixon, drawing on his experience attacking Alger Hiss in the 1950s, was keen to "try [Ellsberg] in the press": "Just get everything out . . . leak it out. We want to destroy him in the press." Not only would that help with the tricky problem of leakers; it would also be a useful salvo in the culture war the administration was waging on behalf of the Silent Majority. Ellsberg was a "natural villain," observed one internal memo; prosecuting him would "arouse the heartland." Nixon wanted to tie Ellsberg to Communism and the antiwar movement, and he fantasized about turning him over to the House Un-American Activities Committee: "What a marvelous opportunity for the committee. They can really take this and go. . . . Jesus Christ, they'll be hanging from the rafters. . . . Going after all these Jews." The break-in, as Charles Colson put it, was supposed to "put this bastard in one hell of a situation and discredit the New Left." But it didn't turn up anything useful.[72]

In December 1971 the initial indictment of Ellsberg was torn up, and new charges were issued. Confronting fifteen charges of stealing government documents and violating the Espionage Act, Ellsberg now faced 115 years in jail. Russo was charged as a coconspirator. But when the trial began in July 1972, it was delayed as evidence came to light that the government had wiretapped one of the defendants and their lawyer. In December a mistrial was declared and a new jury formed.[73]

So it wasn't until January 1973 that the trial began. And over the next two months, as witness after witness testified, the full extent of the Watergate break-in the previous summer began to come to light. The break-in at Ellsberg's psychiatrist's office was soon uncovered, along with evidence that the White House had placed illegal wiretaps on Halperin's phone, as well as the phones of sixteen other journalists and staffers, when news of the secret bombing of Cambodia was leaked to the *New York Times* in 1969. Those wiretaps had captured conversations between Ellsberg and fellow Pentagon Papers author Halperin. Ellsberg's lawyer, Leonard Boudin, who had made a name defending radicals prosecuted by the security state, moved to have the case dismissed. He had successfully done the same thing when representing Judith Coplon in her espionage trial in the early 1950s.[74]

In light of the extraordinary government misconduct, the judge dismissed the case against Ellsberg and Russo "with prejudice"—which meant that neither man could be indicted on the same charges again. They were free men; cheers broke out in the courtroom. Nixon was apoplectic: "The son-of-a-bitching thief is made a national hero and is going to get off on a mistrial. And the *New York Times* gets a Pulitzer Prize for stealing documents. . . . What in the name of god have we come to?"[75]

When the mistrial was declared, surveys of the jurors found that they were intending to acquit. It just wasn't easy to sell the case that the leak of historical documents almost two years ago had harmed the national interest. It was plain that the republic had not fallen. In fact, the leaks hadn't even hastened the end of the increasingly unpopular war, which was just now beginning to shift to a new phase, with the signing of the Paris Peace Accords.[76]

It is impossible to know what the impact of an acquittal might have been. But there was good reason to think that if the case had reached its natural end, it might have made it clear that the secrecy regime was not fit for purpose. Robert Manning, editor of the *Atlantic Monthly* and a former public-relations official in the State Department, testified that "the entire system of classification is . . . obscure, contradictory and open to a wide variety of interpretations." Meanwhile, leaks were habitual: "If the letter of the regulations was firmly applied, certainly hundreds of public servants could be found to be in persistent violation." An acquittal might have helped undermine the presumption that the Espionage Act could be used to enforce the classification rules, making it far harder to prosecute future leaks to the press. The mistrial meant that the rickety laws of state secrecy weren't really put to the test. The outcome, as Tony Russo declared on the day the charges against him were dismissed, was a "great partial victory."[77]

If anything, the reputation of the Pentagon Papers as a great victory for civil liberties made it even harder to grapple with the legal status of the nation's improvised secrecy regime. Both newspapers and leakers went free. And the public could read classified details of an unpopular war. But however happy that outcome was for the case at hand, it made the letter of the law seem far more liberal than it was. It was less a defeat for the structures of secrecy than a tactical retreat, a moment of crisis avoided.

Over time, we have forgotten how controversial, confusing, and ambiguous the Pentagon Papers case was. It has been turned, like so much US history, into a neat morality tale. Ellsberg is the hero of the story, a wise insider who realized the error of the war and then revealed the truth to the public—and for all its efforts, the government could not stop his act of conscience.

Ellsberg has become the textbook instance of the noble whistleblower—the "right" kind of leaker, a truth teller, a true patriot. Subsequent leakers are forced to measure up to this image and are often found wanting. In the *New Yorker* in 2016, for instance, Malcolm Gladwell compared Edward Snowden, unfavorably, to Ellsberg: "Snowden did not study under a Nobel prize winner, or give career advice to the likes of Henry Kissinger. He was a community college dropout, a member of the murky hacking counterculture." Ellsberg was an elite insider, to be trusted; Snowden was not.[78]

Yet such a story entirely misrepresents Ellsberg's arc. His was not a lone act of conscience. His decision to leak the papers was forged by engagement with the collective politics of the antiwar movement—his conversations with Natarjan, his experience at War Resisters International, his relationship with Patricia Marx, the help he received from Tony Russo and Gar Alperovitz and the rest of the Lavender Hill mob.

And when he acted in solidarity with that movement, he was greeted not as a wise insider acting out of conscience but as a radical narcissist connected to the worst excesses of the Left. Barry Goldwater criticized his "conceited arrogance": "Here is a college professor who casually places his judgment above that of all the fficials in the executive branch." The *Arizona Republican* compared Ellsberg to the Berrigan brothers, Angela Davis, Eldridge Cleaver, and "assorted criminals and misfits who believe that their commitment to leftist orthodoxy justifies any illegal attack." "What is it," asked the *Chicago Tribune*, "that deludes so many well-meaning American liberals into treating these people as heroes?" *Rolling Stone* called Ellsberg "vain, egocentric"; *Newsweek* thought he had a "martyr complex" and was on an "Ego trip." Kissinger called him "unbalanced," a fanatic, a drug abuser, a sexual pervert, and the "most dangerous man in America." Hence the effort to break into Ellsberg's psychiatrist's office to further discredit him in the public eye.[79]

To forget these dynamics is to strip all the politics from the story. What was at stake in the Pentagon Papers was not a polite dispute about policy. It was a fundamental clash between two cultures: an imperialist security apparatus waging violent war and an antiwar movement committed to stopping it.

And the comforting, nostalgic version of the Pentagon Papers myth even more dramatically misrepresents the legal history of the case. Far from securing Ellsberg's right to dissent, the law heavily favored the secretive security apparatus. No leakers went to jail, and the press won its case at the Supreme Court, but these were superficial victories. The press confirmed that it had the right to publish state secrets without prior injunction. But it was still unclear if the state had the right to criminally prosecute journalists for that act. As for the leakers, their liability for providing information to the press seemed as great as ever.[80]

In the aftermath of the Pentagon Papers case, this uneasy state of affairs was embraced as proof of the great vitality of American democracy. In 1975 Bickel, who had represented the *Times* before the Supreme Court, developed the most theoretically sophisticated justification for the status quo. Democracies, he asserted, needed both secrecy (to ensure security) and transparency (to preserve democracy). But how to balance these competing interests? In a Solomonic moment, Bickel argued that the government had to have the right to withhold information at the source but that the press also had to have the right to publish secret information if it could get its hands on it. ("If we should let the government censor as well as withhold, that would be too much dangerous power. . . . If we should allow the government neither to censor nor to withhold, that would provide . . . too much power in the press and in Congress.") In this highly abstract fashion, Bickel turned the problem of public knowledge over to the rough-and-tumble of competition between the press and the executive branch. It was a procedural fix for a normative problem.[81]

Appropriately enough, given the role of the RAND Corporation in the Pentagon Papers affair, Bickel called this the "game theory of the First Amendment." He thought that the permissive ambiguity of the secrecy laws created space for the sort of self-righting process so beloved by liberal theorists.

As would soon become clear, the game was rigged for the security state.

Chapter 9

LONG LIVE THE
SECRECY STATE

Dick Cheney, Gerald Ford's chief of staff, in dialogue with another member of the
Ford administration at the White House, September 30, 1976. Cheney helped the
administration manage fallout from revelations about abuses by the security state.
Ever after, he would be a champion of presidential secrecy. (Library of Congress, photograph by Marion S. Trikosko)

J ust before Christmas, 1974, the Sunday edition of the *New York Times* published a blockbuster scoop: the CIA had been secretly surveilling the antiwar movement. That weekend, President Gerald Ford was on a skiing trip in Colorado. His chief of staff, Donald Rumsfeld, was with him. So the task of coordinating the White House response fell to Rumsfeld's thirty-three-year-old assistant, Dick Cheney.[1]

In the short term, Cheney's efforts to limit the fallout from the revelations failed. The CIA disclosures triggered so many government hearings, so many leaks, so many investigations into the abuses of the security state that the *Times* dubbed 1975 the "Year of Intelligence." Decades of state secrets spilled out, revealing security agencies involved in coups and wiretapping and assassinations. It was an unparalleled legitimacy crisis for the secrecy regime. "The heyday of the national security state," observed the *Nation*, "appears to be over."[2]

In the years to come, however, Cheney and a tight cluster of conservatives managed to defuse the crisis. Reforms were enacted—the Freedom of Information Act, the creation of new intelligence-oversight committees—but these turned out to be astonishingly timid, carving out only narrow channels of disclosure. There was no reform of the classification system, no effort to limit the reach of the Espionage Act.

Even so, the lesson that Cheney and his allies took from the Year of Intelligence was that there was too much transparency, that the presidency had become overly constrained by Congress and by public opinion. They wanted to restore the president's power to act in secret but had little faith that the Espionage Act was up to the task. In the years after 1975, they therefore pioneered a series of new techniques and laws to secure secrets.

By the Reagan years, the nation's secrecy regime had grown yet more elaborate and robust. Not even the scandal of Iran-Contra could dent it. In fact, the only meaningful reform effort came in the 1990s, when a congressional commission on secrecy proposed major changes to the classification system. But by then it was too late: the reform impulse had faded, and little came of the commission's sensible recommendations.

In 2001, when Cheney returned to the White House as George W. Bush's vice president, he would find the Espionage Act waiting for him, its power undimmed in its ninth decade of life.

If you squinted hard enough at the Year of Intelligence, you might be able to see it as proof of the "game theory" of the First Amendment that had been articulated after the Pentagon Papers decision. According to that theory, the US public was supposed to rely on principled government leakers to inform them about the misdeeds of the security state.

The antiwar movement *had* mobilized some CIA equivalents to Daniel Ellsberg. *Ramparts*, a left-leaning Catholic magazine, published insider exposés of a secret Michigan State University program to train a Vietnamese paramilitary squad, of secret CIA funding of the National Student Association, of the secret wiretapping being conducted by the other NSA: the National Security Agency. There were also a handful of ex–CIA officers who began publishing critical memoirs about their clandestine activities.[3] But given what the CIA had been up to, there were far fewer whistleblowers than one might expect—or that democratic theory required.

And the CIA turned out to be unusually prone to leaks. J. Edgar Hoover's FBI, by contrast, was watertight.

In his fifth decade in charge of the Bureau, Hoover had built a culture of absolute deference and loyalty. Agents were recruited according to exacting, if idiosyncratic, standards designed to ensure homogeneity: those with "pear-shaped heads" were nonstarters; the "male, Yale and pale" employees of the CIA snottily joked that FBI agents were all "Fordham Bronx Irish." (The first female agent wouldn't be hired until 1972, a few months after Hoover died.) Once hired, Bureau agents were, like minor-league baseball prospects, rotated through short-term assignments in far-flung field offices, which meant they could not easily develop cultural networks independent of the Bureau. Even then they were monitored closely, every sign of deviance policed carefully. For the rest of their careers, agents would be routinely weighed. They could be fired for putting on too many pounds.[4]

Hoover's FBI showed that it was possible to build an organizational culture that would not leak, in which employees would stay loyal to their bureaucracies even when that bureaucracy was undeniably engaged in wrongdoing. It showed that you could not rely on leakers as a check on governmental abuse.

For the FBI of the late 1960s was certainly doing deeds that ought to have inspired the Bureau equivalent of an Ellsberg. These were the years of the infamous COINTELPRO program, a secret "counterintelligence" effort to "expose, disrupt, misdirect, discredit, or otherwise neutralize" all those whom the FBI took to be subversives. It was a sweeping program, involving hundreds of illegal acts of monitoring and surveillance. Agents broke into the headquarters and homes of civil-rights and antiwar activists. They swarmed the Haverford meeting of War Resisters International at which Ellsberg had his 1969 breakdown. At nearby Swarthmore, every Black student was being surveilled by the FBI.[5]

Efforts to infiltrate and undermine radical social movements were crude but nevertheless effective. Prostitutes with sexually transmitted diseases were hired to sleep with antiwar leaders; oranges injected with laxatives were circulated before protests. FBI agents used their control over communications networks to sow disruption and doubt within the civil-rights and Black power movements. Martin Luther King Jr. was pressured and harassed with the threat that illegally obtained recordings revealing his infidelity would be made public; the FBI provided Chicago police with the map of Black Panther headquarters that was used to assassinate Fred Hampton.[6]

This was all the subject of open rumor among the New Left, which knew it was being surveilled and harassed. "Want to find the agents in any room?" advised Bill Ayers of the Weather Underground: "Look at their shoes." The ubiquity of the wingtips mandated by Hoover was more than a tell. It revealed the still-intact cultural loyalty of the FBI. Nothing about COINTELPRO leaked to the press.[7]

The public began to learn about it only because of one of the most effective acts of civil disobedience in the nation's history. In 1971 eight antiwar activists broke into a small FBI office in a Pennsylvania town called, of all things, Media. They had been organized by William Davidon, a physics professor at Haverford College who was deeply involved with the Catholic antiwar movement. Inspired by earlier efforts to steal draft cards, they called themselves the Citizens Committee to Investigate the FBI and planned to steal documents that would prove FBI malfeasance. They spent months casing the nondescript downtown office building, long nights drafting getaway plans. They practiced lock picking in the attic of John and Bonnie Raines's comfortably middle-class home in suburban Philadelphia. John and Bonnie made plans for their in-laws to raise their three young children if they went to jail.

The burglary was timed to take place while neighbors and potential witnesses were distracted by the broadcast of the Ali-Frazier "Fight of the Century," and it went off without a hitch. Despite frantic investigations, none of the eight were ever arrested. Hoover, panicked, closed 103 FBI offices and ramped up security at the remainder. And when the burglars began reviewing the documents at their hideout, a Quaker conference center just outside Philadelphia, they realized they had hit pay dirt. The files that they stole provided proof that the FBI was engaged in illegal surveillance. One of the documents even contained the code word COINTELPRO, the first time that name had been seen outside of the FBI.[8]

Ellsberg, dissident CIA vets, professors robbing FBI offices—the repercussions of the antiwar movement were starting to shake loose some of the secrets of the security state. But it had taken an astonishing political mobilization against a deeply unpopular war; leaks alone had been insufficient. And none of it was enough to produce the legitimacy crisis of the Year of Intelligence.

That was a consequence of institutional dynamics triggered by another unusual and even more unlikely break-in: at the Watergate Hotel in June 1972, when the Nixon presidential campaign broke into Democratic Party headquarters to install secret wiretaps. It wasn't just that the Watergate affair further undermined American trust in all state institutions. (But it certainly did that: by 1974, 62 percent of Americans distrusted their government, up from 22 percent a decade earlier.[9]) It was that the CIA and FBI were directly implicated in the dirty business. The Plumbers arrested in the Watergate had connections to the CIA, as did Howard Hunt, who had previously orchestrated the burglary of Ellsberg's psychiatrist's office—a break-in, it turned out, aided by cameras, fake IDs, and disguises that Hunt had borrowed from the CIA. Richard Nixon then tried to cover up Watergate by telling the CIA to tell the FBI to lay off the investigation in the interests of national security: recordings of his instructions to that effect were the "smoking gun" that forced him out of office. "I see now," reflected head Plumber Egil Krogh ruefully as he went to jail, "that the key is the effect that the term 'national security' had on my judgment. The very word seemed to block critical analysis."[10]

Recently installed CIA director James Schlesinger was as shocked as anyone to learn of his agency's role in Watergate. To avoid any future surprises, he issued a directive to his staff to report all activities that might have been illegal or questionable. The document tallying up the responses ended up running to 693 pages. It became known as the Family Jewels.[11]

Amid the institutional chaos—Schlesinger was also laying off some 7 percent of the agency's personnel—the document soon leaked to Seymour Hersh, perhaps the leading antiwar journalist in the country. An investigative journalist of the old school, Hersh had no patience with cant—"I'm a bitchy sort of kvetch," he admitted—as well as an indefatigable work ethic and a skill at gaining the trust of disgruntled officials within the defense sector. As a freelancer, he had uncovered the My Lai massacre and exposed, in *Ramparts*, the details of America's experimentation with chemical and biological weapons.[12]

With the Family Jewels, Hersh had delivered a winner for the *Times*. On December 22, the prime position on the front page was devoted to a seven-thousand-word story that the CIA had "conducted a massive, illegal domestic intelligence operation . . . against the antiwar movement and other dissident groups in the U.S." It was the first of thirty-two stories on the CIA that the *Times* would run in the next three weeks.[13]

Five days later, Dick Cheney wrote the memo that outlined the White House's strategy for damage control. Congress would want to investigate, Cheney noted, and the ensuing "debate will take place within the context of Watergate [and] the Ellsberg case." It was therefore not enough to work out whether the CIA had broken the law or to adopt safeguards to prevent future problems. It was equally important to "protect CIA from overreaction by Congress," which could both impair the CIA's ability to function and amount to a "serious legislative encroachment on executive power."[14]

Of itself, this was hardly a surprising way for a young White House staffer to game out the crisis at hand. But the memo also encapsulated ideas about presidential power that Cheney would hold for the rest of his long political career and that would make him a great champion of the secrecy regime.

Why Cheney was so committed to the power of the presidency is something of a mystery. Nothing in his early life foreshadowed it. Indeed, his meteoric political rise seemed defined by the absence of any driving ideological commitments. Raised in Wyoming, he had received a scholarship to Yale because his girlfriend, Lynne, had impressed her boss, a Yale grad working at a Casper-based oil company. Yale wasn't yet accepting women, so the oilman pulled the old-boy strings for Dick instead. Dick partied too hard in New Haven and was asked to leave after three semesters. He had more academic success back in Wyoming, then got himself accepted to graduate school at the University of Wisconsin, which was one of the epicenters of the antiwar movement. Cheney casually disapproved of the protests he saw on the way to class—they were "an aggravation"—but betrayed no great commitment to the war either, seeking and receiving multiple draft deferments. When questioned about them during his later confirmation as defense secretary, Cheney explained, truthfully, that "I had other priorities in the '60s than military service."[15]

First among them was making a career as a political staffer. Cheney quit his PhD program to take up a job as a congressional aide, where he caught the eye of Rumsfeld, then a hotshot conservative congressman from Illinois. It was the forging of a fateful political partnership. When Rumsfeld moved into the Nixon administration, to run the antipoverty Office of Equal Opportunity, he took Cheney with him. In the rancorous, paranoid Nixon White House, Cheney received an education in the arts of executive power and the benefits of discretion. "Don and I survived and prospered in that environment," he later recalled, "because we didn't leave a lot of paper laying around." He still had no particular ideological agenda. But his run of good fortune continued. He avoided the Watergate minefield that ensnared so much of the Republican political elite—he had nearly joined the Committee to Reelect the President but ultimately declined the opportunity. When Rumsfeld left the White House in 1972, so did Cheney. That meant that in 1974, when Gerald Ford was looking to put together an untainted staff, he could call Rumsfeld back from the political wilderness to serve as his chief of staff. Cheney picked Rumsfeld up at the airport in Washington and followed him back into the White House.[16]

It was the experience of working for the beleaguered Ford presidency that shaped the convictions that drove the rest of Cheney's career. The political atmosphere, he later recalled, was "grim. One participant at the time said that no matter what problems or crises lay ahead . . . nothing could be as perilous as the collapse of executive authority. That fact defines the period. . . . The ability of the president to fulfill his responsibilities was being eroded by the congressional assertion and usurpation of presidential power."[17]

This was, of course, a highly ideological interpretation of the political issues involved and of the structure of the US Constitution.

Cheney never really sought to justify it philosophically; he was interested in wielding political power more than theorizing it. In later years he would sometimes seek to buttress his view of presidential power by selectively quoting from the Federalist Papers, but his attitudes seemed to stem more from a preexisting set of assumptions about the way the world worked. The international climate was "dangerous and hostile," which meant that the United States had to be able to act decisively to protect itself; there wasn't always the time to consult with Congress. Moreover, Congress was hardly a responsible, trustworthy steward of the national interest: it "was all too often swayed by the public opinion of the moment." This was the same logic that for generations had led national-security hawks to prefer acting in secret. Indeed, it was telling that the need for "secrecy" was one of the key justifications for Cheney's expansive vision of the presidency.[18]

This desire to protect the president's powers guided Cheney's response to Hersh's wiretapping revelations, as it would guide his politics for decades to come. In his Christmas memo, Cheney recommended appointing a presidential commission, stacked with sympathetic members, to investigate the alleged abuses and thus "head off congressional efforts to further encroach on the Executive Branch." Ford agreed.[19]

But Congress wasn't placated by the attempted whitewash. Both houses of Congress soon established their own committees to investigate the shadowy world of the intelligence community. The Senate's Church Committee held 126 meetings over the next fifteen months, interviewing 800 witnesses and reviewing 110,000 documents before issuing a six-volume report that ran to almost 2,700 pages. Another fifty-four public hearings were held by the House's Pike Committee. CIA director Bill Colby alone testified to Congress thirty-seven times from March to June.[20]

By the end of 1975, the public had received a crash course about all the things that the secretive security state had been up to since World War II. Individually, the revelations were shocking. Taken together, they suggested that something had gone very wrong in America.

There was illegal surveillance of staggering proportions. At the New York post office, the CIA had monitored some 28 million letters, taken photographs of 2.7 million envelopes ("metadata," in today's parlance), and steamed open more than 200,000. The information was used particularly by the FBI, which had opened investigations on half a million Americans in the previous fifteen years, simply because it distrusted their politics. The NSA, about which nothing was previously known, was discovered to be collecting vast quantities of telegrams leaving the country and eavesdropping on the phone calls of Americans who had been placed on a watch list. And if that all seemed a little colorless, the existence of the CIA's LSD experiments also came to light for the first time.[21]

The scale of CIA meddling overseas was equally shocking. Since 1961, the Church Committee reported, the CIA had "conducted some 900 major or sensitive covert actions plus several thousand smaller projects." Political and media coverage fixated on the lurid details of assassination plots: the poison, rubber gloves, and syringe sent by diplomatic pouch to CIA operatives in the Congo to assassinate Patrice Lumumba (Belgian-backed assassins got to him first), a sequence of plots to assassinate Fidel Castro with poison-laced scuba suits, or exploding seashells, or poisonous cigars. But more important was evidence of the hand of the CIA in destabilizing so many nations. The recent funneling of support to antidemocratic forces in Chile in the lead-up to General Augusto Pinochet's coup—one more example of chaotic, freewheeling, clumsy interventionism—was a particular focus.[22]

It all added up to an unparalleled legitimacy crisis. A decade earlier, 84 percent of Americans had a "highly favorable" view of the FBI. Now it was 37 percent. Only 14 percent of Americans approved of the CIA; bills to permanently ban covert operations were introduced in Congress. And the secrecy regime that had been slowly constructed over previous decades was directly implicated. "Abuse," concluded the Church Committee in its final report, "thrives on secrecy."[23]

Yet the secrecy regime would survive the crisis. If anything, it would only grow stronger.

Even in the midst of 1975, Cheney and his allies in the Ford administration were fighting tooth and nail to maintain control over information and shore up the credibility of the security state. They challenged congressional subpoenas, treating information turned over to the committees as the extension of a revocable privilege.

It was a formative experience for a small network of Republicans who would dominate the nation's politics for the next three decades. Rumsfeld and Cheney were at the center of things; so was a young Antonin Scalia, then working for the Office of Legal Counsel. In November 1975, in what became known as the Halloween Massacre, Ford reshuffled the security positions in his cabinet in an effort to prove his conservative bona fides. Bill Colby was out as CIA director—he had spoken too truthfully to Congress. He was replaced by George H. W. Bush, who was prepared for congressional hearings by a young William Barr, fresh from a stint as a CIA lawyer. Brent Scowcroft became national security advisor, and Rumsfeld became defense secretary. Cheney was promoted to chief of staff.[24]

Control over classified information became a central political project of this conservative phalanx, keen to preserve the power of the presidency over foreign policy. "The irresponsible release of classified information by people who should know better must cease," declared Ford as he swore in his new CIA director. "George Bush shares my commitment to these principles." So did Ford's new chief of staff. By 1976, a colleague in the White House later recalled, Cheney's "sensitivity over news leaks rose almost to the paranoid level."[25]

These Republican champions of secrecy were gifted a cause célèbre when CIA officer Richard Welch was assassinated outside of his home in Athens, Greece, in the midst of the season of congressional inquiries. Most commentators pointed the finger at *Counterspy*, a magazine funded by Norman Mailer, who wanted to establish a "people's FBI, and a people's CIA" that would provide intelligence to the public about the secretive organizations. In a recent series of articles, rogue ex–CIA officer Phillip Agee had been outing undercover CIA officers, such as Welch, by cross-checking the list of employees at embassies with State Department employee lists. The assassinated spy was offered to the public as a martyr of feckless transparency: his funeral shown live on television, Ford in attendance; his body carried to its burial site in Arlington Cemetery on the same buggy that had carried JFK's to his grave. Only later would a government investigation clear *Counterspy* of responsibility for the death—Welch's name had already been published, and in an act of stunningly poor operational security, he had moved into the same home that previous CIA officers had occupied in the troubled and violent Greek capital. Such details could not muddy the simpler story being pushed by secrecy hawks. The public was not concerned about intelligence abuses, argued Strom Thurmond during Bush's confirmation hearings, but about "disclosures which are tearing down the CIA."[26]

In this context an internally divided Pike Committee decided it had the authority to release its final report, including classified information, without getting the approval of the White House. It was a delicate, controversial political question about interbranch relations, about the control of information, about the public's right to know. But the White House offensive on the need for secrecy had shifted the political atmosphere. The Pike Committee needed an extension on its deadline to report; the House Rules Committee voted 9–7 to grant the extension only if the White House was given the opportunity to approve the report and to request redactions. Otis Pike argued that the president alone should not have the power to declare something secret. "A secret," he had learned, was nothing more than "a fact or opinion to which some bureaucrat has applied a rubber stamp." When Pike would not accede to the demand that the White House be allowed to review the report, the House voted to suppress it. A report into the abuses of state secrecy was now itself secret.[27]

As the suppression of the Pike Report revealed, there was no congressional counterweight to the focused efforts of the secrecy hawks clustered around Cheney. The Democrats, who did not hold the White House, were the natural agents for reforming the system.

And they held large majorities in both houses of Congress. Yet for a variety of reasons, they had little appetite for taking on either the security state or the secrecy regime.

The Democrats had always had a fraught relationship with the Left, particularly on questions of foreign policy. A key lesson taken from the 1972 presidential election, in which George McGovern had lost so badly to Richard Nixon, was that the country had little appetite for even a flirtation with the antiwar movement. Moreover, grappling seriously with the abuses of Cold War foreign policy would have required grappling with the legacies of the Kennedy and Johnson administrations—undesirable both for older politicians who saw the 1960s as their salad days and for younger aspirants seeking to claim both the approval of the party establishment and the mantle of past glories.

Meanwhile, the party's leading geopolitical critics may have had their complaints about the war in Southeast Asia, but they were equally worried about the decline of US power. America, J. William Fulbright feared, was being torn apart by an "inquisition psychology." The revelations about the CIA were "not the kind of truths we most need now; these are truths which must injure if not kill the nation."[28] And the party's swollen junior ranks, the so-called Watergate Babies, had won elections before the intelligence abuses had come to light. They had their broader suspicions of government and a desire for a more involved Congress, but they were hardly antiwar radicals—in fact, many had won in normally Republican seats, benefiting from a quite specific backlash to Nixon. Their key issues were domestic reform, not foreign policy. And domestic politics, amid the rancorous backlash to civil-rights successes and the economic shocks of stagflation, cut in all sorts of complicated ways.[29]

There was neither a large party constituency nor an obvious opening in the political culture for a serious challenge to decades-old pieties about national security. In fact, much of the party was seeking to distance itself from the antiwar Left to make a play for centrist credibility. That might have been smart politics. When Frank Church took the helm of his investigative committee, he was a rising star, with an eye on the White House. But he lost his next election, swept away by the Reagan Revolution.[30]

After 1975, the political agenda was set not by advocates for transparency but by an increasingly pugnacious conservative movement keen to protect secrets. In fact, the only congressional efforts to reform the Espionage Act would have made it tougher: expanding the definition of "information relating to the national defense," lowering the intent requirements, and explicitly covering newspapers. Had the law passed, Hersh's revelations of My Lai and CIA surveillance would both have been illegal. Under press protest, the proposed revisions were quickly dropped.[31]

The only meaningful transparency reform of the period was the passage of a new Freedom of Information Act (FOIA). It had been passed in 1974, *before* the Year of Intelligence, and was itself an amendment to the first Freedom of Information Act (1966). In many ways the 1966 FOIA was an astonishing piece of liberal reform. The product of years of slow campaigning by a network of journalists, scientists, and politicians seeking to make the government more transparent, the FOIA allowed anyone, citizen and noncitizen alike, to petition the government for the release of records and to go to court to force their disclosure if they were denied.[32]

But in the field of national security, it had a fatal flaw. The law had nine exemptions listing nine types of information that could not be requested under the act. The first was information that was classified by the executive branch in the interests of national defense or foreign policy. "None of us," explained one of the most important advocates of the law, journalist James S. Pope, "wants security information—genuine security information—revealed."[33]

In theory, this was an understandable concession—not only a piece of shrewd politics but also entirely defensible on philosophical grounds. The problem was that the logic of the FOIA assumed that the actually existing classification system covered only "genuine security information." Not only did the exemption defang the FOIA in the realm of the security state; it also meant that the *Freedom of Information* Act, of all acts, was the first time that Congress conceded the legitimacy of the classification system that Harry Truman had unilaterally created fifteen years before.

As a result, the FOIA made little difference in the great national-security scandals of its early years—it played no role in the Pentagon Papers or in Watergate, did nothing to minimize CIA adventurism or the secret bombing of Cambodia. There was only one important exception. After reading the FBI documents stolen by the Media activists, Carl Stern, a legal-affairs reporter at NBC, filed an FOIA request for the release of all documents relating to COINTELPRO. The case revealed the persistence and fortune needed to successfully pry loose national-security secrets. For ten months in 1972, Stern asked the FBI time and again for the documents; each time, the Bureau declined. In 1973 he sued, and nine months later the judge ruled in his favor. Surprisingly, Acting Attorney General Robert Bork decided not to appeal—amid the fallout from Watergate, it was perhaps one fight too many. COINTELPRO documents were released; the world learned what the FBI had been up to. It was a sign of what the FOIA could do when judges refused to defer to the security branches.[34]

But another case unfolding simultaneously was more typical. In 1971 thirty-three congressional representatives, headed by Patsy Mink, the Japanese American representative from Hawaii, sued for the release of information about underground nuclear testing in Alaska. The government declined, citing the national-security exemption, and won in court. In 1973 the Supreme Court upheld the decision, ruling that judges could not question classification decisions. Even if the decision to classify was "cynical, myopic or even corrupt," the court said, classified material was exempt from the FOIA.[35]

It was an invitation to revise the law, and in 1974 Congress amended the FOIA to explicitly allow judges to review classification decisions and force the release of improperly classified information. But the Ford White House was deeply opposed to the change, and Congress, worried about a veto, flinched at the last moment, advising courts to "accord substantial weight" to executive claims for secrecy. (This concession was neither philosophically defensible nor politically savvy—Ford vetoed the amendment anyway, and Congress had the votes to override.) Thereafter, courts have been remarkably deferential to expansive executive branch claims that disclosure would harm the national security. The role of the courts has not been to balance the public right to know against the need for classification. Rather, it has been to determine whether the classification procedures were adequately followed.

Indeed, representatives of the security state were soon making two new sorts of claims that exerted great influence on the courts in FOIA cases. In what was known as the "mosaic theory," they argued that even apparently innocuous pieces of information might, in the hands of shrewd enemies, be arranged to reveal something damaging. On this logic, almost nothing could be disclosed: anything could be valuable to those who knew how to use it. Judges, on the outside of the intelligence community, were poorly positioned to dismiss such claims.[36]

Going one step further, the executive branch also began arguing that some things were so sensitive that their very existence could be neither confirmed nor denied—let alone reviewed by judges. This became known as the "Glomar response," after the 1975 case in which it was first used. The *Glomar Explorer* was an experimental deep-sea salvage vessel, built by the Howard Hughes company on a $350 million contract from the CIA. It was designed to raise a sunken Soviet submarine from the floor of the Pacific Ocean, but it didn't really work—as with an arcade claw machine, most of the sub had slipped out of the *Glomar*'s grasp. News of the *Glomar* leaked out to journalists, including Hersh, but the CIA convinced the press to sit on it in the interests of national security. Finally, Jack Anderson, Drew Pearson's old partner from the Nickerson leak, got word and ran stories that called the whole thing a boondoggle. The US taxpayer had paid hundreds of millions of dollars, run the risk of antagonizing the Soviets, and received in return only some outdated codebooks and the remains of some Soviet submariners. Two journalists then applied under the FOIA to get all the

CIA documents about the project, including information about the CIA's efforts to quash the story. The CIA replied that it wasn't even going to respond. To claim an FOIA exemption, it said, would itself confirm the existence of the program, which would spill vital secrets. The court approved, and although the government did concede the existence of the *Glomar* project shortly thereafter, it would be another thirty-five years before the CIA began releasing documents about it (themselves heavily redacted). By then, the FBI, the Justice Department, the State Department, the Marshals Service, and the Customs Service were all using the Glomar response to neither confirm nor deny that they had records that could be requested.[37]

The FOIA, the most meaningful piece of transparency reform in the nation's history, thus failed to directly challenge the logic of national-security secrecy. It left the core of the secrecy regime— the Espionage Act and the classification system—intact. It did not place requirements on government to actively disclose information. It settled for creating an additional, ancillary mechanism for individuals to extract individual pieces of information from what was presumed to be a secretive state. It was a reactive, deferential form of transparency.

The reforms that followed 1975 bent even further to the presumption that the executive branch held secrets that the public could not be trusted to learn. The preferred fix was to create new institutions *within* the secret state that were supposed to check and monitor the security agencies and thus prevent abuses. To prevent warrantless surveillance of citizens by the FBI and the NSA, Congress passed the Foreign Intelligence Surveillance Act (FISA), which established a secret foreign intelligence surveillance court to provide the warrants. The legislation had been drawn up by Cheney and his allies in the Ford White House as a way to ward off more radical reform, and it worked. The FISA court, operating in secret, wouldn't decline an application for a wiretap for the next twenty-five years.[38]

CIA reform had a similar arc. In 1974, in an effort to prevent secret CIA adventurism, Congress passed a new rule that required the CIA to receive presidential approval for covert operations and to inform six congressional committees of them in a "timely" fashion—a number that was expanded to eight following the creation of permanent intelligence committees in the Senate in 1976 and the House in 1977. That was all a stopgap. The permanent solution was supposed to be the creation of a comprehensive, legislative charter, in which Congress would set clear guidelines around what the CIA could and could not do, and give itself powers to enforce them. In the late 1970s a 263-page charter for the intelligence community was drawn up.

But that vision of reform ran into powerful opposition, not merely from the intelligence community but also from its allies in Congress and, increasingly, in the Carter White House, which had come to a renewed appreciation of the security apparatus as it sought to navigate the Iranian Revolution and the Soviet invasion of Afghanistan. Instead of a comprehensive charter, in 1980 Congress passed a two-page Intelligence Oversight Act. It reduced the number of oversight committees from eight to two. (The CIA complained that reporting to eight committees created too many risks that congressional staffers would leak secrets.) And although it did require that those oversight committees be given advance notice of any covert operations, it ultimately included an important exception. In 1980, when the Carter administration had made its disastrous effort to rescue hostages held in Iran—the helicopters crashed in desert storms—it had proposed a new workaround: when the president thought that covert operations were sufficiently sensitive, the only people who needed to be briefed were the senior party leaders of both chambers and both intelligence committees, the so-called Gang of Eight. The 1980 law formalized this exception and brought to an end the window of reform that had opened in 1975.[39]

Thereafter, although congressional committees did play a new role in overseeing the intelligence community, they proved an uneven and inadequate check on secrecy. They were entirely dependent on the executive branch to provide them with information—they did not know what they did not know. ("We are like mushrooms," joked one member of the House Intelligence Committee. "The CIA "keep[s] us in the dark and feed[s] us a lot of manure.") There were few political incentives for any member of Congress to speak out strongly against the intelligence community. And many members of the intelligence committees liked getting the inside access, liked proving themselves as "responsible" as their peers in the executive branch. They installed secure rooms in the bowels of the Congress in which they could be briefed without fear of eavesdroppers and worked to inculcate cozy relationships with legislative liaisons from within the security state.[40]

Although the oversight committees added more checks on the security branches, ones that formally reside outside of the executive branch, it would be a mistake to see these changes as increasing transparency. They did not increase the flow of information to the public. Rather, they incorporated a piece of the legislature into the veiled wing of the state. "Members of the committee," said one staffer, "see themselves as being inside the circle." "Keeping secrets," added another, "was the *sine qua non* for this Committee."[41]

At the same time that they blunted transparency reforms, the champions of secrecy also sought new laws to overcome what they took to be the inadequacies of the Espionage Act.

For instance, an effort to prosecute ex–CIA officer Agee for his program of outing CIA officers collapsed amid uncertainties about the scope of the 1917 law. In 1977 Agee's lawyers cut a deal with the Justice Department that he would not be prosecuted under the Espionage Act if he would stay out of the United States. In lieu of prosecution, the US government had to content itself with canceling Agee's passport. "Of course we're upset," said a CIA spokesperson. "We don't have laws to prevent people from disclosing classified information." In 1982 an Intelligence Identities Protection Act was passed to make it illegal to disclose the names of intelligence officers: one more patch to the old law.[42]

Nor was Agee's the only failed Espionage Act prosecution of the period. In May 1975 Cheney had called for the prosecution of Hersh for a story revealing that the United States was secretly deploying submarines deep into Soviet waters to tap underground communication cables—a violation of the sovereignty of the USSR and a dangerous provocation. By making an example of Hersh, Cheney hoped to prevent future leaks and also to "create an environment" that would "bolster" the White House's efforts to keep information out of the hands of congressional investigative committees. But he got pushback from Attorney General Edward Levi, who explained that the prospects of an Espionage Act conviction were weak. The law was not intended to prosecute journalists, Levi explained. And there wasn't, it turned out, all that much new in Hersh's story. In any case, the Soviets had not responded to it, so the submarine operations had continued. Prosecuting now would require both confirming that the program existed and that it was classified. Better to let the story die, to maintain plausible deniability, than to "put the official stamp of truth on the article."[43]

And then there was the case of the Pike Report, in theory suppressed by the House but soon leaked to journalist Dan Schorr, who published major portions in the *Village Voice*. An effort to prosecute Schorr also collapsed after a six-month DOJ investigation. The material in the report, even if once classified, had entered the public domain by the time of the leak. A House ethics investigation that sought to identify Schorr's source also collapsed; he refused to cooperate, and a supportive petition signed by five thousand journalists led the congressional committee to back down from a contempt citation.[44]

In 1977 newly elected senator Joe Biden chaired a yearlong Senate Subcommittee on Secrecy and Disclosure that set out to understand why the government had so spectacularly failed to prosecute leaks. There were plenty of people who wanted to blame the Espionage Act: CIA director Stansfield Turner thought the sixty-year-old law was "not very effective"; his general counsel, Anthony Lapham, dismissed it as "so vague and opaque as to be virtually worthless."

Biden also thought that the Espionage Act was "a good deal less useful today than it was in 1917," but his committee focused on the procedural problems that were preventing the Justice Department from pursuing leak prosecutions: the unwillingness to turn classified information over to judges or juries and the fear of confirming the accuracy of stolen secrets. Biden's committee therefore proposed an omnibus bill that would create complex new mechanisms to guide the handling of classified evidence in criminal trials, intending to make it easier for leaks—and other crimes committed by those in the secret state—to be prosecuted. Four decades after the *Gorin* court had first called for similar legislation in 1941, Congress finally enacted the Classified Information Procedures Act in 1980.[45]

By the early 1980s, the perceived inadequacies of the Espionage Act had thus led to yet another flurry of legislative fixes, layering new laws on top of old problems. There was the FOIA regime and its mandated exemptions, then the Classified Information Procedures Act of 1980, and then the Intelligence Identities Protection Act of 1982. Amid a fear of hackers, sparked in no small part by the 1983 Hollywood film *War Games*, the Computer Fraud and Abuse Act was soon added to the mix, one clause of which made it illegal to use a computer to access classified information without authorization—a cybersecurity update on the Espionage Act's old list of banned places.[46]

Those seeking to secure secrets in the future would have a variety of legal tools to choose from.

Yet the period's most important addition to the secrecy regime was a piece of administrative reform that was unilaterally implemented by the executive branch. To end the spate of critical books by former officers, the CIA began to insist on a right to review materials before publication to ensure that no "sources or methods" would be revealed. The former officers claimed, fairly, that this was prior restraint and thus a violation of their First Amendment rights. Had the standards of the Pentagon Papers decision applied, the CIA would have needed to show that publication would "inevitably, directly and immediately" cause a serious harm before insisting on such an extreme form of censorship. But those were not the standards that the courts applied because they treated the cases as matters of contract law, ruling that the CIA had a right to enforce the secrecy agreements that it made its employees sign. It was the logical culmination of the truncated vision of employee-speech rights articulated by Oliver Wendell Holmes many years before, now updated for the spy age: one had no right to be a CIA officer; ergo, one had no right to speak about what one learned by virtue of employment as a CIA officer.[47]

The problem was that prepublication review gave the CIA incredible power to censor political speech even if it involved information that did not need to be classified. In 1972 Victor Marchetti was the first ex-officer subject to the new technique. The CIA said he had to cut 20 percent of his book manuscript. The 339-item list included the innocuous (descriptions of the lavish furnishings of the office of CIA director John McCone), the plainly political (Henry Kissinger's declaration that Chile would not be allowed to go Communist just because of the "irresponsibility of its own people"), and the absurd (plans to eavesdrop on conversations by training cats surgically enhanced with bugging devices). Marchetti called the agency's bluff. When they went back to court, the CIA blinked, and it sought the redaction of only 168 passages. The judge ultimately concluded that only 27 of those requests were plausible, but before the matter was resolved, Marchetti, whose book had been delayed for years and whose legal expenses were crippling, went ahead and published with all 168 passages blacked out. To mock the CIA's predilection for censorship, he also published in bolded text all the passages the CIA had initially claimed were dangerous. But the precedent had been set. The deputy general counsel for the CIA boasted that it was a "significant victory in a landmark legal case." In contrast to the clunky provisions of the Espionage Act, a "workable tool in a court of law, based on simple contract theory," had now been developed.[48]

In 1976 George H. W. Bush established a permanent CIA Publication Review Board, tellingly located in the Public Relations Division. Ostensibly tasked with protecting classified information, it was in fact a political tool to maintain agency control over its public image. In 1977 former officer Frank Snepp published a book charging that the CIA had abandoned its allies in South Vietnam during the hasty US withdrawal. He did not submit the book to prepublication review because it did not contain classified material. The CIA conceded that that was true, but it nevertheless took him to court for violating his employment contract and won a favorable decision from conservative judge "Roarin'" Oren Lewis—a former Hearst newspaperman who had made a name giving antiwar protestors tough sentences and who ordered Snepp to surrender all profits earned on the book to the CIA as well as submit all future publications for review.

Snepp appealed to the Supreme Court, claiming that his right to free speech had been violated. The Supreme Court then did something unusual. In a 6–3 decision, it declined to hear the appeal. But even though it had not technically taken the case, and had not heard arguments about the First Amendment issues, the majority declared in a bland three-sentence footnote that the CIA's vital interest in protecting secrets trumped Snepp's First Amendment claims. Only by checking for classified materials, ruled the judges, could the agency be sure that no classified materials were being disclosed. It was as close as the court has ever come to considering the constitutionality of prepublication review. A small board had been given enormous discretion to censor anyone who had ever worked for the CIA. Unsurprisingly, it was tougher on those who sought to criticize their former employer than on those who sought to mythologize it.[49]

In 1982 a working group in the Reagan administration tasked with preventing leaks proposed extending prepublication review across the federal government. It was a controversial order that proposed mandatory lie-detector tests to identify leakers as well as new lifetime secrecy oaths, but after congressional blowback it was delayed and then quietly abandoned. Prepublication review boards were nevertheless soon established across the national-security state, and the absence of a central directive establishing their procedures has, if anything, made their confusing and idiosyncratic sprawl even more repressive of speech. Today, there are at least seventeen separate pre-publication review systems covering more than five million federal employees and contractors, requiring them to receive approval from a secretive board if they want to speak or write on matters relating to their former employment—which can mean the entire field of national security or foreign policy or intelligence. It is an astonishing, largely hidden system of censorship, all built on the thin reed of the *Snepp* precedent.[50]

The report of that 1982 working group on leaks also had another important consequence: it unexpectedly resuscitated the Espionage Act, showing that the old law could be more effective in prosecuting leaks than anyone had realized. The members of the working group shared the belief that the 1917 law was hamstrung by a "variety of legal and practical problems" and conceded that "the past approach to leak investigations has been almost totally unsuccessful and frustrating to all concerned." But they nevertheless called for more aggressive Espionage Act investigations, on the hope that even if criminal prosecutions would likely fail, they might change the climate and hence make it easier to identify leakers who could be punished administratively.[51]

In the late summer of 1984, *Jane's Defense Weekly*, a British magazine, published photographs of a Soviet aircraft carrier that had been taken by a US spy satellite, the KH-11. Following the new procedures, the FBI launched a leak investigation and hit pay dirt. *Jane's*, following British press practices, turned over the originals of the photos; US publications, keen to protect their sources and sticklers for their First Amendment rights, would likely have refused. (It helped that *Jane's* was no crusading muckraker but a hawkish trade journal for the defense industry, with no desire to fall out of the good graces of its official contacts.) When the glossy photographs were dusted in FBI offices, they turned up one very clear fingerprint.[52]

It belonged to Samuel Loring Morison, a civilian employee in naval intelligence who had handled the photographs while cutting the "Secret" labels off their borders before mailing them to the magazine. Morison had been moonlighting for *Jane's* and, in addition to getting paid, was trying to curry favor at the magazine in the hopes of landing a full-time job there. It soon became clear to Justice Department officials that this was an ideal test case to show that the Espionage Act could be used to prosecute leakers. Morison was not a sympathetic figure or one likely to be defended by civil-liberties activists. He was no Ellsberg but a "right-wing boat nut"—an aloof, eccentric, arrogant advocate of American naval power. His defense lawyers wouldn't put him on the stand or even let him speak to the press. "Have you ever met Morison?" was their simple explanation.[53]

Even better, the KH-11 satellite was due to be replaced, which meant that it was possible to show the court the classified information at the heart of the matter without further harming national security. In fact, information about the KH-11 hadn't been secret for years. In the late 1970s an ex–CIA officer had sold the Soviets the technical manual for the KH-11 and received forty years in jail for Espionage Act violations. Photos from the KH-11 had also been published both in another US magazine and in the Iranian press (satellite images had been found on board the wreckage from Carter's failed mission to rescue the hostages in 1980). A former CIA officer who had been responsible for satellite intelligence testified on Morison's behalf that there was "zero" damage to the United States from the disclosure. But the trial judge asserted that all that needed to be shown was "potential damage" to national security. The jury took just six hours to find Morison guilty. He was sentenced to two years in jail.[54]

Morison appealed, claiming that such a use of the Espionage Act was overly broad and threatened the First Amendment. The politics of the case made it a heavy lift. The leaked photos didn't do anything much to meaningfully inform public debate, and Morison's efforts to claim that he was blowing the whistle to call for increased

defense spending were neither particularly sympathetic nor particularly plausible. And despite the fact that Morison was freelancing
as a journalist at *Jane's*, the institutional press kept a wary distance
during the case, reluctant to pick a fight with the national-security
state on behalf of such a disreputable cause—particularly after the
DOJ met privately with press representatives to explain that the
Espionage Act, in the department's theory of the prosecution, applied only to government employees and not to the media. Although
press representatives ultimately did file an amicus brief raising
concerns about the First Amendment implications of the case,
they also took pains to clarify that Morison's case was "unique and
unsympathetic."[55]

In 1988 the Fourth Circuit Court of Appeals, in Richmond, Virginia, upheld Morison's conviction 3–0. The majority opinion concluded flatly that "we do not perceive any First Amendment rights
to be implicated here," although the two concurring judges did express some concern about the breadth of the Espionage Act, and
one of them called on Congress to step in and revise the "unwieldy
and imprecise" law. That was good enough for members of the press,
who bailed on Morison's effort to appeal to the Supreme Court: they
didn't want the court setting precedent for such important matters
on such an unfavorable set of facts. In October 1989 the court quietly declined to hear the case.[56]

"The successful prosecution of Morison is a major accomplishment," crowed an internal DOJ memorandum. A "carefully selected
case" had produced a ruling that affirmed that the Espionage Act
could be used to prosecute leakers.[57] Seven decades after the passage
of the law, thirty-five years after Truman established the modern
classification system, Morison was the first leaker of state secrets to
go to jail. Given the precedent that was established, given the uses to
which the Espionage Act would later be put, it was a deeply significant moment. But few outside the Justice Department were paying
attention. It seemed an odd and isolated case about an odd and isolated man. It was no match for the great scandal about the secretive
state that dominated Reagan's second term: Iran-Contra.

In October 1986, in the window between Morison's conviction and his unsuccessful appeal, a young Nicaraguan soldier had shot down a cargo plane running weapons to the Contras, right-wing rebels waging war on his left-leaning Sandinista government. One of the crew members survived, and he confessed to be working for the CIA. The next month, a small Lebanese newspaper reported that members of the Reagan administration had been selling arms to the revolutionary Islamic government in Iran in exchange for the release of hostages held in Lebanon. Both supplying the Contras and selling weapons to Iran had been banned by Congress and were therefore illegal. It turned out that they were also connected. A small group operating out of the Reagan White House had been secretly transferring the profits made on weapons sales to Iran to fund the Contras.[58]

Covert ops had begun to come back into favor amid the geopolitical turmoil that marked the end of Jimmy Carter's presidency. The ascension of Ronald Reagan promised a full restoration. Two weeks after the 1980 election, Reagan's incoming chief of staff, James Baker, met with Dick Cheney to receive a briefing on best practices for running the White House. Alongside advice on scheduling, Baker's handwritten notes of the meeting included Cheney's advice on the "central theme we ought to push": "Pres. Seriously weakened in recent yrs. Restore powers & authority to Exec branch—Need strong ldr'ship. Get rid of War Powers Act—restore independent rights." Baker underlined the note, twice, and then marked it with six asterisks for good measure. The new director of the CIA, Bill Casey, was also a throwback, a dyed-in-the-wool Cold Warrior who had run operations for the Office of Strategic Services during World War II and now fancied a return to the devil-may-care aggression of yesteryear's anti-Soviet spies. He hung a portrait of "Wild Bill" Donovan on his office wall and expanded the agency's covert operations around the world. "Secrecy," Casey explained, was the "lifeblood" of the CIA. The "business of Congress," he added, "is to stay out of my business."[59]

The post-1975 reforms had been tepid; the return of an executive branch committed to unilateral action now revealed their inadequacies. In 1981 Reagan authorized covert operations aimed at the Sandinista government, which in 1979 had taken power from the Somoza regime, backed by the United States since the occupation decades earlier. News of these covert operations made their way into the newspapers, where they were found by the chair of the House Intelligence Committee, Edward Boland, who successfully amended an appropriations bill to prohibit the use of funds to overthrow the Sandinistas. The Reaganites continued sending money to the Contras anyway, claiming implausibly that their goal was not overthrowing the government but simply stopping the flow of weapons into neighboring countries.[60]

Then, in 1984, the CIA mined the harbors of Nicaragua. It was an illegal act, an act of war, and exactly the sort of thing that was supposed to be reported to the intelligence oversight committees. But the CIA dissembled before the Senate committee, further undermining Congress's trust. Congress soon passed another amendment, Boland II, which barred any intelligence agency from providing *any* funding for the Contras. Boland II was included in an emergency funding bill that was needed to prevent a government shutdown, so Reagan had no choice but to sign it into law.[61]

When one loophole closed, the Reaganites opened others. Support for the Contras would flow not through the CIA but through a working group in the National Security Council, which insiders decided was not technically an intelligence agency and hence not covered by Boland II. And if Congress would not appropriate funds for the Contras, then other means would have to be found, such as the diverting of funds from the sales of weapons to the Iranians, which were themselves highly secret because even negotiating for hostages was a violation of White House policy. "I'm one of the few people that know fully the details," Vice President Bush confessed to his diary as news of the deals with Iran began to dribble out in late 1986. "This is one operation that had been held very, very tight and I hope it will not leak."[62]

It was public within days. "We did not, repeat, did not trade weapons or anything else for hostages," said Reagan, trying his darndest to charm the scandal away.[63] Within the White House, those responsible for Iran-Contra were shredding documents at a frenetic pace.

The ensuing season of inquiries and congressional hearings should have been a rerun of the Year of Intelligence, a wide-ranging consideration of the dangers of the secretive security state. Instead, it was more like a rerun of Watergate, with all attention focused on what the president knew and when he knew it. There was no doubt that Reagan supported both the Iran and Nicaragua policies in their broadest contours; what was unclear was whether he knew about the particular use of Iranian money to supply the Contras, the connective tissue that had come to be the heart of the scandal. This time, there was no smoking gun. Reagan, never a micromanager of his staff and possibly suffering from the early stages of dementia, made a plausible enough case to have been ignorant of the details. No single document could be found to prove otherwise. Bill Casey's role in the scandal also remained mysterious—he suffered a massive seizure days before he was to testify to Congress. He had a malignant brain tumor and would be in and out of consciousness for the remaining five months of his life.[64]

Meanwhile, conservatives in Congress went to bat to defend the administration. First among them was Cheney, who had been elected to Wyoming's lone House of Representatives seat in 1978. Most politicians will become advocates for whatever branch of government they currently occupy. Not Cheney. Throughout Reagan's presidency, Cheney would use his secure position in the House to serve as cheerleader for the Republican Party's radical project of executive restoration.

By the time that Iran-Contra broke, Cheney had risen to a prominent position in the House as well as on the House Intelligence Committee: it was no surprise that he was the leading Republican appointed to the House committee to investigate the scandal. He had no objections to the substance of the Nicaragua policy. "From a strategic standpoint," Cheney wrote to his constituents, "the U.S. cannot sit back and allow the Communists to take over Central

America. They already control centrally located Nicaragua, and have vowed to export their war to other nations." So he was opposed to Boland II, which he dubbed a "killer amendment" that would lead to the defeat of the Contras. And once Congress started investigating, there were bigger principles at stake. "I didn't want to see the president and his administration damaged," he later recalled. "I thought there were people . . . who were trying to damage the president and I took it as my responsibility as the senior Republican on the House side to do everything I could to support and defend him." The lessons of the Ford years remained front of mind.[65]

During the hearings, Cheney was an invaluable ally of the beleaguered administration. He used his leadership position to help the accused take control of the narrative. When his congressional colleagues were deep into a cross-examination, he would interrupt to throw in a softball, breaking the flow of questions and steering the testimony back to safer ground. He turned over a portion of his time to Oliver North, the conservative ex-marine who had run operations out of the White House, so that North had an opportunity to justify his actions as patriotic. North testified in dress uniform, assuming the role of the decorated war hero. It played well on television.[66]

That was perhaps standard-issue harm minimization. But Cheney, like others in the administration, also made the remarkable claim that Iran-Contra was evidence not of the dangers of a secret executive branch but of precisely the opposite problem: a presidency hamstrung and hemmed in by an overreaching Congress.

When the congressional committee issued a final report condemning Iran-Contra—an affair "characterized by pervasive dishonesty and inordinate secrecy"—Cheney oversaw the production of a dissenting minority report. More than 150 pages long, it concluded that the administration's policy was legal throughout the affair. And it blamed congressional meddling for the scandal, for waging "guerrilla war" against the president's foreign policy with "vaguely worded and constantly changing laws to impose policies in Central America that went beyond the law itself." The architects of Iran-Contra, Cheney argued, had been motivated by "legitimate frustration with abuses of power and irresolution by the Legislative branch."[67]

Congress's worst sin, Cheney emphasized, was a "track record of leaks of sensitive information sufficient to worry even the most apologetic advocate of an expansive role for the Congress in foreign policy-making." The architects of Iran-Contra had tried to justify their secrecy by claiming that Congress couldn't be trusted to keep secrets. A whole chapter of Cheney's minority report was devoted to documenting congressional leaks. Ultimately, his report made only five recommendations based on what had been learned during Iran-Contra. One was to "restore presidential power" by limiting the ability of Congress to pass resolutions tied to appropriations bills. The rest aimed to roll back transparency by replacing the oversight committees with a single joint congressional committee and reducing the Gang of Eight to be briefed on exceptional matters with a "Gang of Four" ("on the principle that notifying fewer people is better"). Two of them were aimed explicitly at securing classified information by making members of Congress sign strict secrecy oaths with "stiff penalties" and by passing a new law to criminalize the disclosure of classified information. As of 1987—and despite the unfolding administration victory in the *Morison* case—Cheney continued to believe that the Espionage Act was an inadequate tool to punish leakers.[68]

Iran-Contra did no lasting damage to the Reaganites. The only person who served jail time in the fallout was an ex–CIA officer who had been involved in the weapons sales but had not disclosed his profits on his tax return. Bush, unharmed by his role in the affair, won the White House in 1988, and he soon appointed Cheney as his defense secretary. Four years later, weeks before the end of his term, Bush pardoned six of the key architects of the scheme and its cover-up.[69]

Nor did the scandal lead to any reform of the secrecy regime. There was serious discussion of amending the Intelligence Oversight Act, and in 1988 the Senate passed a bill requiring the president to inform the oversight committees of any covert operations within forty-eight hours. But just before the House was to take it up, Cheney and other House Republicans accused Democratic Speaker Jim Wright of spilling classified information about covert operations in Nicaragua to reporters. It was a trumped-up charge; Wright had discussed only publicly available information and was later cleared of any wrongdoing. But it was an effective diversionary tactic that killed the momentum for reform. In February 1989, as "an opening gesture of good faith" to the new Bush administration, Wright shelved the reform bill. Once more, Cheney had wielded the need for secrecy as a club to beat away reform.[70]

In the wake of Iran-Contra, one new and improbable champion of transparency did emerge: Daniel Patrick Moynihan, senator from New York. To say he was late to the cause is an understatement. While his Democratic colleagues were investigating the intelligence community in the 1970s, Moynihan was serving as Ford's ambassador to the UN, where his advocacy of a more aggressive US foreign policy won praise from Ronald Reagan. Then he won the democratic nomination for the New York Senate seat in 1976 by running to the right of Bella Abzug—an antiwar activist and champion of transparency who herself had been subject to illegal CIA surveillance. On the Hill, as the leading Democrat on the Senate Intelligence Committee, Moynihan worked to protect the CIA from serious reform, arguing that any legislative charter would be the equivalent of a "tax code" that would enmesh the CIA in bureaucratic red tape and make it overly cautious—exactly, he said, "what we don't want in the intelligence services." His chief of staff in these early years was Elliot Abrams, who would later join the Reagan administration and help orchestrate Iran-Contra.[71]

For Moynihan, Iran-Contra marked a turning point. In 1983 he visited Nicaragua and was convinced that the CIA obsession with overthrowing the Sandinistas was dangerous nonsense. In 1984, when he learned about the CIA's illegal mining operations,

Daniel Patrick Moynihan, mid-speech on March 25, 1976. (Library of Congress, photograph by Marion S. Trikosko)

he publicly resigned from the Intelligence Committee, only to back down when Casey apologized. In 1989, in a last-ditch effort to ensure there could be no repeat of Iran-Contra, he introduced a bill that would make it illegal for the executive branch to solicit or divert funds for activities banned by Congress. Bush vetoed it. Then, exasperated by the CIA's ongoing failure to produce good intelligence—particularly its failure to predict the fall of the Soviet Union—Moynihan introduced legislation to abolish the CIA entirely and to replace it with a new intelligence operation housed under the State Department. The proposal was a piece of symbolism more than anything, and it never went anywhere.[72]

Finally, Moynihan turned on secrecy itself. In 1993 he introduced legislation calling for a holistic review of the classification system that had grown up in the Cold War and was now in dire need of reform. The Commission on Protecting and Reducing Government Secrecy was duly established, with Moynihan as its head. In 1995 and 1996 it held thirteen formal meetings, visited seventy-five agencies and associations, and interviewed hundreds of individuals. It was the most comprehensive study of the secrecy regime since the Wright Commission had handed down its report at the time of the Nickerson trial four decades earlier.[73]

Its three-hundred-page final report, issued in March 1997, announced in its opening sentence that "it is time for a new way of thinking about secrecy." This was the most powerful critique of the secrecy regime ever issued by the US government. Secrecy was expensive and wasteful: it cost the taxpayers more than $5 billion annually. That didn't stop spies from stealing secrets, and it encouraged a culture of politics by leaking. Meanwhile, Moynihan argued, the secrecy regime was seriously undermining democratic faith in the government. He was particularly incensed by the conspiracy theories that had grown up around the JFK assassination. Oliver Stone's pulsatingly paranoid *JFK* had been a blockbuster movie in 1991.[74]

The commission therefore proposed major reform. Five decades of classification by executive order had done nothing to arrest the bloat of the secrecy regime. Congress should instead pass a statute to guide the classification system, said the commission, one that established clearer rules about what information should be kept secret. Rather than asking the classifier simply to consider harms that might flow from disclosure, as the current system did, it should also force the classifier to weigh those risks against the costs of secrecy. The commission did not consider amending the Espionage Act itself, but this change to the classification rules would have been a serious reform. "The initial decision to classify is critical," argued the commission. Reduce the number of secrets, and the rest of the secrecy regime would begin to shrink to a more manageable size. The commission also suggested other reforms, such as mandatory declassification after ten years (or thirty years in special circumstances) and the standardization of secrecy practices across the executive branch. A bill to make these changes was soon introduced to Congress.[75]

It seemed a sensible, pragmatic approach to the problem. The commission was bipartisan and reported unanimously. The reform legislation was cosponsored in the Senate by Moynihan and fellow commissioner Jesse Helms, a far-right conservative. Yet after the Committee on Governmental Affairs unanimously recommended passage of the law in 1998, nothing ever came of it.[76]

Part of the problem was that Moynihan was never a great leg-
islator, never very good at forcing an issue to the top of the agenda
and then through Congress. He sought to champion causes as a
public intellectual—rhetorical, controversial, flamboyant—not as a
backroom deal maker. The contrast with the devastatingly effective
Cheney was instructive, for Cheney was the consummate insider, a
dour and reserved man, so unobtrusive in the 1970s that his Secret
Service code name was Backseat. It was fitting that the main result
of the Moynihan Commission was a 300-page report, parts of which
Moynihan then adapted for a 270-page history of secrecy published
by Yale University Press. It was a useful academic intervention, but
that was the end of it.[77]

The deeper problem was that there was no great passion for reform,
no reason for either political party to expend political capital to take
on an entrenched set of bureaucratic practices. In an effort to forge
a consensus, and to appeal to the political center in this era of small
government, Moynihan had taken to describing secrecy as a problem
of overregulation. (Secrecy, he said, was the "ultimate mode of regulation."[78]) He was correct, but it was a coolly intellectual argument,
one that sought to co-opt the antiregulatory rhetoric of the Right. It
failed to make headway with conservatives, who were happy to carve
out an exception for the national-security state, and it made secrecy
reform seem like a technocratic adjustment. The nation's politics was
dominated by the scandal of Bill Clinton's relationship with Monica Lewinsky, by the increasingly partisan clashes between Clinton
Democrats and a GOP mobilizing under Newt Gingrich. By comparison, classification reform was a snoozefest.

To make the case for secrecy reform, it would have helped to have
a big, troubling case study, a symbol of the sorts of problems that
secrecy wrought. The year 1975 had plenty of symbolic scandals, and
then there was Iran-Contra. But by the mid-1990s, when the Cold
War had been won, the economy was humming, and America was
indisputably the dominant power, there was no great anxiety about
the security state or US foreign policy or the health of democracy.
Moynihan's reform came too late.

Tellingly, for his political symbol, Moynihan turned to the history books, to the great spy scare of the McCarthy period. Perhaps the Moynihan Commission's most significant accomplishment was that it forced the declassification of the Venona transcripts. For Moynihan, Venona was a sign of the democratic perils of secrecy as regulation: if Venona had been revealed at the time, he thought, it would have prevented the whole maddened fury of the second red scare. It was a textbook example of Moynihan's idiosyncratic centrism, of his inopportune political timing. It was too clever by half to think that the lesson of Venona was that the rabid right wing of the McCarthy era could have been calmed if spies had been publicly identified and neutralized. For rather than make the debate about the Cold War more rational, the revelation of Venona reanimated partisan conflict over the historical memory of McCarthyism. It bolstered the anticommunist Right and led to a culture war not about the post-Soviet world order but about the political morality of the 1940s. And headlines that there had indeed been spies in the Cold War did not help make the case that the secretive security state was a redundant waste. Triumphantly revealing such code-breaking success after fifty years of secrecy made it seem as if counterintelligence work was both necessary and effective. Far from condemning the US security state, Moynihan helped rehabilitate its reputation.[79]

Meanwhile, the fear of spies remained despite the collapse of the Soviet Union. The new threat was China, not only a Communist holdover from the Cold War but also a throwback to the fears of a rising Asian power that had animated the country's first espionage laws. In 1999 Taiwanese-born physicist Wen Ho Lee was accused of stealing nuclear secrets for the Chinese from his workplace at Los Alamos. He was hit with fifty-nine counts under the Espionage Act and the Atomic Energy Act, and kept in solitary confinement for nine months, before the government's case collapsed. Lee ultimately pled guilty to one count of improperly retaining defense information (the sprawling 793(e) clause created in 1950) and then sued the government and the media for violating his privacy in their rush to depict him as a spy. The government settled by paying him $1.6 million. But it was a sign of spy scares to come. In 1996 the Economic Espionage Act was passed to regulate the disclosure of trade secrets to foreign powers. It would soon be used to disproportionately target Chinese Americans.[80]

Security hawks were also seeking to further *strengthen* the secrecy regime. In 2000 the Senate Intelligence Committee introduced new legislation that would dispense with the Espionage Act's intent requirements and make it illegal to leak any classified information. But once again, this latest patch to the old secrecy laws was drawn broadly and proved controversial among civil libertarians. Newspaper publishers complained that it was essentially an "Official Secrets Act" that would "shatter the delicate balance that has been achieved in this country between the public's right to know and the legitimate demands of national security." Moynihan also lobbied against it. Congress nevertheless passed the law, and only a Clinton veto prevented it from going into force. Later that year, as he was leaving office, Clinton also pardoned Morison, the only man who had gone to prison for leaking information to the press. The pardon was a result of Moynihan's lobbying and the closest the Moynihan Commission ever came to taking on the Espionage Act.[81]

So a third great moment to reform the secrecy system had passed. The Espionage Act and the classification system had survived 1975 and Iran-Contra, and now they had outlived the Cold War itself. In fact, they had grown only stronger with age. In 1995 Clinton had issued a new classification order that made some noise about rolling back classification. The next year, when six million documents were stamped as secret, classification increased by 62 percent. It would continue to increase each year after that.[82]

Moynihan was at the end of his very long political career. He decided not to run for office in 2000, announced his retirement, and blessed Hillary Rodham Clinton to succeed him as senator from New York.

Nine months later, the towers fell. The 9/11 attacks were perhaps the US security state's most abject failure. For decades, money had been poured into intelligence and counterintelligence and surveillance to secure the homeland, to prevent American deaths. Despite it all, three thousand US lives had been lost in horrific scenes of violence and destruction in the very seat of American affluence and influence.

The finger-pointing started immediately. The afternoon of the attacks, Reagan's old chief of staff James Baker was on the air blaming the reforms of the 1970s. The Church Committee, claimed Cheney's friend of many decades, "had unilaterally disarmed . . . our intelligence capabilities."[83]

In truth, as the 9/11 Commission revealed, there had been plenty of intelligence on the threat. The systems were, famously, "blinking red." But the signal was lost in the noise. Forty times that year, Bush's presidential daily briefings warned that Osama Bin Laden was a threat, but in such vague and nebulous terms that nothing was done. On August 6 the briefing was titled "Bin Laden Determined to Strike in U.S." "OK," Bush told his briefer, "you've covered your ass." It was a reasonable enough response—the CIA didn't have anything specific. It had traced two of the hijackers to a meeting in Kuala Lumpur but then lost track of them, and it failed to put them on a watch list. That meant they could easily enter the United States. The CIA had also failed to inform the FBI of the meeting, which meant that no one tracked them once they entered the country. Nor was the FBI blameless. It failed to follow up on reports of suspiciously underqualified students attending flight schools to learn how to pilot commercial planes. On September 10 the NSA had intercepted intelligence suggesting that 9/11 would be the date of the attack but failed to translate it. The 9/11 Commission later criticized security practices in the agencies that "nurture over-classification and excessive compartmentation of information" and had contributed to the failure to see the attack coming.[84]

And in a deeper sense, the attacks were a product not of a shackled security apparatus but of the same sort of adventurist militarism that had been the subject of so much concern in 1975. When the

Soviet Union invaded Afghanistan in 1979, the CIA had secretly begun funding the mujahideen to resist them. Under Reagan, the support they received dwarfed the funding of the Contras in Nicaragua. By the end of his presidency, Afghanistan was receiving 80 percent of the money spent on covert operations, some $700 million per year. It was the kind of open, technically deniable "secret" produced by the post-1975 reforms. Members of Congress loved the idea of funding anti-Soviet freedom fighters.[85]

The problems came later. The Taliban emerged victorious in the vicious civil war that followed Soviet withdrawal. And a minor player among the mujahideen, Osama Bin Laden, had seen a superpower defeated. He formed Al-Qaeda and began plotting to force the United States out of the Middle East. He was particularly upset by the presence of a US military base in his native Saudi Arabia. It had been opened during the First Gulf War when Dick Cheney had personally flown to Jeddah to meet with King Fahd to secure US rights to the base. He got them on the promise that the United States would withdraw at the end of Operation Desert Storm. That never happened. Bin Laden, enraged, went to ground in the Taliban's Afghanistan, then launched attacks on US embassies in Kenya and Tanzania and on the USS *Cole*.[86]

By then, America was in the midst of an election season in which the subject of terrorism barely came up. It was a bitterly close campaign, but thanks to some hanging chads and a divided Supreme Court, George W. Bush emerged the victor. Back in the spring, as the inexperienced Texas governor eyed the campaign, he had decided he needed a running mate with foreign-policy experience. He asked Dick Cheney to run the search to help him find a suitable vice president. Although it wouldn't quite be fair to say that Cheney picked himself, his was the name that ended up on the ticket. After spending the 1990s making a small fortune in the energy business, Cheney was back in the White House. He brought with him a team of neoconservative staffers he had accumulated across his long political career: Scooter Libby, Paul Wolfowitz, and, perhaps most important of all, David Addington, an ex–CIA lawyer with a grand vision of the powers of the presidency, who had met Cheney as a staffer on the House Intelligence Committee in the 1980s and been his right-hand man ever since.[87]

On the morning of 9/11, Bush was away from Washington, promoting his education policy in a Florida classroom. When the attacks came, it was Cheney who held down the fort in the White House, just as he had done in 1975 when Hersh's story about CIA surveillance had broken while Ford was skiing. It was a chaotic moment; no one knew if there were more hijackers, if more planes were about to be turned into missiles. But Cheney was quiet, stern, and decisive. He gave the military permission to shoot down a hijacked plane if they believed it necessary. It was an astonishing call for a vice president, so astonishing, in fact, that Cheney would later tell the 9/11 Commission that he was simply relaying orders that Bush had given him in a phone call that no one else had heard. The 9/11 Commission found no evidence of such a call on the White House phone logs.[88]

For a quarter of a century, Cheney had been arguing that the executive branch needed the capacity to act decisively, unilaterally, and secretly to protect the nation's security. Five days after 9/11, he went on the Sunday talk shows to tell a vengeful American public that "it's going to be vital for us to use any means at our disposal basically, to achieve our objective."

It was time, he said, to "work the dark side."[89]

Chapter 10

WHISTLEBLOWERS IN THE WAR ON TERROR

A meeting outside the Oval Office on September 10, 2003. From left to right: Michael Hayden (NSA director, later to serve as CIA director), George Tenet (director of Central Intelligence), Alberto Gonzales (White House counsel, later to serve as attorney general), and David Addington (Vice President Dick Cheney's legal counsel, later to serve as his chief of staff). During the war on terror, secret legal memos prepared by lawyers like Addington would expand the powers of the security state. (National Archives and Records Administration)

A FTER 9/11, THE BUSH-CHENEY ADMINISTRATION MASSIVELY expanded the secrecy regime that had been slowly constructed over the previous century. Secrecy shrouded and shaped US policy during the war on terror: the torture and surveillance programs, the planning for the invasion of Iraq, the increasing reliance on drones to police foreign battlefields. The reaction to this unprecedented secrecy was a burst of disclosures from government employees within the security state, who tried to inform the US public what was being done in its name.

History had provided the guardians of national security with an array of tools to silence and punish these leakers. But the best tool turned out to be the oldest one. For decades, the Espionage Act had seemed an inadequate law to protect secrets. Beginning in 2005, the Bush-Cheney government began to use it more aggressively to send leakers to jail. The Obama and Trump administrations continued the trend.

In its ninth decade of life, the Espionage Act was reborn.

Even before 9/11, the Bush administration had revealed a predilection for secrecy. In the summer of 2001, Dick Cheney had headed up an energy task force that met with industry stakeholders in secret, raising legal challenges from transparency groups that worried about the possibility of corruption. (It later turned out that the task force spent at least some time looking at maps of Iraq.)[1]

Then came the war on terror and a new obsession with national security. From 2001 to 2005, the number of documents being classified every year doubled—every minute of the year, 125 documents were being stamped as secret. George Bush's classification order in 2003 removed Bill Clinton's instructions to underclassify marginal cases and allowed for the reclassification of previously declassified material. Federal agencies were instructed to withhold "sensitive but unclassified" information and to make full use of the exemptions in the FOIA.[2]

Secrecy spilled out to cover the vast national-security economy that was built over the next two decades of war and counterterrorism. A recent study estimates that the war on terror has cost the US nearly six trillion dollars—money diverted from education, health, and infrastructure. Much of it flowed through the intelligence and military agencies and into the pockets of private contractors. Someone had to build the weapons, the hardware and software needed for surveillance, even the buildings in which the expanding labor force of the security state worked. Massive, multibillion-dollar development projects threw up new office complexes, which in turn bolstered local economies: Washington was ringed by ever-more-affluent suburbs and a new tech economy centered on defense contracting. All of these new buildings had to have a sensitive compartmented information facility (SCIF), a government-approved, impenetrable room in which secrets could be discussed without fear of eavesdropping or surveillance. "In DC, everyone talks SCIF, SCIF, SCIF," said the owner of a construction company that specialized in installing them. "They've got the penis envy thing going. You can't be a big boy unless you're a three-letter agency and you have a big SCIF."[3]

By 2011, almost one in every three of the 850,000 people with a top-secret clearance worked for a contractor. The revolving door that had upset John Nickerson half a century before was spinning at a dizzying rate. Bush's second director of national intelligence was J. Michael McConnell, a former Naval Intelligence officer who had headed the NSA under Bush 1. He had spent the intervening years running the national-security branch of Booz Allen Hamilton, and he would return to the firm as a senior VP on a multimillion-dollar contract when his second tour in the public sector came to an end.[4]

Inevitably, such a secretive political economy bred corruption. There was corruption in the technical, textbook sense, such as the $2.4 million bribe paid to California congressman Randy "Duke" Cunningham of the Intelligence Oversight Committee to ensure that a San Diego businessman got a CIA contract (delivered, of course, via a classified earmark in a military-spending bill). But there was also something rotten about such a small network of politicians and contractors spending so much of the nation's money, about a closed circle making so many consequential decisions about the political and economic future of so many citizens. That some of the most affluent sectors of the economy quietly relied on government spending was hard to square with the residual libertarian rhetoric of America's political culture. And there was something sordid and uncomfortable about the fact that so much of the world's leading economy was devoted to policing and violence and repression.[5]

Under the cloak of secrecy, new forms of counterterrorism were adopted. Six days after 9/11, President Bush secretly authorized the CIA to capture terrorism suspects abroad, to detain and interrogate them, and to transfer them to foreign governments. It was an unprecedented set of powers. Even twenty years later, the details of how the CIA used them remain murky. But at least 119 individuals were held in CIA custody. In a process known as "extraordinary rendition," some were transferred to the prisons of foreign states with appalling human-rights records: Hosni Mubarak's Egypt, Bashar Al-Assad's Syria.[6]

That was a way of outsourcing torture, but the CIA also tortured at least thirty-nine individuals itself. In secret prisons on foreign soil—known as "black sites"—it subjected its detainees to a nauseating array of what it called "enhanced interrogation techniques." Prisoners were deprived of sleep, forced into stress positions for long periods of time, tormented by isolation and sensory deprivation and psychological abuse. Some were waterboarded, which is often called a form of simulated drowning but is really a form of slow-motion, controlled suffocation.[7]

Under both international and domestic law, it all should have been illegal. But in secret legal opinions, Bush administration lawyers had written themselves get-out-of-jail-free cards, asserting that such abuse was torture only if "death, organ failure or permanent damage resulting in loss of significant bodily function" was likely to occur.[8]

There was no good reason to classify these torture memos. There was nothing operational in them. They were policy documents outlining the interpretation of the law. J. William Leonard, who oversaw the classification system in his role as director of the Information Security Oversight Office, thought the decision to stamp them secret "one of the worst abuses of the classification process" he had ever seen. But the issuance of secret law was the preferred mode of the small coterie of conservative lawyers, including Cheney's old aide David Addington, who were guiding the Bush administration's sweeping new counterterrorism programs. Secrecy gave these legally minded security hawks control over the policy process and space to stretch the powers of the executive branch.[9]

Inevitably, torture spread beyond the CIA. In early January 2002 the first detainees began arriving at Guantánamo Bay ("Gitmo"), where they were held in hastily built cages before being moved to more permanent facilities, which were being built on a no-bid contract by Kellogg, Brown, and Root, a subsidiary of Cheney's old employer, Halliburton. In all, some 780 individuals would be held at Gitmo. Cheney told the press that they were "the worst of a very bad lot," but later studies suggested that only about 40 percent of them had any connection to a terrorist group whatsoever and that fewer than one in ten had been involved in any attack on the United States. Many had been seized by mistake or after being falsely named by local warlords or rivals to receive the bounties that the United States was paying for intelligence on terrorism suspects.[10]

There was also a black site at Guantánamo, and it wasn't long before military officials began requesting permission to use the same techniques they heard that the CIA had been using. (Prophetically, the black site was called "Strawberry Fields"—because detention there could last "forever." Two decades later, there are still thirty-nine detainees held at Guantánamo, twenty-seven of whom have never been charged with any crime. In 2022 the Pentagon requested $88 million to build an old-age hospice on the base.[11])

In secret legal memos, the Bush administration authorized "enhanced interrogation" at Gitmo too. Some lawyers in the armed forces protested the decision. Their dissenting memos were classified and suppressed. Hoods and sleep deprivation and stress positions came to Gitmo. When personnel moved from Cuba to a prison in Iraq known as Abu Ghraib, they took their new techniques with them.[12]

There was something eerily familiar about these abuses. Waterboarding had been used to torture Filipino nationalists in the imperial wars a century earlier. Guantánamo Bay had been leased from a recently occupied Cuba at around the same time, its nebulous legal status—not subject to US law but not subject to any other nation's law either—making it a useful space for this new era of extralegal policing.[13]

The legal architects of the war on terror were rummaging through the repressed excesses of the security state in decades past, cherry-picking precedents and programs that they stitched together to expand the power of the executive branch. By 2004, Cheney, who thought that waterboarding was a "no-brainer," could reflect on his long-term project with deep satisfaction, telling the History Channel that "I think, in fact, that there has been over time a restoration, if you will, of the power and authority of the President." The decision to try political prisoners via military commission, for instance, was based on FDR's 1942 decision to do the same to Nazi saboteurs.[14]

Selective sampling of the legal record was also a preferred technique of the lawyer in the Office of Legal Counsel who wrote the torture memos, as well as a number of other important legal memos expanding the powers of the president. This was John Yoo, a thirty-four-year-old law professor with deeply conservative convictions who had made his name in a series of provocative articles arguing that the US president had remarkably sweeping powers. Yoo was the child of South Korean immigrants. His faith in the unilateral powers of the presidency rested on a deep belief that South Korea had been saved by Harry Truman's decision to declare war on North Korea without waiting for congressional approval.[15]

The constellation of torture techniques that were deployed with Yoo's blessing also had their origins in the Korean war. They were a result of the same fears about Communist brainwashing that had led to the CIA's mind-control programs in the 1950s. In 1955 the US military had begun a new "Survive, Evade, Resist, and Escape" program (SERE) to instruct members of special forces how to resist torture programs designed to break them down and extract false confessions that the Communists could use for propaganda purposes. When the CIA began to torture its detainees, it turned for advice to James Mitchell, a psychologist who had been involved in the SERE program. Having simulated torture to teach Americans how to resist it, he was the closest thing the United States had to a torture expert. Mitchell and his colleagues were paid $81 million to reverse engineer an active torture program for the CIA.[16]

The fact that the torture program could trace its origins to SERE revealed its central flaw. Beyond its immorality, the torture program wasn't fit for its ostensible purpose, which was to extract useful intelligence to protect the United States from terrorism. The torture programs that SERE was designed to evade were intended not to produce usable intelligence but false confessions: they were designed to so break the will of the tortured that they would say whatever their torturers wanted to hear. And, to give credit where credit is due, Mitchell and his team did reproduce precisely that sort of program. Detainees did confess to being involved in terrorist plots; they named collaborators; they detailed future plans. The problem was that it was bunk, desperate fabrications by desperate men, saying whatever they thought would stop the torture. "I was going out of my mind," explained Shafiq Rasul, a British man who confessed to being in a video with Osama Bin Laden, even though it was later shown he had been in England at the time that the footage was taken. After weeks of isolation and brutal interrogation, he said, "I just gave in and admitted to being in the video."[17]

The torture program thus polluted the stream of US intelligence. One Libyan member of Al-Qaeda, Ibn al-Shayhkh al-Libbi, was tortured for weeks, waterboarded, and forced to stand overnight, naked in a cold cell while being doused with water, before he gave up and told his interrogators a made-up story that he knew would satisfy them. Iraq, he said, had offered to show Al-Qaeda how to use biological and chemical weapons.[18]

Within the administration were a number of neoconservative hard-liners who had been hoping to overthrow Saddam Hussein even before 9/11. They were predisposed to use the tragedy to pursue the cause. Late in the night of September 11, Deputy Defense Secretary Paul Wolfowitz was already requesting an intelligence summary of information about Iraq's involvement in international terrorism. Al-Libbi's false confession fed suspicions of a connection between Saddam and 9/11. So did a report from an unnamed informant in Czechoslovakia that 9/11 hijacker Mohammed Atta had met an Iraqi diplomat in Prague in the months before the attack. It was dodgy intel—Atta had apparently been in the United States at the time of the meeting—but Cheney repeated the story on *Meet the Press*.[19]

In the end, there was simply no way to connect Saddam to 9/11. But the case for war had its own momentum and began to mutate. What mattered now was not whether Saddam had aided the hijackers but whether he was developing weapons of mass destruction (WMD). The intel on WMD was similarly flimsy: an Iraqi defector—code-named Curveball—who made up stories about mobile weapons labs; facially implausible and ultimately false reports that Iraq had been trying to buy uranium in Niger; and an Australian report that Iraq had purchased mapping software of the United States (the software had been included in a standard package deal when Iraq bought Garmin GPS equipment).[20]

In September 2002 the administration began a public-relations offensive to sell the war. ("From a marketing point of view," explained White House chief of staff Andrew Card, "you don't introduce new products in August.") *New York Times* reporter Judith Miller was given classified information that Iraq had purchased aluminum tubes that could be used to build a nuclear centrifuge. This, too, was shoddy intelligence—the assessment had been made by just one CIA analyst and was disputed by experts in the Department of Energy who said that the tubes could not be used in a nuclear program but were simply for rockets. But Miller wasn't told that, and the centrifuge story was on the front page of the Sunday *Times*. The same day, administration officials flooded the Sunday talk shows. On *Meet the Press*, Cheney cited Miller's story to bolster his case for war.[21]

In such ways did control over the flow of information allow the administration to build the case for war. Poor intelligence was selectively leaked to the press, then cited as if it were independent verification. Classification meant that no one could check the administration's work, which meant that the administration could lie with impunity. A Center for Public Integrity study later concluded that the administration made 935 false statements to the public in the lead-up to the war.[22]

It all had a devastating effect on the quality of public debate about the consequential decision to invade Iraq. Media insiders were swept up; the *New York Times* later criticized its own coverage as "credulous" and overly deferential to anonymous disclosures. The public was simply confused and misled. By the end of the year, nine out of ten Americans believed that Iraq was developing WMD. Six months after the invasion, 69 percent of Americans thought that Saddam had been complicit in 9/11.[23]

Nor was Congress immune to the impact of the administration's savvy deployment of secrets. Initially, Congress was kept in the dark. As Cheney complained about the risks of congressional leaks, Rumsfeld held briefings in secure rooms on the Hill, in which legislators had to swear secrecy oaths and wait patiently while the room was performatively swept for listening devices. Then they were told information that was already public; John McCain dismissed it all as a "joke" and walked out in disgust. But some Democratic members of the Senate Select Committee on Intelligence had access to classified information that undermined the White House claims. They called for the production of a formal National Intelligence Estimate. It was ready within weeks—a rushed job that downplayed the doubts and made the case for war seem stronger than it was. Even so, it was enough to convince some senators to vote against the war. The problem was that very few read the full, ninety-two-page report.

Most read instead a declassified, twenty-five-page white paper that was released to the public and that smoothed away all doubts. Or they relied on the briefings they had received from administration officials. They had little incentive to look too closely at what had become a type of political common sense. The White House got its authorization to invade.[24]

Everything that followed—the deaths, the disastrous occupation, the rise of ISIS—can be blamed in no small part on the ways that secrecy distorted the initial debate about the need for war.

As the wars in Afghanistan and Iraq dragged on, as the passions and panic of 9/11 faded, word of US torture began to dribble out. The first rumors of secret torture at Bagram Air Base had been published in the *Washington Post* in late 2002. Similar allegations popped up in other outlets in 2003, and in January 2004 the US Command in Baghdad issued a bland, one-paragraph notice that it was beginning an internal investigation into detainee abuse. Evidence from the internal investigations soon began to leak. The key disclosure, as had been the case in the Year of Intelligence, was to Seymour Hersh, who also learned that CBS's *60 Minutes* was sitting on particularly shocking photos of abuse at Abu Ghraib. When it became clear that Hersh was about to go public, in the late spring of 2004 *60 Minutes* aired photos of hooded, strung-up, and sexually humiliated prisoners. It was an international outrage. Within months, the torture memos leaked. By the end of 2005, the *Washington Post* was running stories on the CIA's black-site interrogation programs.[25]

In the midst of it, news of a massive surveillance program also broke. In the fearful days after 9/11, Cheney had approached Michael Hayden, head of the NSA, to ask what more could be done to secure the nation. He then had David Addington and John Yoo prepare secret legal memos authorizing dragnet collection of phone and internet metadata, as well as warrantless surveillance of terrorism suspects on US soil. Under the terms of the 1978 Foreign Intelligence Surveillance Act, these were all illegal practices—the government was supposed to go to the FISA court to get approval for such eavesdropping. This was hardly an onerous burden: by 2001, the government had applied for 13,087 warrants and had never been turned down. And it would have been easy enough in the panicked patriotism of the moment to have revised the old law. But Cheney saw the 1978 law in terms of his broader struggle to expand the power of the presidency. Yoo's memorandum claimed a constitutional right for the president to unilaterally bypass FISA and establish new surveillance programs. In October, Bush signed orders that did just that. For over two years, the NSA's new program, known as STELLARWIND, was a tightly held secret.[26]

Then there was a personnel change in the Office of Legal Counsel. Jack Goldsmith, new to the position, revised Yoo's legal authorization. Even for the staunchly conservative Goldsmith, himself a believer in a powerful presidency, Yoo's opinions were clearly flawed and far too broad. Goldsmith now grounded STELLARWIND not in the president's constitutional powers but in Congress's Authorization to Use Military Force, passed after 9/11 to facilitate the war in Afghanistan. As a result of the change, Goldsmith was unwilling to reauthorize some parts of the program when they came up for renewal. In March 2004 this secret clash over surveillance came to a dramatic head in a hospital room in Washington, when White House officials tried to pressure Attorney General John Ashcroft, groggily recovering from emergency gallbladder surgery, into reauthorizing STELLARWIND. Ashcroft refused. When Bush made moves to continue the program anyway, it came close to triggering a mass resignation in the Department of Justice.[27]

Amid the hubbub, news of the program leaked to two *New York Times* journalists, James Risen and Eric Lichtblau. They were ready to go public just weeks before the 2004 election, but the Bush administration convinced their editors to kill the story on the grounds that revealing the surveillance program would harm national security. It did not run until the following year, after Bush had been returned to the White House for a second term, once Risen was preparing to publish it in a book and the hand of the newspaper was forced.[28]

For patriotic partisans of the Bush administration, the upsetting thing was the simple fact of publication. Much had been invested in secrecy; much had been made of the need to defend national security. Leaks promised to create a deep legitimacy crisis. Two weeks after the *New York Times* NSA story, the Justice Department announced it was opening an investigation to find the leakers and prosecute them under the Espionage Act. Some—including conservative legal commentator Gabriel Schoenfeld and a politically ambitious army lieutenant by the name of Tom Cotton—called for the prosecution of the *New York Times* as well.[29]

Since the prosecution of Samuel Morison two decades earlier, the Espionage Act had lain dormant in leak cases. But amid the broader revitalization of secretive presidential power after 9/11, lawyers in the Bush administration had taken another look at the ambiguous law and decided that it was more powerful than anyone had realized. As recently as the year 2000, conservatives in Congress were still trying to patch the Espionage Act by passing a new law to criminalize leaks, only to be defeated by a Bill Clinton veto. In 2001 they asked the Bush administration to carry out a comprehensive review of leak law with an eye to finally remedying its deficiencies. But the next year, Ashcroft reported that there was no need for a new law because there were already sufficient laws on the books. What was needed to stanch the flow of harmful leaks was simply "rigorous investigation" and "vigorous enforcement."[30]

In early 2006 the Justice Department announced the creation of a new task force devoted to pursuing leaks. The DOJ had come to believe that the Espionage Act was very powerful indeed. In May the new attorney general, Alberto Gonzales, was asked on national television if the administration might prosecute journalists who published secret information. There were statutes, he said, that if "you read the language carefully, would seem to indicate that that is a possibility." The next month, a DOJ lawyer told Congress that Sections 793 and 798 of the Espionage Act "do not exempt a class of professionals, any class of professionals, including reporters, from their reach."[31]

This aggressive interpretation of the law was reinforced by a for-tuitous court opinion in an unusual Espionage Act case unfolding simultaneously. For a number of years the FBI had been investigat-ing the American-Israel Public Affairs Committee (AIPAC) on sus-picion that it was engaged in espionage. During the investigation, the Bureau had recorded two AIPAC lobbyists talking to Lawrence Franklin, an analyst in the Defense Department who believed that current US policy on Iran was too soft. A subsequent raid on Frank-lin's house found a stash of classified documents. It was a kind of right-wing remake of the *Amerasia* case, and its denouement revealed how much more powerful the Espionage Act was in the war on terror than in the early Cold War. Franklin pleaded guilty, but his twelve-year sentence was reduced to probation and ten months in community confinement when he cooperated with efforts to prose-cute the two lobbyists with Espionage Act violations.

The pair argued that the unprecedented charges were a violation of the First Amendment: they were not government employees, they were engaged in simple political lobbying, and if they could be found guilty of receiving classified documents and passing them on to oth-ers, then so too could the press. One of the crimes of "espionage" that the lobbyists were alleged to have committed was providing Frank-lin with a fax number so he could send them some information con-taining national-defense information. But the district court judge, T. S. Ellis III, dismissed their constitutional arguments by drawing on the precedents of *Gorin*, *Heine*, *Snepp*, and *Morison*. Although the prosecution of the pair was ultimately dropped, the case revealed a new theory about the scope of the Espionage Act. In sentencing Franklin, Ellis had gone out of his way to clarify that the law would apply to "all persons" who had disclosed classified information with-out authorization and to all who had received it. "That applies," he said, "to academics, lawyers, journalists, professors, whatever."[32]

In the ramp-up of leak prosecutions that followed, the press was un-derstandably anxious that it might find itself a victim of this freshly invigorated Espionage Act. And although a direct prosecution of the press never came, its rights were threatened by the effort to more tightly police its confidential sources.

The big showdown took place over what is known as a "reporter's privilege," the right of a journalist to decline to share information about their sources with criminal investigations, in the same fashion that patient-doctor and attorney-client communications are privileged. Given that the Espionage Act made leaking a crime, the press argued, it had to be able to shield its sources. Otherwise, the fragile truce between press freedom and state secrecy that had developed since the Pentagon Papers decision would be broken: no source would run the risk of leaking even important information to the press if the press could be forced to turn them in. The public interest in promoting the free flow of information at a structural level justified the inconvenience posed to law enforcement in any particular case.

The uncomfortable fact for the press was that the legal standing of the "reporter's privilege" was weak. In 1972, in reviewing a series of cases about the press's right to protect the identities of Black Panthers and drug dealers, the Supreme Court had been asked to find such a privilege implied in the First Amendment right to a free press. Four judges had thought that there was such a privilege, four that there was not, and the ninth had issued a confusing ruling in which he said he did not recognize such a privilege in the cases at hand but thought that it might exist in other cases. In the three years following the decision, no fewer than seventeen bills were introduced to Congress to establish the privilege by statute. None of them passed. But three decades later, almost every state in the nation recognized a reporter's privilege either by statute or court decision—lawyers for the newspaper industry had managed to massage the ambiguities of that 1972 ruling and received favorable rulings in a number of lower courts. And in practice, Justice Department guidelines tightly restricted the subpoenas that were issued to journalists. On shaky legal ground, the press had managed to construct a fairly robust privilege for itself.[33]

In 2005 it all fell apart. The idea of a reporter's privilege was an unexpected casualty of the recriminations that followed from the deceptive case for war in Iraq. In July 2003, former diplomat Joseph Wilson argued that Bush administration claims that Saddam Hussein had tried to purchase uranium in Niger were false. He also said he had written a report telling the CIA so the previous year. To discredit the accusation, and perhaps also exact a pound of flesh, Bush administration officials charged that Wilson's Niger trip was a junket set up by his wife, Valerie Plame, who worked in the CIA. Cheney also instructed his chief of staff, Scooter Libby, to share with Judith Miller classified intelligence briefings that supported the claims about Niger's uranium.[34]

Sensing a political opportunity, Democrats in Congress pushed for the appointment of a special prosecutor, J. Patrick Fitzgerald, to see if the disclosure of Plame's identity violated the Intelligence Identities Protection Act, passed in the wake of the Agee affair and basically forgotten ever since. By the time Fitzgerald was in place, it was already known that Plame's name had first been shared with the press by three members of the administration, each of whom had confessed to the FBI. None of them were ever charged. But Fitzgerald also wanted to know who had given Plame's identity to Miller. And because he was a special prosecutor and not bound by the Justice Department's guidelines for investigating journalists, he was willing to put her on the stand and force her to name her sources. Miller refused and served eighty-five days in prison for contempt of court. The US Court of Appeals for the DC Circuit reaffirmed that she had no constitutional privilege to protect her sources.[35]

In the end, it became clear that Libby was Miller's source and that Libby had lied to investigators to cover up his role in the sordid mess. But it was unlikely that Libby had violated the Intelligence Identities Protection Act: Plame was likely not a "covert agent," as the statute required. In theory, Libby could nevertheless have been charged with the Espionage Act because he had shared classified information with someone—Miller—not entitled to receive it. But Fitzgerald dismissed such charges because Section 793 "is a difficult statute to interpret. It's a statute you want to carefully apply."[36] In any case, in the typical fashion of Washington scandals, it was easier to get a conviction for the cover-up than for the crime. Libby was found guilty of perjury, although Bush promptly commuted his prison sentence.

"Plamegate" revealed the highly uneven way in which the sweeping clauses of the Espionage Act were being applied in a war on terror in which off-the-record disclosures were standard political practice: leaks benefiting the administration were never prosecuted. And it revealed how vulnerable the press was when confronted by a criminal leak investigation willing to press for information about sources. That the first journalist to take a stand for the principle of press autonomy was Miller—poster child for the insider dealing that had led to Iraq—was one of the grand ironies of the period.

The next journalist to try to claim a reporter's privilege was James Risen, who had revealed the NSA surveillance programs. Although no charges were ever filed against his sources for that story—the investigation against DOJ lawyer Trevor Tamm was dropped in 2011, for reasons unclear—Espionage Act charges were brought against the source for another story that Risen had published in his 2006 book on the security state. This was Jeffrey Sterling, a former CIA officer who had worked with Risen on an earlier story about racial discrimination in the CIA. Now he was alleged to be the source for passages in Risen's book that documented a flawed CIA plan to disrupt Iranian nuclear weapons development in the Clinton era. (The idea was to sell the Iranians a blueprint with errors, thus setting back their program. The problem was that the errors were obvious, and obviously remedied, and the Russian scientist being used as a go-between told the Iranians what they were.) To get at Sterling, Risen's credit card, bank, and airline travel records were subpoenaed. It was part of an aggressive new era in which the DOJ also subpoenaed the phone records of the Associated Press and the email records of a *Fox News* journalist in an effort to identify the sources of leaks.[37]

Sterling maintained his innocence, and the Justice Department wanted to put Risen on the stand to name his source. Years of legal wrangling followed. The initial subpoena lapsed; a recently elected Obama administration renewed it. Then the trial judge recognized Risen's right to maintain the confidentiality of his source, until the Obama administration appealed and won a 2–1 Fourth Circuit Court ruling that the First Amendment provided no such privilege. The Supreme Court declined to hear an appeal.[38]

But having established the principle, the Justice Department backed down. Risen was not forced to give up his source, and in 2013 Attorney General Eric Holder issued new guidelines restricting the tactics that could be used to investigate journalists. It was one more example of the same old dynamics that had shaped the Espionage Act for a century. To secure its secrets, the government had stretched its legal powers and encroached on the liberties of the press. The press had cried blue murder. "The Obama administration is the greatest enemy of the press in a generation," charged Risen. "Eric Holder has been the nation's top censorship officer."[39]

There was some truth in the claim, but it was a subtler affair than Risen's rhetoric suggested. This was not the same kind of censorship that had existed in earlier wars. In fact, for all the civil-liberties violations of Bush's war on terror, there was no frontal assault on the right to free speech—no new sedition act, no prosecutions for speech crimes. And although there had been a mob-like rush to the flag after 9/11, this hostility to criticism of the government, this stifling of dissent, had been accomplished largely through the private sector. When the members of the Dixie Chicks, a country-music band, said they were ashamed of Bush in the run-up to the Iraq war, a highly consolidated media industry refused to play their songs on its own initiative. The state had not needed to get involved.[40]

Instead, the Bush and Obama administrations focused their ire on the leaker. Risen's rights had been threatened only as a way to get to Sterling. And it turned out that the government didn't ultimately need Risen's testimony to win a conviction against Sterling.

The Espionage Act, for so long assumed to be a weak and ambiguous tool, turned out to be incredibly effective when wielded with sufficient intent. The law offered leakers no possible defenses; the only evidence needed to convict was evidence that classified documents had been disclosed. From 2009 to 2012, seven people were indicted for violating the Espionage Act. The government won convictions in every case. Six of the accused, fearing the stigma and penalties of the Espionage Act, took plea deals. The seventh was Sterling, who was found guilty and sentenced to forty-two months in jail.[41]

The new crackdown on leaks chilled the willingness of sources to talk to journalists. And even when material leaked out, it did so in a partial, garbled, and delayed form. The consequence was a deformation of public opinion, as America's stunted efforts to come to terms with its torture program reveal.[42]

The Bush administration acknowledged the existence of the black sites in 2006, closed them down, and transferred the fourteen men still detained in them to Guantánamo. But there was no effort to hold those responsible for the programs accountable. In fact, claims of secrecy were used to keep important details of what had happened under wraps. Maher Arar was a Canadian software engineer with no ties to terrorism who had been mistakenly seized at JFK Airport and then interrogated and tortured for a year in Syria. When he tried to sue for justice, the case was dismissed to protect state secrets, one of a rash of cases in which the Bush administration used the precedent established in the Reynolds B-29 accident of the early Cold War to close down legal proceedings. Meanwhile, as CIA officers retired and began to talk about what they had done, prepublication review boards examined the public statements of those involved, redacting names and details.[43]

Journalists struggled to piece together a clearer image of what had happened. At the end of 2007 the *New York Times* revealed that the CIA had destroyed videotapes of abusive interrogations of Abu

Zubaydah in a black site in Thailand. On *ABC News* a few days later, retired CIA officer John Kiriakou gave the first public acknowledgment that waterboarding had been used. He didn't, at first, criticize the decision, and he got important things wrong. He said that Zubaydah had been waterboarded once, for about thirty seconds, and then had offered valuable information that prevented future terrorist attacks. In fact, Zubaydah had been waterboarded eighty-three times in August 2002 alone, and he had shared no valuable information. He was not Al-Qaeda's number 3, as the CIA assumed at the time, but a kind of freelance logistics man who worked with Al-Qaeda but had never been a member. Even after being waterboarded to the point of catatonia, bubbles forming in his open mouth, even after being locked in a coffin for days and thrown against a wall and deprived of sleep and blasted with loud music, he couldn't give the CIA what it wanted. He didn't have knowledge of future plots to disclose.[44]

A leak investigation into Kiriakou was soon opened, and his increasingly frequent contacts with journalists on the trail of the torture story were closely scrutinized. For sharing with journalists information about two officers involved in the interrogation program, he was charged in 2012 with three counts of espionage and one count of violating the Intelligence Identities Protection Act. Facing decades in jail, he pled guilty to the Intelligence Identities Protection Act charges in exchange for the dropping of the espionage charges. He received a sentence of thirty months.[45]

The day of Kiriakou's plea deal, David Petraeus, then director of the CIA, called the conviction an "important victory." "Oaths do matter," said Petraeus, "and there are indeed consequences for those who believe they are above the laws that protect our fellow officers and enable American intelligence agencies to operate with the requisite degree of secrecy." Three days later, Petraeus himself was interviewed by the FBI for spilling secrets. He had shared his notebooks with his biographer, with whom he was also having an affair. "They are highly classified," Petraeus had told her. They included code-word information, the identities of covert officers, high-level deliberative discussions, top-secret national-security information, and intelligence capabilities and mechanisms. No Espionage Act charges were filed. Petraeus pled guilty to the misdemeanor of mishandling classified documents and was given two years of probation and a $100,000 fine, costs easily covered when he returned to the lucrative speaker circuit.[46]

Such selective enforcement of the broad rules against disclosing secrets gave the CIA the ability to manage the public narrative about the torture program. There was never a commission, never an effort at truth and reconciliation. The closest thing the United States had was a long-running Senate Intelligence Committee investigation into the torture program. It was hamstrung by the control that the CIA continued to exert over its classified files. The agency insisted that the Senate investigators, headed by staffer Daniel Jones, would have to access its files only in a CIA-run "saferoom": the CIA would post files to a secure network where they could be read by Jones and his small team. Documents came and went from the network, and piecing the story together was difficult. But then a thousand-page internal CIA history of the torture program turned up on the network. Whether it was placed there by mistake, or by a still-anonymous whistleblower, it was a kind of Family Jewels of the war on terror, showing how brutal the torture was and how utterly useless it had been in extracting intelligence. Jones copied sections of the report and removed them from the CIA saferoom to an Intelligence Committee safe in the Senate building. When senators started calling for the public release of this history, the CIA put the Senate under surveillance and formally requested that Jones be charged with violating the Espionage Act. It then fought tooth and nail to prevent the Senate from releasing its 6,700-page final report, the product of years of labor, on the grounds that it would disclose secrets and harm national security.[47]

In the end, only a redacted, executive summary of the report was released. And it was countered in the political culture not only by a CIA rebuttal but also by memoirs and media briefings from some of the key players that told things in a more favorable light.

During the long delay as the torture report was fought over, the CIA had worked with Kathryn Bigelow as she made the blockbuster movie *Zero Dark Thirty*, which made it seem that the torture programs, however ugly, had produced the intelligence that led to the assassination of Osama Bin Laden. It was self-mythologizing masquerading as hard-eyed realism. The screenwriter, who lacked a security clearance, had been invited to a CIA ceremony celebrating the team that had killed Bin Laden, at which the CIA director had revealed secret information and named individuals involved in the program. Kiriakou had gone to jail for less. But Kiriakou's leaks had hurt the reputation of the CIA, not helped it.[48]

It is hard to calculate the impact of this ongoing guerrilla war over information. But the slow disclosures, the constant both-siding of the issue, must have done important work in blunting the shock from the revelation of what was done after 9/11. In 2005, when the Abu Ghraib story broke, only 38 percent of the public said that they would support torture if it could prevent a future terrorist attack. By 2017, 48 percent of Americans thought torture was acceptable under some circumstances. Half the country disagreed. But the modern security state does not need unanimous support; it does not require a public regimented in lockstep behind it. Division, confusion, and indifference are good enough. Secrecy is a powerful tool of legitimation.[49]

Meanwhile, Abu Zubaydah remains locked in Gitmo. He has never been charged with a crime. Gina Haspel, who oversaw the black site in Thailand where Zubaydah was tortured and helped order the destruction of the tapes of those interrogations, was promoted to head of the CIA, which she led from 2018 to 2021. And the only member of the CIA who has served jail time in connection with the torture program is John Kiriakou.[50]

In April 2010 an organization known as WikiLeaks released video footage of a 2007 Apache helicopter attack in Iraq that had killed twelve people, including two Reuters employees. It was not an unknown incident. Transcripts had been published in a recent book by a journalist embedded with the US Army; Reuters had been trying, in vain, to get access to the video footage. But the video was nevertheless a news event. There was power in directly confronting the quotidian brutality of the war, of hearing, in live time, the bureaucratic chatter of modern violence and the macho indifference of the crew as they killed. It turned out that one of the vans that had been fired on was not full of insurgents but contained a father taking his kids to school. "Their fault," said the gunmen, "for bringing kids into a battle." The video was released in two forms, one raw, one edited. WikiLeaks called the edited version "Collateral Murder."[51]

It had been provided to WikiLeaks by Chelsea Manning, a young intelligence analyst in the US Army. Manning had signed up to get out of her small hometown in Oklahoma and acquire money for college. She had been stationed in Iraq and was upset by what she saw unfolding there: torture of detainees, heavy-handed political censorship in the lead-up to much touted elections, the savage consequences of "low-intensity" warfare that never made headlines back home. Manning thought that publicizing the intelligence files she had access to "could spark a domestic debate" on the war. During a leave back in the United States, she tried to make contact with newspapers but had no success. She turned instead to WikiLeaks, an organization she knew of because of her involvement in online chat groups interested in hacking. Along with the "Collateral Murder" video, she began sharing hundreds of thousands of files documenting the everyday conduct of the US war and foreign policy.[52]

Until now, WikiLeaks had been a relatively obscure organization. It had been founded in 2006 as a platform to allow leakers to anonymously upload secret documents. Its releases thus far had been scattershot: documentation of political assassinations in Somalia, corruption and extrajudicial killings in Kenya, banking abuses in Iceland, Sarah Palin's emails from her ill-fated vice-presidential run. For such transparency work, WikiLeaks had won praise from both Amnesty International and the *Economist*.[53]

But WikiLeaks was also nursing a more radical agenda. Its driving force was Julian Assange, who had emerged out of the anarchist-inflected hacking cultures of the 1990s, particularly what was known as the cypherpunk movement (a portmanteau of William Gibson–inspired cyberpunk aesthetics and the cipher of the code-breaking world of cryptology). In the early 1990s Assange had been convicted in his native Australia of hacking into the networks of the US defense sector. One hack of the era, possibly attributable to Assange himself, was the so-called Wank Worm, which took over NASA systems to display prankish antinuclear messages.[54]

There was an obvious affinity between the radical politics of Assange's hacking background and the antiwar movement. In some senses, Assange was an heir to the antisecrecy crusaders of the Vietnam era. In fact, the first person he asked to join the WikiLeaks board was Daniel Ellsberg. (Ellsberg wished Assange success with his "terrific" concept but declined the offer.) Another influence was cypherpunk John Young, who had been active in the 1960s student movement and was publishing the names of intelligence agents on his website like a latter-day version of the *Counterspy* magazine put out by Phillip Agee and associates in the 1970s. In a direct echo of Norman Mailer's call in that era for a people's CIA, Assange would at one point say that WikiLeaks' ambition was to become "the most powerful intelligence agency on earth, an intelligence agency of the people."[55]

But in its vision of radically decentralized power, of information flowing freely, cypherpunk had its adherents on the anarchist/libertarian right as well as the anarchist left. Although Assange himself always seems to have identified with the Left, a radical transparency agenda could make such distinctions blurry. In an early manifesto, "Conspiracy as Governance," Assange made a vague and sweeping case that exposing the internal communications of governing organizations would lead to their collapse—it was mainly aimed at "authoritarian regimes," but it wasn't clear what Assange meant by this or how his theory would distinguish between legitimate and illegitimate governments. There was always something messianic about

Assange, which made his flights of theoretical fancy hard to pin down. And he was himself a tricksterish figure, a slippery, self-styled controversialist. Back in the day, he had taken his hacking handle from Horace: "Mendax," someone who lies for noble causes.[56]

Much of the initial public discussion about WikiLeaks focused on the medium as much as the message. The blowback to the releases was astonishing. Vice President Joe Biden called Assange a "high-tech terrorist." Right-wing politicians and pundits called for his assassination, and Dianne Feinstein called for his prosecution under the Espionage Act. In the *New York Times*, Thomas Friedman concluded that the stability of the world order was threatened by two things: the rise of China and the rise of "super-empowered individuals, as represented by the WikiLeakers."[57]

Amid the moral panic, what had actually been disclosed, and how, was often hard to glean. This was not actually a simple data dump. The first tranche of documents released were 92,000 Afghan war logs, and WikiLeaks teamed with three traditional news organizations to analyze them before all four rolled out the news on the same day. The *New York Times*, the *Guardian*, and *Der Spiegel* all ran traditional stories sampling from what they found newsworthy in the logs. WikiLeaks released all but 15,000 of the logs directly. Lacking sufficient staff or experience to correctly vet them, it did not properly redact the names of Afghan civilians who had collaborated with the Americans. This was an important, unforgivable error, but WikiLeaks seemed to learn from it. In October it posted 400,000 field reports from Iraq after developing automated processes to redact names. The next month, WikiLeaks shared 250,000 State Department cables with a number of news organizations, asked the State Department for help redacting them—they were rebuffed—and then published only a few hundred of them directly online.[58]

In the furor that met the releases, such distinctions were ignored. Because of the errors with the Afghan logs, many assumed that WikiLeaks had "blood on their hands." There was no evidence that this was the case: a 2011 Pentagon task force on WikiLeaks concluded that no one had suffered physical harm as a result of the leak, and no such instance has come to light in the decade since. But the errors colored the treatment of all the disclosures that followed. For instance, Hillary Clinton called the diplomatic leaks an "attack on the international community," although Defense Secretary Robert Gates was more circumspect, admitting that the disclosures were "embarrassing" and "awkward" but would have only "fairly modest" consequences for US foreign policy.[59]

Given the scale of the disclosures, people also seemed to expect apocalyptic, world-historical consequences. What was actually revealed was the casual violence of twenty-first-century military adventurism, the everyday corruption and cynicism of geopolitics. The Afghan logs documented 144 incidents in which US forces fired on civilians. The Iraq logs revealed that civilian casualties were higher than previously reported and that the US-supported Iraqi Army was torturing prisoners. The *New York Times* downplayed the Iraq logs that it was publishing as "provid[ing] no earth-shaking revelations." Headlines abroad were less blasé: "Protocol of Barbarity" (*Der Spiegel*), "Huge Wikileaks Release Shows US Ignored Iraq Torture" (BBC). The impact of the diplomatic cables was greater abroad, too. Although US headlines made much of the casual, impolitic gossip on the wire, there was also serious information disclosed. Yemen was seen to acquiesce to US bombing in its own territory. Confirmation of the corruption of Tunisian president Ben Ali added fuel to the Tunisian Revolution, which in turn helped sparked the Arab Spring.[60]

In the 1970s the Pentagon Papers were received by an expansive, and expanding, antiwar movement, but Ellsberg was a product of that movement, not a cause of it. By the 2010s, antiwar politics was far less mobilized, and the disclosures alone could not lead to meaningful political change. The wars, already an unpopular sideshow amid economic collapse and the increasingly carnivalesque theater of American politics, simply trundled along.

At the eye of the storm, Assange was hardly the sort of figure to catalyze a broader political movement. WikiLeaks, a young, small organization, was placed under incredible strain. Their servers were subject to distributed-denial-of-service attacks. Joe Lieberman, chair of the Senate Homeland Security Committee, called on companies to ostracize WikiLeaks: it was ejected from Amazon's cloud software and found itself cut off from revenues when financial services such as PayPal and Mastercard refused to work with it. Even Assange's Swiss bank closed his account.[61]

Meanwhile, Assange was accused of rape in Sweden. He said the charges were political, an effort to bring him to Sweden, from where he would be extradited to the United States to be prosecuted for the leak. It wasn't the most compelling claim: there was no great bar to extradition from the UK, as would become clear almost a decade later. But in the heated politics of the moment, Assange's personal legal travails became intertwined with the broader issues of transparency and antiwar politics. Key members of WikiLeaks quit the organization because they thought it was becoming more an appendage to the cult of Assange than anything else. In the turmoil, more mistakes were made. Unredacted versions of the diplomatic cables had been placed in a password-protected file that had been distributed online as a form of poison pill—if anything happened to Assange, the password would be released. But then the password was accidentally published in September 2011, and WikiLeaks became what it was always accused of being: a dumper of data.[62]

Assange himself was an increasingly isolated figure. The journalists who had happily worked with him to publish his documents distanced themselves. In 2012, worried about being deported to the United States to face Espionage Act charges, he was offered asylum by Ecuador and entered the Ecuadorian embassy in London. For the next seven years he would run WikiLeaks from the small room that had become his entire world.

Chelsea Manning was even more alone. WikiLeaks had been designed to allow leakers to share documents anonymously and thus to avoid persecution. In this sense, it was a logical reaction to the clampdown on leaks that had taken place during the war on terror—if WikiLeaks didn't know the source of its documents, it couldn't be forced to name the leaker in court. But this did nothing to lessen the psychological costs of leaking. If anything, by depriving the leaker of even solidarity with their contact in the press, it heightened those pressures, leaving the leaker completely alone to bear the burden of what they had done.

For Manning, those pressures were particularly intense. She was trying to make sense of how to be in the world as a woman while being identified by the army as a man. Gay in the last days of the "don't ask, don't tell" era, she had also been subject to homophobia in the army. In May 2010, not long after "Collateral Murder" was published, a supervisor found her in a storage room in a fetal position; later she punched a colleague. Facing disciplinary proceedings, with no one to speak to, she reached out in an online chatroom to Adrian Lamo, well-known in the hacking community, and confessed to what she had done. Lamo turned her in.[63]

Manning was kept in solitary confinement for the next eleven months. Her conditions in Kuwait and then Quantico, ostensibly to prevent her from self-harm, were a troubling echo of the "enhanced interrogation techniques" of the period—enforced nudity, continuous surveillance, being told that she would be sent to Gitmo. The UN said that the treatment might constitute torture.[64]

When her trial began, in March 2013, Manning pleaded guilty to ten of the twenty-two charges against her. She took "full responsibility" for leaking the information but rejected the most severe charges of espionage and aiding the enemy. A few months later, Manning was acquitted of aiding the enemy, which could have brought the death penalty. But she was found guilty of seven Espionage Act violations and sentenced to thirty-five years in Fort Leavenworth, a men's prison. In 2016 she twice tried to kill herself. In 2017, in his last days in office, Obama commuted her sentence, and she went free later that year. Even so, her seven years in jail was the longest sentence ever served for a leak to the press.[65]

For all the chatter about mega-leaks, for all the speculations about techno-dystopias and digital utopias, the WikiLeaks affair followed a familiar pattern. An insider had become disillusioned by what she had learned about the politics of national security, shared it with more-famous figures in the media, and suffered the consequences of an alarmist effort to punish the leak. All that was different was the scale. And that was a response to the evolution of secrecy since 9/11. The fact that there were so many banal secrets to reveal was a product of entrenched overclassification, the willingness to experiment with new methods to disclose them a function of the eroded legitimacy of secrecy and the harsh punishment of leakers.

In politics as in physics, actions produce reactions. In the arms race between secrecy and transparency, the security hawks had been first to radicalize. WikiLeaks, with all of its flaws, was the inevitable consequence.

Three days into Manning's trial, the *Guardian* published a story that the National Security Agency had been secretly collecting millions of telephone records from Verizon. The story was based on an order from the FISA court that had been given to the paper. It was marked "Top Secret//SI//NOFORN," meaning that it was supposed to be restricted only to those with access to signals intelligence and was not to be shown to any foreigners. It was the first time a FISA court order had ever been seen by the US public.[66]

It was just the beginning of disclosures about the secretive NSA. The next day, on the basis of an equally classified slide deck, the *Washington Post* revealed that the NSA was collecting vast amounts of information from internet companies such as Google, Apple, Facebook, and Yahoo!. Three days later, the *Guardian* posted a twelve-minute video in which Edward Snowden went public as the source of these documents, which he clarified were but a small taste of the millions of documents he had removed from the NSA. Over the coming months they would reveal a surveillance apparatus of dizzying scope and trigger an intense debate about privacy rights in the digital age.

They also sparked a debate about Snowden himself and his decision to spill state secrets. Within days, the twenty-nine-year-old contractor had been charged with violating the Espionage Act. Once again, Americans sought to adjudicate the ethics of secrecy and disclosure by arguing about the leaker.[67]

From Snowden's perspective, the ethics were simple. From his privileged position as a systems administrator within the NSA—a perch from which he could survey the totality of NSA's programs— Snowden had come to realize just how surveilled contemporary communications really were. The state had developed ominous new capacities, reined in only by its own policies. Snowden was personally appalled by the surveillance, worried that it created the capacity for a "turnkey tyranny." But he also hated the fact that the electorate had never consented to these programs, that they weren't democratically legitimate. "My sole motive," he explained, "is to inform the public as to that which is done in their name and that which is done against them."[68]

Some welcomed him as a hero. Bonnie Raines, who had been the same age as Snowden when she broke into FBI offices in 1971 and revealed the COINTELPRO program, thought that Snowden was a "legitimate whistleblower." Daniel Ellsberg immediately embraced Snowden as his heir, proclaiming that the NSA disclosures were the most important leaks in American history, even more important than his release of the Pentagon Papers four decades earlier.[69]

Many in the commentariat disagreed. Snowden was "no hero," argued Jeffrey Toobin in the *New Yorker*, but a "grandiose narcissist who deserves to be in prison." Geoffrey Stone, one of the nation's leading First Amendment scholars, agreed that Snowden had broken the law. Snowden, he complained, had decided "on the basis of his own ill-informed, arrogant, and amateurish judgement that he knows better than everyone else in government how best to serve the national interest."[70]

Picking among the details of a very online life, Snowden's critics painted an unflattering portrait of a loner, a loser, a radical right-winger. Snowden was a "paranoid libertarian," argued Sean Wilentz—a Rand Paul fan who had bounced around low-level government jobs while decrying the very legitimacy of governance itself. David Brooks saw in Snowden an avatar of an atomized generation, the "ultimate unmediated man," a man bereft of friends or social connections, unable to discern—let alone serve—the "common good." Apart from the millennial-era flourishes, it all sounded a lot like the 1970s attack on Daniel Ellsberg's narcissism.[71]

Snowden's critics had not invented this image out of thin air. Yes, Snowden was an internet geek from a young age, an anime fan, a frequenter of often obnoxious chat boards, a Tekken player—but so were many shy, suburban kids whose parents divorced in the 1990s. Yes, he had dropped out of high school (after a bout of mono) and then moved through a sequence of jobs in the intelligence community, oscillating back and forth between contract and direct employment. But that career path was hardly atypical of the booming political economy that had been created in the antiterror security state, and it ignored both his youthful patriotism—he had volunteered for the Special Forces after 9/11, only to break his legs in a training accident—and the considerable tech savvy that saw him find work, variously, for the CIA in Geneva and the NSA in Japan. And yes, he had donated to Ron Paul and expressed libertarian attitudes about economic policy, but if there was ever a point of political principle on which libertarians and liberals could agree, surely opposition to massive state surveillance was it.

Indeed, for all of his alleged techno-libertarianism, it was significant that Snowden had not dumped his documents online, nor had he gone to WikiLeaks. (In fact, he would later criticize the WikiLeaks approach to radical transparency.) Rather, he partnered with journalists, trusting them to decide which documents deserved to be published, which deserved to be redacted.[72]

Getting journalists involved meant exposing himself to considerable legal jeopardy. In his cubicle in an underground NSA base in

Hawaii—originally built as an airplane factory after Pearl Harbor, since repurposed into a vast, lightless office complex—he had copied millions of documents onto SD cards and smuggled them out inside a Rubik's cube or in his mouth or in the bottom of his pocket. At home, he encrypted them on laptops that had never been connected to the internet. Driving out from his home to tap into random wireless systems, he used anonymous, encrypted messaging services to reach out to documentary filmmaker Laura Poitras and *Guardian* columnist Glenn Greenwald, both known for their frequent clashes with the national-security state and for their fierce civil-libertarian commitments. To avoid detection by the NSA, he flew to Hong Kong, where he holed up in a hotel room to meet with the journalists in early June. The *Guardian* sent veteran reporter Ewen MacAskill to Hong Kong to work with Greenwald. Poitras had also brought Barton Gellman, a former *Washington Post* reporter, into the mix. Gellman received documents but never traveled to Hong Kong.

By the letter of the Espionage Act, this was all illegal. And, in a funny case of life imitating the law, the measures taken to avoid arrest under the Espionage Act forced Snowden and the journalists into acting like spies. To read the various memoirs written about Snowden's leak, to watch Poitras's documentary, is to be plunged into a paranoia-inducing swirl of amateur tradecraft: crash courses in encrypted communication and air-gapped hard drives, cell phones stashed in fridges during clandestine meetings, Snowden typing passwords under a blanket to avoid hidden cameras, the smearing of glitter glue across the screws on the base of laptops to be able to check to see if they had been opened while you weren't looking.

Such clandestine behavior led, inevitably, to charges that Snowden wasn't just acting like a spy but actually was one. Snowden's decision to go to Hong Kong was cited as evidence that he was a traitor, his stance as a whistleblower a form of ingenious cover for treason. "I'm suspicious," said Dick Cheney, "because he went to China." John Bolton compared Snowden to Phillip Agee and Benedict Arnold. In fact, Snowden had chosen Hong Kong, not mainland China, because he thought it offered him geopolitical protection from unilateral US efforts to silence him—Snowden seems to have feared rendition—without placing himself firmly at the mercy of a rival global power.[73]

Facing Espionage Act charges, Snowden then began looking for political asylum and made an effort to fly to Ecuador. But his passport was canceled mid-flight, and he was stranded in the Moscow airport for a biblical forty days—eating at Burger King and reading a copy of *Crime and Punishment* given to him by his Russian lawyer. In the end, Snowden was offered asylum in Russia, a fact that only added to suspicions that he was a spook. There has never been any evidence that Snowden was working for the Russians or the Chinese, or that he leaked secrets to them, either deliberately or accidentally. And if anyone had the technical skills to keep his documents secure, it was probably Snowden—he had, at one point in his career, run training sessions on anti-Chinese information security within the defense sector. But the accusations persist, and the suspicions linger. By treating leakers like spies, the Espionage Act helps to reproduce its own paranoid logic.[74]

When asked to make sense of a complex political controversy like the revelation of a secret surveillance program, Americans frequently fall back on questions of procedure. Whether or not Snowden was a "callow Ron Paul donor," a "traitor," or a brave whistleblower, it would surely have been better, many suggested, if he had aired his concerns through internal channels. Why not bring his complaints to responsible officials rather than taking things into his own hands? Snowden later claimed, in fact, that he had complained to his superiors, although we have no way to verify the claim, given the ongoing classification of NSA records. But whatever happened inside the NSA, and however much this appeal to internal channels may appear a neutral, sensible approach to the problem, the simple fact is that no internal channels existed that would have helped Snowden. The procedures available to Snowden were established by the Intelligence Community Whistleblower Protection Act of 1998. They are deeply flawed.[75]

To begin with, they are not designed to reveal concerns about systemic policy failures. They are designed to uncover fraud, waste, false statements to Congress, and other cut-and-dried instances where the law or the policy is not being followed and higher-ups need to know so they can put the train back on the tracks. What Snowden was complaining about was not a rogue employee but a massive surveillance program that had been laundered through an elaborate legal process. This program may have been unethical or immoral, and it may even have been potentially unconstitutional—Snowden and his advocates thought that it was—but you couldn't say it was unlawful in any simple sense.[76]

After the internal DOJ revolt of 2004 and then the leaking of the warrantless wiretapping program to Risen and Lichtblau, the Bush administration had turned to damage control, seeking to shore up the legitimacy of what it now dubbed, in an act of spin doctoring, the Terrorist Surveillance Program. Behind the scenes, it worked to find legal authorization for its dragnet programs that were collecting phone and email metadata. In decisions in 2004 and 2006 the FISA court secretly granted it that authority in creative readings of obscure clauses in the 1978 FISA law and the Patriot Act, which had been passed in the weeks after 9/11. Efforts to get the FISA court to authorize warrantless surveillance of foreign suspects were less successful, and the Bush administration was eventually forced to turn to Congress, which initially authorized warrantless wiretapping for six months, before the FISA Amendments Act did so permanently in 2008.[77]

The NSA, once reliant on voluntary compliance from telecommunications companies to access data, could now legally compel the transfer of communications records—including the records of Silicon Valley companies that had declined to participate in the voluntary program. In fact, Yahoo! tried to challenge the new legal orders as a violation of the Fourth Amendment's ban on unreasonable searches. A secret court ruling rejected the claim and then levied astronomical fines that forced Yahoo! to comply. The cornucopia of warrantless surveillance programs that Snowden would reveal in 2013 was now approved by statute. The NSA began collecting records from Microsoft in 2007, Google and Facebook in 2009, YouTube in 2010, and Apple in 2012.[78]

These policies were all facially lawful. In fact, they had been so cleverly lawyered that they were almost incomprehensible to the layperson. "NSA was operating under statute," explained one NSA inspector general, "but ordinary, intelligent, educated Americans could not have looked at that statute and understood that it meant what the FISA Court interpreted it to mean."[79]

The problem for Snowden was not that there were illegal activities taking place in the NSA that his superiors needed to know about. The problem was that his superiors had helped craft programs that had been legally authorized in such secrecy that they lacked democratic legitimacy.

This was a second reason that the 1998 whistle-blowing statute would have provided no help to Snowden. In deference to state secrecy, it was designed not to make complaints generally transparent but to channel them into narrow, secure outlets. It established a carefully scripted process, in which an NSA whistleblower would go first to the NSA inspector general and then the head of the NSA, neither of whom, as insiders, would have been surprised by Snowden's revelations or inclined to view them as evidence of unlawful behavior.

In the last instance, the 1998 law did allow a whistleblower to take their complaint to Congress's intelligence oversight committees. In theory, Congress could have provided a democratic check on executive overreach, providing a forum for public debate about the legality and propriety of the surveillance program.[80]

But in practice, the oversight committees already knew what the NSA was doing. They had been briefed. So, technically, had Congress as a whole. In 2009 and 2011, before Congress voted to reauthorize the Patriot Act, the Obama administration had made a classified report on NSA activity available to members of Congress to read in a secure room on the Hill. Many didn't bother; even those who did often lacked the technical skills to make sense of the report and were barred from discussing what they learned with others (including staffers who lacked security clearances).[81] And those few who were concerned about what they learned remained highly deferential to the need for secrecy. In 2009 three Democratic senators wrote to Attorney General Eric Holder to ask for the declassification of the bulk-surveillance programs so that there could be proper debate before they were reauthorized. Their request was classified, as was Holder's rejection. Even so, any of the senators could have unilaterally declassified the surveillance programs on the Senate floor—yet none did, out of fear of seeming "irresponsible."[82]

Had Snowden followed the internal channels, it is hard to see how he would have accomplished anything more than informing people who already knew what the NSA was doing. And he would have done so at risk to himself. This was a third problem with the whistle-blowing laws: they did not protect whistleblowers in the intelligence community from retaliation. Unlike the Whistleblowing Act of 1989, which applies to the rest of the civil service, the 1998 law governing intelligence-community whistle-blowing does not provide any means to prevent an agency from punishing a whistleblower, even for a legitimate complaint. A presidential directive in October 2012 began to offer some relatively weak protections for employees in the intelligence agencies, but it did not apply to contractors like Snowden. Had he pushed hard on internal channels, he would have risked losing his security clearance, and hence his job, without doing anything that would have helped inform the US public about what was going on.[83]

Whatever else one might think about Snowden's disclosures, there is no denying that they triggered a significant debate about NSA surveillance. In an era marked by low public interest in the news, nine out of ten Americans knew about his disclosures, and one in three reported taking new steps to protect their online privacy in their wake. Internet companies began investing more in encryption. Revelations that the NSA was surveilling millions of foreigners—including, awkwardly, German chancellor Angela Merkel—led to hearings in Europe and Latin America, and to diplomatic tensions.[84]

It was not always the most edifying debate. Americans mainly cared about whether *their* rights were being interfered with; the surveillance of foreigners was accepted with a cynical, world-weary shrug. It didn't help that there was no great symbolic scandal in the Snowden disclosures, no simple story to demonstrate the illegality of these programs—there was no intentional targeting of journalists or political figures, no equivalent to Hoover's efforts to blackmail Martin Luther King Jr. The occasional story of abuse— horny NSA analysts sharing pornographic sexts and video chats they had stumbled across, lovesick desk jockeys using databases to stalk exes and crushes and spouses—received disproportionate attention. In general, the threats that the programs posed to privacy were abstract and hypothetical. And they turned on highly technical matters—how, precisely, the NSA was capturing and storing information, how law enforcement was authorized to access it. Those details were not easily reducible to the sound bite or the hot take. The fact that so many of them were still classified made it all even murkier.[85]

Attitudes to surveillance and privacy thus remained deeply ambivalent. A year after Snowden's revelations, Americans were gifting each other Alexas, welcoming little surveillance units into their homes.[86]

On the other side of the ledger, it was very hard to judge how effective these programs were in improving national security. There was a tendency to assume that there was a central, simple trade-off between privacy and security. "You can't have 100% security and also then have 100% privacy," said Obama. "You know, we are going to have to make some choices as a society." But such a framing presumed that eliminating privacy actually improved security. It presumed that the programs worked.[87]

After Snowden's disclosures, it was often said that the NSA programs had "thwarted" fifty-four terrorist attacks. But NSA head Keith Alexander had actually made a much vaguer and more limited claim: surveillance programs had "contributed to our understanding" of forty-two terror plots and twelve cases of material support. How much they contributed is difficult to know; we are dependent on information that has been disclosed by the still-secretive agency. The gold standard would be something that would not have been on the NSA's radar if not for the bulk-surveillance programs. Only one such case has ever been disclosed for the phone-records program, that of a cab driver in San Diego who was involved in no terrorist plot and had simply sent $8,500 to al-Shabab in Somalia. The House Intelligence Committee has also declassified three other examples in which bulk internet surveillance was said to be helpful. The most convincing of them is the case of Najibullah Zazi, who was convicted of plotting to bomb the New York City subway in 2009. The difficulty is that there was plenty of other intelligence that could have led the FBI to Zazi, as there was in the other two examples. Did bulk surveillance make it easier to find them, as its champions claim? Or by soaking up resources and creating a vast pool of noise in intelligence fields, did it in fact make it harder to deploy more targeted, traditional means of counterterrorism?[88]

These are close to impossible questions to answer definitively. But against such ambivalent successes, one should also stack up the cases of terrorism that bulk collection did *not* stop even though it was running full tilt at the time they took place: the Boston Marathon bombing or the Fort Hood shooting or any of the numerous acts of white-supremacist violence that took place with increasing regularity. When Umar Farouk Abdulmutallab, the "underwear bomber," tried to detonate a bomb on a passenger flight to Detroit in 2009, he was stopped not by any high-tech surveillance but by a passenger noticing him fumbling to set his pants on fire. A few weeks earlier, Abdulmutallab's father had actually contacted the US embassy in Nigeria to warn them that his son had radicalized and might be planning an attack. Nothing was done with that good old-fashioned intelligence. His name had been incorrectly entered into a database and then disappeared in an ocean of information.[89]

The NSA programs that Snowden revealed should not be judged on a simple spectrum in which privacy and security are the only poles. There is another axis to the issue: whether such surveillance is an effective and efficient tool of security in the first place. It is an easier problem to focus on when we remember that Snowden was not the first NSA whistleblower to face Espionage Act charges.

That was Thomas Drake, an air force veteran who had joined the NSA as a senior executive on, of all days, September 11, 2001. Drake was a patriot, a GOP voter, and a true believer in the organization's mission. But he was one of a small cluster of NSA employees who came to believe that the warrantless programs were not only an unnecessary violation of privacy. They were also a corporate boondoggle.

Drake had been a champion of a program for analyzing collected data called Thinthread, which had been developed in house at a cost of $3 million. But the NSA had instead given the contract to a rival program, Trailblazer, being pushed by Northrup Grumman. Trailblazer cost $1.2 billion, was less protective of privacy than Thinthread, and never worked. In 2006 it was abandoned, and the NSA turned once again to the Thinthread program (although the NSA also stripped out the privacy protections). Drake, along with a handful of other insiders, complained through all the internal channels he could. An internal report concluded that he was right, but this report was classified and buried. When nothing happened, Drake discussed some unclassified information with a reporter from the *Baltimore Sun* looking into mismanagement at the NSA.

Then came the Bush administration's crackdown on leaks. Drake was suspected of being the leaker who had given the *New York Times* the 2005 warrantless wiretapping story, and in November 2007, armed FBI agents raided his home. He was stripped of his security clearance and placed on leave. Then he was charged with ten counts. They included five counts of violating the Espionage Act, not for sharing classified information with a journalist but for retaining classified information without authorization. In 2011, after a long struggle that drained his savings, Drake pleaded guilty to a single misdemeanor of unauthorized use of a work computer.

He was, on multiple levels, the rightful heir to John Nickerson. Simply being charged with espionage had ruined his career. During the ordeal he had quit his job at the NSA to avoid being fired and ended up working in an Apple store. He had been charged, he said, "to send a chilling message" to other whistleblowers. It didn't quite work. "If there had been no Thomas Drake," said the next man to leak from the NSA, "there would be no Edward Snowden."[90]

Drake's effort to blow the whistle on the Thinthread contract is a reminder that the post-9/11 surveillance state was also a massive economic enterprise. In 2013, according to a budget document released by Snowden, the NSA was spending $10.8 billion per year. Much of that money sloshed out to private contractors. At the time of 9/11, the NSA had 55 contracts with 144 companies. Four years later, it had more than 7,000 contracts with 4,388 firms.[91]

A tight circle of influence ran from Silicon Valley to the security state. Via In-Q-Tel, a venture-capital firm backed by the CIA, money was invested in a satellite mapping company called Keyhole, which was later sold to become Google Earth. Keyhole's founder then went on to create the company that gave the world the five-minute wonder of Pokemon Go. In 2004 In-Q-Tel gave libertarian Peter Thiel's young start-up Palantir a $2 million data-mining contract. Palantir subsequently sold its services to Immigration and Customs Enforcement and numerous police departments, and also sued to win an $800 million contract with the army. How effective Palantir actually is remains unclear, but its reputation as an Orwellian project has been good for the business model. Thiel has confessed that he'd "rather be seen as evil than incompetent."[92]

National-security surveillance thus helped to subsidize the rise of a broader digital economy devoted to the collection and manipulation of aggregated data. Its implications for democracy are unclear.

So, frankly, is its economic viability. Mostly, it has surveilled in order to micro-target advertising, fueled by a bubble of investment speculating on its future profitability.[93]

Even in the realm of consumer advertising, it hasn't quite lived up to the hype. And sorting through masses of consumer behavior looking for patterns and matches is relatively simple. Finding two Amazon book buyers with similar tastes is a much easier task than finding two terrorists with similar profiles, for terrorists are statistically much rarer, and hence much more idiosyncratic. Keith Devlin, a Stanford statistician funded by the Defense Department to explore how to extrapolate useful intelligence from bulk-collected data, concluded that it couldn't be done. "Based on everything I learned in those five years," he said, "blanket surveillance is highly unlikely to prevent a terrorist attack and is a dangerous misuse of resources that, if used in other ways, possibly could prevent attacks."[94]

Snowden had asked Americans to engage in a debate about cost and benefit, about risk and reward, about fundamentals of privacy and security and public expenditure. And although he provided much new information, the high walls of secrecy surrounding the NSA made the debate almost impossible to resolve. It wasn't even entirely clear how many documents Snowden had taken or what percentage of them he had released, let alone what harm his disclosures had done to ongoing programs or whether those programs were effective enough to warrant protecting.[95] And the fact that this was the second round of disclosures, several years after the first stories of warrantless wiretapping, no doubt muffled their impact.

Yet for all that ambivalence, Snowden's revelations did trigger a sudden burst of political reform. In July 2013 a measure to end bulk-phone-records collection fell just seven votes short of passage in the House. It had drawn trans-partisan support from the libertarian right and the civil libertarian left, only to be narrowly beaten by vigorous opposition from the White House, the security branches, and the bipartisan center of congressional leadership. (Those voting to continue the program had received, on average, twice as many campaign contributions from defense lobbyists as those voting to end it.)[96]

The next month, because of the "rapid and passionate response" to Snowden's disclosures, Obama established a review of NSA policy that led to new presidential procedures designed, for the first time, to protect the privacy of foreign citizens subject to surveillance. A dragnet surveillance program that the Drug Enforcement Agency had been conducting in secret since 1992 was brought to an end, and proposals to allow easier wiretapping of encrypted communications, which had been gathering momentum within the administration, quietly died. The NSA began releasing more documents in response to FOIA requests, posting them on a new website—by March 2014, it had released twice as many documents as had the journalists working with Snowden. And in 2015, Congress passed the USA Freedom Act, which revised the way that the NSA accessed phone records and introduced new FISA procedures intended to protect privacy.[97]

These reforms hardly resolved, once and for all, the difficult questions that Snowden's disclosures raised about the value and danger of the NSA. Surveillance continued, to the chagrin of privacy advocates. But public debate and cautious reform are exactly how democracies are supposed to run, and none of it would have happened had Snowden not leaked information to the press. "We can certainly argue about the way in which Snowden did what he did," conceded Eric Holder in 2016, "but I think that he actually performed a public service by raising the debate that we engaged in and by the changes that we made."[98]

Of course, Holder said that only after he had left office. The Obama administration continued to insist that Snowden had violated the Espionage Act. "He should man up," blustered Secretary of State John Kerry, and "come back" to the United States. "He should come home and face the music," added Robert Gates, "much as earlier whistleblowers like Daniel Ellsberg and others did." Snowden explained that he would be happy to do so if he had any chance of a meaningful trial. The problem was that the "hundred-year old law under which I've been charged" meant "there's no chance to have a fair trial." When Ellsberg had leaked the Pentagon Papers, the legal reach of the Espionage Act was entirely untested. By 2013, its meaning was all too clear. Given the way that it was being applied, the jury would not need to consider whether or not Snowden's actions did more harm than good, whether he served the public interest in blowing the whistle on surveillance. Nor would the prosecution need to show any actual harm flowing from the disclosures.[99]

All that would be considered was whether or not Snowden had disclosed classified information to those not entitled to receive it, a fact that he had confessed to in the interview he recorded in the Hong Kong hotel room in June 2013. The extremities of the Espionage Act mean that the public has been denied the opportunity for a final reckoning of the justice of Snowden's disclosures and the opportunity for further reflection about the morality and value of the surveillance programs that he revealed.

Snowden also remains in limbo. He is still in exile in Russia.

In the final scenes of Laura Poitras's Oscar-winning documentary about the Snowden disclosures, Glenn Greenwald travels to Russia to show Snowden a set of classified documents that his new organization, the *Intercept*, has received from a copycat whistleblower revealing information about the rise of drone warfare. It was a fitting coda to the politics of secrecy in the war on terror.[100]

The man who turned out to be the *Intercept*'s source was, like Snowden and Manning, an employee of the lower echelons of the vast security state who had become disillusioned with what he had learned about the never-ending war on terror. In 2008, at age twenty-one, Daniel Hale had joined the air force out of a sense of desperation. Lacking a job, unable to live with a father with whom he clashed, he had walked into a recruitment center in a strip mall on the border of Virginia and Tennessee, aced his test, and ended up assigned to intelligence work. His job was to help identify cars and homes that would be struck by missiles fired from drones controlled by operators located thousands of miles away. By 2014, his tour over, Hale was attending antiwar events and working as a contractor with the Geospatial Intelligence Agency. Frustrated by the lack of public debate about the secret drone program, he gave the *Intercept* seventeen secret documents that provided new insight into the bureaucratic process by which targets were selected, confirmation of the ways that the US government was undercounting civilian casualties, and proof, in one document, that 90 percent of the casualties in one five-month stretch in Afghanistan had not been the intended targets of strikes.[101]

Like the torture and surveillance programs, the drone program had been lawyered to a fine point. No statute directed or constrained it. Obama's Office of Legal Counsel wrote memos that allowed the drone program to expand beyond the battlefield into what were considered lawless areas in Yemen, Libya, Somalia, and Pakistan. Taking advantage of the Bush administration's porous Authorization for the Use of Military Force, strikes against a range of organizations and individuals considered to be "associated forces" of Al-Qaeda were considered a legitimate part of the war on terror. Targets thought to pose a "continuing and imminent" threat were selected based on intelligence fed into an internal "disposition matrix," known colloquially as the "kill list." The executive branch was waging a secret air war according to rules it had written for itself.[102]

And like the torture and surveillance programs, the drone war had grown in secret. Only in 2012 did the Obama administration finally acknowledge the existence of what CNN called "the worst kept secret in Washington and Pakistan." The pretense of secrecy gave the administration space to spin the program. "We're exceptionally precise and surgical," boasted Obama's counterterrorism adviser John Brennan in 2011, before the program was technically public—there had never, he added, been a single civilian casualty. In reality, as Hale's leaks helped to show, there were many civilian casualties. In 2016 Obama for the first time disclosed some statistics about the drone program, claiming that between 64 and 166 noncombatants had been killed. Compared to the figures produced by watchdog groups, those numbers were radically, implausibly low—likely a product of the fact that the administration was counting all military-age males killed in a strike as enemy combatants except when explicitly proven innocent after the fact.

But partial transparency sowed doubt and confusion, creating space for cynical acceptance of a program that might have landed differently if revealed all at once. Debate necessarily centered on the ethics and legality of particular actions—such as the killing of a US citizen like Anwar Al-Awlaki or the accidental murder of his sixteen-year-old son—that were already over by the time they were revealed. At no point was there public debate about the strategic value of the program, about whether the risk of alienating and radicalizing its foreign victims actually made the United States more secure.[103]

The drip-drip disclosures meant that the American public never came face-to-face with the reality of the drone war; that was reserved for the victims of the program in the fields of Pakistan, Yemen, and Somalia. The half-seen drone program "play[ed] well domestically," according to Dennis Blair, the director of national intelligence, "and [wa]s unpopular only in foreign countries." It was also unpopular with those, like Hale, who knew what their country was doing overseas. Many drone operators were traumatized by the disjuncture between the violence they wreaked and the anodyne rooms in which they watched it unfold on grainy screens, as well as their inability to discuss it with friends and relatives who lacked security clearances.[104]

By disclosing secrets to the *Intercept*, Hale was trying to inform the public about the realities of the drone program. It "was necessary," he said, "to dispel the lie that drone warfare keeps us safe, that our lives are worth more than theirs." For that effort, Hale was charged with five counts of violating the Espionage Act.[105]

In this sense, Hale's story is a fitting coda not merely to the history of the Espionage Act in the war on terror but also to the slow rise of

America's secrecy regime. For the development of the secret air war required the existence of two technologies—the military technology of the drone and the legal technology of the Espionage Act—which had each taken nearly a century to perfect.

When the United States had copied the laws of secrecy from European empires at the time of World War I, it had also copied the first uses of aerial power as a tool of imperial policing. Just as the British bombed and strafed restive populations in postwar Yemen and Iraq, as the French did the same in Morocco and Syria, so too did US marines deploy the airplane to suppress the Sandino uprising in Nicaragua in the late 1920s. Thereafter, to the chagrin of army men like John Nickerson, airpower was the key to American geopolitical primacy, and the quest for automation had already begun. As early as World War II, there were experiments with flying B-17s remotely: JFK's older brother, Joe, was killed in 1944 when one of them exploded. The Pentagon Papers revealed another failed effort to automate the air war—a multibillion-dollar program to drop sensors in the Cambodian jungle that would instruct circling American planes to open fire.[106]

The breakthroughs came in the Reagan years, when the CIA and the army began experimenting with a new generation of small drones at around the same time that Samuel Loring Morison became the first person to serve time for a leak. A few years later, a pair of Contra-supporting defense contractors built the first successful prototype of the Predator. In 2002 the Bush administration ordered the first of forty-eight drone strikes conducted during Bush's presidency. Obama ordered fifty-two in his first year alone, and hundreds more before he left the Oval Office. As with drone strikes, so with leak prosecutions. There was one Espionage Act leak charge during the Bush administration, eight under Obama.[107]

So when Daniel Hale sought to leak documents about the unprecedented scale of the drone program, he confronted an Espionage Act that was more powerful than ever before. The prosecutions of previous whistleblowers had revealed that there was no effective defense. While awaiting trial, Hale updated his Tinder profile. "Soo, full disclosure: I was charged last year with espionage . . . if you know anything about these types of cases, you know that my chances of winning are next to none ;P. In the meantime, I'm hoping to meet someone genuine to hang out with."[108]

Inevitably, Hale pleaded guilty and was sentenced to forty-five months in prison. The drone war continued.

Conclusion

GOOD-BYE TO THE ESPIONAGE ACT?

T HE RAGE AND RESENTMENT THAT FUELED DONALD TRUMP'S path to the White House had many roots. The fault lines in American politics run deep. But the role of the secretive war on terror should not be underestimated. Part of what made Trump look like an outsider was his willingness to criticize the national-security pieties of the post-9/11 GOP. Before winning the South Carolina primary, Trump criticized Bush for lying America into the war in Iraq and also touched what was supposed to be the third rail of the political culture. On 9/11, said Trump on the way to delivering the death blow to Jeb Bush's presidential hopes, George W. hadn't kept the country safe.[1]

The anger at fifteen years of failed wars was channeled not into pacifism but into a juvenile fury. Trump doubled down on the callous cruelty of the preceding years. He would "bomb the shit out of ISIS." He would restock Gitmo. He would "bring back a hell of a lot worse than waterboarding." If the United States was going to expend lives and money in places like Iraq, it might as well go ahead and take the oil that was its rightful due. It was surprisingly hard to object to Trump's callous vision of foreign policy. "Do you think our country's so innocent?" he sneered at critics who still spoke in the language of American moral righteousness. Given the secrets that had been revealed in the previous decades, it wasn't as easy to dismiss him as one might hope.[2]

The Islamophobia that had wormed its way through so much security policy since 9/11 also opened a sluice through which the darkest undercurrents of American racism returned to the center of political life. In the run-up to the 2016 election, sixteen of the top twenty Breitbart stories attacking immigrants focused on the threat posed by radical Muslims. The fear of another terrorist attack, cultivated by years of "See something, say something" politics, cross-fertilized with the other bugbears of the surging Far Right. One of the most shared Breitbart stories was headlined "Clinton Cash: Khizr Khan's Deep Legal, Financial Connections to Saudi Arabia, Hillary's Clinton Foundation Tie Terror, Immigration, Email Scandals Together."[3]

And what about her emails? When FBI director James Comey announced that he was reopening an investigation into Clinton's use of a private server to store classified State Department email, providing a final blow from which her star-crossed campaign could not recover, the ensuing scandal reflected the deeper pathologies of the politics of secrecy. The revelation of the server was a consequence of the endless Benghazi hearings, in which conservatives sought to blame the Obama administration for failing to defend the US diplomatic compound in Libya when it was attacked in 2012. The secrecy that surrounded US security policy provided enough air to sustain allegations that there was some sort of cover-up involved. And it made it hard to dismiss the revelation that Clinton was, in the words of Comey's unprecedented public scolding, "lacking in the kind of care for classified information that's found elsewhere in the U.S. government." Trump rushed to claim that Clinton had threatened the security of the United States. Obama responded that there was nothing to it, that although there was classified information on the server, this was no necessary danger because "there's classified and then there's classified." The use of the server reflected the habitual hypocrisy of the security state's pieties about secrecy in an era of routine overclassification. But having railed so hard against leakers, having made so much of the need for secrecy, it was not easy for the Democrats to quash suspicions that the server was a sign of something more nefarious.[4]

After the shock of the November election result, things turned truly strange. In the confusing swirl of conspiracist theorizing that followed, the politics of secrecy was a bright thread. Anti-Trumpers, struggling to make sense of an outcome that shook their faith in US democracy, sought to blame Russian interference, seeing a dark conspiracy emanating from the old Cold War nemesis. They put their faith in the security branches, trusting the generals, the CIA, and the FBI, sheltered as they were from political oversight by their secretive autonomy, to do the right thing and keep the US state on the rails.

Trump and his supporters returned fire, seeing a "deep state" conspiracy aligned against them, an unelected phalanx of security hawks seeking to subvert the will of the people. (Well, the will of the electoral college, at least, but that's another story.) Unforced errors by the FBI added fuel to the fire. A wiretap on Trump adviser Carter Page was opened on the basis of a misleading and error-filled application to the FISA court, the kind of abuse of surveillance powers that civil libertarians had long been worried about but that now provided them with the least appealing test case imaginable. And it turned out that two of the FBI agents investigating allegations of corrupt Trump ties to Russia were having an affair and texting each other little missives of elitist self-satisfaction. "Just went to a southern Virginia Walmart," one said. "I could SMELL the Trump support." Don't worry about losing the country to the Right, said the other. "We'll get it back. We're America. We rock."[5]

The claims about Russia and the deep state were both exaggerated, and they frequently slid into the improbable and the imaginary. But their form was instructive. For years, one of the central fronts of US political life was shaped by dueling conspiracy theories. Both sides deployed little scraps of decontextualized information to explain what was going on: the key action was always presumed to be secret, walled away from prying eyes. This wasn't politics on anything like the model of a liberal public sphere, in which self-interested actors rationally parse competing policies and muddle their way to a middle ground. It was eighteenth-century court intrigue or a postmodern spy thriller, an all-or-nothing war between subterranean forces in which the truth could never be known.

The Espionage Act did play a small role in this drama of leaks and anonymous tips and secret disclosures. Reality Winner, a young contractor working for the NSA, leaked a document outlining failed Russian efforts to hack election machines—a separate issue from allegations that fake news had "hacked" the political culture—and pled guilty when charged with the Espionage Act. She received a sixty-three-month sentence.[6]

Overall, though, the Espionage Act prosecutions of the Trump years were of a piece with those of his predecessors in the White House. The number of leak investigations tripled in his first seven months in office. Daniel Hale went to jail for leaking details of the ongoing drone program, Terry Albury for leaking details of the FBI's discriminatory counterterrorism programs. And the administration also used the law to prosecute those who disclosed secrets for more ambiguous reasons. Josh Schulte was found guilty of leaking the code for CIA hacking tools to WikiLeaks, apparently less out of a desire to inform the public than out of vengeance for personal, nonpolitical disagreements he had had in the workplace.[7] Henry Kyle Frese, an analyst in the Defense Intelligence Agency, shared information about the weapons systems of foreign nations with two journalists, one of whom he was dating.[8] In this sense, at least, the Trump administration broke no norms.

But in August 2022 the Justice Department investigated Trump himself for violating the Espionage Act. The case stemmed from Trump's departure from the White House, when, it had become clear, he had not turned over to the National Archives all documents that were required by the Presidential Records Act, which had been passed in the wake of the Watergate scandal. Instead, Trump had retained a number of records at Mar-a-Lago, his resort in Florida. In January 2022 the National Archives belatedly received fifteen boxes from the resort, which contained, mingled among newspaper clippings and dinner menus, 184 classified documents. Negotiations to take possession of yet more withheld records stalled out, and in August the Justice Department raided Mar-a-Lago, seizing twenty boxes of documents. Amid the ensuing public controversy, the DOJ released the warrant for the raid, which revealed that Trump was under investigation for violating Section 793 of the Espionage Act as well as other crimes relating to records management. At the end of August, it also released a photograph of seized documents laid out on the Mar-a-Lago carpet, their classified markings clearly visible.[9]

At the time of writing, it is too soon to tell what will come of the affair. Many of the central details, such as what was in the documents in question, remains unknown. There can be no doubt that democratic government requires careful management of genuine national-security information as well as compliance with the laws of record keeping and transparency. If the Trump administration, as has been charged, violated these rules, if it destroyed or falsified records, it should be held accountable.

But the Espionage Act is a poor tool for the task, as the ensuing debate revealed. For some liberal critics of Trump, the fact that he was being investigated under the Espionage Act seemed proof that improper storage of documents had actually endangered the nation's security. (In some corners, old fears of a Russian connection were re-animated by the raid, the layperson understandably assuming that a charge of espionage meant that Trump was suspected of classic spying.) But that is to presume that everything stamped as secret is truly vital to national security. Meanwhile, it is Trump's defenders who claim that the secrecy stamp is nothing more than a bureaucratic fiction, dictated at the whim of the president. Trump has even claimed that he declassified all documents at Mar-a-Lago "by thinking about it," so he cannot be charged with the Espionage Act. On one level, the exchanges highlight the confusions that still surround the meaning of the old law. Even if the documents were properly declassified, legal commentators explained, they could still be "information relating to the national defense" and thus their unauthorized retention unlawful anyway.[10]

Then classified documents were found in Joe Biden's garage, and in Mike Pence's home. It all reveals the impossible situation produced by the vague terms of the Espionage Act and the bloat of classification. The law and the classification system cover so much that they cannot be applied literally. In all cases, the decision to use the Espionage Act can therefore seem entirely political, governed by power and self-interest rather than justice. Indeed, the selective enforcement of the law over the past fifteen years has essentially boxed the Justice Department in; almost any application of the law will seem hypocritical or biased. Whatever comes of it, the Mar-a-Lago affair reveals the broken politics of the secrecy regime.[11]

The ultimate significance of the Espionage Act in the Trump years was deeper still. The steady ratcheting up of secrecy, the prosecutions of leakers, had fueled an ever-larger disconnect between the public and its politics, between citizens and their state. Foreign policy was being conducted out of sight and out of mind, its experiential costs borne overwhelmingly by a small fraction of the populace, themselves increasingly isolated in the polarizing and fragmenting cultural landscape of the modern United States. The fiscal toll of the security state, of course, was borne much more broadly as money flowed away from schools and health care and infrastructure. And into the gaps had grown a paranoid and angry politics. It was no accident that the Q-Anon conspiracy featured as its protagonist an all-powerful political insider deep inside the secret state who knew what was really going on. He was known as Q, of course, for the level of his security clearance.[12]

To grapple with the world that the Espionage Act has made, it is important to begin with such political atmospherics, however hard they are to fully measure. The secrecy laws and the security state are supposed to keep the United States safe in a threatening world, and their champions will often paint nightmarish pictures of tragedies that may follow from any effort to roll them back. If we start from a presumption that the high walls of secrecy have helped keep the wolves from the door, it will be hard to begin experimenting with reform. What possible improvements could justify any risk of weakness in the face of violent attack?

We need to start instead by acknowledging that things are already in a pretty bad way. Runaway secrecy has been producing real harms for decades, and it continues to do so today. There are all the familiar harms: torture and corruption and death and waste. And there are the costs to democracy itself, harder to get your hands around but nevertheless very real. The cynicism about and mistrust of American politics today have been bred, in no small part, by the cult of secrecy that the Espionage Act helped to construct.

We also need to acknowledge that secrecy has not, in fact, made us secure. People have lost their lives as a result of abuses and incompetence made possible by secrecy. The nation has started wars on the basis of policies begun in secret. Secretive politics have led, often many years later, to blowback. The 9/11 attacks can be seen as a consequence of secrecy as much as a cause of it. The geopolitical costs of the war on terror will not be known for decades.

And although the secrecy regime has been very effective in blunting democratic oversight, it has not actually been all that effective at securing secrets. The mega-leaks of Snowden and Manning proved that it was actually pretty easy for a low-level employee to exfiltrate huge quantities of data from the supposedly impregnable bowels of the security state. Manning needed just a couple of blank CDs with a Lady Gaga label. It is only because of good fortune that American leakers have, thus far, been motivated by the desire to inform the public about wrongdoing rather than by more sinister goals.

It would have been just as easy to sell those secrets to a rival power. From 2011 to 2013, a petty officer in the supply corps of a US Navy base in Japan was walking into a secure room on the USS *Blue Ridge*,

printing out the schedules of upcoming ship movements, and walking off the boat to give them to a Singapore-based firm that supplied
navy ships in the Indian and Pacific Oceans. The movement of vessels is the kind of operational detail that was held up as the gravest
risk to national security in the Pentagon Papers case. Thankfully,
this was a low-level case of political corruption. Detailed knowledge
about shipping schedules, and what the US was paying its rivals,
helped the firm win millions of extra dollars from the US taxpayer.
But all the firm had to do to get the secrets was give the officer about
$1,000 per month, some free nights in luxury hotels, and a handful
of consumer electronics (an iPad, a Wii, a digital camera).[13]

The simple fact is that the more secrets one tries to keep, the
harder it is to actually secure them. The sheer size of the secretive
state means that more than four million Americans need security
clearances to do their work. In the 1990s the job of managing those
security clearances was privatized, and the firms that are responsible are inevitably cutting corners to try to get through the backlog
and meet their required quotas. This is security theater, producing
profit for the contractors more than any genuine peace of mind.[14]

Meanwhile, efforts to compensate for increasingly frequent leak-
ages are causing problems *within* the security branches. In 2011
State Department employee Peter Van Buren had his Top Secret
clearance indefinitely suspended because he linked to WikiLeaks on
a blog post. He could not appeal and was assigned to a dead-end job
where he did not need access to secrets. Even more absurdly, for almost three years the head of Naval Intelligence was not able to read,
see, or hear any classified information. His clearance had been suspended when his name surfaced during a corruption investigation,
and although he was ultimately never charged, the case remained
open for years, and he remained in his position throughout. Every
time he entered the room of a colleague, they had to secure all classified material.[15]

The whole song and dance about secrecy is an expensive production, costly both in simple budgetary terms and in its broader
political consequences. Too much information is being kept secret,

including information that should, by rights, be public. It leaks all the time, mostly to serve the needs of those in power. Yet rare acts of disclosure that are intended to inform the public are prosecuted harshly, and the vague clauses of the Espionage Act provide a powerful cudgel to shape the flow of information in the polity.

It is past time to reform the system.

The secrecy regime is such a complex tangle of laws and orders and bureaucratic practices that it is hard to know where to begin. That complexity is in fact a large part of the problem. Since the passage of the Espionage Act in 1917, the system has grown like weeds, guided by no overall vision but a century-long process of improvisation and adjustment. Momentary controversies have had a disproportionate impact on its shape, pushback by particular interest groups a disproportionate hand in guiding its development. The risk of tinkering with one part of the regime is that it will create new problems somewhere else as the delicate ecology of the bureaucracy evolves to deal with changes.

So the ideal solution would be to begin again, to think about the system as a whole and to draw up laws that try to accommodate the competing interests in a more rational way. This would be no permanent solution, of course, and future experience would guide yet further tinkering. But root-and-branch reform is needed. Thankfully, people have been calling for reforms to the espionage laws since at least the time Herbert Yardley published his memoir in the early 1930s. Law reviews called for updating the laws after the *Gorin* decision in 1941. So did some of the judges ruling on Samuel Loring Morison's case in 1988. In 2006, in the decision that launched the new era of Espionage Act prosecutions under George W. Bush, Judge T. S. Ellis III observed that it was remarkable that the "basic terms and structure of [the Espionage Act] have remained largely unchanged since the administration of William Howard Taft." A lot had changed in US law and politics and foreign policy since then. "These changes," Ellis said, "should suggest to even the most casual observer that the time is ripe for Congress to engage in a thorough review and revision of these provisions."[16]

That hasn't happened. But the past ninety years of complaints about secrecy have provided a well-stocked pantry of reform ideas. Putting them together, we can begin to imagine what a new secrecy regime might look like.

The most basic starting point is an omnibus information bill that will consolidate and coordinate the various moving pieces of the law. At present, the structure of the laws is shaped by history. The Espionage Act, in all of its vagueness, came first. Then came patches to deal with what were once seen as the inadequacies of the Espionage Act: the classification system, prepublication review, the Intelligence Identities Protection Act. Then came reform measures intending to make that secretive state more transparent: the FOIA and whistle-blowing laws. But because the secrecy laws came first, both historically and logically, the reform measures have largely deferred to them. The whistle-blowing laws and the FOIA exempt classified information. At present, the right of the public to know what its government is doing is not actually being balanced against the need for the state to keep some things secret. It is being sacrificed to the presumption of secrecy.

An omnibus public-information law could consider all of these things at once, building in balancing tests at the crucial junctures that would serve to better protect the public's interest in knowing what its government is up to. The precise form of such a law would be a matter for democratic debate. But history suggests that any effective law would need to do two things.

First, it would need to prevent the routine overclassification of information that distorts so much of the secrecy regime. The obvious solution is to put the classification regime on a statutory basis, as the Moynihan Commission suggested. The current system, a patch to the founding flaw of the Espionage Act, asks classifiers to stamp as secret any potential risks to national security. Alongside this executive order, which changes with differing administrations, exist statutory add-ons—covering atomic information or CIA sources and methods—as well as administrative flourishes to guard particular operations. A new statute should standardize the stamps, require a clearer articulation of the need for secrecy in any given case, and also require classifiers to weigh that need for secrecy against the harms posed by a lack of transparency.

However nicely drawn the standards, the only way to ensure that they will be effective is to enforce them. In 1951, when Truman first established the classification system, William Benton and the ACLU proposed creating a "people's advocate" or "anti-censor" who could audit and police classification decisions. It is still a good idea and should be enacted. The Information Security Oversight Office, established in the 1970s to oversee the classification system, should be transformed into an Office of Public Knowledge, with powers to audit classification decisions and impose sanctions. Individuals who repeatedly classify incorrectly would see that reflected in evaluations of their work performance. Agency-wide failures could be punished by forcing the agency to cover the costs of overclassification in its budget. Reform could be incentivized by allowing agencies to redirect money saved on classification to other needs. Limited experiments since the 1990s with the Interagency Security Classifications Appeals Panel have shown that such review panels do reverse classification decisions and do increase transparency. This panel has worked on historical materials, and on a tiny scale, but there is every reason to think that expanding such processes within the administrative state, creating new checks and balances, would also work to arrest the sprawl of secrecy.[17]

The second area for reform is the Espionage Act itself. Its murky, confusing provisions should be revised to more clearly distinguish between the crime of espionage and the crime of improperly disclosing classified information. This latter law should make clear that it only applies to government employees and contractors and that it exempts the press and the public. The liability for improperly spilling secrets should be strict, covering both negligent disclosures and willful disclosures. If overclassification is really kept in check, then one doesn't want the small class of properly secret information spilling out willy-nilly. But there should be an important exception: if you disclose information that actually informs the public about a matter of importance, you should not be found guilty of violating the public-information law. Legal scholar Yochai Benkler has outlined one model for such a public-interest defense that strikes me as both sensible and workable. It would require the leaker to prove three things: (1) that they had a reasonable belief that their leak discloses a substantial violation of law or a substantial systemic error; (2) that they took efforts to avoid causing imminent, specific harms from disclosure that outweigh the benefits of the disclosure; and (3) that they communicated their disclosures to a channel likely to result in actual exposure to the public—that they went to a journalist, say, rather than tipped off an acquaintance.[18]

Beyond the public-interest defense, it would also help to vary the penalties for leaking depending on the severity of the disclosure. One of the quirks of the current secrecy laws is that the level of classification is completely irrelevant. It doesn't matter if you leak "confidential" information or "top-secret-code-word" information. A lot of bureaucratic effort is put into distinguishing different levels of classification, into working out who can have access to information that will "harm" the United States and that will "gravely harm" the United States. It is absurd that the same penalties apply to both. Greater proportionality of punishment would allow for more fine-grained prosecutions of genuine leaks without granting prosecutors the power to win plea deals by leaning on the draconian punishments of the current law. One could imagine, too, requiring that prosecutors show that the information was properly classified as part of this process. A more nuanced and precise criminal law would provide an important safety valve and check on abuse while also securing genuine secrets.

Obviously, these two sets of reforms would not resolve, once and for all, the democratic dilemmas posed by secrecy. But much of the current tension is caused by the swollen bloat of the classification system and the imprecise criminal laws used to enforce it. Creating mechanisms to ensure that improperly or unnecessarily classified information cannot be kept secret will make it much easier to enforce prohibitions against disclosing a much smaller class of properly classified information. Reducing the amount of information kept secret will reduce the temptation, and need, to leak.

Foundational reform to the classification and espionage laws would also, I believe, remove much of the need for reform in all the ancillary organizations and structures that have grown up, barnacle-like, around the secrecy regime. The Freedom of Information Act, for instance, has failed to live up to its initial promise. It takes time to use the law, which means that it is of little use to journalists on deadline and that its revelations do little to inform the public about unfolding policy. It is today mainly used by three groups: dogged historians and investigative journalists, who patiently wait for national-security files about distant wrongs to be released and then closely parse their heavily redacted pages; antigovernment trolls, who use the FOIA process against regulatory agencies like the Environmental Protection Agency to gum up the administrative works and search for nuggets to weaponize; and corporations, who use the FOIA to gain economic advantage by reading the bid contracts or regulatory filings of their rivals. There is understandable frustration with the FOIA, which sometimes seems to harm good governance as much as ensure it.[19] But if overclassification was reduced, pressure on the FOIA would be reduced, making it much more effective. The same is true of the whistle-blowing laws. Such transparency laws could nevertheless be reexamined as they were being incorporated into the omnibus public-information law. So, too, could other reform proposals such as standardizing and liberalizing the prepublication review boards or passing a law to create a federal reporter's privilege.[20]

Improvisation, inertia, and evolution have produced a deeply flawed secrecy regime. Only an intentional program of reform can repair it.

How likely is such a reform program? Amid the controversial leak prosecutions of recent years, there have been occasional proposals to revise the Espionage Act. In 2020 Ron Wyden and Ro Khanna introduced a bill to explicitly exempt journalists from Espionage Act prosecutions. Two years later they reintroduced the law with an additional sponsor: Kentucky Republican Thomas Massie. Tulsi Gabbard suggested a "Protect Brave Whistleblowers Act," which proposed tweaking the act's intent requirements to protect those seeking to inform the public rather than aid an enemy. Rashida Tlaib has recently proposed a similar bill.[21]

Each of these proposals, while partial, would be helpful. But they have gone precisely nowhere. Seemingly technocratic, they have failed to mobilize any broader political passions and have withered on the vine. Whether a more holistic program of reform may inspire more determined support is unclear. And there are plenty of people who fear that trying to enact foundational reform would be a dangerous enterprise, as likely to produce a more censorial secrecy regime as a more liberal one. Given the current dysfunctions of American politics, this is a reasonable concern, although I think it underestimates the damage that the current secrecy regime is doing.

At this point in a book on the problems of the US security state, when the author is faced with both a need for reform and a lack of any meaningful political movement calling for it, it is typical to call on the public to become more concerned about the abuses being conducted in their name, to ask them, like good Madisonians, to become more informed and more engaged.

There's nothing wrong with the sentiment, but it's a little bit of a cop-out. The average citizen is never going to go to bat for reforming the Espionage Act. They are too busy worrying about other things— work and family and economic precarity and public health and education. And the political system, flush with campaign contributions, gerrymandered beyond recognition, is not particularly responsive to even those concerns that are close to home. By definition, the problems of state secrecy are out of sight and out of mind. It is naive to think that voters are going to push the issue to the top of their representative's policy agenda.

But that's the fairy-tale version of democratic politics; it's not really how politics works in the modern United States. As the history of the Espionage Act demonstrates, policy is made not by a diffuse process of public engagement. It is shaped by the strategic intervention of relatively small interest groups, positioning themselves as champions of broader philosophical dispositions. Politicians and bureaucrats within the security state championed heightened restrictions on civil liberties to unilaterally protect the nation from a threatening world, sculpting and stretching the laws to allow them to do so. Pushback came from civil-liberties groups, which favored instead a more confident vision of the nation's security, one that prioritized the benefits of robust debate for producing a more democratic and just national-security policy.

As these competing visions clashed across the twentieth century, they reached a kind of uneasy accommodation. The security state could police its own domain, but it could not interfere with the liberties of speech and press in the public sphere. Time and again, efforts by the state to censor the press were defeated. But as civil-liberties and media groups played defense, seeking to preserve their autonomy from an aggressive security state, their First Amendment claims did not check the increasing power of the state to protect its own secrets. The individual leaker was the sacrificial lamb of this settlement, offered up to prosecution under the Espionage Act as long as the press that published their leaks was not policed. However, the ultimate victim was the public's right to know, for even a completely unregulated press could not publish information that it did not have.

The prospects for reform of the Espionage Act therefore rest on the willingness of the press and civil-liberties groups to take the offensive for the first time, to seek not only to protect their own autonomy from the security state but also to roll back the state's control over information.

There are signs that this is beginning to happen. The Reporter's Committee on Freedom of the Press filed amicus briefs in the *Hale* and *Albury* cases arguing that prosecutions of leakers raised serious First Amendment concerns.[22] Seventeen law professors filed a

similar amicus brief in the *Albury* case.[23] In May 2022 the ACLU
and the Knight First Amendment Institute filed a lawsuit on behalf
of five former public servants challenging the prepublication review
system as an unconstitutional interference with civil liberties.[24] To
date, such First Amendment arguments have been unsuccessful in
the courts. But they reveal the slow crystallization of a reform coalition, and if the history of the Espionage Act reveals anything, it
is that a small group of committed activists can decisively shape the
political culture and the law.

The most important case in the coming years will be the
long-delayed prosecution of Julian Assange in connection with the
WikiLeaks affair of 2010. Assange has few friends among the institutional press or even the civil-liberties community. In the 2016
election, WikiLeaks published internal Democratic Party emails
that appear to have been stolen by Kremlin hackers, a decision that
has come to appear particularly controversial because it became intertwined with fears of Russian electoral hacking (a slightly different
issue) and the impact of Comey's investigation of Clinton's server (a
completely different issue), and because those emails provided the
seedbed for some truly bizarre conspiracy theorizing about a satanic
pedophilia ring being run by the Democrats out of the basement
of a DC pizzeria (an issue so strange as to be unclassifiable). Even
if the disclosure of those emails could be justified on transparency
grounds—no one has claimed they were false; they did inform the
public about Democratic National Committee (DNC) practices—
Assange's broader willingness to flirt with the chaotic fringes of
contemporary politics has left him politically isolated. It is hard, for
instance, to wholeheartedly embrace an organization that offered
$20,000 for any information on the death of Seth Rich, a DNC
staffer whose 2016 murder was subject to wild speculation on the Far
Right that he had been a victim of political assassination.[25]

So when the Trump administration first charged Assange with
computer fraud—he is alleged to have helped Chelsea Manning
hack passwords, which led to the WikiLeaks disclosures—the institutional press was not upset. Assange "is not a free-press hero," said

the *Washington Post*, or even a "real journalist": he was "long overdue for personal accountability."[26] The *New York Times* kept a cautious distance, observing coolly that the "administration has begun well by charging Mr. Assange for an indisputable crime."[27] It seemed another case of the press tightly protecting its own privileges. Meanwhile, Manning refused to testify in the case and spent sixty-two days in jail for contempt of court.[28]

In May of 2019, however, the Trump administration also charged Assange with seventeen counts of violating the Espionage Act. Handing down the charges, the Justice Department spokesperson tried to avoid riling up the press, clarifying that it was charging Assange because he was not a journalist. But if Assange could be found guilty of soliciting, receiving, and publishing classified information, a precedent would be set that would certainly cover the institutional press. The practices that Assange is said to have engaged in—such as creating a secure drop for anonymous disclosures—are the same as those that the press has instituted after the war on leakers. And there is nothing in the murky language of the Espionage Act that could be read to distinguish between an organization like WikiLeaks and an organization like the *New York Times*.[29]

The press and civil-liberties groups have responded by denouncing the prosecution as a threat to press freedom. However much they may have to hold their noses, it is important that they stand in solidarity with Assange lest the Espionage Act expand into new territory.[30] Even still, it is important to remember that the opposition to the Assange prosecution is another case of defense, an effort to contain the growth of the Espionage Act. It is unlikely that it will bring much clarity to the deeper ambiguities and pathologies of the secrecy regime, no matter how it resolves.

What we need is a true reckoning with the laws of secrecy that have developed during the century-long life of the Espionage Act. Such a reckoning will come only if the press and civil-liberties activists force it. The newspaper industry is not what it once was, but it still has political clout. It also has the powerful weapon of the First Amendment's guarantee of the right to free speech.

"The press must take up the cause of the brave men and women who leak vital information to them," announced the *Pittsburgh Post-Gazette* in 2019 as it called for much needed revisions to the antiquated Espionage Act. "We cannot afford to remain silent on this issue. Silence is complicity."[31]

ACKNOWLEDGMENTS

Writing a book is never easy, but there were times when this one seemed particularly hard. And it felt that way despite the unbelievable help I received on so many fronts. It's a pleasure to thank all these good people and institutions here. If they hadn't smoothed the way, making the work on the book imaginable, doable, and worthwhile, you wouldn't be reading it now.

When I finished my first book, in 2016, I thought I was probably finished working on the Espionage Act. Then I met Hannah Gurman and Kaeten Mistry, who were putting together a working group on the history of national-security whistle-blowing. Conversations with them, and all the fantastic scholars in that group, led me to write a new piece on the early evolution of the Espionage Act, subsequently published as a chapter in their terrific volume. I thank everyone involved in that group—especially Lloyd Gardner for early comments on my draft chapter—for helping me realize that there was more to be said about the law.

But I was already working on other things, and that might have been the end of it, if not for an email from Connor Guy, who wrote in early 2020 to see if I might be interested in writing a narrative history of the law for Basic Books. We had some preliminary conversations in the spring of 2020, before the bottom fell out of the world in March. But the idea stuck with me, and actually provided some distraction in those dark days, and by the summer of 2020, I had worked up a book proposal. Connor's enthusiasm convinced me that it was a book worth writing and that I could be the one to write it. Don Fehr handled the technical details of getting the book under contract, and me on my way, with remarkable efficiency and reassuring professionalism.

That would all have been fortunate enough, but then I had a run of stupid good luck. Thanks to the hard work of many colleagues at George Mason, the Center for Humanities Research (CHR) was established in 2020, offering a small group of faculty and graduate students a semester of research support to work on a common theme. The inaugural theme was "dissent," and I found myself blessed with a semester freed from teaching, as well as the opportunity to meet twice a week with inspiring colleagues to think about the theory and practice of dissent, social movements, and politics. My first draft of the Pentagon Papers chapter was written in dialogue with my amazing cohort—Ashley Gaddy, Nate Greenberg, Annie Hui, Niklas Hultin, and Jessica Scarlata—and shaped by their work. Extra thanks to Alison Landsberg for running CHR so ably and for bringing her contagious enthusiasm for political and cultural theory to our meetings.

Then I won the lottery again, this time in the form of a National Endowment for the Humanities Public Scholar Fellowship, which provided a year of leave to work on the manuscript. Thanks to the incredible support of Matt Karush, chair of the History Department, and the College of Humanities and Social Sciences, I was able to add this NEH leave to an already scheduled semester-long sabbatical. Two years freed from classroom obligations was, and is, a guilt-inspiring luxury. Without that space to grow in, the book you are reading now would be a very different thing, and likely still unfinished. Of course, if it hadn't been for years of teaching, the book would also be a very different, far clunkier thing. My deep thanks to all my students who have helped me think through problems of democracy, national security, and foreign policy in the classroom.

As I was finishing my first draft, I was also fortunate to receive a grant from the Nelson fund at George Mason that made possible two short archival trips: one to Independence, Missouri, to work at the Truman Library on the early years of classification, and the other to the archives at the University of Huntsville–Alabama to look at papers on the *Nickerson* case. Archivists in both places were remarkably helpful in helping me make the most of my limited time. Sue Woods handled the George Mason travel bureaucracy with her usual but nevertheless remarkable efficiency and grace.

By this point, Connor had left Basic Books, and Emma Berry had inherited the manuscript. This could have been awkward, but from our first meetings, Emma was enthusiastic and supportive, understanding what I wanted to do with the book and offering wise counsel to help me accomplish it. Her careful reading and astonishingly sharp notes have made this book so much better: being edited by Emma was a dream. Donald Pharr gave the book a brilliant copyedit; Melissa Veronesi and Madeline Lee made the production process run perfectly.

A murderers' row of colleagues were kind enough to read drafts of various chapters: Kate Epstein, Justin Evans, Sam Huneke, Richard Immerman, Heidi Kitrosser, Chase Madar, Emily Marker, Peter Roady, Laura Weinrib, and John Fabian Witt. That's an intimidating, humbling group, who made sure that I avoided some real clangers. Extra thanks to Kaeten Mistry, who not only read the entire manuscript in draft but also shared key sources and the inspiring example of his own brilliant work, as well as many great chats about secrecy, soccer, and the struggles of writing history.

Plenty of other people helped, perhaps without realizing. As the pandemic waned, it was a great joy to reconnect with our far-flung network of friends and family. I did much of the work on Chapter 2 during an unexpected trip to Sydney in 2021 to help out with a family medical emergency. Things worked out happily, and I'm looking forward to giving Mum and Dad a copy of this book as one more inadequate token of love and gratitude for all they have done to support me over the years. Justin Evans, Judy Choi, Persy, and Claudia—our DC family—were constant sources of support and friendship. (I complained plenty to them; they knew they were helping.) Studying Tai Chi under the guidance of Paul Ramos has improved every part of my life, including this book: Paul is a master teacher, and what he has taught me is a true gift.

Even with all this help, I'm embarrassed to say, I still found writing the book hard. Perhaps because of the subject matter, or the speed with which it was written, or all the other shit that went down in the world the last couple of years—or simply because I'm now an undeniably middle-aged man—working on the book often made me a bit of a grump. Emily Jane Weaver was remarkably understanding throughout, even during what were some difficult times for her as well. Anyone who knows Em is aware of her generosity; even if you don't know her, you are benefiting from that generosity anyway, for she once again let me read her the manuscript in draft, where her incredible ear helped smooth out all sorts of clunky passages. But that's an easy thing to say thanks for. For all the rest, well, words don't quite work. Em, I can't express how grateful I am for our life together, how happy being with you makes me, and how excited I am to see what we do next.

It's not enough, but this one's for you too.

ABBREVIATIONS

AC	*Atlanta Constitution*
APP	Gerhard Peters and John T. Woolley, American Presidency Project online at www.presidency.ucsb.edu
BG	*Boston Globe*
CSM	*Christian Science Monitor*
CT	*Chicago Tribune*
EP	*Editor and Publisher*
HC	Commission on Freedom of the Press Records, Special Collections Research Center, University of Chicago Library, Chicago, IL
JNP	Col. John C. Nickerson, Jr. Papers, University of Alabama in Huntsville Archives and Special Collections, Huntsville, AL
JNP-CMT	Court-martial transcript, series 2, box 1, folder 11–12, Col. John C. Nickerson, Jr. Papers, University of Alabama in Huntsville Archives and Special Collections, Huntsville, AL
LAT	*Los Angeles Times*
LOC	Library of Congress, Washington, DC
NYT	*New York Times*
OC	Record Group 216, Records of the Office of Censorship, National Archives and Records Administration II, College Park, MD

OWI   Record Group 208, Records of the Office of War Information, National Archives and Records Administration II, College Park, MD

RG   233 Records of the US House of Representatives, 61st Congress, National Archives and Records Administration I, Washington, DC

TOF   Truman Official File, Harry S. Truman Library, Independence, MO

WP   *Washington Post*

NOTES

Introduction

1. Janet Reitman, "I Helped Destroy People," *NYT Magazine*, September 1, 2021; Julian Joslin, "A Counterterrorism Informant's Drama of Trust and Betrayal," *New Yorker*, November 18, 2021; "I'm Part of Something That's Really Evil," *Daily*, September 9, 2021; Josh Gerstein, "Feds Seek 4-Year-Plus Sentence for FBI Agent in Leak Case," *Politico*, October 5, 2018; JaneAnne Murray and Joshua Dratel, "Position on Sentencing on Behalf of Terry Albury—Redacted," Court Filing, October 10, 2018, www.politico.com/f/?id=00000166-4276-d5d9-ab67-de76ae5c0001; Brief of Amici Curiae Scholars of Constitutional Law, First Amendment Law, and Media Law in Support of Defendant at 7–12, *United States v. Albury*, No. 18-cr-00067 (D. Minn., October 4, 2018), https://fas.org/sgp/jud/albury-amicus.pdf.

2. Cora Currier, "Based on a Vague Tip, the Feds Can Surveil Anyone," *Intercept*, January 31, 2017.

3. Reitman, "I Helped Destroy People."

4. Reitman.

5. Reitman; Michael Price, "Community Outreach or Intelligence Gathering? A Closer Look at 'Countering Violent Extremism' Programs," Brennan Center for Justice, January 29, 2015; Michael Hirsch, "Inside the FBI's Secret Muslim Network," *Politico*, March 24, 2016; Amanda Sperber, "Somalis in Minnesota Question Counter-extremism Program Targeted at Muslims," *Guardian*, September 14, 2015.

6. Cora Currier, "Hidden Loopholes Allow FBI Agents to Infiltrate Political and Religious Groups," *Intercept*, January 31, 2017; Cora Currier, "Despite Anti-profiling Rules, the FBI Uses Race and Religion When Deciding Who to Target," *Intercept*, January 31, 2017; Faiza Patel, "Ending the 'National Security' Excuse for Racial and Religious Profiling," Brennan Center for Justice, July 22, 2021.

7. Reitman, "I Helped Destroy People."

8. Charlie Savage and Mitch Smith, "Ex–Minneapolis F.B.I. Agent Is Sentenced to 4 Years in Leak Case," *NYT*, October 18, 2018.

9. The five early cases were Stanley Johnston (1942) and the Pentagon Papers (1971), in which charges were dismissed; *Amerasia* (1946), in which some charges were dropped and two defendants pled out; John Nickerson (1957), who took a plea deal; and the fifth, successful case, that of Samuel Loring Morison. See Reporters Committee for Freedom of the Press, "Federal Cases Involving Unauthorized

Disclosures to the News Media, 1788 to Present," www.rcfp.org/wp-content /uploads/2018/12/12-8-2019-Leaks-Chart-1.pdf.

10. Peter Galison, "Removing Knowledge," *Critical Inquiry* 31 (2004): 229–243; Information Security Oversight Office, "2017 Report to the President," www .archives.gov/files/isoo/reports/2017-annual-report.pdf; Oona A. Hathaway, "Secrecy's End," *Minnesota Law Review* 106 (2021): 719.

11. *New York Times Company v. United States*, 403 US 713 (1971), at 753.

12. Harold Edgar and Benno C. Schmidt, "The Espionage Statutes and Publication of Defense Information," *Columbia Law Review* 73 (May 1973): 929.

Chapter 1: The Fear of Spies

1. "Hyphen Disloyalty Attacked by Wilson," *AC*, June 15, 1916, 1; "Wilson and 60,000 March for Defense," *WP*, June 15, 1916, 1; Patricia O'Toole, *The Moralist: Woodrow Wilson and the World He Made* (New York: Simon and Schuster, 2018), 209–214.

2. "Wilson Braves Rain, Makes War Speech," *WP*, June 15, 1917, 1; Woodrow Wilson, "Address on Flag Day," APP.

3. Joan M. Jensen, *Army Surveillance in America, 1775–1980* (New Haven, CT: Yale University Press, 1991), 113–115; Kenneth Campbell, "Major General Ralph H. Van Deman: Father of Modern American Military Intelligence," *American Intelligence Journal* 8 (1987): 13–19.

4. "Spies Caught in Russia," *NYT*, May 24, 1904, 1; "Russian Spies Convicted," *NYT*, June 17, 1897, 1; "Russian Spies on Watch in New York Libraries," *NYT*, June 23, 1906, 1; "Spies Watch Baltic Fleet?," *NYT*, October 14, 1904, 1; "Spies at Niu-Chwang," *NYT*, April 7, 1904, 1; "Got Plans of Vladivostok," *NYT*, April 11, 1905, 1; "Russian in British Jail," *NYT*, May 7, 1905, 1; "A Japanese Spy Caught at a Fort," *NYT*, July 12, 1907, 1; "Every Nation Has Spies at Work All the Time," *NYT*, March 13, 1904, SM3; "Women Spies at All Capitals of the Nations," *NYT*, May 29, 1904, 12.

5. John Fabian Witt, *Lincoln's Code: The Laws of War in American History* (New York: Free Press, 2012), 25, 127.

6. Christopher Andrew, *The Secret World: A History of Intelligence* (New Haven, CT: Yale University Press, 2018), 17, 24–29, 60, 87–88.

7. Daniel N. Hoffman, *Governmental Secrecy and the Founding Fathers: A Study in Constitutional Controls* (Westport, CT: Greenwood, 1981); Frederick A. O. Schwarz, *Democracy in the Dark: The Seduction of Government Secrecy* (New York: New Press, 2015), 19–20, 254.

8. Anna Kasten Nelson, "Secret Agents and Security Leaks: President Polk and the Mexican War," *Journalism Quarterly* 52 (1975): 9–14, 98; Everette E. Dennis, "Stolen Peace Treaties and the Press: Two Case Studies," *Journalism History* 2 (1975): 6–14; Donald A. Ritchie, "'No Secrecy Possible:' One Aspect of the Relationship Between the U.S. Senate and the Press in the Nineteenth Century," *Government Publications Review* 18 (May 1991): 239–244; Daniel Larsen, "Creating an American Culture of Secrecy: Cryptography in Wilson-Era Diplomacy," *Diplomatic History* 44 (2020): 114.

9. Lindsay Schakenbach Regele, "'Confidence': Private Correspondence in Daniel Parker's War Department, 1811–1846," *Journal of the Early Republic* 41 (2021): 39–68; James G. Randall, "The Newspaper Problem in Its Bearing upon Military Secrecy

During the Civil War," *American Historical Review* 23 (1918): 303–323; Harold Holzer, *Lincoln and the Power of the Press: The War for Public Opinion* (New York: Simon and Schuster, 2014).

10. Arvin S. Quist, *Security Classification of Information*, vol. 1, chap. 2 (2002), https://sgp.fas.org/library/quist; Dallas Irvine, *Origin of Defense Markings in the Army and Former War Department* (Washington, DC: National Archives Staff Information Paper, 1972); Harold C. Relyea, "The Evolution of Government Information Security Classification Policy: A Brief Overview (1775–1973)," in *Government Secrecy, Hearings Before the Subcommittee on Intergovernmental Relations of the Committee on Government Operations*, 93d Cong., 846–857 (1974).

11. "To Prevent the Disclosure of National Defense Secrets," H.R. No. 61–1942 (1911), 2; Andrew, *Secret World*, chap. 20.

12. Richard J. Evans, *The Pursuit of Power: Europe 1815–1914* (New York: Viking, 2016), 643; Jeffery T. Richelson, *A Century of Spies: Intelligence in the Twentieth Century* (Oxford: Oxford University Press, 1995), chap. 1; Christopher M. Andrew, *Her Majesty's Secret Service: The Making of the British Intelligence Community* (New York: Viking, 1986), 7–13; Richard J. Samuels, *Special Duty: A History of the Japanese Intelligence Community* (Ithaca, NY: Cornell University Press, 2019), 32–44; Roy Talbert, *Negative Intelligence: The Army and the American Left, 1917–1941* (Jackson: University Press of Mississippi, 1991), chap. 1.

13. Arthur S. Hulnick, "The Dilemma of Open Sources Intelligence: Is OSINT Really Intelligence?," in *The Oxford Handbook of National Security Intelligence*, ed. Loch K. Johnson (Oxford: Oxford University Press, 2010), 228–241.

14. Samuels, *Special Duty*, 13; Holger H. Herwig, "Imperial Germany," 65–70, and Norman Stone, "Austria-Hungary," 42–44, both in *Knowing One's Enemies: Intelligence Assessment Before the Two World Wars*, ed. Ernest R. May (Princeton, NJ: Princeton University Press, 1984); Gerald Morgan, "Myth and Reality in the Great Game," *Asian Affairs* 60 (February 1973): 55–65; Danny Orbach, "The Military-Adventurous Complex: Officers, Adventurers, and Japanese Expansion in East Asia, 1884–1937," *Modern Asian Studies* 53 (March 2019): 339–376; Andrew, *Her Majesty's Secret Service*, 26–27.

15. Christopher M. Andrew, "France and the German Menace," in *Knowing One's Enemies: Intelligence Assessment Before the Two World Wars*, ed. Ernest R. May (Princeton, NJ: Princeton University Press, 1984), 133.

16. Andrew, *Her Majesty's Secret Service*, 27.

17. Christopher R. Moran, *Classified: Secrecy and the State in Modern Britain* (Cambridge: Cambridge University Press, 2013), chap. 1; K. G. Robertson, *Public Secrets: A Study in the Development of Government Secrecy* (New York: St. Martin's, 1982), chap. 4; David Vincent, *The Culture of Secrecy: Britain, 1832–1998* (Oxford: Oxford University Press, 1998), chaps. 2–3; Lucinda Maer and Oonagh Gay, "Official Secrecy," Research note SN/PC/02023, December 30, 2008, House of Commons Library, https://commonslibrary.parliament.uk/research-briefings/sn02023.

18. Allan Mitchell, "The Xenophobic Style: French Counterespionage and the Emergence of the Dreyfus Affair," *Journal of Modern History* 52 (1980): 414–425; Hannah Arendt, *The Origins of Totalitarianism* (San Diego: Harcourt, 1968), chap. 4; William C. Fuller, *The Foe Within: Fantasies of Treason and the End of Imperial Russia* (Ithaca, NY: Cornell University Press, 2018).

19. Herwig, "Imperial Germany," 65.

20. William C. Fuller, "The Russian Empire," in *Knowing One's Enemies: Intelligence Assessment Before the Two World Wars*, ed. Ernest R. May (Princeton, NJ: Princeton University Press, 1984), 115; Ian D. Armour, "Colonel Redl: Fact and Fantasy," *Intelligence and National Security* 2 (1987): 170–183; Richelson, *Century of Spies*, 14–15.

21. Nicholas Hiley, "The Failure of British Counter-espionage Against Germany, 1907–1914," *Historical Journal* 28 (1985): 847; Robertson, *Public Secrets*, 64–67; David French, "Spy Fever in Britain, 1900–1915," *Historical Journal* 21 (1978): 361; Rosamund Thomas, *Espionage and Secrecy: The Official Secrets Acts 1911–1989 of the UK* (London: Routledge, 1991), 5–9; Maer and Gay, "Official Secrecy."

22. Andrew, *Her Majesty's Secret Service*, 34–85; French, "Spy Fever in Britain"; Michael Denning, *Cover Stories: Narrative and Ideology in the British Spy Thriller* (London: Routledge, 1987).

23. French, "Spy Fever in Britain," 355; Richelson, *Century of Spies*, 9, 14; Andrew, *Her Majesty's Secret Service*, 61–69; Hiley, "Failure," 839, 854.

24. Hiley, "Failure," 841–844; Richelson, *Century of Spies*, 9; Robertson, *Public Secrets*, 64.

25. Andrew, *Her Majesty's Secret Service*, 20–21, 59; Bernard Porter, *Plots and Paranoia: A History of Political Espionage in Britain 1790–1988* (Abingdon, UK: Routledge, 2016), chap. 6; Andrew, *Secret World*, 428.

26. Daniel Bruckenhaus, *Policing Transnational Protest: Liberal Imperialism and the Surveillance of Anti-colonialists in Europe 1905–1945* (Oxford: Oxford University Press, 2017), chap. 1; Porter, *Plots and Paranoia*, 130.

27. Talbert, *Negative Intelligence*, chap. 1; Rhodri Jeffreys-Jones, "The Montreal Spy Ring of 1898 and the Origins of 'Domestic' Surveillance in the United States," *Canadian Review of American Studies* 5, no. 2 (1974): 119–134; Jensen, *Army Surveillance in America*, chap. 4.

28. Jensen, 112–113; Alfred W. McCoy, *Policing America's Empire: The United States, the Philippines, and the Rise of the Surveillance State* (Madison: University of Wisconsin Press, 2009); Talbert, *Negative Intelligence*, chap. 1; Campbell, "Major General Ralph H. Van Deman."

29. Kari Frederickson, "Manhood and Politics: The Bankhead-Hobson Campaigns of 1904 and 1906," *Alabama Review* 69 (April 2016): 104; Daniel Wayne Stewart, "The Greatest Gift to Modern Civilization: Naval Power and Moral Order in the United States and Great Britain, 1880–1918" (PhD diss., Temple University, 1999), 343; Barton Shaw, "The Hobson Craze," *US Naval Institute Proceedings* 102 (1976): 54–60; Walter Earl Pittman Jr., "Richmond P. Hobson, Crusader" (PhD diss., University of Georgia, 1969); T. B. Pearson, "Richmond Pearson Hobson: Naval Hero, Reformer, and 'The Most-Kissed Man in America,'" *Alabama Review* 50 (1997): 174–180.

30. Patrick S. Grant, "Hell with the Lid Off!—Lt. Hobson and the Sinking of the *Merrimac* at Santiago, Cuba, 1898," *Sea History* 155 (2016): 32–37.

31. Stewart, "Greatest Gift to Modern Civilization," 344.

32. "Capt. Hobson Sees Peace in Great Navy," *WP*, August 8, 1906, 4; "Perkins Expects a Conflict," *NYT*, February 2, 1907, 1; "Hobson to Speak on Yellow Peril," *AC*, June 18, 1911, 5; Hobson, "The Japanese Crisis," July 9, 1907, box 31, folder 5, Richmond P. Hobson Papers, LOC.

33. John Rieder, "John Henry Palmer's *The Invasion of New York, or, How Hawaii Was Annexed*: Political Discourse and Emergent Mass Culture in 1897," in *Future Wars: The Anticipations and the Fears*, ed. David Seed (Liverpool: Liverpool University Press, 2012), 85–102; Edlie L. Wong, "In a Future Tense: Immigration Law, Counterfactual Histories, and Chinese Invasion Fiction," *American Literary History* 26 (2014): 511–535.

34. Richmond Hobson, "If War Should Come," *Cosmopolitan*, May 1908, 588–593; June 1908, 40–47; September 1908, 382–387.

35. Richmond Pearson Hobson, "Japan Is Trying to Force War upon America," *AC*, April 26, 1908, E3; Masuda Hajimu, "Rumors of War: Immigration Disputes and the Social Construction of American-Japanese Relations, 1905–1913," *Diplomatic History* 33 (2009): 1–37.

36. "H.R. 25292, a Bill to Prevent the Disclosure of National Defense Secrets," folder: HR 26656, Records of the Committee on the Judiciary: HR 61A-D8, box 405, RG 233.

37. "Sees War in 10 Months," *Sun*, February 21, 1911, 1; Pittman, "Richmond P. Hobson, Crusader," 56, 86; "To Prevent the Disclosure of National Defense Secrets," 3; Chief of Second Section, "Memorandum for the Secretary: The Necessity of Legislation to Prevent Espionage in Time of Peace," folder: HR 26656, Records of the Committee on the Judiciary: HR 61A-D8, box 405, RG 233; "Spies to Be Punished," *Baltimore Sun*, February 7, 1911, 15; "Jap Spies in Every Nation," *Detroit Free Press*, April 6, 1908, 1; HW Loomis to Major WHH Llewellyn, January 22, 1908, box 31, folder 2, Hobson Papers; Jay Hughes to TW Jones, February 10, 1908, box 31, folder 2, Hobson Papers.

38. "Want to Punish Spies," *NYT*, December 30, 1910, 5; "To Prevent the Disclosure of National Defense Secrets," 5.

39. *Annual Report of Attorney-General of the United States for the Year 1916*, H. Doc. No. 64–1483, 19.

40. Stephen Irving Max Schwab, "Sabotage at Black Tom Island: A Wake-Up Call for America," *International Journal of Intelligence and Counterintelligence* 25 (2012): 367–391; Michael J. Sulick, *Spying in America: Espionage from the Revolutionary War to the Dawn of the Cold War* (Washington, DC: Georgetown University Press, 2012), chap. 13; Tracie Lynn Provost, "The Great Game: Imperial German Sabotage and Espionage Against the United States, 1914–1917" (PhD diss., University of Toledo, 2003); Francis MacDonnell, *Insidious Foes: The Axis Fifth Column and the American Home Front* (New York: Oxford University Press, 1995), 16–17.

41. Seema Sohi, *Echoes of Mutiny: Race, Surveillance and Indian Anticolonialism* (Oxford: Oxford University Press, 2014); Leon Comber, "The Singapore Mutiny (1915) and the Genesis of Political Intelligence in Singapore," *Intelligence and National Security* 24 (2009): 529–541.

42. French, "Spy Fever in Britain," 364–365; Andrew, *Her Majesty's Secret Service*, 73, 179–188.

43. Andrew, 231.

44. Andrew, 177–183, 233; Richard C. Thurlow, *The Secret State: British Internal Security in the Twentieth Century* (Oxford: Blackwell, 1995), 55.

45. Daniel Patrick Moynihan, *Secrecy: The American Experience* (New Haven, CT: Yale University Press, 1999), 89; John B. Stanchfield, "The Peril of Espionage," *North*

American Review 203 (June 1916): 830–840; "Need a Spy System to Protect Our War Secrets," *NYT*, January 30, 1916, SM4.

46. David M. Rabban, *Free Speech in Its Forgotten Years* (Cambridge: Cambridge University Press, 1997), 249–250; Jensen, *Army Surveillance in America*, 132; Aziz Rana, "Constitutionalism and the Foundations of the Security State," *California Law Review* 103 (2015): 375–377; House Committee, Unpublished Committee Hearing with Warren, April 10, 1917, 7–8; Michael Allan Wolfe, "Charles Warren: Progressive, Historian" (PhD diss., Harvard University, 1991), 275; M. A. DeWolfe Howe, "Charles Warren," *Proceedings of the Massachusetts Historical Society* 71 (1953): 390–398.

47. Charles Warren, "War Notes," 603–616, box 6, folder 3, Charles Warren Papers, LOC.

48. 64th Cong. Rec. 3486–3493 (February 17, 1917); 64th Cong. Rec. 3600 (February 19, 1917).

49. Ralph Mills Sayre, "Albert Baird Cummins and the Progressive Movement in Iowa" (PhD diss., Columbia University, 1958); Elbert Harrington, "A Survey of the Political Ideas of Albert B. Cummins," *Iowa Journal of History and Politics* 39 (1941): 339–386; David R. Berman, *Governors and the Progressive Movement* (Louisville: University Press of Colorado, 2018), 57–59.

50. "Espionage Bill Called Despotic," *NYT*, February 20, 1917, 2; Harold Edgar and Benno C. Schmidt, "The Espionage Statutes and Publication of Defense Information," *Columbia Law Review* 73, no. 5 (May 1973): 947.

51. House Committee, Unpublished Committee Hearing with Warren, April 10, 1917, 29; 64th Cong. Rec. 3610 (February 19, 1917).

52. "Senator Overman Dies in 77th Year," *NYT*, December 12, 1930, 25; "Espionage Bill Called Despotic," *NYT*, February 20, 1917, 2; 65th Cong. Rec. 783 (April 18, 1917); 65th Cong. Rec. 878 (April 20, 1917).

53. "Senate Passes Bill to Punish Spies," *NYT*, February 21, 1917, 6.

54. George C. Herring, *From Colony to Superpower: U.S. Foreign Relations Since 1776* (New York: Oxford University Press, 2008), 408–410.

55. Woodrow Wilson, Address to a Joint Session of Congress Requesting a Declaration of War Against Germany, April 2, 1917, APP; Michael Kazin, *War Against War: The American Fight for Peace, 1914–1918* (New York: Simon and Schuster, 2017), 172–179; Provost, "The Great Game," 159–160; "Congress Maps Out Big War Program," *Sun*, April 9, 1917, 1.

56. "Publishers Assail the Espionage Bill," *NYT*, April 23, 1917, 9; "The Censorship," *NYT*, April 11, 1917, 12; "The Espionage Bill," *NYT*, April 13, 1917, 12; "Undermining Democracy," *NYT*, April 20, 1917, 12.

57. "Anti-censorship Tide Floods House," *NYT*, May 4, 1917, 1; "Censorship Vote 39 to 38," *NYT*, May 13, 1917, 1; 65th Cong. Rec. 1816 (May 4, 1917); Edgar and Schmidt, "Espionage Statutes," 961; "Wilson Demands Press Censorship," *NYT*, May 23, 1917, 1; "President Calls Conferees, Urges Press Censorship," *NYT*, May 24, 1917, 1; "Censorship Clause Out," *NYT*, June 5, 1917, 11.

58. "Espionage Bill Passed," *NYT*, June 8, 1917, 20.

59. Alasdair Palmer, "The History of the D-Notice Committee," in *The Missing Dimension: Governments and Intelligence Communities in the Twentieth Century*, ed. Christopher Andrews and David Dilks (Urbana: University of Illinois Press, 1984), 227–249.

60. Unpublished Committee Hearing with Warren, April 10, 1917, 12, 15.

61. Edgar and Schmidt, "Espionage Statutes," 973.

Chapter 2: The Speech Crimes of Eugene Debs

1. Jill Lepore, "Eugene V. Debs and the Endurance of Socialism," *New Yorker*, February 18 and 25, 2019; Ray Ginger, *The Bending Cross: A Biography of Eugene Victor Debs* (New Brunswick, NJ: Rutgers University Press, 1949), 281–282, 357; Nick Salvatore, *Eugene V. Debs: Citizen and Socialist* (Urbana: University of Illinois Press, 1982), 233.

2. J. Michael Sproule, "Clyde Miller: Twentieth Century Pioneer of Free Speech," *Free Speech Yearbook* 24 (1985): 27–37; Ernest Freeberg, *Democracy's Prisoner: Eugene V. Debs, the Great War, and the Right to Dissent* (Cambridge, MA: Harvard University Press, 2008), 69.

3. Geoffrey R. Stone, *Perilous Times: Free Speech in Wartime: From the Sedition Act of 1798 to the War on Terrorism* (New York: W. W. Norton, 2004), 197.

4. "The Canton, Ohio Speech," June 16, 1918, www.marxists.org/archive/debs/works /1918/canton.htm.

5. Freeberg, *Democracy's Prisoner*, 78; "Debs Invites Arrest," *WP*, June 17, 1918, 2.

6. Salvatore, *Eugene V. Debs*, 127–140; Richard White, *The Republic for Which It Stands: The United States During Reconstruction and the Gilded Age, 1865–1896* (New York: Oxford University Press, 2017), 773–789; Steven Hahn, *A Nation Without Borders: The United States and Its World in an Age of Civil Wars, 1830–1910* (New York: Viking, 2016), 485–486; Erik Loomis, *A History of America in Ten Strikes* (New York: New Press, 2018), 73–74.

7. Margaret A. Blanchard, *Revolutionary Sparks: Freedom of Expression in Modern America* (New York: Oxford University Press, 1992), 13–15.

8. David M. Rabban, *Free Speech in Its Forgotten Years* (Cambridge: Cambridge University Press, 1997), 170.

9. *Snyder v. Phelps*, 562 U.S. 443 (2011).

10. Joseph Story, *Commentaries on the Constitution of the United States* (Boston: Hilliard, Gray, 1833), 703; Margaret A. Blanchard, "Filling in the Void: Speech and Press in the State Courts Prior to Gitlow," in *The First Amendment Reconsidered: New Perspectives on the Meaning of Freedom of Speech and Press*, ed. Bill F. Chamberlin and Charlene J. Brown (New York: Longman, 1982), 18, 27; David Yassky, "Eras of the First Amendment," *Columbia Law Review* 91 (1991): 1699–1755.

11. Paul Starr, *The Creation of the Media: Political Origins of Modern Communications* (New York: Basic Books, 2004), 231–250; Michael Kent Curtis, *Free Speech, "The People's Darling Privilege": Struggles for Freedom of Expression in American History* (Durham, NC: Duke University Press, 2000), 117–271.

12. Frederick Schauer, "The Boundaries of the First Amendment: A Preliminary Exploration of Constitutional Salience," *Harvard Law Review* 117 (April 2004): 1765–1809.

13. Rabban, *Free Speech in Its Forgotten Years*, 171; Laura M. Weinrib, *The Taming of Free Speech: America's Civil Liberties Compromise* (Cambridge, MA: Harvard University Press, 2016), 34–35.

14. Beverly Gage, *The Day Wall Street Exploded: A Story of America in Its First Age of Terror* (Oxford: Oxford University Press, 2009), 5.

15. Howard Zinn, *A People's History of the United States, 1492–Present* (New York: Harper, 1995), 272–273; White, *Republic for Which It Stands*, 654–674; D. G. Thiessen and Carlos A. Schwangtes, "Industrial Violence in the Coeur d'Alene Mining District: The Visual Record," *Pacific Northwest Quarterly* 78 (1987): 83–90.

16. Ginger, *Bending Cross*, 93, 208–209.

17. Robert K. Murray, *Red Scare: A Study in National Hysteria, 1919–1920* (Minneapolis: University of Minnesota Press, 1955), 19; Salvatore, *Eugene V. Debs*, 222; Dave Burns, "The Soul of Socialism: Christianity, Civilization and Citizenship in the Thought of Eugene Debs," *Labor: Studies in Working Class Histories of the Americas* 5 (2008): 83–116.

18. Ginger, *Bending Cross*, 51–52, 303–304.

19. James Weinstein, *The Decline of Socialism in America, 1912–1925* (New Brunswick, NJ: Rutgers University Press, 1984), 11.

20. B. Ronald Genini, "Industrial Workers of the World and Their Fresno Free Speech Fight, 1910–1911," *California Historical Quarterly* 53 (1974): 101–114; Rabban, *Free Speech in Its Forgotten Years*, 77–128; Robert L. Tyler, "The Everett Free Speech Fight," *Pacific Historical Review* 23 (1954): 19–30; Melvyn Dubofsky, *We Shall Be All: A History of the Industrial Workers of the World* (Chicago: Quadrangle, 1969), 173–197.

21. William Preston, *Aliens and Dissenters: Federal Suppression of Radicals, 1903–1933* (Urbana: University of Illinois Press, 1994), 52; Grace I. Miller, "The IWW Free Speech Fight: San Diego, 1912," *Southern California Quarterly* 54 (1972): 223, 229; Matthew S. May, *Soapbox Rebellion: The Hobo Orator Union and the Free Speech Fights of the Industrial Workers of the World, 1909–1916* (Tuscaloosa: University of Alabama Press, 2013), 77–78.

22. Freeberg, *Democracy's Prisoner*, 31.

23. Salvatore, *Eugene V. Debs*, 185, 263, 275.

24. Weinstein, *Decline of Socialism in America*, 125.

25. Roland Marchand, *The American Peace Movement and Social Reform, 1889–1918* (Princeton, NJ: Princeton University Press, 2015), 202–203.

26. Weinstein, *Decline of Socialism in America*, 125–126; Leslie Marcy, "The Emergency National Convention," *International Socialist Review* 11 (May 1917): 665–672, www.marxists.org/history/usa/pubs/isr/v17n11-may-1917-ISR-riaz-ocr.pdf.

27. Freeberg, *Democracy's Prisoner*, 64.

28. 65th Cong. Rec. 2087 (May 11, 2017).

29. Espionage Act of 1917, Pub. L. No. 65-24, 40 Stat. 217.

30. Freeberg, *Democracy's Prisoner*, 50–52; Stone, *Perilous Times*, 149–151; Rabban, *Free Speech in Its Forgotten Years*, 249–255.

31. Weinstein, *Decline of Socialism in America*, 144; Jeanette Keith, *Rich Man's War, Poor Man's Fight: Race, Class, and Power in the Rural South During the First World War* (Chapel Hill: University of North Carolina Press, 2004), 89–101; Paul L. Murphy, *World War I and the Origin of Civil Liberties in the US* (New York: W. W. Norton, 1979), 97–99; Freeberg, *Democracy's Prisoner*, 57–58; Patricia O'Toole, *The Moralist: Woodrow Wilson and the World He Made* (New York: Simon and Schuster, 2018), 293–294.

32. Michael Kazin, *War Against War: The American Fight for Peace, 1914–1918* (New York: Simon and Schuster, 2017), 245; Stone, *Perilous Times*, 171–173.

33. *Shaffer v. US*, 255 F. 886 (1919); "Rich Farmer Sentenced for Mailing 'Finished Mystery,'" *New York Tribune*, July 11, 1918, 7.

34. Stone, *Perilous Times*, 170–171.

35. Richard Polenberg, *Fighting Faiths: The Abrams Case, the Supreme Court, and Free Speech* (New York: Viking, 1987), 314; Stone, *Perilous Times*, 211–212; Weinstein, *Decline of Socialism in America*, 161, 168; "Victor Berger Indicted for Opposing War," *San Francisco Chronicle*, March 10, 1918, 45; Freeberg, *Democracy's Prisoner*, 90; Murphy, *World War I*, 96.

36. Freeberg, *Democracy's Prisoner*, 43; Christopher McKnight Nichols, *Promise and Peril: America at the Dawn of a Global Age* (Cambridge, MA: Harvard University Press, 2011), 206.

37. Christopher M. Finan, *From the Palmer Raids to the Patriot Act: A History of the Fight for Free Speech in America* (Boston: Beacon, 2007), 12; Murphy, *World War I*, 87, 124–125.

38. O'Toole, *Moralist*, 293; Christopher Capozzola, *Uncle Sam Wants You: World War I and the Making of the Modern American Citizen* (Oxford: Oxford University Press, 2008), 183–184, 191; Ginger, *Bending Cross*, 351–352.

39. Freeberg, *Democracy's Prisoner*, 65, 81; Salvatore, *Eugene V. Debs*, 288; Capozzola, *Uncle Sam Wants You*, 117, 163; Murphy, *World War I*, 117–118, 128–131.

40. Murphy, 87; Kazin, *War Against War*, 254; Clemens P. Work, *Darkest Before Dawn: Sedition and Free Speech in the American West* (Albuquerque: University of New Mexico Press, 2005), 79; Freeberg, *Democracy's Prisoner*, 53, 61.

41. Dubofsky, *We Shall Be All*, 383–384; "Get out the Hemp," *Tulsa Daily World*, November 9, 1917, 4; "IWW Members, Flogged, Tarred and Feathered," *Tulsa Daily World*, November 10, 1917, 1.

42. Work, *Darkest Before Dawn*, 60, chap. 5; Eric Thomas Chester, *The Wobblies in Their Heyday: The Rise and Destruction of the Industrial Workers of the World During the World War 1 Era* (Santa Barbara, CA: Praeger, 2014), 30–31, 49, 84–85.

43. Work, *Darkest Before Dawn*, 93–94; Gage, *Day Wall Street Exploded*, 116; Dubofsky, *We Shall Be All*, 391–392; Chester, *Wobblies in Their Heyday*, 35–37, 92–102; Fredrick Allen, "Montana Vigilantes and the Origins of 3-7-77," *Montana: The Magazine of Western History* 51, no. 1 (2001): 2–19.

44. Dubofsky, *We Shall Be All*, 392; Work, *Darkest Before Dawn*, 99.

45. Gage, *Day Wall Street Exploded*, 114; Weinrib, *Taming of Free Speech*, chap. 3; Dubofsky, *We Shall Be All*, chaps. 16–17; Preston, *Aliens and Dissenters*, chap. 5; Work, *Darkest Before Dawn*, 100.

46. Arnon Gutfeld, "The Ves Hall Case, Judge Bourquin, and the Sedition Act of 1918," *Pacific Historical Review* 37 (1968): 163–178; Stone, *Perilous Times*, 160–161.

47. Gutfeld, "Ves Hall Case," 170; Polenberg, *Fighting Faiths*, 29–31; Work, *Darkest Before Dawn*, 194–196.

48. Gutfeld, "Ves Hall Case," 173–174.

49. "Suggestions of Attorney General Gregory to Executive Committee in Relation to the Department of Justice," April 16, 1918, *American Bar Association Journal* 4 (1918): 305–316.

50. Gutfeld, "Ves Hall Case," 177; Murphy, *World War I*, 83; Polenberg, *Fighting Faiths*, 32–33; Stone, *Perilous Times*, 160–169, 185–191; O'Toole, *Moralist*, 298–299.

51. Freeberg, *Democracy's Prisoner*, 65, 68; Salvatore, *Eugene V. Debs*, 288–289; Eugene V. Debs, "The Class War and Its Outlook," *International Socialist Review* 17

(September 1916): 135–136; Eugene V. Debs, "The IWW Bogey," *International Socialist Review* 18 (February 1918): 395–396.

52. Freeberg, *Democracy's Prisoner*, 68.

53. Freeberg, 75.

54. Sproule, "Clyde Miller"; Clyde Miller, "The Man I Sent to Prison," *Progressive*, October 1963, 33–35.

55. Freeberg, *Democracy's Prisoner*, 78–79; Thomas Healy, *The Great Dissent: How Oliver Wendell Holmes Changed His Mind—and Changed the History of Free Speech in America* (New York: Metropolitan, 2013), 88–89.

56. "Debs Arrested; Sedition Charged," *NYT*, July 1, 1918, 1.

57. Freeberg, *Democracy's Prisoner*, chap. 5; Ginger, *Bending Cross*, 366–367.

58. Freeberg, *Democracy's Prisoner*, 86; Ginger, *Bending Cross*, 364.

59. Eugene Debs, "Statement to the Court upon Being Convicted of Violating the Sedition Act," September 18, 1918, www.marxists.org/archive/debs/works/1918/court.htm; Freeberg, *Democracy's Prisoner*, 105–107.

60. David Pietrusza, *1920: The Year of the Six Presidents* (New York: Basic Books, 2007), 271.

Chapter 3: 1919, Year of the Bombs

1. David Pietrusza, *1920: The Year of the Six Presidents* (New York: Basic Books, 2007), 143–144; David M. Kennedy, *Over Here: The First World War and American Society* (Oxford: Oxford University Press, 2004), 288; Frederick Lewis Allen, *Only Yesterday: An Informal History of the 1920s* (New York: Perennial Classics, 2000), 43–44; Laura M. Weinrib, *The Taming of Free Speech: America's Civil Liberties Compromise* (Cambridge, MA: Harvard University Press, 2016), 116.

2. "Radical Outrages Stir Washington," *NYT*, May 3, 1919, 1.

3. Seema Sohi, *Echoes of Mutiny: Race, Surveillance and Indian Anticolonialism* (Oxford: Oxford University Press, 2014), 172–173; Erez Manela, *The Wilsonian Moment: Self-Determination and the International Origins of Anticolonial Nationalism* (Oxford: Oxford University Press, 2007); Kim Wagner, "'Calculated to Strike Terror': The Amritsar Massacre and the Spectacle of Colonial Violence," *Past and Present* 233 (2016): 185–225.

4. "Tanks Used in Cleveland Riot," *New York Tribune*, May 2, 1919, 1; Geoffrey R. Stone, *Perilous Times: Free Speech in Wartime: From the Sedition Act of 1798 to the War on Terrorism* (New York: W. W. Norton, 2004), 221–222; Robert K. Murray, *Red Scare: A Study in National Hysteria, 1919–1920* (Minneapolis: University of Minnesota Press, 1955), 75–76; Ann Hagedorn, *Savage Peace: Hope and Fear in America, 1919* (New York: Simon and Schuster, 2007), 185–186; Stanley Coben, *A. Mitchell Palmer: Politician* (New York: Da Capo, 1972), 204.

5. Hagedorn, *Savage Peace*, 317, 321, 379–380; Erik Loomis, *A History of America in Ten Strikes* (New York: New, 2018), 110; Chris Myers Asch and George Derek Musgrove, *Chocolate City: A History of Race and Democracy in the Nation's Capital* (Chapel Hill: University of North Carolina Press, 2017), 232–235; Rhonda Pavlu, "Chicago Race Riot of 1919," and Matthew Nichte, "Elaine Massacre of 1919," both in *Encyclopedia of Race and Crime*, ed. Helen Taylor Greene and Shaun Gabbidon (Thousand Oaks, CA: Sage, 2009), 102–105; "Blames Race Riots on Negro Leaders," *NYT*, August 26, 1919, 14; Murray, *Red Scare*, 178–179; "Reds Try to Stir Negroes to Revolt," *NYT*, July 28, 1919, 4.

6. Coben, *A. Mitchell Palmer*, 196; Richard Polenberg, *Fighting Faiths: The Abrams Case, the Supreme Court, and Free Speech* (New York: Viking, 1987), 86–87; "A National Danger," *WP*, May 3, 1919, 6.

7. "Debs Appeals to Supreme Court," *NYT*, October 23, 1918, 7.

8. "The Canton, Ohio Speech," June 16, 1918, www.marxists.org/archive/debs /works/1918/canton.htm.

9. Thomas C. Grey, "Holmes and Legal Pragmatism," *Stanford Law Review* 41 (1989): 812; Morton J. Horwitz, *The Transformation of American Law, 1870–1960: The Crisis of Legal Orthodoxy* (New York: Oxford University Press, 1995), 123; Thomas Healy, *The Great Dissent: How Oliver Wendell Holmes Changed His Mind—and Changed the History of Free Speech in America* (New York: Metropolitan, 2013), 142, 464–479.

10. Grey, "Holmes and Legal Pragmatism," 846; Louis Menand, *The Metaphysical Club: A Story of Ideas in America* (New York: Farrar, Straus and Giroux, 2001).

11. Healy, *Great Dissent*, 6, 38; Benjamin Patrick Newton, "Mr. Justice Hobbes? On the Jurisprudence of Oliver Wendell Holmes Jr.," *American Political Thought* 7 (June 2018): 470.

12. Newton, "Mr. Justice Hobbes?," 468; Grey, "Holmes and Legal Pragmatism," 812.

13. Healy, *Great Dissent*, 25; Grey, "Holmes and Legal Pragmatism," 846; Vincent Blasi, "Holmes and the Marketplace of Ideas," *Supreme Court Review* (2004): 1–46.

14. Edward White, *Justice Oliver Wendell Holmes: Law and the Inner Self* (New York: Oxford University Press, 1993), 290–291, 328–333; Horwitz, *Transformation of American Law*, 132–142; Newton, "Mr. Justice Hobbes?," 469.

15. Polenberg, *Fighting Faiths*, 210; White, *Justice Oliver Wendell Holmes*, 363; Healy, *Great Dissent*, 6.

16. White, *Justice Oliver Wendell Holmes*, 341–343.

17. White, 286, 348–352; Healy, *Great Dissent*, 38.

18. Newton, "Mr. Justice Hobbes?," 472.

19. Healy, *Great Dissent*, 12.

20. *Schenck v. United States*, 249 U.S. 47 (1919).

21. Polenberg, *Fighting Faiths*, 214.

22. Ernest Freeberg, *Democracy's Prisoner: Eugene V. Debs, the Great War, and the Right to Dissent* (Cambridge, MA: Harvard University Press, 2008), 102; Corey Robin, "Falsely Shouting Fire in a Theater," February 17, 2013, https://corey robin.com/2013/02/17/falsely-shouting-fire-in-a-theater-how-a-forgotten-labor -struggle-became-a-national-obsession-and-emblem-of-our-constitutional-faith; Corey Robin, "New Information on That False Shout of Fire in a Theater," February 19, 2013, https://coreyrobin.com/2013/02/19/new-information-on-that-false-shout -of-fire-in-a-theater; L. A. Powe, "Searching for the False Shout of Fire," *Constitutional Commentary* 19 (2002): 345–352.

23. *Frohwerk v. United States*, 249 U.S. 204, at 208–209 (1919).

24. *Debs v. United States*, 249 U.S. 211 (1919).

25. White, *Justice Oliver Wendell Holmes*, 421.

26. "Palmer and Family Safe," *NYT*, June 3, 1919, 1; Pietrusza, *1920*, 145–146; "Flynn Called to Track Reds in Bomb Plots," *Detroit Free Press*, June 4, 1919, 1.

27. Hagedorn, *Savage Peace*, 222; "Palmer and Family Safe," 1.

28. Pietrusza, *1920*, 145; Coben, *A. Mitchell Palmer*.

29. Pietrusza, *1920*, 193; Kennedy, *Over Here*, 311–313; Coben, *A. Mitchell Palmer*, 127–150; "Gregory Going to Paris with Wilson as General Adviser on Peace Questions," *NYT*, March 3, 1919, 1.

30. Coben, *A. Mitchell Palmer*, 200.

31. "Palmer Warns Societies," *NYT*, April 1, 1919, 9; Coben, *A. Mitchell Palmer*, 206, 215; Freeberg, *Democracy's Prisoner*, 135; Hagedorn, *Savage Peace*, 225, 227.

32. "Flynn to Direct Search for Reds," *NYT*, June 4, 1919, 2; Beverly Gage, *G-Man: J. Edgar Hoover and the Making of the American Century* (New York: Vintage, 2022), 64–68; Coben, *A. Mitchell Palmer*, 60, 207–211; "Palmer and Family Safe"; "2000 Reds on List," *WP*, June 19, 1919, 1; Hagedorn, *Savage Peace*, 229; Murray, *Red Scare*, 193; Pietrusza, *1920*, 146; Polenberg, *Fighting Faiths*, 164–165.

33. Technically, the Espionage Act remained in force until the legal end of the war in 1921, but a decision was made within the DOJ not to use it during this gray period. Palmer apparently worried that juries would not convict under wartime statutes when the war was over—in fact, if not in law. "Radical Outrages Stir Washington," *NYT*, May 3, 1919, 1; "New Law Needed for Alien Enemies," *NYT*, March 29, 1919, 9; Coben, *A. Mitchell Palmer*, 209, 241; "War Law Repeal Signed," *NYT*, March 4, 1921, 2; "Letter from the Attorney-General, Investigative Activities of the Department of Justice," S.doc. 153, 66th Cong., November 17, 1919, 6–7.

34. Coben, *A. Mitchell Palmer*, 214; Hagedorn, *Savage Peace*, 382; "Deport the Agitators, Demands Poindexter," *NYT*, November 1, 1919, 4; "Attorney General Palmer on Immigration," *NYT*, October 17, 1919, 16.

35. Coben, *A. Mitchell Palmer*, 218; "Letter from the Attorney-General"; Margaret A. Blanchard, *Revolutionary Sparks: Freedom of Expression in Modern America* (New York: Oxford University Press, 1992), 115; "200 Caught in New York," *NYT*, November 8, 1918, 1.

36. "Letter from the Attorney-General."

37. "Letter from the Attorney-General," 8; "Unpreparedness in the War Against Radicalism," *NYT*, November 23, 1919, XX1; Freeberg, *Democracy's Prisoner*, 217–218; "Proposed Anti-Red Law Imposes Heavy Penalty on Guilty," *Arizona Republic*, January 11, 1920, 1; "A Sedition Bill with Teeth," *Pittsburgh Gazette-Times*, January 13, 1920, 6; "Passes Anti-Red Bill," *WP*, January 11, 1920, 1.

38. "President Eliminated as Third-Term Candidate," *Wall Street Journal*, November 10, 1919, 8; "391 Alien Reds Now Under Arrest," *NYT*, November 11, 1919, 1.

39. Polenberg, *Fighting Faiths*, 36–42, 180; Hagedorn, *Savage Peace*, chap. 6.

40. Healy, *Great Dissent*, 176–180.

41. Polenberg, *Fighting Faiths*, 145. A fifth surviving defendant, Hyman Rosansky, was given a lighter sentence for his cooperation and confession during the investigation.

42. Healy, *Great Dissent*, 134–137; Ray Ginger, *The Bending Cross: A Biography of Eugene Victor Debs* (New Brunswick, NJ: Rutgers University Press, 1949), 383–384.

43. Healy, *Great Dissent*, 33–35; Stone, *Perilous Times*, 202.

44. Healy, *Great Dissent*, 160.

45. "Opposes Spy Bill Section," *NYT*, February 21, 1917, 6; Weinrib, *Taming of Free Speech*; David M. Rabban, *Free Speech in Its Forgotten Years* (Cambridge: Cambridge University Press, 1997); Christopher M. Finan, *From the Palmer Raids to the Patriot Act: A History of the Fight for Free Speech in America* (Boston: Beacon, 2007),

14–28, 705–763; Paul L. Murphy, *World War I and the Origin of Civil Liberties in the US* (New York: W. W. Norton, 1979), 153–171.

46. John Fabian Witt, "Crystal Eastman and the Internationalist Beginnings of American Civil Liberties," *Duke Law Journal* 54 (December 2004): 747.

47. Polenberg, *Fighting Faiths*, 85.

48. Finan, *From the Palmer Raids to the Patriot Act*, 30–31; Healy, *Great Dissent*, 57–60, 158–159; White, *Justice Oliver Wendell Holmes*, 427–430.

49. *Abrams v. United States*, 250 U.S. 616 (1919).

50. *Abrams*; Healy, *Great Dissent*, 205–206; Blasi, "Holmes and the Marketplace of Ideas," 5–6.

51. Healy, *Great Dissent*, 182–186; Isaac Kramnick and Barry Sheerman, *Harold Laski: A Life on the Left* (New York: Penguin, 1993), 96–150; Stone, *Perilous Times*, 199.

52. Polenberg, *Fighting Faiths*, 236; Healy, *Great Dissent*, 1–6; Hagedorn, *Savage Peace*, 393; Blasi, "Holmes and the Marketplace of Ideas."

53. Polenberg, *Fighting Faiths*, 242–243, 285–303, 341–342.

54. Murray, *Red Scare*, 207; Torrie Hester, *Deportation: The Origins of U.S. Policy* (Philadelphia: University of Pennsylvania Press, 2017), 115; Coben, *A. Mitchell Palmer*, 221.

55. "Palmer Pledges War on Radicals," *NYT*, January 1, 1920, 17.

56. Hagedorn, *Savage Peace*, 421–422; Allen, *Only Yesterday*, 49; Stone, *Perilous Times*, 223–224; Coben, *A. Mitchell Palmer*, 227–229; Gage, *G-Man*, 81; Hester, *Deportation*, 127; Murray, *Red Scare*, 210–222; "The Red Assassins," *WP*, January 4, 1920, 26.

57. "Palmer Promises More Soviet Arks," *NYT*, February 29, 1920, E1; "Reds by the Thousand," *NYT*, January 4, 1920, 10.

58. A. Mitchell Palmer, "The Case Against the Reds," *Forum* 63 (February 1920): 173–185; William Preston, *Aliens and Dissenters: Federal Suppression of Radicals, 1903–1933* (Cambridge, MA: Harvard University Press, 1963), 193–194; Ellen Schrecker, *Many Are the Crimes: McCarthyism in America* (Princeton, NJ: Princeton University Press, 1998), 57; Stone, *Perilous Times*, 224; Coben, *A. Mitchell Palmer*, 250.

59. "Palmer Pushing War on Radicals," *NYT*, January 5, 1920, 1; *Sedition: Hearing Before the Committee on the Judiciary*, 66th. Cong. 22 (February 4, 6, 1920); "Sedition Bill Ready for House," *NYT*, January 12, 1920, 4; "Sterling Bill Fails in House Committee," *NYT*, January 16, 1920, 3; "Gompers Fights Sedition Bill," *NYT*, January 19, 1920, 15; "Wage Labor Fight on Sedition Bills," *NYT*, January 23, 1920, 3; Murray, *Red Scare*, 230–231.

60. "Senate Passes Sedition Bill," *CT*, January 11, 1920, 5; "Find Sedition Bills Must Be Modified," *NYT*, January 25, 1920, 3; "New Sedition Bill Is to Be Drafted," *NYT*, February 1, 1920, 14; "Palmer Lets Sedition Bill Go Undefended," *New York Tribune*, January 23, 1920, 3.

61. *Sedition: Hearing Before the Committee on the Judiciary*; Tim Weiner, *Enemies: A History of the FBI* (New York: Random House, 2013), 37; "Lawyers Denounce Raids on Radicals," *NYT*, May 28, 1920, 6; Coben, *A. Mitchell Palmer*, 238.

62. Adam Goodman, *The Deportation Machine: America's Long History of Expelling Immigrants* (New Brunswick, NJ: Princeton University Press, 2020), 29; Coben, *A. Mitchell Palmer*, 232; "Calls Post Factor in Revolution Plan," *NYT*, June 2, 1920, 4.

63. Coben, *A. Mitchell Palmer*, 186, 255; "Strike Traced to IWW," *NYT*, April 15, 1920, 1.

64. "Nation-Wide Plot to Kill High Officials on Red May Day Revealed by Palmer," *NYT*, April 30, 1920, 1; Coben, *A. Mitchell Palmer*, 235; Pietrusza, *1920*, 147.

65. Coben, *A. Mitchell Palmer*, 236; Editorial cartoon, *CT*, May 4, 1920, 1; Murray, *Red Scare*, 248.

66. Coben, *A. Mitchell Palmer*, 257–259; Pietrusza, *1920*, 247, 254.

67. Pietrusza, *1920*, 254–257.

68. Stephen M. Kohn, *American Political Prisoners: Prosecutions Under the Espionage and Sedition Acts* (Westport, CT: Praeger, 1994), 52–54, 126.

69. Freeberg, *Democracy's Prisoner*, 293–301; Stone, *Perilous Times*, 612.

70. Freeberg, *Democracy's Prisoner*, 315–316; Stone, *Perilous Times*, 230–232.

71. Polenberg, *Fighting Faiths*, 366–367.

Chapter 4: The Creeping Scope of the Secrecy Laws

1. "Russians Go on Trial as Spies, Sale of Navy Secrets Charged," *LAT*, February 22, 1939, 1; *Gorin v. United States, Salich v. United States*, 111 F.2d 712 (1940); *Gorin v. U.S.*, 312 U.S. 19 (1941).

2. "Files on Spy Suspect Lost," *LAT*, February 24, 1939, 1; "Salich Charges Navy Men Approved All His Action," *LAT*, March 8, 1939, 10.

3. "Coast Jury Indicts Two on Spy Charges," *NYT*, December 22, 1938, 10; "Two 'Spies' Guilty in Trial on Coast," *NYT*, March 11, 1939, 9; Harold Edgar and Benno C. Schmidt, "The Espionage Statutes and Publication of Defense Information," *Columbia Law Review* 73, no. 5 (May 1973): 974–981.

4. "Russian Spies Sentenced," *NYT*, March 21, 1939, 10; "2 Spies Who Stole US Navy Files for Soviet Are Sentenced," *CT*, March 21 1939, 4.

5. *Gorin* (1940).

6. E. S. Rosenberg, "World War I, Wilsonianism, and Challenges to U.S. Empire," *Diplomatic History* 38, no. 4 (September 1, 2014): 852–863; Jennifer K. Elsea and Matthew C. Weed, "Declarations of War and Authorizations for the Use of Military Force: Historical Background and Legal Implications," Congressional Research Service Report RL31133 (April 18, 2014); Barbara Salazar Torreon and Sofia Plagakis, "Instances of Use of United States Armed Forces Abroad, 1798–2022," Congressional Research Service Report 42738 (March 8, 2022); Colleen Woods, "Seditious Crimes and Rebellious Conspiracies: Anti-Communism and US Empire in the Philippines," *Journal of Contemporary History* 53, no. 1 (January 2018): 61–88; Alfred W. McCoy, *Policing America's Empire: The United States, the Philippines, and the Rise of the Surveillance State* (Madison: University of Wisconsin Press, 2009), 99–104.

7. Brandon R. Byrd, "'To Start Something to Help These People': African American Women and the Occupation of Haiti, 1915–1934," *Journal of Haitian Studies* 21, no. 2 (2016): 154–180; Brenda Gayle Plummer, "The Afro-American Response to the Occupation of Haiti, 1915–1934," *Phylon* 43, no. 2 (1982): 125–143; Rayford W. Logan, "James Weldon Johnson and Haiti," *Phylon* 32, no. 4 (1971): 396–402; Peter James Hudson, "The National City Bank of New York and Haiti, 1909–1922," *Radical History Review* 2013, no. 115 (2013): 91–114.

8. Robert K. Murray, *Red Scare: A Study in National Hysteria, 1919–1920* (Minneapolis: University of Minnesota Press, 1955), 234–236.

9. Leonard W. Levy, *Emergence of a Free Press* (New York: Oxford University Press, 1985), 258–262, 307.

10. John R. Vile, *"Herndon v. Lowry* (1937)," *The First Amendment Encyclopedia*, https://mtsu.edu/first-amendment/article/268/herndon-v-lowry; Christopher M. Finan, *From the Palmer Raids to the Patriot Act: A History of the Fight for Free Speech in America* (Boston: Beacon, 2007), chap. 2; Edward White, *Justice Oliver Wendell Holmes: Law and the Inner Self* (New York: Oxford University Press, 1993), 441–449; Paul L. Murphy, *The Constitution in Crisis Times, 1918–1969* (New York: Harper Torch, 1972), 84–88, 118–123; Laura M. Weinrib, *The Taming of Free Speech: America's Civil Liberties Compromise* (Cambridge, MA: Harvard University Press, 2016).

11. Sam Lebovic, *Free Speech and Unfree News: The Paradox of Press Freedom in America* (Cambridge, MA: Harvard University Press, 2016), 42–49.

12. *Near v. Minnesota*, 283 U.S. 697 (1931).

13. Jonathan M. Katz, *Gangsters of Capitalism: Smedley Butler, the Marines, and the Making and Breaking of America's Empire* (New York: St. Martin's, 2022), 4, 9.

14. James Bamford, *Puzzle Palace: A Report on America's Most Secretive Agency* (New York: Penguin, 1982), 20–46.

15. Daniel Larsen, "Creating an American Culture of Secrecy: Cryptography in Wilson-Era Diplomacy," *Diplomatic History* 44 (2020): 102–132.

16. David Kahn, *The Reader of Gentlemen's Mail: Herbert O. Yardley and American Intelligence* (New Haven, CT: Yale University Press, 2004), 50; McCoy, *Policing America's Empire*, 298; Roy Talbert, *Negative Intelligence: The Army and the American Left, 1917–1941* (Jackson: University Press of Mississippi, 1991), chap. 2.

17. Christopher Andrew, *The Secret World: A History of Intelligence* (New Haven, CT: Yale University Press, 2018), 5, chap. 11.

18. Kahn, *Reader of Gentlemen's Mail*, 56–58, 79; George C. Herring, *From Colony to Superpower: U.S. Foreign Relations Since 1776* (New York: Oxford University Press, 2008), 454–455.

19. Kaeten Mistry, "A Culture of 'Embarrassing Indiscretions': The Origins of U.S. National Security Whistleblowing," in *The Culture of Intelligence: Germany, Britain, France and the USA*, ed. Andreas Gestrich, Philipp Gassert, Soenke Neitzel, and Simon J. Ball (Oxford: Oxford University Press, 2018), 174.

20. Louis Kruh, "Stimson, the Black Chamber, and the 'Gentlemen's Mail' Quote," *Cryptologia* 12, no. 2 (1988): 65–89.

21. Kahn, *Reader of Gentlemen's Mail*, 108; George T. Bye to Laurence Chambers, February 27, 1931, Reynolds and Goodwin to George T. Bye, January 12, 1931, both in box 391, James O. Brown Associates Records 1927–1992, Rare Book & Manuscript Library, Columbia University. My thanks to Kaeten Mistry for sharing these records with me.

22. Mistry, "Culture of 'Embarrassing Indiscretions,'" 168.

23. Christopher R. Moran, *Company Confessions: Secrets, Memoirs, and the CIA* (New York: Thomas Dunne/St. Martin's, 2016), 23–52, 36.

24. Kahn, *Reader of Gentlemen's Mail*, 107.

25. Mistry, "Culture of 'Embarrassing Indiscretions,'" 179.

26. George H. Manning, "Press Gag Averted in 'Secrets' Bill," *EP*, April 8, 1933, 7.

27. "Editorial," *EP*, April 8, 1933, 20.

28. "Hull Says Code Bill Cannot Curb Press," *NYT*, April 25, 1933, 10.

29. "New Bill Eliminates Press Censorship," *EP*, April 15, 1933, 8; Buel W. Patch, "Protection of Official Secrets," *Editorial Research Reports*, February 25, 1948, 133.

30. *Congressional Record*, May 10, 1933, S.3127–3128.

31. See Max Everest-Phillips, "Reassessing Pre-war Japanese Espionage: The Rutland Naval Spy Case and the Japanese Intelligence Threat Before Pearl Harbor," *Intelligence and National Security* 21, no. 2 (April 2006): 281–282; Michael J. Sulick, *Spying in America: Espionage from the Revolutionary War to the Dawn of the Cold War* (Washington, DC: Georgetown University Press, 2012), 156–158; *Annual Report of the Attorney General of the United States, for Fiscal Year 1937* (Washington, DC: US GPO, 1937), 76; Eric Setzekorn, "The Contemporary Utility of 1930s Counterintelligence Prosecution Under the United States Espionage Act," *International Journal of Intelligence and CounterIntelligence* 29 (July 2, 2016): 545–563. At the end of my research for this book, I did discover another Espionage Act case that happened in 1933. Ralph Osman, a member of the armed forces stationed in the Panama Canal Zone, was accused of mailing secret information—apparently fortification plans—to contacts in Brooklyn who were alleged to be Communists. He was found guilty by court-martial, given a $10,000 fine, and sentenced to two years of hard labor. But then FDR overturned the sentence and ordered a retrial, in which Osman was acquitted of all charges. It seems that Osman had been framed, perhaps a victim of anti-Semitism. It is a strange and mysterious case. The newspaper coverage was patchy and poor, and I did not consult any archival sources that might clarify what happened. Anyway, it was quickly forgotten. Two years later, when Harry Thompson was found guilty of espionage, the navy crowed that this was the first time the law had been used in peacetime. The army reminded everyone of the *Osman* case, but no one paid attention. Thereafter, people remembered Thompson's case as the first peacetime use of the law. See "US Navy Man Found Guilty as Spy for Japan," *New York Herald Tribune*, July 4, 1936, 3; "Osman Acquitted as Canal Zone Spy," *NYT*, May 22, 1934, 13; "Dead Letter Opened Spy Case in Panama," *NYT*, August 29, 1933, 15; "U.S. Soldier on Trial as a Spy; Russia Is Named," *CT*, August 29, 1933, 3; "Corporal Goes on Trial in Canal Zone Spy Case," *New York Herald Tribune*, August 29, 1933, 14; "Red Affiliations Laid to Osman at Spy Hearing," *New York Herald Tribune*, August 30, 1933, 7; "American Jewish Committee 28th Annual Report," *American Jewish Yearbook* 37 (1935): 430.

32. "Russians Convicted as Spies," *LAT*, March 11, 1939, 1; *Gorin* (1940).

33. "Spy Act Scope Under Debate," *LAT*, December 20, 1940, 5.

34. Mary L. Dudziak, *War Time: An Idea, Its History, Its Consequences* (Oxford: Oxford University Press, 2012).

35. David Ekbladh, "The Interwar Foundations of Security Studies: Edward Mead Earle, the Carnegie Corporation and the Depression-Era Origins of a Field," *Global Society* 28 (2014): 40–53; Alexandre Rios-Bordes, "When Military Intelligence Reconsiders the Nature of War: Elements for an Archaeology of 'National Security' (United States, 1919–1941)," *Politix*, 104 (2013/14): 105–132.

36. Andrew Preston, "Monsters Everywhere: A Genealogy of National Security," *Diplomatic History* 38 (2014): 477–500; Dexter Fergie, "Geopolitics Turned Inwards: The Princeton Military Studies Group and the National Security Imagination," *Diplomatic History* 43 (2019): 644–670.

37. Edward Mead Earle, "The Threat to American Security," *Yale Review* 30 (1941): 469.

38. Mark Neocleous, *Critique of Security* (Montreal: McGill-Queen's University Press, 2008), 76; Rios-Bordes, "When Military Intelligence Reconsiders the Nature of War," 24.

39. *Gorin* (1941), at 28.

40. *Gorin*, at 28.

41. *Gorin*, at 27.

42. Edgar and Schmidt, "Espionage Statutes," 960–961, 989, 992–994.

43. *Gorin* (1940), at 715.

44. Edgar and Schmidt, "Espionage Statutes," 990.

45. *Gorin* (1941), at 30.

46. *Gorin* (1940), at 717.

47. *Gorin*, at 722.

48. "High Court Upholds Spy Convictions," *LAT*, January 14, 1941, 1; "Construction of the Espionage Act of 1917," *Illinois Law Review* 36 (1941–1942): 225–229.

49. Joseph Alsop and Stewart Alsop, *The Reporter's Trade* (New York: Reynal, 1958), 23.

50. Rios-Bordes, "When Military Intelligence Reconsiders the Nature of War," xxv, xxvi; David H. Morrissey, "Disclosure and Secrecy: Security Classification Executive Orders," *Journalism & Mass Communication Monographs* 161 (1997): 10–11; Dallas Irvine, *Origin of Defense Markings in the Army and Former War Department* (Washington, DC: National Archives Staff Information Paper, 1972), 29–42; Arvin S. Quist, *Security Classification of Information*, vol. 1, chap. 2 (2002), 9, https://sgp.fas .org/library/quist.

51. Bamford, *Puzzle Palace*, 46–61; Andrew, *Secret World*, 602–612; Kathryn S. Olmsted, *Real Enemies: Conspiracy Theories and American Democracy, World War I to 9/11* (Oxford: Oxford University Press, 2009), 57–58.

Chapter 5: The Nazi Spy Who Wasn't

1. Edmund Carl Heine, FBI Detroit File: 100-7886, October 16, 1942, Robert C. Burns, "Edmund Carl Heine," FBI Detroit File 100-7886, September 27, 1944, both in case file 146-43-278, RG 60, NARA II.

2. Theron L. Caudle to Solicitor General, December 12, 1945, *U.S. v Edmund Carl Heine*, case file 146-43-278, RG 60, NARA II.

3. "Flier Says Heine Bought Army Data," *NYT*, September 19, 1941, 10; Edmund Carl Heine, FBI Detroit File: 100-7886; "Spy Trial Hears Heine Collected Warplane Data," *New York Herald Tribune*, September 20, 1941, 7; David Kahn, *Hitler's Spies: German Military Intelligence in World War II* (New York: Collier, 1982), 332.

4. Hans L. Trefousse, "Failure of German Intelligence in the United States, 1935–1945," *Mississippi Valley Historical Review* 42 (1955): 84–100; Francis MacDonnell, *Insidious Foes: The Axis Fifth Column and the American Home Front* (New York: Oxford University Press, 1995); Thomas H. Etzold, "The (F)Utility Factor: German Information Gathering in the United States, 1933–1941," *Military Affairs* 39 (1975): 77–82.

5. Rhodri Jeffreys-Jones, *The Nazi Spy Ring in America: Hitler's Agents, the FBI and the Case That Stirred a Nation* (Washington, DC: Georgetown University Press, 2020);

Michael J. Sulick, *Spying in America: Espionage from the Revolutionary War to the Dawn of the Cold War* (Washington DC: Georgetown University Press, 2012), chaps. 15–19.

6. Jeffreys-Jones, *Nazi Spy Ring in America*, 20.

7. Trefousse, "Failure of German Intelligence in the United States," 90; "Duquesne Plays a 40-Year Hand Against Britain," *New York Herald Tribune*, July 1, 1941, 9; Peter Duffy, *Double Agent: The First Hero of World War II and How the FBI Outwitted and Destroyed a Nazi Spy Ring* (New York: Scribner, 2014).

8. "Spy Suspects," *BG*, June 30, 1941, 1; "29 Are Held as Nazi Spies in Roundup by FBI," *New York Herald Tribune*, June 30, 1941, 1A; "29 Suspects Show Variety of Talent," *NYT*, June 30, 1941, 3.

9. Kahn, *Hitler's Spies*, 13–22.

10. Etzold, "(F)Utility Factor," 79; Jeffreys-Jones, *Nazi Spy Ring in America*, 8–9; C. G. Sweeting, "Not-So-Secret-Weapon," *Aviation History*, March 2014, 30–35; Kahn, *Hitler's Spies*, 331; Sulick, *Spying in America*, 134–135.

11. Jeffreys-Jones, *Nazi Spy Ring in America*, 125–127; Etzold, "(F)Utility Factor," 78–79; "Spies," *NYT*, December 1, 1938, 22.

12. MacDonnell, *Insidious Foes*, 179.

13. Hanson Baldwin, "A Spy Thriller—in Real Life," *NYT*, June 26, 1938, 57; MacDonnell, *Insidious Foes*, 57.

14. Jeffreys-Jones, *Nazi Spy Ring in America*, chap. 13; "Turrou Spy Story Barred in Press," *NYT*, June 23, 1938, 1; "Free Press Argued at Turrou Hearing," *NYT*, June 24, 1938, 3; "Plans to Print Spy Story Draw Roosevelt Fire," *New York Herald Tribune*, June 25, 1938, 8A; "Judge Delays Decision on Turrou Exposé," *Baltimore Sun*, June 24, 1938, 1; "Spy Story Is Withheld," *NYT*, June 25, 1938, 4.

15. MacDonnell, *Insidious Foes*, 63–71, 133–134; Jeffrey A. Smith, *War and Press Freedom: The Problem of Prerogative Power* (New York: Oxford University Press, 1999), 147.

16. Beverly Gage, *G-Man: J. Edgar Hoover and the Making of the American Century* (New York: Vintage, 2022), 214–215; Jeffreys-Jones, *Nazi Spy Ring in America*, chap. 11; Trefousse, "Failure of German Intelligence in the United States," 89.

17. MacDonnell, *Insidious Foes*, 7–8.

18. Brett Gary, *The Nervous Liberals: Propaganda Anxieties from World War I to the Cold War* (New York: Columbia University Press, 1999), 199–216; Athan Theoharis, *The FBI and American Democracy: A Brief Critical History* (Lawrence: University Press of Kansas, 2004), 49–57; 34–36, 156–157; William J. Maxwell, *F.B. Eyes: How J. Edgar Hoover's Ghostreaders Framed African American Literature* (Princeton, NJ: Princeton University Press, 2015), 93; Gage, *G-Man*, 206, 228.

19. "Spy Suspect Cites Loss of Reich Job," *NYT*, October 28, 1941, 13.

20. Caudle to Solicitor General, December 12, 1945; Duffy, *Double Agent*, 246; "14 Convicted Here as German Spies," *NYT*, December 13, 1941, 1; "33 in Spy Ring Get Heavy Sentences," *NYT*, January 3, 1942, 1; "33 Nazi Spies Get Sentences up to 18 Years," *New York Herald Tribune*, January 3, 1942, 6.

21. Christopher M. Finan, *From the Palmer Raids to the Patriot Act: A History of the Fight for Free Speech in America* (Boston: Beacon, 2007), 26.

22. A History of the Office of Censorship, vol. I, 32–34, box 1, entry 4, OC; Sam Lebovic, *Free Speech and Unfree News: The Paradox of Press Freedom in America*

(Cambridge, MA: Harvard University Press, 2016), chap. 5; Michael S. Sweeney, *Secrets of Victory: The Office of Censorship and the American Press and Radio in World War II* (Chapel Hill: University of North Carolina Press, 2001).

23. Transcript of OC Meeting, April 14, 1942, 20, box 109, folder: Training, entry 1, OC; A History of the Office of Censorship, vol. II, 4, box 1, entry 4, OC; A. D. Surles to Byron Price, August 29, 1942, box 109, folder: New York, entry 1, OC; "Long Vacation in Price's Plans," *EP*, August 18, 1945, 14.

24. Meetings of June 19–20, 1944, 24, doc. 18, box 1, folder 7, HC; Bulletin on Censorship no. 22, December 14, 1943, box 109, folder: New York, entry 1, OC.

25. Walter F. Schneider, "Editors Suggest Improvements in Voluntary Censorship Plan," *EP*, May 3, 1941, 3.

26. Lebovic, *Free Speech and Unfree News*, 133; Patrick S. Washburn, "The Office of Censorship's Attempt to Control Press Coverage of the Atomic Bomb During World War II," *Journalism Monographs* 120 (1990): 1–43; Victor Sebestyen, *1946: The Making of the Modern World* (New York: Pantheon, 2015), 24.

27. Sweeney, *Secrets of Victory*, 195–209; "Knoxville Sat on Atomic News Bombshell," *EP*, August 11, 1945, 59.

28. Claudius O. Johnson, "The Status of Freedom of Expression Under the Smith Act," *Western Political Quarterly* 11, no. 3 (1958): 469–480; Geoffrey R. Stone, *Perilous Times: Free Speech in Wartime: From the Sedition Act of 1798 to the War on Terrorism* (New York: W. W. Norton, 2004), 251–252; Ira Katznelson, *Fear Itself: The New Deal and the Origins of Our Time* (New York: Liveright, 2013), 332.

29. Stone, *Perilous Times*, 243, 255–256.

30. Richard W. Steele, *Free Speech in the Good War* (New York: St. Martin's, 1999), 284; Stone, *Perilous Times*, 235–310; Patrick Scott Washburn, *A Question of Sedition: The Federal Government's Investigation of the Black Press During World War II* (New York: Oxford University Press, 1986).

31. Donna Haverty-Stacke, *Trotskyists on Trial: Free Speech and Political Persecution Since the Age of FDR* (New York: NYU Press, 2016).

32. *Hartzel v. United States*, 322 U.S. 680 (1944).

33. David M. Kennedy, *Freedom from Fear: The American People in Depression and War, 1929–1945* (New York: Oxford University Press, 1999), 486–488.

34. Sam Lebovic, "When the Mainstream Media Was Conservative," in *Media Nation: The Political History of News in Modern America*, ed. Bruce J. Schulman and Julian E. Zelizer (Philadelphia: University of Pennsylvania Press, 2017), 70; Kennedy, *Freedom from Fear*, 472; Richard Norton Smith, *The Colonel: The Life and Legend of Robert R. McCormick, 1880–1955* (Evanston, IL: Northwestern University Press, 1997), 418.

35. Arthur Sears Henning, "White House Calls Cabinet Aid to Draft Reply," *CT*, December 5, 1941, 1; "A.E.F. 'Plan' Laid to Army and Navy," *NYT*, December 5, 1941, 3; "Story of Plans for an AEF Is Not Denied," *WP*, December 5, 1941, 1; "Chicago Tribune Discloses Maximum Plan for AEF of Five Million by 1943," *St. Louis Post-Dispatch*, December 4, 1941, 1; "Army, Navy Start Probe into Story U.S. Plans AEF," *BG*, December 5, 1941, 1; Kennedy, *Freedom from Fear*, 488; Smith, *Colonel*, 415–419.

36. James Bamford, *Puzzle Palace: A Report on America's Most Secretive Agency* (New York, Penguin, 1982), 53.

37. Dina Goren, "Communication Intelligence and the Freedom of the Press: The Chicago Tribune's Battle of Midway Dispatch and the Breaking of the Japanese Naval Code," *Journal of Contemporary History* 16 (1981): 663–690; Oliver S. Cox, "Criminal Liability for Newspaper Publication of Naval Secrets," June 16, 1942, in *Supplemental Opinions of the Office of Legal Counsel of the US Department of Justice*, ed. Nathan A. Forrester (Washington, DC, 2013), 1:93–101; John Prados, "Secrecy and Leaks: When the U.S. Government Prosecuted the Chicago Tribune," National Security Archive Briefing Book, October 25, 2017; Elliot Carlson, *Stanley Johnston's Blunder: The Reporter Who Spilled the Secret Behind the U.S. Navy's Victory at Midway* (Annapolis, MD: Naval Institute Press, 2017), 156.

38. William D. Mitchell, "Report on Chicago Tribune Case for the Attorney General and the Secretary of the Navy," July 14, 1942; Memorandum for the Record, William D. Mitchell (DOJ), "TRIBUNE Case," July 15, 1942; Memorandum, Assistant Attorney General Wendell Berge to Attorney General Francis Biddle, July 27, 1942. See https://nsarchive.gwu.edu/briefing-book/intelligence/2017-10-25/secrecy-leaks-when-us-government-prosecuted-chicago-tribune.

39. "News Story Faces Inquiry," *LAT*, August 8, 1942, 7; "U.S. Jury Clears Tribune," *CT*, August 20, 1942, 1; Goren, "Communication Intelligence and the Freedom of the Press," 666–671; Carlson, *Stanley Johnston's Blunder*, 215.

40. Arvin S. Quist, *Security Classification of Information*, vol. 1, chap. 3 (2002), 9, https://sgp.fas.org/library/quist/chap_3.pdf; "Security Regulations," n.d., box 2, folder: Secret Indoctrinations; and Edward Klauber, "To Heads of All Departments and Agencies," March 13, 1944, box 2, folder: SAB Memo 1, both in entry 12: General Records of Chairman, Security Advisory Board, OWI.

41. Alex Wellerstein, *Restricted Data: The History of Nuclear Secrecy in the United States* (Chicago: University of Chicago Press, 2021), 57–59; William F. Vogel, "The Mighty Microbe Can Go to War: Scientists, Secrecy and American Biological Weapons Research, 1941–1969" (PhD diss., University of Minnesota, 2021), 261–262.

42. "History of Security Office and Security Advisory Board, OWI," December 15, 1944, box 2, folder: Security Advisory Board, entry 6H, OWI; "Common Violations of Security," n.d., box 5, folder: Miscellaneous, entry 12, OWI; "Security of Classified Documents," February 21, 1944; "Security Training," Security Advisory Board Memo no. 4-1944, April 11, 1944, box 1, folder: SAB Memoranda, entry 11, OWI; "Removal of Classified Documents from Official Place of Storage," April 26, 1944, in box 1, folder: SAB Memoranda, entry 11, OWI.

43. 24th Meeting of Security Advisory Board, March 1, 1944, 7, box 1, folder: Security Advisory Board Minutes, entry 11, OWI; "Talk of Lieutenant Commander Theodore Gould to Trainees at the Office of Economic Warfare," n.d., box 5, folder: Miscellaneous, entry 12, OWI; "Security Indoctrination Programs for Civilian Employees of Nonmilitary Federal War Agencies," n.d., box 2, folder: Secret Indoctrinations, entry 12, OWI; "Security Training," April 11, 1944.

44. "Editorial," *EP*, February 28, 1942, 22; Buel W. Patch, "Protection of Official Secrets," *Editorial Research Reports*, February 25, 1948, 134; "White House Writers Hit Justice Bill," *EP*, February 28, 1942, 3; C. P. Trussell, "Biddle Presents War 'Secrets' Bill," *NYT*, February 25, 1942, 1; "Biddle Proposes Law to Tighten Censorship,"

EP, February 21, 1942, 6; Richard L. Worsnop, "Secrecy in Government," *Editorial Research Reports*, August 18, 1971, 642.

45. "Laws Applicable to Officers or Employees of the Government Giving Out Information or Copies of Papers or Results of Investigations Which Are of a Confidential Character," n.d., box 2, folder: SAB Memo 7, entry 12, OWI; Meeting of SAB, May 31, 1944, Meeting of SAB, June 21, 1944, Meeting of SAB, July 26, 1944, 2–3, box 1, folder: SAB Minutes 3, entry 11, OWI.

46. United States Commission on Government Security, *Report of the Commission on Government Security*, S.doc. 64, at 155 (1957); Harold C. Relyea, "The Evolution of Government Information Security Classification Policy: A Brief Overview (1775–1973)," in *Government Secrecy, Hearings Before the Subcommittee on Intergovernmental Relations of the Committee on Government Operations*, U.S. Senate, 93rd Congress, 2nd sess., 1974, 855.

47. Gerald Gunther, *Learned Hand: The Man and Judge* (New York: Oxford University Press, 2010), xvi.

48. Gunther, *Learned Hand*, 127–136; Stone, *Perilous Times*, 160–179.

49. Gunther, *Learned Hand*, 143.

50. Gunther, 221–222.

51. *US v. Heine*, 151 F.2d 813 (1945).

52. Francis Biddle, "Communication of Secret Information to Representatives of Allied Nations," October 28, 1942, *Official Opinions of the Attorneys-General of the United States* 40 (1940–1948): 247–250.

53. *Gorin v. U.S.*, 312 U.S. 19 (1941).

54. Caudle to Solicitor General, December 12, 1945.

55. "Ruling Is Refused in Espionage Case," *NYT*, April 30, 1946, 10; J. Howard McGrath, Petition for a Writ of Certiorari, *U.S. v Heine, Records and Briefs of the U.S. Supreme Court*, October Term, 1945.

56. Charles B. Murray to Director FBI, October 6, 1952, case file 146-43-278, RG 60, NARA II.

57. "Danger in Failure of Voluntary Censorship," *EP*, March 14, 1942, 9; Meetings of June 19–20, 1944, 24–34, document 18, box 1, folder 7, HC.

58. Meetings of March 31 to April 2, 1946, 39, document 94, box 5, folder 4, HC.

59. Gage, *G-Man*, chap. 24; Louis Fisher, "Military Tribunals: The Quirin Precedent," *CRS Report for Congress RL 31340*, March 26, 2002.

60. Peter H. Irons, *Justice at War: The Story of the Japanese-American Internment Cases* (Berkeley: University of California Press, 1993), 249; Stone, *Perilous Times*, 298–307.

Chapter 6: Red Herrings, or, the Cold War Spy Scare

1. 1948 Pulitzer Prize citation, www.pulitzer.org/winners/nat-s-finney.

2. "Chances Slim for Truman Approval of Censorship Plan," *Minneapolis Morning Tribune*, October 25, 1947, 2; "Secrecy Rules Softened in Response to Protests," *EP*, November 1, 1947, 5; Nat Finney, "Cloak of Secrecy Seen as Means to Hide Inefficiency in Office," *Minneapolis Star*, October 22, 1947, 6; "US Censorship Plan Revealed," *Minneapolis Sunday Tribune*, October 19, 1947, 1; Richard M. Freeland, *The Truman Doctrine and the Origins of McCarthyism: Foreign Policy, Domestic Politics and Internal Security, 1946–1948* (New York: Alfred A. Knopf, 1972), 224.

3. Jeffrey Frank, *The Trials of Harry Truman: The Extraordinary Presidency of an Ordinary Man, 1945–1952* (Simon and Schuster, 2022); David G. McCullough, *Truman* (New York: Simon and Schuster, 1992).

4. Frank, *Trials of Harry Truman*, 52; Mary Graham, *The President's Secrets: The Use and Abuse of Hidden Power* (New Haven, CT: Yale University Press, 2017), 80, 84; Martin J. Sherwin, *A World Destroyed: The Atomic Bomb and the Grand Alliance* (New York: Vintage, 1977), 146–149.

5. Sherwin, *World Destroyed*, 159, 172–173.

6. Report by the Policy Planning Staff, "Review of Current Trends of U.S. Foreign Policy," February 24, 1948, *Foreign Relations of the United States, 1948: General; the UN*, vol. 1, part 2, document 4.

7. Frank, *Trials of Harry Truman*, 29, 48; Garry Wills, *Bomb Power: The Modern Presidency and the National Security State* (New York: Penguin, 2010), 22.

8. Amy Knight, *How the Cold War Began: The Igor Gouzenko Affair and the Hunt for Soviet Spies* (New York: Carroll and Graf, 2005).

9. Kathryn S. Olmsted, *Red Spy Queen: A Biography of Elizabeth Bentley* (Chapel Hill: University of North Carolina Press, 2002).

10. Christopher Andrew, *The Secret World: A History of Intelligence* (New Haven, CT: Yale University Press, 2018), 672–676; Michael J. Sulick, *Spying in America: Espionage from the Revolutionary War to the Dawn of the Cold War* (Washington, DC: Georgetown University Press, 2012), 173–180; Richard Gid Powers, "Introduction," in Daniel Patrick Moynihan, *Secrecy: The American Experience* (New Haven, CT: Yale University Press, 1999), 15, 70–71; Joseph W. Esherick and Michael E. Parrish, "Looking for Spies in All the Wrong Places," *Reviews in American History* 25 (1997): 174–185.

11. Athan G. Theoharis, *Chasing Spies: How the FBI Failed in Counterintelligence but Promoted the Politics of McCarthyism in the Cold War Years* (Chicago: Ivan R. Dee, 2002), 4–10.

12. Kate Brown, *Plutopia: Nuclear Families, Atomic Cities, and the Great Soviet and American Plutonium Disasters* (Oxford: Oxford University Press, 2013), 77; Katherine A. S. Sibley, *Red Spies in America: Stolen Secrets and the Dawn of the Cold War* (Lawrence: University Press of Kansas, 2004), 77, 92–93, 98.

13. Olmsted, *Red Spy Queen*, 47.

14. Alex Wellerstein, *Restricted Data: The History of Nuclear Secrecy in the United States* (Chicago: University of Chicago Press, 2021), 65, 433; Victor Sebestyen, *1946: The Making of the Modern World* (New York: Pantheon, 2015), 309–310.

15. Wills, *Bomb Power*, 23; Barton J. Bernstein, "The Quest for Security: American Foreign Policy and International Control of Atomic Energy, 1942–1946," *Journal of American History* 60 (1974): 120; Sibley, *Red Spies in America*, 169; Moynihan, *Secrecy*, 143–144; David Holloway, *Stalin and the Bomb: The Soviet Union and Atomic Energy, 1939–1956* (New Haven, CT: Yale University Press, 1994), 222–223; Daniel Hirsch and William G. Mathews, "Who Really Gave Away the Secret?," *Bulletin of the Atomic Scientists* (January 1990): 10.

16. Wellerstein, *Restricted Data*, 222–224; Sibley, *Red Spies in America*, 25, 36–38.

17. Ellen Schrecker, *Many Are the Crimes: McCarthyism in America* (Princeton, NJ: Princeton University Press, 1998), 178–179.

18. Walter Schneir and Miriam Schneir, *Final Verdict: What Really Happened in the Rosenberg Case* (Brooklyn: Melville House, 2010), 109.

19. Sulick, *Spying in America*, chap. 31; Wellerstein, *Restricted Data*, 251–255; Schneir and Schneir, *Final Verdict*, 26; "Atom Spy Couple Sentenced to Die," *NYT*, April 6, 1951, 1; "Death for Spies Bill Introduced in Senate," *NYT*, April 10, 1951, 10.

20. Wellerstein, *Restricted Data*, 227–228; Lori Clune, *Executing the Rosenbergs: Death and Diplomacy in a Cold War World* (New York: Oxford University Press, 2016), 16.

21. "Pair Silent to End," *NYT*, June 20, 1953, 1.

22. Theoharis, *Chasing Spies*, 98–105; Harvey Klehr and Ronald Radosh, *The Amerasia Spy Case: Prelude to McCarthyism* (Chapel Hill: University of North Carolina Press, 1996); "Memorandum of the Department of Justice on the Amerasia Case," in John Service, *The Amerasia Papers: Some Problems in the History of US-China Relations* (Berkeley: University of California Press, 1971), 39.

23. Klehr and Radosh, *Amerasia Spy Case*, 98–100.

24. Gerald Gunther, *Learned Hand: The Man and Judge* (New York: Oxford University Press, 2010), 509–512; Tim Weiner, *Enemies: A History of the FBI* (New York: Random House, 2012), 163–165; Sulick, *Spying in America*, chap. 27; Theoharis, *Chasing Spies*, 90–95; Betty Medsger, *The Burglary: The Discovery of J. Edgar Hoover's Secret FBI* (New York: Alfred A. Knopf, 2014), 130–133.

25. Sibley, *Red Spies in America*, 125; Landon R. Storrs, *The Second Red Scare and the Unmaking of the New Deal Left* (Princeton, NJ: Princeton University Press, 2013), 2; Graham, *President's Secrets*, 104.

26. Sibley, *Red Spies in America*, 115, 126; Olmsted, *Red Spy Queen*, 63–66.

27. David Rohde, *In Deep: The FBI, the CIA, and the Truth About America's "Deep State"* (New York: W. W. Norton, 2020), 41.

28. Theoharis, *Chasing Spies*, 42–43; Knight, *How the Cold War Began*, 107–108; Olmsted, *Red Spy Queen*, 116–123, 125, 132, 151, 170, 186.

29. Olmsted, 114; David Caute, *The Great Fear: The Anti-Communist Purge Under Truman and Eisenhower* (New York: Simon and Schuster, 1978), 27; Sam Tanenhaus, *Whittaker Chambers: A Biography* (New York: Modern Library, 1998), 234; David Greenberg, *Nixon's Shadow: The History of an Image* (New York: W. W. Norton, 2003), 1–34.

30. David Oshinsky, *A Conspiracy So Immense: The World of Joe McCarthy* (New York: Free Press, 1983), 207–209; Michael J. Ybarra, *Washington Gone Crazy: Senator Pat McCarran and the Great American Communist Hunt* (Hanover, NH: Steerforth, 2004).

31. Schrecker, *Many Are the Crimes*, 203–239; Beverly Gage, *G-Man: J. Edgar Hoover and the Making of the American Century* (New York: Vintage, 2022); Sam Lebovic, "No Right to Leave the Nation: The Politics of Passport Denial and the Rise of the National Security State," *Studies in American Political Development* 34, no. 1 (April 2020): 170–193.

32. Geoffrey R. Stone, *Perilous Times: Free Speech in Wartime: From the Sedition Act of 1798 to the War on Terrorism* (New York: W. W. Norton, 2004), 363–366; Richard Perlstein, *Invisible Bridge: The Fall of Nixon and the Rise of Reagan* (New York: Simon and Schuster, 2014), 356–370.

33. Murray L. Schwartz and James C. N. Paul, "Foreign Communist Propaganda in the Mails: A Report on Some Problems of Federal Censorship," *University of*

Pennsylvania Law Review 107 (March 1959): 634–644; Note, "Government Exclusion of Foreign Political Propaganda," *Harvard Law Review* 68 (June 1955): 1393–1409.

34. *Dennis v. United States*, 341 U.S. 494 (1951); Claudius O. Johnson, "The Status of Freedom of Expression Under the Smith Act," *Western Political Quarterly* 11 (1958): 469–480; Stone, *Perilous Times*, 312–426.

35. Lebovic, "No Right to Leave the Nation."

36. Schrecker, *Many Are the Crimes*, 286, 371–373; Storrs, *Second Red Scare*; David K. Johnson, *The Lavender Scare: The Cold War Persecution of Gays and Lesbians in the Federal Government* (Chicago: University of Chicago Press, 2004); Robert D. Dean, *Imperial Brotherhood: Gender and the Making of Cold War Foreign Policy* (Amherst: University of Massachusetts Press, 2001), 66.

37. Jessica Wang, *American Science in an Age of Anxiety: Scientists, Anticommunism, and the Cold War* (Chapel Hill: University of North Carolina Press, 1999), 265.

38. Tanenhaus, *Whittaker Chambers*, 266; K. A. Cuordileone, *Manhood and American Political Culture in the Cold War* (London: Routledge, 2005), 45.

39. Tanenhaus, *Whittaker Chambers*, 277.

40. Tanenhaus, 227–228, 283, 287; Olmsted, *Red Spy Queen*, 143.

41. Tanenhaus, *Whittaker Chambers*, 435–439.

42. Caute, *Great Fear*, 52; "Seems the People Can't Be Trusted," *Minneapolis Morning Tribune*, October 27, 1947, 6.

43. "Seems the People Can't Be Trusted," 6.

44. Wellerstein, *Restricted Data*, chap. 4; Wang, *American Science in an Age of Anxiety*, chap. 1; Frank, *Trials of Harry Truman*, chap. 7; Mario Daniels and John Krige, *Knowledge Regulation and National Security in Postwar America* (Chicago: University of Chicago Press, 2022), 67; Peyton Ford to Frederick J. Lawton, May 4, 1950, Roger Jones to William Hopkins, May 9, 1950, both in folder: May 13, 1950, box 63, White House Records Office, Bill Files, Truman Library; Harold Edgar and Benno C. Schmidt, "The Espionage Statutes and Publication of Defense Information," *Columbia Law Review* 73 (May 1973): 1064–1065; H. Rep. 81-1895 (1950).

45. 81st Cong. Rec. 3409, 3413 (March 15, 1950); Edgar and Schmidt, "Espionage Statutes," 1021–1031.

46. 81st Cong. Rec. 12069 (August 9, 1950).

47. Amendment in the Nature of a Substitute to S.595, Unpublished Hearings Before the Subcommittee of the Senate Committee on the Judiciary, April 5, 1949, 24–26, 29; Tom Clark to McCarran, June 23, 1949, box 55, folder: Pat McCarran, 1945–1949, Tom Clark Papers, Truman Library; 81st Cong. Rec. 9748 (July 20, 1949).

48. 81st Cong. Rec. 3409 (March 15, 1950).

49. Stone, *Perilous Times*, 333–335; Paul L. Murphy, *The Constitution in Crisis Times, 1918–1969* (New York: Harper, 1972), 290–292, 448–449.

50. Raymond Whearty, Chairman ICIS, Memorandum: EO 10290, June 17, 1952, TOF 285-M: Classified Information, June 25, 1952–October 1952, box 982; Roger Jones to Joe Short, January 23, 1951, Eben Ayers to Charlie Ross, October 26, 1950, both in TOF 285-M Classified Information, October 50–October 51, Preservation Copy, folder 1, box 144.

51. Harry S. Truman, Executive Order 10290, APP; *US v. Rosen and Weissman*, No. 445 F.Supp.2d 602 (US District Court, E.D. Virginia, August 9, 2006).

52. Franklin D. Roosevelt, Executive Order 8381, APP; Harry Truman, Executive Order 10104, APP; David H. Morrissey, "Disclosure and Secrecy: Security Classification Executive Orders," *Journalism and Mass Communication Monographs* (February 1997): 2, 39; Robert M. Pallitto and William C. Weaver, *Presidential Secrecy and the Law* (Baltimore: Johns Hopkins University Press, 2008), 71–73; Oona A. Hathaway, "Secrecy's End," *Minnesota Law Review* 106 (2021): 709, 715.

53. Pallitto and Weaver, *Presidential Secrecy*, 61; Jack N. Rakove, *Original Meanings: Politics and Ideas in the Making of the Constitution* (New York: Alfred A. Knopf, 1996), chap. 9; Arthur Schlesinger Jr., *The Imperial Presidency* (Boston: Mariner, 2004); Jack N. Rakove, "Making Foreign Policy—the View from 1787," in *Foreign Policy and the Constitution*, ed. Robert A. Goldwin and Robert A. Licht (Washington, DC: AEI, 1990), 1–19; Michael W. McConnell, *The President Who Would Not Be King: Executive Power Under the Constitution* (Princeton, NJ: Princeton University Press, 2020).

54. Schlesinger, *Imperial Presidency*, 124.

55. Paul A. C. Koistinen, *State of War: The Political Economy of American Warfare, 1945–2011* (Lawrence: University Press of Kansas, 2012), 45; Schlesinger, *Imperial Presidency*, 131; Morrissey, "Disclosure and Secrecy," 14; Graham, *President's Secrets*, 107.

56. Louis Fisher, *Judicial Interpretations of Egan* (Washington, DC: Law Library of Congress, Global Legal Research Directorate, 2009).

57. Nathan Brooks, "The Protection of Classified Information: The Legal Framework," CRS Report for Congress, August 5, 2004, 2; Harold J. Koh, *The National Security Constitution: Sharing Power After the Iran-Contra Affair* (New Haven, CT: Yale University Press, 1990), 171; Frank, *Trials of Harry Truman*, chap. 25.

58. Joseph Short's Press and Radio Conference, September 24, 1951, box 1, folder: September 1951, Joseph Short Files, Truman Library.

59. Harry S. Truman, The President's News Conference, October 4, 1951, APP; Arthur Krock, "Truman's Press Views Mystify the Capital," *NYT*, October 7, 1951, 157; David Greenberg, "The Tale of the Upside-Down Recipe Cake: Harry Truman, the Press, and Executive Confidentiality in the Cold War Years," in *Civil Liberties and the Legacy of Harry S. Truman*, ed. Richard S. Kirkendall (Kirksville, MO: Truman State University Press, 2013); Anthony Leviero, "Yale Men, Acting Like Spies, Bared Grave Security Leaks," *NYT*, October 14, 1951, 1; Kathleen L. Endres, "National Security Benchmark: Truman, Executive Order 10290, and the Press," *Journalism Quarterly* 67 (1990): 1071–1077; James E. Pollard, "Truman and the Press: Final Phase, 1951–53," *Journalism Quarterly* 30 (1953): 273–286.

60. Krock, "Truman's Press Views Mystify the Capital," 157; "Text of Truman Security Statement," *NYT*, October 5, 1951, 12.

61. Transcript of Columbus Town Meeting, "Should Government Decide What the People Can Be Told?," October 7, 1951, folder: Security 3 of 3, box 2, Joseph Short Files, Truman Library.

62. Sam Lebovic, *Free Speech and Unfree News: The Paradox of Press Freedom in America* (Cambridge, MA: Harvard University Press, 2016), 167; Morrissey, "Disclosure and Secrecy"; Schlesinger, *Imperial Presidency*, 340.

63. Moynihan, *Secrecy*, 175; Koh, *National Security Constitution*, 201, 320; Jason Ross Arnold, *Secrecy in the Sunshine Era: The Promise and Failures of U.S. Open Government Laws* (Lawrence: University Press of Kansas, 2014), 5, 21–22.

64. Morrissey, "Disclosure and Secrecy," 36; Schlesinger, *Imperial Presidency*, 343; Executive Order 10290.

65. Elizabeth Gotein and David M. Shapiro, *Reducing Overclassification Through Accountability* (New York: Brennan Center for Justice, 2011), 28; Hathaway, "Secrecy's End," 798.

66. J. Patrick Coyne Memorandum for Mr. Lay, "Minimum Standards for the Handling and Transmission of Classified Information," July 10, 1951, TOF 285-M Classified Information, October 50–October 51, Preservation Copy, folder 3, box 144; Minutes of the Third Meeting ICIS Subcommittee on EO 10290, February 15, 1952, TOF 285-M: Classified Information, November 1951 to January 10, 1952, folder 1 of 2, box 981; Joseph Short's Press and Radio Conference, September 24, 1951, box 1, folder: September 1951; ACLU News Release, October 23, 1951, folder: Security 2 of 3, box 2; William Benton to James Pope, October 18, 1951, folder: Security 3 of 3, box 2 all in Joseph Short Files, Truman Library.

67. Executive Order 12065, Executive Order 12356, Executive Order 12958, Executive Order 13292, and Executive Order 13526.

68. "OPS Bans 'Embarrassing' News," *NYT*, September 28, 1951, 1; Erwin Griswold, "Secrets Not Worth Keeping," *WP*, February 15, 1989, A25.

69. Gotein and Shapiro, *Reducing Overclassification*, 22; Hathaway, "Secrecy's End," 722.

70. *Freedom of Information and Secrecy in Government, Part 2: Hearing Before the Subcommittee on Constitutional Rights of the Committee on the Judiciary*, 85th Cong, 548–557.

71. Pallitto and Weaver, *Presidential Secrecy*, 80.

72. *Espionage Laws and Leaks: Hearing Before the Subcommittee on Legislation of the Permanent Select Committee on Intelligence, House of Representatives*, 96th Cong., 1st sess. (January 24, 25, 31, 1979), 7, 36; Hathaway, "Secrecy's End," 737; "Developments in the Law: The National Security Interest and Civil Liberties," *Harvard Law Review* 85 (1972): 1233.

73. "Developments in the Law," 1196–1197; Lebovic, *Free Speech and Unfree News*, 174.

74. James Bamford, *The Puzzle Palace: Inside the National Security Agency, America's Most Secret Intelligence Organization* (New York: Penguin, 1983); Stephen Budiansky, *Code Warriors: NSA's Codebreakers and the Secret Intelligence War Against the Soviet Union* (New York: Alfred A. Knopf, 2016), 157, 170.

75. Ira Katznelson, *Fear Itself: The New Deal and the Origins of Our Time* (New York: Liveright, 2013), 439; Scott Anderson, *Quiet Americans: Four Spies at the Dawn of the Cold War* (New York: Anchor, 2020), 27–28; Graham, *President's Secrets*, 82; Wills, *Bomb Power*, 59–60.

76. Hugh Wilford, *The Mighty Wurlitzer: How the CIA Played America* (Cambridge, MA: Harvard University Press, 2009), 23; Tim Weiner, *Legacy of Ashes: The History of the CIA* (New York: Doubleday, 2007), 3–14; Keith E. Whittington and Daniel P. Carpenter, "Executive Power in American Institutional Development," *Perspectives on Politics* 1 (September 2003): 505; Richard H. Immerman, *The Hidden Hand: A Brief History of the CIA* (Hoboken, NJ: Wiley, 2014), chap. 1; Katznelson, *Fear Itself*, 444, Graham, *President's Secrets*, 95.

77. Immerman, *Hidden Hand*, 36; Weiner, *Legacy of Ashes*, 57, 123–129.

78. Weiner, 46–47, 54; Kenneth Alan Osgood, *Total Cold War: Eisenhower's Secret Propaganda Battle at Home and Abroad* (Lawrence: University Press of Kansas, 2006); Immerman, *Hidden Hand*, 43.

79. Weiner, *Legacy of Ashes*, 81–104; Greg Grandin, *Empire's Workshop: Latin America, the United States, and the Making of an Imperial Republic* (New York: Picador, 2021), 60–67; Ray Takeyh, *The Last Shah: America, Iran, and the Fall of the Pahlavi Dynasty* (New Haven, CT: Yale University Press, 2021), 87–116; Nick Cullather, *Secret History: The CIA's Classified Account of Its Operations in Guatemala, 1952–1954* (Stanford, CA: Stanford University Press, 2006).

80. Chris Whipple, *The Spymasters: How the CIA Directors Shape History and the Future* (New York: Scribner, 2020), 94–99.

81. David Shamus McCarthy, *Selling the CIA: Public Relations and the Culture of Secrecy* (Lawrence: University Press of Kansas, 2018), 15–16; Wilford, *Mighty Wurlitzer*, 225–231; Weiner, *Legacy of Ashes*, 180.

82. Weiner, 65; Frederick A. O. Schwarz, *Democracy in the Dark: The Seduction of Government Secrecy* (New York: New Press, 2012), 122; "Report Says CIA Agents Picked up Bar Patrons for LSD Experiments," *NYT*, April 27, 1976, 25; Tim Weiner, "Sidney Gottlieb, 80, Dies," *NYT*, March 19, 1999, C22; Nicholas M. Horrock, "Drugs Tested by CIA on Mental Patients," *NYT*, August 3, 1977, 1; Stephen Kinzer, *Poisoner in Chief: Sidney Gottlieb and the CIA Search for Mind Control* (New York: Henry Holt, 2019).

83. Kathryn S. Olmsted, *Challenging the Secret Government: The Post-Watergate Investigations of the CIA and FBI* (Chapel Hill: University of North Carolina Press, 1996), 42–43; Whittington and Carpenter, "Executive Power," 505; McCarthy, *Selling the CIA*, 15; Andrew, *Secret World*, 679.

84. Lebovic, *Free Speech and Unfree News*, 160–162; Oshinsky, *Conspiracy So Immense*, 108–111, 139–158.

85. D. J. Mulloy, *The World of the John Birch Society: Conspiracy, Conservatism, and the Cold War* (Nashville: Vanderbilt University Press, 2014).

86. Richard Hofstadter, *The Paranoid Style in American Politics: And Other Essays* (New York: Vintage, 1967); Thomas Milan Konda, *Conspiracies of Conspiracies: How Delusions Have Overrun America* (Chicago: University of Chicago Press, 2019); Kathryn S. Olmsted, *Real Enemies: Conspiracy Theories and American Democracy, World War I to 9/11* (Oxford: Oxford University Press, 2009); "CIA Acknowledges Its Mysterious Area 51 Test Site for First Time," Reuters, August 16, 2013.

87. Gregg Herken, *The Georgetown Set: Friends and Rivals in Cold War Washington* (New York: Alfred A. Knopf, 2014), 104; Jefferson Morley, *The Ghost: The Secret Life of CIA Spymaster James Jesus Angleton* (New York: St. Martin's Griffin, 2017); Weiner, *Legacy of Ashes*, 45–46.

88. Herken, *Georgetown Set*, 228; Whipple, *Spymasters*, 25; Anderson, *Quiet Americans*, 467.

89. Melvyn P. Leffler, *A Preponderance of Power: National Security, the Truman Administration, and the Cold War* (Stanford, CA: Stanford University Press, 1992), 17; Graham, *President's Secrets*, 99; Michael J. Hogan, *A Cross of Iron: Harry S. Truman and the Origins of the National Security State, 1945–1954* (Cambridge: Cambridge University Press, 1998), 184–206; Douglas T. Stuart, *Creating the National Security State:*

A History of the Law That Transformed America (Princeton, NJ: Princeton University Press, 2008), 47–229.

90. Townsend Hoopes and Douglas Brinkley, *Driven Patriot: The Life and Times of James Forrestal* (New York: Alfred A. Knopf, 1992), 422–468; Weiner, *Legacy of Ashes*, 37–38.

Chapter 7: Missile Gaps

1. Testimony of Andrew Kinney, December 31, 1956, by Ogden and Conran, series 2, box 1, folder 9, JNP; Testimony of Jane Nelson, January 9, 1957, Testimony of John Nickerson, January 10, 1957, both in series 2, box 1, folder 10, JNP; Drew Pearson and Jack Anderson, *USA—Second Class Power?* (New York: Simon and Schuster, 1958), 158; Testimony of Jane S. Nelson, January 3, 1957, series 2, box 1, folder 9, JNP.

2. Thomas F. Hickey, General Court Martial Order, No. 85, July 8, 1957, series 2, box 1, folder 8, JNP; Testimony of John Nickerson, January 2, 1957, 11 a.m., series 2, box 1, folder 9, JNP.

3. "The Nickerson Case," *NYT*, June 30, 1957, 134; M. Martin Gross, "Would Do It Again," *BG*, September 12, 1957, 19; Pearson and Anderson, *USA*, 149; CF Cordes, Review of Army Staff Judge Advocate, July 8, 1957, series 2, box 1, folder 8, JNP.

4. Sam Lebovic, "The Forgotten 1957 Trial That Explains Our Country's Bizarre Whistleblowing Laws," *Politico*, March 27, 2016; Ian MacDougall, "The Leak Prosecution That Lost the Space Race," *Atlantic*, August 15, 2016.

5. "Nickerson Trial Likely to Focus Conflicts of Era," *Huntsville Times*, April 5, 1957, series 4, box 2, folder 1, JNP.

6. Ira Katznelson, *Fear Itself: The New Deal and the Origins of Our Time* (New York: Liveright, 2013), 452–453; Benjamin O. Fordham, "Paying for Global Power: Assessing the Costs and Benefits of Postwar US Military Spending," in *The Long War: A New History of US National Security Policy Since World War II*, ed. Andrew J. Bacevich (New York: Columbia University Press, 2007), 370–404.

7. Berkeley Rice, *The C-5A Scandal: An Inside Story of the Military-Industrial Complex* (Boston: Houghton Mifflin, 1971), 76; Julian E. Zelizer, *Arsenal of Democracy: The Politics of National Security—From World War II to the War on Terrorism* (New York: Basic Books, 2010), 125; Paul A. C. Koistinen, *State of War: The Political Economy of American Warfare, 1945–2011* (Lawrence: University Press of Kansas, 2012), 103–104; Gary Gerstle, *Liberty and Coercion: The Paradox of American Government from the Founding to the Present* (Princeton, NJ: Princeton University Press, 2018), 261–265; Ann Markusen, Scott Campbell, Peter Hall, and Sabina Deitrick, *The Rise of the Gunbelt: The Military Remapping of Industrial America* (New York: Oxford University Press, 1991).

8. Monique Laney, *German Rocketeers in the Heart of Dixie: Making Sense of the Nazi Past During the Civil Rights Era* (New Haven, CT: Yale University Press, 2015), chaps. 1–2; John Gimbel, "Project Paperclip: German Scientists, American Policy, and the Cold War," *Diplomatic History* 14, no. 3 (1990): 343–365.

9. JNP-CMT, 250.

10. Gerstle, *Liberty and Coercion*, 261; Michael H. Armacost, *The Politics of Weapons Innovation: The Thor-Jupiter Controversy* (New York: Columbia University Press, 1969), 31.

11. Armacost, *Weapons Innovation*, 25–27.

12. Armacost, 39; Koistinen, *State of War*, 67–68; Donald Quarles, "Memo for Secretary of the Defense: Adjustment of Army/Air Force Differences," August 14, 1956, series 2, box 1, folder 13, JNP.

13. Robert R. Brunn, "Whose Mission Is the Missile?" *CSM*, May 10, 1957, 11; "Army Colonel Facing Court Martial Sticks to His Guns in Missile Feud," *WP*, March 10, 1957, A2.

14. Walter A. McDougall, *The Heavens and the Earth: A Political History of the Space Age* (Baltimore: Johns Hopkins University Press, 1997), 119.

15. McDougall, *Heavens and the Earth*, 119–122.

16. Armacost, *Weapons Innovation*, 50, 283; "Considerations on the Wilson Memorandum," n.d., series 2, box 1, folder 13, JNP; Charles E. Wilson, "Memorandum for the Secretaries of Army and Navy: Mgmt. of the IRBM #2 Development Program," November 8, 1955, series 2, box 1, folder 13, JNP.

17. McDougall, *Heavens and the Earth*, 128; Armacost, *Weapons Innovation*, 101, 133–134.

18. Gross, "Would Do It Again," 19.

19. Testimony of John Nickerson, made at Army Ballistic Missile Agency, February 15, 1957, before Wilbur Wilson, series 2, box 1, folder 8, JNP; JNP-CMT, 233.

20. JNP-CMT, 165, 173, 233, 252, 331, 376; Testimony of Colonel James S. Killough, February 13, 1957, before Wilbur Wilson, series 2, box 1, folder 8; Testimony of William Pritchard, January 8, 1957, by Wootten, series 2, box 1, folder 9; CF Cordes, Review of Army Staff Judge Advocate, July 8, 1957 all in JNP.

21. Armacost, *Weapons Innovation*, 90–91, 99.

22. Armacost, 115, 123; "Court-Martial Head Is Named," *Sun*, March 8, 1957, 1; JNP-CMT, 205; Testimony of Charles A. Lundquist, February 15, 1957, before Wilbur Wilson, series 2, box 1, folder 8, JNP; McDougall, *Heavens and the Earth*, 123.

23. Testimony of John Nickerson, January 2, 1957, by Ogden and Conran, 4 p.m., series 2, box 1, folder 9; JNP-CMT, 176, 199, 358.

24. Armacost, *Weapons Innovation*, 114; Charlie Wilson, "Memorandum for Members of the Armed Forces Policy Council: Clarification of Roles and Missions to Improve the Effectiveness of the Dept of Defense," November 26, 1956, series 2, box 1, folder 13, JNP; Testimony of John Medaris, January 12, 1957, series 2, box 1, folder 10, JNP.

25. Testimony of John Nickerson, January 10, 1957, series 2, box 1, folder 10, JNP; Anand Toprani, "Budgets and Strategy: The Enduring Legacy of the Revolt of the Admirals," *Political Science Quarterly* 134 (2019): 133–138.

26. JNP-CMT, 94, 199; McDougall, *Heavens and the Earth*, 130–131.

27. Armacost, *Weapons Innovation*, 126; Donald Quarles, "Memo for Secretary of the Defense: Adjustment of Army/Air Force Differences," August 14, 1956, series 2, box 1, folder 13, JNP; Erik Bergaust, *Reaching for the Stars* (Garden City, NY: Doubleday, 1960), 219; Pearson and Anderson, *USA*, 154; "Considerations on the Wilson Memorandum," n.d., series 2, box 1, folder 13, JNP; "Interservice Row over Missile Case Foreseen," *LAT*, February 24, 1957, 36.

28. *Life* magazine clipping, November 5, 1956, series 2, box 1, folder 13, JNP; Summary of Pretrial Investigation Testimony in Nickerson Case, series 1, box 1, folder 3, JNP; JNP-CMT, 250, series 2, box 1, folder 12, JNP.

412 Notes to Pages 216–221

29. Testimony of Lieutenant Colonel James S. Killough, January 6, 1957, series 2, box 1, folder 10, JNP; JNP-CMT, 373; Gross, "Would Do It Again," 19.

30. JNP-CMT, 287, 350; Further Testimony of Walter Wiesman, January 4, 1957, series 2, box 1, folder 9, JNP; Testimony of John Nickerson, January 10, 1957; Stipulation, *US v. John C. Nickerson*, June 25, 1957, series 2, box 1, folder 13, JNP.

31. JNP-CMT, 301, 376.

32. Gross, "Would Do It Again," 19; CF Cordes, Acting Army Staff Judge Advocate, Memorandum for Commanding General, February 28, 1957, series 2, box 1, folder 14, JNP; Court-Martial Transcript, 367–368, series 2, box 1, folder 12, JNP; Further testimony of Lt. Col. Lee B. James, January 3, 1957, series 2, box 1, folder 8, JNP; Testimony of John Nickerson, January 4, 1957, by Ogden and Conran, series 2, box 1, folder 9, JNP; Summary of Pretrial Investigation Testimony in Nickerson Case, series 1, box 1, folder 3, JNP; Testimony of John Nickerson, January 4, 1957.

33. Pearson and Anderson, *USA*, 157; Testimony of Andrew Kinney, December 31, 1956, series 2, box 1, folder 9, JNP.

34. CF Cordes, Review of Army Staff Judge Advocate, July 8, 1957; JNP-CMT, 158, 362; Exhibit XVII: "Affidavits Prepared by Mr. Erik Bergaust and Mr. Ed Hull," February 11, 1957, series 2, box 1, folder 14, JNP.

35. CF Cordes, Review of Army Staff Judge Advocate, July 8, 1957; Charge Sheet: John C. Nickerson, January 28, 1957, series 2, box 1, folder 8, JNP; JNP-CMT, 367.

36. Wilbur Wilson, Investigating Officers Report, February 20, 1957, series 2, box 1, folder 8, JNP; CF Cordes, Colonel JAGC, Acting Army Staff Judge Advocate, Memorandum for Commanding General, February 28, 1957, series 2, box 1, folder 14, JNP; Charles Zimmer, Defense Counsel, to Matthew Ridgway, March 15, 1957, series 1, box 1, folder 1, JNP.

37. US Department of Defense, Committee on Classified Information, *Report to the Secretary of Defense*, November 6, 1956.

38. Defense Counsel, "Notes on the Nickerson case," n.d., series 3, box 1, folder 15, JNP; Jenkins form letter to John Sherman Cooper, Karl Mundt, Stuart Symington et al., May 15, 1957, series 1, box 1, folder 5, JNP.

39. John Sparkman to Robert K. Bell, May 11, 1957, series 1, box 1, folder 5, JNP.

40. "Rocket Expert Modern Version of Billy Mitchell," *BG*, April 14, 1957, B20; Bergaust, *Reaching for the Stars*, 215; "Prepare Trial in Hush-Hush Atmosphere," *CT*, June 24, 1957, 18.

41. "Prepare Trial in Hush-Hush Atmosphere," 18; Arthur J. Sabin, *In Calmer Times: The Supreme Court and Red Monday* (Philadelphia: University of Pennsylvania Press, 1999); Geoffrey R. Stone, *Perilous Times: Free Speech in Wartime: From the Sedition Act of 1798 to the War on Terrorism* (New York: W. W. Norton, 2004), 413–415; Willard Edwards, "Demands Ban on High Court Red Decisions," *CT*, July 27, 1957, 1.

42. Detlev F. Vagts, "Free Speech in the Armed Forces," *Columbia Law Review* 57 (February 1957): 187–218; Jason Steck, "Dissent Without Disloyalty: Expanding the Free Speech Rights of Military Members Under the 'General Articles' of the UCMJ," *Minnesota Law Review* 96 (April 2012): 1606–1632; "Nickerson Trial Likely to Focus Conflicts of Era."

43. Arch Dotson, "The Emerging Doctrine of Privilege in Public Employment," *Public Administration Review* 15, no. 2 (1955): 77–88; Edward White, *Justice*

Oliver Wendell Holmes: Law and the Inner Self (New York: Oxford University Press, 1993), 285.

44. David H. Rosenbloom, "Public Personnel Administration and the Constitution: An Emergent Approach," *Public Administration Review* 35 (January 1975): 52–59; Robert Roberts, "The Supreme Court and the Deconstitutionalization of the Freedom of Speech Rights of Public Employees," *Review of Public Personnel Administration* 27 (June 2007): 171–184; Heidi Kitrosser, "The Special Value of Public Employee Speech," *Supreme Court Review* 2015 (January 2016): 301–344; Stephen I. Vladeck, "The Espionage Act and National Security Whistleblowing After Garcetti," *American University Law Review* 57, no. 5 (June 2008): 1531–1546.

45. JNP-CMT, 79, 175, 177; "Ex-Nazi Missile Scientists Testify for Colonel Nickerson," *BG*, June 27, 1957, 1.

46. Jason Ross Arnold, *Secrecy in the Sunshine Era: The Promise and Failures of U.S. Open Government Laws* (Lawrence: University Press of Kansas, 2014), 185–189; Garry Wills, *Bomb Power: The Modern Presidency and the National Security State* (New York: Penguin, 2010), 140–147; Barry Siegel, *Claim of Privilege: A Mysterious Plane Crash, a Landmark Supreme Court Case, and the Rise of State Secrets* (New York: Harper, 2008).

47. "Study Asks Tightening of Government Leaks," *NYT*, June 20, 1957, 60; "Security Report Urges Revamping of U.S. Program," *NYT*, June 23, 1957, 1; United States Commission on Government Security, *Report of the Commission on Government Security*, S.doc. 64, at xvi, xxiii, 619–620 (1957); "Editorial," *EP*, June 29, 1957, 6; "Five Bills Support Security Revision," *NYT*, June 28, 1957, 35; "Betrayal of US Laid to Newsmen," *NYT*, July 1, 1957; James Reston, "Security v. Freedom," *NYT*, June 25, 1957, 17.

48. "Text of Wright's Statement on Journalists and U.S. Security," *NYT*, July 1, 1957, 14; "Wright Tells Moss He Will Specify Security Leaks," *EP*, June 29, 1957, 8; "Security Seals up Evidence for Press Betrayal Charge," *EP*, July 6, 1957, 9; "Pearson to Figure in Court Martial," *EP*, March 9, 1957, 70.

49. "Col. Nickerson Cleared of Spying and Perjury," *LAT*, June 26, 1957, 1; Ray Jenkins, Robert Bell, Charles Zimmer, to Major General Crump Garvin, President of the General Court Martial, June 13, 1957, series 2, box 1, folder 14, JNP.

50. Memorandum of Phone Call, January 16, 1957, series 2, box 1, folder 14, JNP; Defense Counsel, "Notes on the Nickerson case," n.d., series 3, box 1, folder 15, JNP; Testimony of John Nickerson, February 15, 1957, before Wilbur Wilson, series 2, box 1, folder 8, JNP.

51. "Strange Trial of the Colonel," *Newsweek*, July 8, 1957, 29, series 4, box 2, folder 3, JNP.

52. "Medaris Sinks Nickerson Hope for Career in Rockets," *Huntsville Times*, June 30, 1957, 1, series 4, box 2, folder 1, JNP; Court-Martial Transcript, 390, series 2, box 1, folder 12, JNP.

53. David Bowman, "Nickerson May Have Been a Hero," *Huntsville News*, November 30, 1990, A4, series 4, box 2, folder 3, JNP; Thomas F. Hickey, General Court-Martial Order, No. 85, July 8, 1957, series 2, box 1, folder 8, JNP; Gross, "Would Do It Again," 19; "News of a Forgotten Man," *BG*, December 19, 1957, 22; Leada Gore, "Mystery, Intrigue and High Drama," *Huntsville Times*, July 27, 2014, series 4, box 2, folder 3, JNP.

54. McDougall, *Heavens and the Earth*, 131.

55. McDougall, 154; Pearson and Anderson, *USA*, chap. 11; "Huntsville Celebrates Until Dawn," *BG*, February 2, 1958, 14; Robert K. Bell to John Nickerson, February 5, 1958, series 5, box 2, folder 9, JNP.

56. Laney, *German Rocketeers in the Heart of Dixie*, 10.

57. McDougall, *Heavens and the Earth*, 129; William I. Hitchcock, *The Age of Eisenhower: America and the World in the 1950s* (New York: Simon and Schuster, 2018), 388–389; Armacost, *Weapons Innovation*, chaps. 6–7.

58. James Ledbetter, *Unwarranted Influence: Dwight D. Eisenhower and the Military-Industrial Complex* (New Haven, CT: Yale University Press, 2011), 156; Hitchcock, *Age of Eisenhower*, 394.

59. Annie Jacobsen, *The Pentagon's Brain: An Uncensored History of DARPA, America's Top Secret Military Research Agency* (New York: Little, Brown, 2015); Sharon Weinberger, *The Imagineers of War: The Untold History of DARPA, the Pentagon Agency That Changed the World* (New York: Alfred A. Knopf, 2017); Margaret Pugh O'Mara, *The Code: Silicon Valley and the Remaking of America* (New York: Penguin, 2019); Tim Wu, *The Master Switch: The Rise and Fall of Information Empires* (New York: Alfred A. Knopf, 2010), 168–175.

60. Hitchcock, *Age of Eisenhower*, 379–380, 396; Zelizer, *Arsenal of Democracy*, 121; Roy E. Licklider, "The Missile Gap Controversy," *Political Science Quarterly* 85 (December 1970): 605; Christopher A. Preble, "Who Ever Believed in the 'Missile Gap'? John F. Kennedy and the Politics of National Security," *Presidential Studies Quarterly* 33 (December 2003): 801–826.

61. Weinberger, *Imagineers of War*, 63–65; Jacobsen, *Pentagon's Brain*, 48; Gregg Herken, *The Georgetown Set: Friends and Rivals in Cold War Washington* (New York: Alfred A. Knopf, 2014), 243; Koistinen, *State of War*, 138; Robert J. Watson, *Into the Missile Age* (Washington: Historical Office, Office of the Secretary of Defense, 1997), 305–310; Preble, "Who Ever Believed in the 'Missile Gap'?"; James C. Dick, "The Strategic Arms Race, 1957–61: Who Opened a Missile Gap?," *Journal of Politics* 34 (1972): 1062–1110.

62. Hitchcock, *Age of Eisenhower*, chap. 19.

63. Ledbetter, *Unwarranted Influence*.

64. Aaron L. Friedberg, *In the Shadow of the Garrison State: America's Anti-statism and Its Cold War Grand Strategy* (Princeton, NJ: Princeton University Press, 2000), chap. 7; O'Mara, *Code*, 50–51; Ledbetter, *Unwarranted Influence*, 140; Koistinen, *State of War*, 92–93.

65. Ledbetter, *Unwarranted Influence*, 114–115; "Nickerson Flays Aircraft Industry," *Huntsville Times*, June 27, 1957, 1, series 4, box 2, folder 1, JNP.

66. Testimony of Dr. Wernher von Braun, February 13, 1957, before Wilbur Wilson, series 2, box 1, folder 8, JNP; Rice, *C-5A Scandal*, 19, 208.

67. Rice; Andrew Feinstein, *The Shadow World: Inside the Global Arms Trade* (New York: Farrar, Straus and Giroux, 2011), 250–260; Koistinen, *State of War*, 102.

68. Rice, *C-5A Scandal*, 203.

69. JNP-CMT, 258.

70. Elie Abel, *Leaking: Who Does It? Who Benefits? At What Cost?* (New York: Priority, 1987); Herken, *Georgetown Set*; Robert W. Merry, *Taking on the World: Joseph and Stewart Alsop—Guardians of the American Century* (New York: Penguin, 1996); Oliver Pilat, *Drew Pearson: An Unauthorized Biography* (New York: Harper and Row,

1973); Kathryn McGarr, "We're All in This Thing Together: Cold War Consensus in the Exclusive Social World of Washington Reporters," in *Media Nation: The Political History of News in America*, ed. Bruce J. Schulman and Julian E. Zelizer (Philadelphia: University of Pennsylvania Press, 2017); David E. Pozen, "The Leaky Leviathan: Why the Government Condemns and Condones Unlawful Disclosures of Information," *Harvard Law Review* 127, no. 2 (2013): 528.

71. Oona Hathaway, "Secrecy's End," *Minnesota Law Review* 106 (2021): 733–735; Pozen, "Leaky Leviathan," 523.

72. Pozen; Abel, *Leaking*, 34–35; William E. Lee, "Deep Background: Journalists, Sources, and the Perils of Leaking," *American University Law Review* 57 (2008): 1469–1470.

73. John Nickerson to Mrs. Brownlow, March 9, 1957, series 1, box 1, folder 4, JNP; Testimony of John Nickerson, January 2, 1957, 4 p.m., series 2, box 1, folder 9, JNP; "Letter to Editor," *WP*, March 16, 1957, A10.

Chapter 8: Papers from the Pentagon

1. Daniel Ellsberg, *Secrets: A Memoir of Vietnam and the Pentagon Papers* (New York: Viking, 2002), 302–303.

2. Campbell Craig and Fredrik Logevall, *America's Cold War: The Politics of Insecurity*, 2nd ed. (Cambridge, MA: Harvard University Press, 2020), 218; Betty Medsger, *The Burglary: The Discovery of J. Edgar Hoover's Secret FBI* (New York: Alfred A. Knopf, 2014), 46; Viet Thanh Nguyen, *Nothing Ever Dies: Vietnam and the Memory of War* (Cambridge, MA: Harvard University Press, 2016), 7; Marilyn Blatt Young, *The Vietnam Wars, 1945–1990* (New York: HarperCollins, 1991), 130.

3. Ellsberg, *Secrets*; Daniel Ellsberg, *The Doomsday Machine: Confessions of a Nuclear War Planner* (New York: Bloomsbury, 2017); David Rudenstine, *The Day the Presses Stopped: A History of the Pentagon Papers Case* (Berkeley: University of California Press, 1996), chap. 2; Bruce Kuklick, *Blind Oracles: Intellectuals and War from Kennan to Kissinger* (Princeton, NJ: Princeton University Press, 2006), chap. 9.

4. David Hounshell, "The Cold War, RAND, and the Generation of Knowledge, 1946–1962," *Historical Studies in the Physical and Biological Sciences* 27, no. 2 (January 1, 1997): 237–267; Kuklick, *Blind Oracles*, chaps. 3, 5.

5. Ellsberg, *Doomsday Machine*, 36–37; Janet Farrell Brodie, "Learning Secrecy in the Early Cold War: The RAND Corporation," *Diplomatic History* 35, no. 4 (September 2011): 643–670.

6. Young, *Vietnam Wars*, 1–2, 11; Fredrik Logevall, *Embers of War: The Fall of an Empire and the Making of America's Vietnam* (New York: Random House, 2012), 117.

7. Logevall, *Embers of War*, xiii–xiv, 267–270, 341–342.

8. Logevall, 593, 606; Young, *Vietnam Wars*, 42.

9. Young, 52; Frances FitzGerald, *Fire in the Lake: The Vietnamese and the Americans in Vietnam* (Boston: Little, Brown, 1972), 88; Logevall, *Embers of War*, 655, 676; Seth Jacobs, *America's Miracle Man in Vietnam: Ngo Dinh Diem, Religion, Race, and U.S. Intervention in Southeast Asia, 1950–1957* (Durham, NC: Duke University Press, 2004), 221.

10. FitzGerald, *Fire in the Lake*, 85, 247; Logevall, *Embers of War*, 669.

11. David Milne, *Worldmaking: The Art and Science of American Diplomacy* (New York: Farrar, Straus and Giroux, 2015), 310; David Halberstam, *The Best and the Brightest*, 20th anniversary edition (New York: Ballantine, 1993), chap. 9.

12. Ellsberg, *Secrets*, 3–5; Daniel C. Hallin, *The "Uncensored War": The Media and Vietnam* (New York: Oxford University Press, 1986), 27; Young, *Vietnam Wars*, 82.

13. Sharon Weinberger, *The Imagineers of War: The Untold History of DARPA, the Pentagon Agency That Changed the World* (New York: Alfred A. Knopf, 2017), 127–130; Young, *Vietnam Wars*, 82.

14. Annie Jacobsen, *The Pentagon's Brain: An Uncensored History of DARPA, America's Top Secret Military Research Agency* (New York: Little, Brown, 2015), 127.

15. Lynn Novick et al., *The Vietnam War*, episode 3, "The River Styx (January 1964–December 1965)," and episode 2, "Riding the Tiger (1961–1963)" (Arlington, VA: PBS, 2017).

16. Ellsberg, *Secrets*, 35.

17. Ellsberg, 36–37.

18. Edwin E. Moise, *Tonkin Gulf and the Escalation of the Vietnam War* (Chapel Hill: University of North Carolina Press, 1996), 142; Young, *Vietnam Wars*, 118–119.

19. Robert Dallek, *Lyndon B. Johnson: Portrait of a President* (New York: Oxford University Press, 2005), 179; Young, *Vietnam Wars*, 118–119; Randall Bennett Woods, *Fulbright: A Biography* (Cambridge: Cambridge University Press, 1995), 352–355; Don Stillman, "Tonkin: What Should Have Been Asked," *Columbia Journalism Review* (Winter 1970/1971): 21–25.

20. Kuklick, *Blind Oracles*, 140–141; Hallin, *"Uncensored War,"* 36.

21. Michael X. Delli Carpini, "Vietnam and the Press," in *The Legacy: Vietnam War in the American Imagination*, ed. D. Michael Shafer (Boston: Beacon, 1990), 130; Hallin, *"Uncensored War,"* 33; William M. Hammond, *Public Affairs: The Military and the Media, 1962–1968* (Washington, DC: US GPO, 1988), 15; Sam Lebovic, *Free Speech and Unfree News: The Paradox of Press Freedom in America* (Cambridge, MA: Harvard University Press, 2016), 180.

22. Ellsberg, *Secrets*, 36–40.

23. Ellsberg, 44–46.

24. Ellsberg, 44.

25. James T. Patterson, *Grand Expectations: The United States, 1945–1974* (New York: Oxford University Press, 1996), 516; Young, *Vietnam Wars*, 135.

26. K. A. Cuordileone, *Manhood and American Political Culture in the Cold War* (London: Routledge, 2005), 233; Woods, *Fulbright*, 342; Robert D. Dean, *Imperial Brotherhood: Gender and the Making of Cold War Foreign Policy* (Amherst: University of Massachusetts Press, 2001), 240.

27. Logevall, *Embers of War*, 702; Halberstam, *Best and the Brightest*; Dean, *Imperial Brotherhood*, 226.

28. Dean, 231; Ellsberg, *Secrets*, 81–83; Halberstam, *Best and the Brightest*, 491–499.

29. Lyndon B. Johnson, Remarks in Memorial Hall, Akron University, October 21, 1964, APP; Ellsberg, *Secrets*, 50; Young, *Vietnam Wars*, 130–131.

30. Ellsberg, *Secrets*, 66–71, 95; Young, *Vietnam Wars*, 135–136, 159; Halberstam, *Best and the Brightest*, 598–601.

31. Hallin, *"Uncensored War,"* 60–61, 91–92.

32. Ellsberg, *Secrets*, chaps. 6–11.

33. Ellsberg, 142, 168.

34. David Culbert, "Johnson and the Media," in *The Johnson Years*, ed. Robert A. Divine (Lawrence: University Press of Kansas, 1987), 1:230; Kathleen J. Turner,

Lyndon Johnson's Dual War: Vietnam and the Press (Chicago: University of Chicago Press, 1985); Novick et al., *Vietnam War*, episode 3; Young, *Vietnam Wars*, 197–198; Geoffrey R. Stone, *Perilous Times: Free Speech in Wartime: From the Sedition Act of 1798 to the War on Terrorism* (New York: W. W. Norton, 2004), 439–440.

35. Mary Hershberger, *Traveling to Vietnam: American Peace Activists and the War* (Syracuse, NY: Syracuse University Press, 1998), 2, 24; Christian G. Appy, *American Reckoning: The Vietnam War and Our National Identity* (New York: Viking, 2015), 184.

36. Hershberger, *Traveling to Vietnam*, 42–44.

37. Kuklick, *Blind Oracles*, chap. 9; Rudenstine, *Day the Presses Stopped*, chap. 1.

38. Aurélie Basha i Novosejt, *"I Made Mistakes": Robert McNamara's Vietnam War Policy, 1960–1968* (Cambridge: Cambridge University Press, 2019), chap. 9.

39. Rudenstine, *Day the Presses Stopped*, 70; Ellsberg, *Secrets*, viii, 186.

40. Ellsberg, 205–207.

41. Young, *Vietnam Wars*, 259; Tom Wells, *Wild Man: The Life and Times of Daniel Ellsberg* (New York: Palgrave, 2001), 204–205.

42. Ellsberg, *Secrets*, chap. 13.

43. Ellsberg, 217, 230–234, 262–263; Kuklick, *Blind Oracles*, 175.

44. Ellsberg, *Secrets*, chap. 17.

45. Dwight D. Eisenhower, Executive Order 10501, APP; Louis W. Liebovich, *Richard Nixon, Watergate and the Press* (Westport, CT: Praeger, 2003), 36; Erwin Griswold, "Secrets Not Worth Keeping," *WP*, February 15, 1989, A25; Rudenstine, *Day the Presses Stopped*, 31, 330; Morton Halperin and Daniel N. Hoffman, *Top Secret: National Security and the Right to Know* (Washington, DC: New Republic Books, 1977), 7.

46. Rudenstine, *Day the Presses Stopped*, 31.

47. Ellsberg, *Secrets*, 275–276, 310–317; "A Case Against Staying in Vietnam," *WP*, October 12, 1969, 90.

48. Ellsberg, *Secrets*, chaps. 24–25; Woods, *Fulbright*, 602–606; Rudenstine, *Day the Presses Stopped*, 43–44.

49. Ellsberg, *Secrets*, chap. 26; Jim Naureckas, "What Can Now Be Told by NYT About Pentagon Papers Isn't Actually True," *Fairness and Accuracy in Reporting*, January 14, 2021.

50. Rudenstine, *Day the Presses Stopped*, chap. 3.

51. James Reston, "The McNamara Papers," *NYT*, June 13, 1971, 13.

52. Stanley I. Kutler, *The Wars of Watergate: The Last Crisis of Richard Nixon* (New York: W. W. Norton, 1990), 109; Rudenstine, *Day the Presses Stopped*, chaps. 4–5.

53. Rudenstine, 92.

54. Rudenstine, chap. 6.

55. Ellsberg, *Secrets*, chap. 29.

56. Rudenstine, *Day the Presses Stopped*, chap. 9; David Halberstam, *The Powers That Be* (New York: Alfred A. Knopf, 1979), 565–578; "Documents Reveal U.S. Effort in '54 to Delay Viet Election," *WP*, June 18, 1971, A1; "FBI Seeking Ex-Pentagon Aide in Leak," *WP*, June 18, 1971, A1.

57. Halberstam, *Best and the Brightest*, 417; Erich Lichtblau, "The Untold Story of the Pentagon Papers Co-conspirators," *New Yorker*, January 29, 2018; "Ellsberg, Co-conspirators Share Untold Stories Behind Pentagon Papers Leak," *Daily Hampshire Gazette*, October 28, 2019.

58. Rudenstine, *Day the Presses Stopped*, 178.

59. Rudenstine, 199–200, 206, 221.

60. Rudenstine; *New York Times v. United States*, 403 U.S. 713 (1971), at 727.

61. Alex Wellerstein, *Restricted Data: The History of Nuclear Secrecy in the United States* (Chicago: University of Chicago Press, 2021), 351–368.

62. Edward White, *Justice Oliver Wendell Holmes: Law and the Inner Self* (New York: Oxford University Press, 1993), 3.

63. Brief on Behalf of National Emergency Civil Liberties Committee as Amicus Curiae, June 21, 1971, box 37, folder 23, Howard Zinn Papers, Tamiment Library.

64. Rudenstine, *Day the Presses Stopped*, 102–108, 290–294; Luther A. Huston, "Highest Court Heard Argument for 2 Hours," *EP*, July 3, 1971, 11.

65. *New York Times*, at 720, 730–731, 752; Rudenstine, *Day the Presses Stopped*, chap. 22.

66. William L. Claiborne, "Government Secrets and the Press," *WP*, April 20, 1972, C3.

67. "Ellsberg Gives up, Admits Secrets Leak," *CT*, June 29, 1971, 1.

68. Margaret Pratt Porter and John Prados, *Inside the Pentagon Papers* (Lawrence: University Press of Kansas, 2004), 105.

69. "Ellsberg Witness Put in Solitary," *CT*, August 27, 1971, A1; Rudenstine, *Day the Presses Stopped*, 341–342.

70. Tim Weiner, *Enemies: A History of the FBI* (New York: Random House, 2012), 296–297; Kutler, *Wars of Watergate*, 108–109, 112; Ellsberg, *Secrets*, chap. 31; Rudenstine, *Day the Presses Stopped*, 344–345.

71. Rick Perlstein, *The Invisible Bridge: The Fall of Nixon and the Rise of Reagan* (New York: Simon and Schuster, 2014), 99; Kutler, *Wars of Watergate*, 112–113; Egil Krogh, "Nixon 'Plumber' Who Authorized a Pre-Watergate Break-In, Dies at 80," *WP*, January 20, 2020.

72. Richard Reeves, *President Nixon: Alone in the White House* (New York: Simon and Schuster, 2001), 338; Stone, *Perilous Times*, 514–515.

73. "2 Indicted in Pentagon Papers Case," *CT*, December 31, 1971, 1; "Ellsberg Case Expanded," *CSM*, January 15, 1972, 1; "Mistrial Declared in Viet Papers Case," *CT*, December 12, 1972, 3; Rudenstine, *Day the Presses Stopped*, 341–342.

74. David Greenberg, *Nixon's Shadow: The History of an Image* (New York: W. W. Norton, 2003), 80–81; Medsger, *Burglary*, 196–197; "Pentagon Papers Case Thrown Out," *CT*, May 12, 1973, 1; Julia Rose Kraut, "The Devil's Advocate: Leonard B. Boudin, Civil Liberties and the Legal Defense of Whistleblowing," in *Whistleblowing Nation: The History of National Security Disclosures and the Cult of State Secrecy*, ed. Kaeten Mistry and Hannah Gurman (New York: Columbia University Press, 2020), 69–94.

75. Stone, *Perilous Times*, 515.

76. "The Ellsberg Dismissal," *CT*, May 6, 1973, 18; Sanford J. Ungar and Leroy F. Aarons, "Most Ellsberg Jurors in Favor of Acquittal," *WP*, May 13, 1973, A1.

77. Robert Manning, Affidavit, June 9, 1972, box 37, folder 24, Howard Zinn Papers; "Deserves Day in Court," *LAT*, May 12, 1973, A18; "The Ellsberg Case's Meaning," *BG*, May 14, 1973, 10; Sanford J. Ungar, "With Questions Unanswered," *WP*, May 14, 1973, A2.

78. Malcolm Gladwell, "Daniel Ellsberg, Edward Snowden and the Modern Whistleblower," *New Yorker*, December 19 and 26, 2016.

79. Barry Goldwater, "Ellsberg Set Self Above Officials," *Arizona Republic*, July 19, 1971, 6; "Some Curious Heroes," *CT*, June 14, 1972, 20; "That 'Indiscreet' Ellsberg," *Arizona Republic*, July 12, 1971, 6; Lida Maxwell, "Celebrity Hero: Daniel Ellsberg and the Forging of Whistleblower Masculinity," in *Whistleblowing Nation: The History of National Security Disclosures and the Cult of State Secrecy*, ed. Kaeten Mistry and Hannah Gurman (New York: Columbia University Press, 2020), 95–121; Young, *Vietnam Wars*, 260–261; Thomas A. Schwartz, *Henry Kissinger and American Power: A Political Biography* (New York: Hill and Wang, 2020), 100; Rudenstine, *Day the Presses Stopped*, 121.

80. Melville B. Nimmer, "National Security Secrets v. Free Speech: The Issues Left Undecided in the *Ellsberg* Case," *Stanford Law Review* 26, no. 1 (1973): 311–333.

81. Alexander M. Bickel, *The Morality of Consent* (New Haven, CT: Yale University Press, 1975), 80–83.

Chapter 9: Long Live the Secrecy State

1. John Prados, *The Family Jewels: The CIA, Secrecy, and Presidential Power* (Austin: University of Texas Press, 2013), 23.

2. Alan Wolfe, "Emergence of the Dual State," *Nation*, March 29, 1975, 369.

3. Tity de Vries, "The 1967 Central Intelligence Agency Scandal: Catalyst in a Transforming Relationship Between State and People," *Journal of American History* 98 (March 2012): 1075–1092; Angus Mackenzie, *Secrets: The CIA's War at Home* (Berkeley: University of California Press, 1997), chap. 1; Kaeten Mistry, "The Rise and Fall of Anti-imperial Whistleblowing in the Long 1970s," in *Whistleblowing Nation: The History of National Security Disclosures and the Cult of State Secrecy*, ed. Kaeten Mistry and Hannah Gurman (New York: Columbia University Press, 2020), 130, 137; Prados, *Family Jewels*, 199–201, 236–237.

4. William J. Maxwell, *F.B. Eyes: How J. Edgar Hoover's Ghostreaders Framed African American Literature* (Princeton, NJ: Princeton University Press, 2015), 133; Betty Medsger, *The Burglary: The Discovery of J. Edgar Hoover's Secret FBI* (New York: Alfred A. Knopf, 2014), 66, 72, 240; David Cunningham, *There's Something Happening Here: The New Left, the Klan, and FBI Counterintelligence* (Berkeley: University of California Press, 2004), 81–83.

5. Cunningham, *There's Something Happening Here*, 6; Medsger, *Burglary*, 170, 233–234.

6. Medsger, 342; Beverly Gage, *G-Man: J. Edgar Hoover and the Making of the American Century* (New York: Vintage, 2022), 583, 608–609, 690–692; Sean L. Malloy, *Out of Oakland: Black Panther Party Internationalism During the Cold War* (Ithaca, NY: Cornell University Press, 2018), 2, 10, 13, 113, 183.

7. Cunningham, *There's Something Happening Here*, 169.

8. Medsger, *Burglary*; Johanna Hamilton (dir.), *1971* (New York: First Run Features, 2015).

9. Kathryn S. Olmsted, *Challenging the Secret Government: The Post-Watergate Investigations of the CIA and FBI* (Chapel Hill: University of North Carolina Press, 1996), 17.

10. Chris Whipple, *The Spymasters: How the CIA Directors Shape History and the Future* (New York: Scribner, 2021), 46; Prados, *Family Jewels*, 16; Stanley I. Kutler, *The Wars of Watergate: The Last Crisis of Richard Nixon* (New York: W. W. Norton, 1990),

464; Leslie Gelb, "Watergate Case Viewed as Peril to the Concept of National Security," *NYT*, May 16, 1974.

11. Prados, *Family Jewels*, chap. 1.

12. Whipple, *Spymasters*, 54–55; Seymour M. Hersh, *Reporter: A Memoir* (New York: Alfred A. Knopf, 2018); Olmsted, *Challenging the Secret Government*, 31.

13. Olmsted, 11–12; "Huge CIA Operation Reported in US Against Antiwar Forces, Other Dissidents in Nixon Years," *NYT*, December 22, 1974, 1.

14. Dick Cheney, "CIA—Colby Report," December 27, 1974, box 5, Richard B. Cheney Files, Gerald Ford Library, Ann Arbor, MI.

15. James Mann, *The Great Rift: Dick Cheney, Colin Powell, and the Broken Friendship That Defined an Era* (New York: Henry Holt, 2020), 15–17; Stephen F. Hayes, *Cheney: The Untold Story of America's Most Powerful and Controversial Vice President* (New York: HarperCollins, 2007), 44; Chris Whipple, *The Gatekeepers: How the White House Chiefs of Staff Define Every Presidency* (New York: Broadway, 2018), chap. 1; Barton Gellman, *Angler: The Cheney Vice Presidency* (New York: Penguin, 2008); Charlie Savage, *Takeover: The Return of the Imperial Presidency and the Subversion of American Democracy* (New York: Little, Brown, 2007); Nicholas Lehman, "Quiet Man: Dick Cheney's Rise to Unprecedented Power," *New Yorker*, May 7, 2001.

16. Mann, *Great Rift*, 21, 27.

17. Dick Cheney, "The Ford Presidency in Perspective," in *Gerald R. Ford and the Politics of Post-Watergate America*, ed. Bernard J. Firestone and Alexei Ugrinsky (Westport, CA: Greenwood, 1993), 3–6.

18. *War Powers and the Constitution*, AEI Forum 61, December 6, 1983 (Washington: AEI for Public Policy Research, 1984), 5, 24; Richard Cheney, "U.S. Foreign Policy: Who's in Charge?," *SAIS Review* 4, no. 1 (1984): 107–115; Dick Cheney, "Congressional Overreaching in Foreign Policy," in *Foreign Policy and the Constitution*, ed. Robert A. Goldwin and Robert A. Licht (Washington, DC: AEI, 1990), 100–122.

19. Cheney, "CIA—Colby Report"; Kenneth Kitts, "Commission Politics and National Security: Gerald Ford's Response to the CIA Controversy of 1975," *Presidential Studies Quarterly* 26(4) (1996): 1081–1098.

20. David Rohde, *In Deep: The FBI, the CIA, and the Truth About America's "Deep State"* (New York: W. W. Norton, 2020), 9, 17; Olmsted, *Challenging the Secret Government*, 118; Leandra Ruth Zarnow, *Battling Bella: The Protest Politics of Bella Abzug* (Cambridge, MA: Harvard University Press, 2019), 219; Loch K. Johnson, *A Season of Inquiry Revisited: The Church Committee Confronts America's Spy Agencies* (Lawrence: University Press of Kansas, 2015).

21. Anthony Lewis, "The Church Committee: A Return to Basics," *NYT*, May 2, 1976, E1; Olmsted, *Challenging the Secret Government*, 175; Prados, *Family Jewels*, chap. 4; Frank John Smist, *Congress Oversees the U.S. Intelligence Community, 1947–1994*, 2nd ed. (Knoxville: University of Tennessee Press, 1994), 73–74; Peter Roady, "The Ford Administration, the National Security Agency, and the 'Year of Intelligence': Constructing a New Legal Framework for Intelligence," *Journal of Policy History* 32 (2020): 325–359.

22. "Excerpts from Report of Intelligence Unit," *NYT*, April 27, 1976, 21; Prados, *Family Jewels*, chap. 6; Johnson, *Season of Inquiry Revisited*, chap. 4; "Panel Clears CIA of a Direct Role in '73 Chile Coup," *NYT*, December 5, 1975, 1; Olmsted,

Challenging the Secret Government, 107; Tim Weiner, *Legacy of Ashes: The History of the CIA* (New York: Doubleday, 2007), 307–314.

23. Olmsted, *Challenging the Secret Government*, 17, 45; Art Swift, "Gallup Vault: An FBI Under Fire," November 3, 2016, https://news.gallup.com/vault/197075/gallup-vault-1975-fbi-fire.aspx; Lewis, "Church Committee," E1.

24. James Wilderotter, discussant, "Reforming the Intelligence Community," in *Gerald R. Ford and the Politics of Post-Watergate America*, ed. Bernard J. Firestone and Alexei Ugrinsky (Westport, CT: Greenwood, 1993), 493–495; Roady, "Ford Administration"; Rohde, *In Deep*, 19–20; Olmsted, *Challenging the Secret Government*, 92, 134.

25. Mackenzie, *Secrets*, 63–64; Savage, *Takeover*, 37.

26. Mackenzie, *Secrets*, 58–59, 89–90; Mistry, "Rise and Fall of Anti-imperial Whistleblowing," 131–134; Kaeten Mistry, "A Transnational Protest Against the National Security State: Whistle-Blowing, Philip Agee, and Networks of Dissent," *Journal of American History* 106 (2019): 374; Weiner, *Legacy of Ashes*, 334; Prados, *Family Jewels*, 222; Jonathan Stevenson, *A Drop of Treason: Philip Agee and His Exposure of the CIA* (Chicago: University of Chicago Press, 2021), 111–116; Olmsted, *Challenging the Secret Government*, 151–158; Rohde, *In Deep*, 16–17.

27. Olmsted, *Challenging the Secret Government*, 158–161.

28. Olmsted, 39.

29. Jeffrey Bloodworth, *Losing the Center: The Decline of American Liberalism, 1968–1992* (Lexington: University Press of Kentucky, 2013), chaps. 7–8; John A. Lawrence, *The Class of '74: Congress After Watergate and the Roots of Partisanship* (Baltimore: Johns Hopkins University Press, 2018).

30. Olmsted, *Challenging the Secret Government*, 55, 191–192.

31. Martin Arnold, "Proposed New Criminal Code Arouses Press's Fears on Secrecy," *NYT*, May 28, 1975, 69; Ronald L. Gainer, "Federal Criminal Code Reform: Past and Future," *Buffalo Criminal Law Review* 2 (2022): 116–118; Ronald Keith Silver, "National Security and the Freedom of the Press: The Constitutionality of S.1's National Defense Information Provisions," *Loyola of Los Angeles Law Review* 9 (March 1976): 323–349.

32. David E. Pozen, "Freedom of Information Beyond the Freedom of Information Act," *University of Pennsylvania Law Review* 165 (2017): 1097–1158; Lebovic, *Free Speech and Unfree News: The Paradox of Press Freedom in America* (Cambridge, MA: Harvard University Press, 2016), 181–189, 212–215; Sam Lebovic, "How Administrative Opposition Shaped Freedom of Information," in *Troubling Transparency: The Freedom of Information Act and Beyond*, ed. David Pozen and Michael Schudson (New York: Columbia University Press, 2018), chap. 1.

33. "Moss Committee Vital to Public Information," *EP*, January 26, 1957, 62.

34. Medsger, *Burglary*, chap. 18.

35. *EPA v. Mink*, 410 U.S. 73 (1972); Patsy T. Mink, "The Mink Case: Restoring the Freedom of Information Act," *Pepperdine Law Review* 2 (1974–1975): 8–27.

36. Adam M. Samaha, "Government Secrets, Constitutional Law, and Platforms for Judicial Intervention," *UCLA Law Review* 53 (2005): 938–940, 972; Philip J. Cooper, "The Supreme Court, the First Amendment, and Freedom of Information," *Public Administration Review* 46 (November–December 1986): 625; Robert P. Deyling, "Judicial Deference and De Novo Review in Litigation over National Security Information Under the Freedom of Information Act," *Villanova Law Review* 37 (1992):

67–112; David E. Pozen, "The Mosaic Theory, National Security and the Freedom of Information Act," *Yale Law Journal* 115 (2005): 638–639; Christina E. Wells, "'National Security' Information and the Freedom of Information Act," *Administrative Law Review* 56, no. 4 (2004): 1195–1221.

37. Hersh, *Reporter*, 227–228; Robert M. Pallitto and William C. Weaver, *Presidential Secrecy and the Law* (Baltimore: Johns Hopkins University Press, 2008), 82; Olmsted, *Challenging the Secret Government*, 67–74; Nathan Freed Wessler, "'(We) Can Neither Confirm nor Deny the Existence or Nonexistence of Records Responsive to Your Request': Reforming the Glomar Response Under FOIA," *New York University Law Review* 85, no. 4 (2010): 1381–1415.

38. Roady, "Ford Administration," 341; Diane Carraway Piette and Jesselyn Radack, "Piercing the 'Historical Mists': The People and Events Behind the Passage of FISA and the Creation of the 'Wall,'" *Stanford Law & Policy Review* 17, no. 2 (2006): 437–486; Pallitto and Weaver, *Presidential Secrecy*, 174–175; Jason Ross Arnold, *Secrecy in the Sunshine Era: The Promise and Failures of U.S. Open Government Laws* (Lawrence: University Press of Kansas, 2014), 146–151, 431.

39. Harold J. Koh, *The National Security Constitution: Sharing Power After the Iran-Contra Affair* (New Haven, CT: Yale University Press, 1990), 57–58; Smist, *Congress Oversees the U.S. Intelligence Community*; Jennifer Kibbe, "Congressional Oversight of Intelligence: Is the Solution Part of the Problem," *Intelligence and National Security* 25 (2010): 24–49; "Effort to Enact Intelligence Charter Is Abandoned by Senate Advocates," *NYT*, May 2, 1980, A1; "Intelligence Bill: Half a Loaf," *NYT*, June 10, 1980, A11; "CIA Triumphant," *NYT*, May 6, 1980, A27.

40. Michael J. Glennon, *National Security and Double Government* (New York: Oxford University Press, 2015), 52; Amy Zegart and Julie Quinn, "Congressional Intelligence Oversight: The Electoral Disconnection," *Intelligence and National Security* 25 (2010): 744; Rohde, *In Deep*, 27; Loch K. Johnson, "Ostriches, Cheerleaders, Skeptics, and Guardians: Role Selection by Congressional Intelligence Overseers," *SAIS Review of International Affairs* 28 (2008): 93–108.

41. Smist, *Congress Oversees the U.S. Intelligence Community*, 229.

42. "Ex-CIA Man May Be Prosecuted," *NYT*, January 8, 1977, 17; Mistry, "Transnational Protest Against the National Security State"; Stevenson, *Drop of Treason*; Anthony Marro, "US Won't Charge Ex-agent over Book on CIA Operations," *NYT*, March 21, 1977, 7; Andrew M. Szilagyi, "Blowing Its Cover: How the Intelligence Identities Protection Act Has Masqueraded as an Effective Law and Why It Must Be Amended," *William and Mary Law Review* 51 (2010): 2269–2312.

43. Olmsted, *Challenging the Secret Government*, 74–76; Hersh, *Reporter*, 229, 249; Savage, *Takeover*, 35.

44. "Moves by House Against Schorr Raise Issue of Freedom of the Press," *NYT*, February 21, 1976, 9; Richard D. Lyons, "Schorr Bids Congress Define Issues in Intelligence Data Disclosure," *NYT*, September 9, 1976, 15; Richard D. Lyons, "House Panel Says Schorr Case Lags," *NYT*, April 1, 1976, 45; Olmsted, *Challenging the Secret Government*, 163–172; "Probe of Spy-Report Leaks Is Faltering," *Arizona Republic*, April 2, 1976, 12.

45. Wendell Rawls, "Carter and New CIA Director Divided on Need for Criminal Penalties to Prevent Security 'Leaks,'" *NYT*, March 10, 1977, 12; *Espionage Laws and Leaks: Hearing Before the Subcommittee on Legislation of the Permanent Select*

Committee on Intelligence, House of Representatives, 96th Cong., 1st sess. (January 24, 25, 31, 1979), 14; *Use of Classified Information in Litigation, Hearings Before the Senate Subcommittee on Secrecy and Disclosure*, 95th Cong., 2nd sess. (March 1, 2, 6, 1977), 47; *National Security Secrets and the Administration of Justice: Report of the Senate Select Committee on Intelligence Subcommittee on Secrecy and Disclosure*, 95th Cong., 2nd session, 1978; Brian Z. Tamanaha, "A Critical Review of the Classified Information Procedures Act," *American Journal of Criminal Law* 13 (1986): 277–328.

46. Ralph Engelman and Carey Shenkman, *A Century of Repression: The Espionage Act and Freedom of the Press* (Urbana: University of Illinois Press, 2022), 152–153; Stephanie Ricker Schulte, "'The WarGames Scenario': Regulating Teenagers and Teenaged Technology (1980–1984)," *Television & New Media* 9 (November 2008): 487–513.

47. Richard Immerman, "From the Mundane to the Absurd: The Advent and Evolution of Prepublication Review," in *Whistleblowing Nation: The History of National Security Disclosures and the Cult of State Secrecy*, ed. Kaeten Mistry and Hannah Gurman (New York: Columbia University Press, 2020), 187–212.

48. Christopher R. Moran, *Company Confessions: Secrets, Memoirs, and the CIA* (New York: Thomas Dunne/St. Martin's, 2016), 113–122; Mackenzie, *Secrets*, 47–52; Mistry, "Rise and Fall of Anti-imperial Whistleblowing," 139; Prados, *Family Jewels*, 237–239.

49. Moran, *Company Confessions*, chap. 5; Jack Goldsmith and Oona Hathaway, "Prepublication Review and the Quicksand Foundation of Snepp," *Just Security*, January 31, 2022; David Shamus McCarthy, *Selling the CIA: Public Relations and the Culture of Secrecy* (Lawrence: University Press of Kansas, 2018), 37–56; Jonathan C. Medow, "The First Amendment and the Secrecy State: *Snepp v. United States*," *University of Pennsylvania Law Review* 130 (April 1982): 775–884.

50. Mackenzie, *Secrets*, 108–110, 126–128; Eve Pell, *The Big Chill: How the Reagan Administration, Corporate America, and Religious Conservatives Are Subverting Free Speech and the Public's Right to Know* (Boston: Beacon, 1984), 39–45; Donna Demac, *Keeping America Uninformed: Government Secrecy in the 1980s* (New York: Pilgrim, 1984), 19–25; Jack Goldsmith and Oona Hathaway, "How the U.S. Government Built the Largest System of Prior Restraint in U.S. History," *Just Security*, February 7, 2022; Ramya Krishnan, "The Government's Own Documents Show That Prepublication Review Is Broken," *Just Security*, April 4, 2019; Immerman, "From the Mundane to the Absurd"; Kevin R. Casey, "Till Death Do Us Part: Prepublication Review in the Intelligence Community," *Columbia Law Review* 115 (2015): 417–460.

51. *Report of the Interdepartmental Group on Unauthorized Disclosures of Classified Information*, 1982, Digital National Security Archive, Proquest, https://search.proquest.com/dnsa, A2, A4.

52. James W. Tankard Jr., "Samuel L. Morison and the Government Crackdown on the Leaking of Classified Information," *Journalism History* 24 (1998): 17–26, 54–65; Mackenzie, *Secrets*, 135–141; Wallace B. Eberhard, "The Press & *U.S. v. Morison*: Sounding the Alarm or Crying 'Wolf'?," *Newspaper Research Journal* 12, no. 1 (1991): 64–75; *United States v. Morison*, 844 F.2d 1057 (1988).

53. Philip Weiss, "The Quiet Coup," *Harper's*, September 1989, 59; Mackenzie, *Secrets*, 140.

54. "Secrecy Is Sought in Analyst's Trial," *NYT*, September 15, 1985, 35; "Judge Sentences Kampiles to 40 Years in Spy Case," *WP*, December 23, 1978, A7.

55. Weiss, "Quiet Coup," 62; David H. Topol, "*United States v. Morison:* A Threat to the First Amendment Right to Publish National Security Information," *South Carolina Law Review* 43 (1992): 598.

56. *Morison.*

57. Tankard, "Samuel L. Morison," 24.

58. Theodore Draper, *A Very Thin Line: The Iran-Contra Affairs* (New York: Hill and Wang, 1991).

59. Bob Woodward, *Veil: The Secret Wars of the CIA* (New York: Simon and Schuster, 1987), 46–48, 130; Gellman, *Angler*, 100–101; Savage, *Takeover*, 42; Judith Miller, "Reagan Urged to Reorganize U.S. Intelligence," *NYT*, December 8, 1980, A1; Glennon, *National Security and Double Government*, 52; Mackenzie, *Secrets*, 83; Rohde, *In Deep*, 49; Richard H. Immerman, *The Hidden Hand: A Brief History of the CIA* (Chichester, UK: Wiley-Blackwell, 2014), chap. 4.

60. Smist, *Congress Oversees the U.S. Intelligence Community*, 247–248; *Report of the Congressional Committees Investigating the Iran-Contra Affair with Supplemental, Minority and Additional Views*, H.Rep. 100-433, November 13, 1987 (Washington, DC: GPO), 33 (hereafter *Iran-Contra Report*).

61. "White House Approval Is Sought on a Compromise Spending Plan," *NYT*, October 10, 1984, A1; "Conferees Agree on Spending Bill, Ending Deadlock," *NYT*, October 11, 1984, A1; *Iran-Contra Report*, 42.

62. Weiner, *Legacy of Ashes*, 408.

63. David Hoffman, "Reagan's 'Worst' Speech," *WP*, July 20, 1987.

64. Rohde, *In Deep*, 53; Woodward, *Veil*, 514–518; Sean Wilentz, *The Age of Reagan: A History, 1974–2008* (New York: HarperCollins, 2008), 224–241.

65. Hayes, *Cheney*, 190–199; Draper, *Very Thin Line*, 24.

66. Prados, *Family Jewels*, 307–308; Hayes, *Cheney*, 198.

67. *Iran-Contra Report*, 13, 437–438.

68. *Iran-Contra Report*, 575–585; "Final Remarks by Leaders of the Panels," *NYT*, August 4, 1987, A6.

69. "Text of President Bush's Statement on the Pardon of Weinberger and Others," *NYT*, December 25, 1992, A22; James T. Patterson, *Restless Giant: The United States from Watergate to Bush v. Gore* (New York: Oxford University Press, 2005), 212–213.

70. Cheney, "Congressional Overreaching in Foreign Policy," 114–115; "House Unit Bars Data for Inquiry on Wright," *NYT*, September 29, 1988, D30; "Wright Formally Denies Breach on Nicaragua," *NYT*, October 6, 1988, A5; "Wright Is Denying Secret Data Leak," *NYT*, September 23, 1988, A5; "Wright Disclosure Termed Accurate," *NYT*, September 25, 1988, 15; Mann, *Great Rift*, 77; Koh, *National Security Constitution*, 61; Julian Zelizer, *Burning Down the House: Newt Gingrich, the Fall of a Speaker, and the Rise of the New Republican Party* (New York: Penguin, 2020), 158; "Senate Votes Bill on Covert Action," *NYT*, March 16, 1988, A8; "Wright, in Gesture to Bush, Shelves Bill on Covert Acts," *NYT*, February 1, 1989, A12; "Panel Mulls Second Probe of Speaker," *WP*, September 24, 1988.

71. "Schlesinger Assails a Charter for CIA," *NYT*, April 3, 1980, 1; Geoffrey Hodgson, *Gentleman from New York: Daniel Patrick Moynihan: A Biography* (Boston: Houghton Mifflin, 2000); Zarnow, *Battling Bella*, chap. 9; "Sorry Moynihan Quit, Reagan Says," *LAT*, February 4, 1976, B11.

72. Smist, *Congress Oversees the U.S. Intelligence Community*, 319; Draper, *Very Thin Line*, 592–595; Moran, *Company Confessions*, 217–218; Immerman, *Hidden Hand*, 150; Paul McGarr, "'Do We Still Need the CIA?' Daniel Patrick Moynihan, the Central Intelligence Agency and US Foreign Policy," *History* 100 (April 2015): 290–292.

73. Richard Gid Powers, "Introduction," in Daniel Patrick Moynihan, *Secrecy: The American Experience* (New Haven, CT: Yale University Press, 1998), 9–10.

74. Commission on Protecting and Reducing Government Secrecy, *Secrecy: Report of the Commission on Protecting and Reducing Government Secrecy* (Washington, DC: GPO, 1997), xxi; *Government Secrecy Act of 1997, Report on the Committee of Government Affairs*, US Senate Report 105-258 (July 22, 1998), 12; E. J. Dionne, "Revealing Some Secrets May Retain Major Ones," *Arizona Republic*, March 7, 1997, 31; R. W. Apple, "Government Is Overzealous on Secrecy, Panel Advises," *NYT*, March 5, 1997, A16.

75. Commission on Protecting and Reducing Government Secrecy, *Secrecy*, xxvi; Tim Weiner, "Bill Seeks to Ease Secrecy Overload," *NYT*, May 8, 1997, 25; Harold C. Relyea, *Managing Secrecy: Security Classification Reform—The Government Secrecy Act Proposal*, Congressional Research Service 98-298, July 8, 1998.

76. "Dismantling the Secrecy System," *NYT*, March 5, 1997, A18; Relyea, *Managing Secrecy*; US Senate Report 105-258.

77. Chris Whipple, *The Gatekeepers: How the White House Chiefs of Staff Define Every Presidency* (New York: Broadway, 2018), 9; Hodgson, *Gentleman from New York*, 22.

78. Apple, "Government Is Overzealous on Secrecy, Panel Advises"; "US Tallies the Cost of Keeping Secrets," *CSM*, May 7, 1997, 3.

79. Moynihan, *Secrecy*, 60; Powers, "Introduction," 15.

80. Reporters Committee for Freedom of the Press, "Federal Cases Involving Unauthorized Disclosures to the News Media, 1778–Present," www.rcfp.org/resources/leak-investigations-chart; "The Making of a Suspect: The Case of Wen Ho Lee," *NYT*, February 4, 2001, 1; "The Prosecution Unravels: The Case of Wen Ho Lee," *NYT*, February 5, 2001, 1; Andrew Chongseh Kim, "Prosecuting Chinese 'Spies': An Empirical Analysis of the Economic Espionage Act," *Cardozo Law Review* 40 (2018): 749–822.

81. "Veto of Anti-leak Bill Urged," *WP*, November 2, 2000, A2; "Anti-leak Bill Splits Clinton Aides," *WP*, November 3, 2000, A31; "Clinton Vetoes Bill Targeting Leaks of Classified Information," *WP*, November 5, 2000, A5; William E. Lee, "Deep Background: Journalists, Sources and the Perils of Leaking," *American University Law Review* 57 (2008): 1467–1468, 1490.

82. Oona A. Hathaway, "Secrecy's End," *Minnesota Law Review* 106 (2021): 796; Garry Wills, *Bomb Power: The Modern Presidency and the National Security State* (New York: Penguin, 2010), 138.

83. Frederick A. O. Schwarz, *Democracy in the Dark: The Seduction of Government Secrecy* (New York: New Press, 2015), 173.

84. Spencer Ackerman, *Reign of Terror: How the 9/11 Era Destabilized America and Produced Trump* (New York: Viking, 2021), 14–15; Gellman, *Angler*, 111–113; Jane Mayer, *The Dark Side: The Inside Story of How the War on Terror Turned into a War on American Ideals* (New York: Doubleday, 2008), 23, 27; Lawrence Wright, *The Looming Tower: Al-Qaeda and the Road to 9/11* (New York: Vintage, 2011), 350–355, 395–396;

Jennifer Stisa Granick, *American Spies* (Cambridge: Cambridge University Press, 2017), chap. 5; Steve Coll, *Ghost Wars: The Secret History of the CIA, Afghanistan, and Bin Laden, from the Soviet Invasion to September 10, 2001* (New York: Penguin, 2004), 488, 570, 579; *The 9/11 Commission Report: Final Report of the National Commission on Terrorist Attacks upon the United States*, official government edition (Washington, DC: US GPO, 2004), 181, 254, 266–267, 272–273, 417; "NSA Intercepts on Eve of 9/11 Sent a Warning," *WP*, June 20, 2002; Terry H. Anderson, *Bush's Wars* (Oxford: Oxford University Press, 2011), 65.

85. Weiner, *Legacy of Ashes*, 420; Immerman, *Hidden Hand*, 156–159; Woodward, *Veil*, 307–310; Andrew Feinstein, *The Shadow World: Inside the Global Arms Trade* (New York: Farrar, Straus and Giroux, 2011), 246–248; Coll, *Ghost Wars*; "Arming Afghan Guerillas: A Huge Effort Led by U.S.," *NYT*, April 18, 1988, A1.

86. Mann, *Great Rift*, 121; Wilentz, *Age of Reagan*, 302; Wright, *Looming Tower*, 178.

87. Gellman, *Angler*, chap. 1; Savage, *Takeover*, 54; Mann, *Great Rift*, 58–59, 184, 196–197; James Mann, *Rise of the Vulcans: The History of Bush's War Cabinet* (New York: Penguin, 2004), 273; Bernard Harcourt, *Exposed: Desire and Disobedience in the Digital Age* (Cambridge, MA: Harvard University Press, 2015), 177–178; Hayes, *Cheney*, 298–301.

88. Savage, *Takeover*, chap. 1; *9/11 Commission Report*, 40–41.

89. Mayer, *Dark Side*, 9–10.

Chapter 10: Whistleblowers in the War on Terror

1. Charlie Savage, *Takeover: The Return of the Imperial Presidency and the Subversion of American Democracy* (New York: Little, Brown, 2007), chaps. 5, 7; Barton Gellman, *Angler: The Cheney Vice-Presidency* (New York: Penguin, 2008), chap. 4.

2. Jason Ross Arnold, *Secrecy in the Sunshine Era: The Promise and Failures of U.S. Open Government Laws* (Lawrence: University Press of Kansas, 2014), 67–72, 81–85; Scott Shane, "Since 2001, Sharp Increase in the Number of Documents Classified by the Government," *NYT*, July 3, 2005, 14.

3. Letta Tayler and Elisa Epstein, "Legacy of the Dark Side: The Costs of Unlawful US Detentions and Interrogations Post-9/11," Watson Institute, January 9, 2022, 37, https://watson.brown.edu/costsofwar/files/cow/imce/papers/2022/Costs%20of%20 War%20-%20Legacy%20of%20the%20%27Dark%20Side%27%20-%20Tayler%20 and%20Epstein%20-%20FINAL%20Jan%209%202022.pdf; Dana Priest and William M. Arkin, *Top Secret America: The Rise of the New American Security State* (New York: Little, Brown, 2011), 66, 71, 163.

4. Priest and Arkin, 179–180, 189–191.

5. Priest and Arkin, 187; "Crooked Congressman Going to Prison," CNN, March 3, 2006; Gabriel Schoenfeld, *Necessary Secrets: National Security, the Media, and the Rule of Law* (New York: W. W. Norton, 2010), 21.

6. *Report of the Senate Select Committee on Intelligence Committee Study of the Central Intelligence Agency's Detention and Interrogation Program*, S. Rep. 113-288 (December 9, 2014), 11; Savage, *Takeover*, 148–149; Spencer Ackerman, *Reign of Terror: How the 9/11 Era Destabilized America and Produced Trump* (New York: Viking, 2021), 39–50, 79–81; Tim Weiner, *Legacy of Ashes: The History of the CIA* (New York: Doubleday, 2007), 481.

7. *Report of the Senate Select Committee on Intelligence Committee Study*, 6; Jane Mayer, *The Dark Side: The Inside Story of How the War on Terror Turned into a War on American Ideals* (New York: Doubleday, 2008), 173.

8. Savage, *Takeover*, 155.

9. Heidi Kitrosser, *Reclaiming Accountability: Transparency, Executive Power, and the U.S. Constitution* (Chicago: University of Chicago Press, 2015), 103.

10. Savage, *Takeover*, 142, 147–148; Terry H. Anderson, *Bush's Wars* (Oxford: Oxford University Press, 2011), 88–90; Tayler and Epstein, "Legacy of the Dark Side," 10–11.

11. Tayler and Epstein; Julian Borger, "An Affront to Justice," *Guardian Weekly*, January 14, 2022.

12. Mayer, *Dark Side*, 183–237.

13. Paul Kramer, "A Useful Corner of the World: Guantánamo," *New Yorker*, July 30, 2013; Paul Kramer, "The Water Cure: Debating Torture and Counterinsurgency—a Century Ago," *New Yorker*, February 25, 2008.

14. Savage, *Takeover*, 154, 158.

15. Savage, 82, 137; Mayer, *Dark Side*, 83–88; Samuel Moyn, *Humane: How the United States Abandoned Peace and Reinvented War* (New York: Farrar, Straus and Giroux, 2021), 238–240; John Richardson, "Is John Yoo a Monster?," *Esquire*, August 24, 2009.

16. "How a Modest Contract for 'Applied Research' Morphed into the CIA's Brutal Interrogation Program," *WP*, July 13, 2016; Savage, *Takeover*, chap. 9; Mayer, *Dark Side*, 157–160.

17. Savage, *Takeover*, 217–218.

18. Savage, 218–219.

19. Robert Draper, *To Start a War: How the Bush Administration Took America into Iraq* (New York, Penguin, 2020), 17, 134–135, 139; "Iraq, 9/11 Still Linked Cheney," *WP*, September 29, 2003.

20. Draper, *To Start a War*; Michael Isikoff and David Corn, *Hubris: The Inside Story of Spin, Scandal, and the Selling of the Iraq War* (New York: Crown, 2006).

21. Elisabeth Bumiller, "Bush Aides Set Strategy to Sell Policy on Iraq," *NYT*, September 7, 2002.

22. Charles Lewis and Mark Reading-Smith, "False Pretenses," Center for Public Integrity, January 23, 2008.

23. Ackerman, *Reign of Terror*, 65; Daniel Okrent, "The Public Editor: Weapons of Mass Destruction or Mass Distraction?," *NYT*, May 30, 2004.

24. Savage, *Takeover*, 377; Jim Vandehei, "Iraq Briefings, 'Don't Ask, Don't Tell,'" *WP*, September 15, 2002; *Report on the U.S. Intelligence Community's Prewar Intelligence Assessments on Iraq, Select Committee on Intelligence US Senate*, 108th Cong., July 7, 2004, 12, 286–297; Richard H. Immerman, "Intelligence and the Iraq and Afghanistan Wars," *Political Science Quarterly* 131, no. 3 (2016): 489–490; "Graham, Iraq Report Prompted 'No' Vote on War," NPR, June 6, 2007; "Few Senators Read Iraq NIE Report," *Hill*, June 19, 2007; B. Judis and Spencer Ackerman, "The Selling of the Iraq War: The First Casualty," *New Republic*, June 30, 2003.

25. Moyn, *Humane*, 253–257; William E. Lee, "Deep Background: Journalists, Sources, and the Perils of Leaking," *American University Law Review* 57 (2008): 1454–1455; Sherry Ricchiardi, "Missed Signals," *American Journalism Review*,

August/September 2004; Seymour M. Hersh, *Reporter: A Memoir* (New York: Alfred A. Knopf, 2018), 309–312; Christopher Hanson, "Tortured Logic," *Columbia Journalism Review* 43 (July/August 2004): 60–62.

26. Gellman, *Angler*, 140–148; Arnold, *Secrecy in the Sunshine Era*, 146–151; Schoenfeld, *Necessary Secrets*, 40; Luke Harding, *The Snowden Files: The Inside Story of the World's Most Wanted Man* (New York: Vintage, 2014), 91; Charlie Savage, *Power Wars: Inside Obama's Post-9/11 Presidency* (New York: Little, Brown, 2015), 183–185.

27. Gellman, *Angler*, chaps. 11–12; Savage, *Power Wars*, 190–194; Ackerman, *Reign of Terror*, 32–37.

28. James Risen, "The Biggest Secret," *Intercept*, January 3, 2018; Savage, *Power Wars*, 196.

29. Scott Johnson, "A Fateful Letter to the Editor of the Times," Powerline blog, October 23, 2012, www.powerlineblog.com/archives/2012/10/a-fateful-letter-to-the-editor-of-the-times.php; Gabriel Schoenfeld, "Has the New York Times Violated the Espionage Act?," *Commentary*, March 2006.

30. John Ashcroft to Dennis Hastert, October 15, 2002, https://sgp.fas.org/other gov/dojleaks.pdf.

31. Savage, *Power Wars*, 351; *DOJ's Investigation of Journalists Who Publish Classified Information: Lessons from the Jack Anderson Case: Hearing Before the S. Comm. on the Judiciary*, 109th Cong., 3–7 (2006); "Gonzales Says Prosecutions of Journalists Are Possible," *NYT*, May 22, 2006, A14.

32. Schoenfeld, *Necessary Secrets*, 240–247; Lee, "Deep Background," 1484–1486; *US v. Rosen and Weissman*, 445 F.Supp.2d 602 (US District Court, E.D. Virginia, August 9, 2006).

33. *Branzburg v. Hayes*, 408 U.S. 665 (1972); Geoffrey Stone, *Top Secret: When Our Government Keeps Us in the Dark* (Lanham, MD: Rowman and Littlefield, 2007), 45–64; Jason M. Shepard, *Privileging the Press: Confidential Sources, Journalism Ethics and the First Amendment* (El Paso, TX: LFB, 2011).

34. Gellman, *Angler*, 360–364; Lee, "Deep Background," 1490–1502.

35. Savage, *Power Wars*, 367; Schoenfeld, *Necessary Secrets*, 235.

36. Lee, "Deep Background," 1496.

37. "No Charges for Man Who Leaked Surveillance Program," *WP*, April 26, 2011; Jennifer Stisa Granick, *American Spies* (Cambridge: Cambridge University Press, 2017), 49–50; "AP Blasts Phone Records Search," CNN, May 14, 2013; Ravi Somaiya, "Head of AP Criticizes Seizure of Phone Records," *NYT*, May 19, 2013; Savage, *Power Wars*, 352–353, 380–381, 395–397.

38. Savage, 402–405; Jonathan Mahler, "Reporter's Case Poses Dilemma for Justice Department," *NYT*, June 27, 2014; Matt Apuzzo, "Times Reporter Will Not Be Called to Testify in Leak Case," *NYT*, January 12, 2015; Ralph Engelman and Carey Shenkman, *A Century of Repression: The Espionage Act and Freedom of the Press* (Urbana: University of Illinois Press, 2022), 184–185.

39. Jack Goldsmith, "The Growth of Press Freedoms in the U.S. Since 9/11," in *National Security, Leaks and Freedom of the Press: The Pentagon Papers Fifty Years On*, ed. Geoffrey R. Stone and Lee C. Bollinger (Oxford: Oxford University Press, 2021), 205; Joanna Walters, "James Risen Calls Obama 'Greatest Enemy of Press Freedom in a Generation,'" *Guardian*, August 17, 2014; Charlie Savage, "Holder Tightens Rules

on Getting Reporters' Data," *NYT*, July 12, 2013; Sari Horwitz, "Holder Tightens Investigators' Guidelines in Cases Involving News Media," *WP*, January 14, 2015.

40. Amanda Petrusich, "Meeting the Moment," *New Yorker*, July 20, 2020, 70–71.

41. Matt Zapotosky, "He Was Fired from the CIA and Jailed for a Leak. Now He's Trying to Hang On," *WP*, February 21, 2016; Reporters Committee for Freedom of the Press, "Federal Cases Involving Unauthorized Disclosures to the News Media, 1778–Present," www.rcfp.org/resources/leak-investigations-chart.

42. Leonard Downie Jr. and Sara Rafsky, *The Obama Administration and the Press: Leak Investigations and Surveillance in Post-9/11 America*, Special Report for the Committee to Protect Journalists, October 10, 2013.

43. Savage, *Takeover*, 149–150, chap. 13; Mayer, *Dark Side*, 130–133, 155; Arnold, *Secrecy in the Sunshine Era*, 194–197; Kevin R. Casey, "Till Death Do Us Part: Prepublication Review in the Intelligence Community," *Columbia Law Review* 115 (2015): 423–424, 445–448; Christopher R. Moran, *Company Confessions: Secrets, Memoirs, and the CIA* (New York: Thomas Dunne/St. Martin's, 2016), 250–280.

44. Alex Gibney, *The Forever Prisoner* (HBO, 2021); Ackerman, *Reign of Terror*, 40–45, 210–211; "CIA Destroyed Tapes of Interrogations," *NYT*, December 6, 2007; "Coming in from the Cold," *ABC News*, December 10, 2007.

45. Savage, *Power Wars*, 384–390; Steve Coll, "The Spy Who Said Too Much," *New Yorker*, March 24, 2013; "Former CIA Agent John Kiriakou Pleads Not Guilty to Leaking Secrets to Journalists," Reporters Committee for Freedom of the Press, April 13, 2012.

46. Savage, *Power Wars*, 410–412; "How David Petraeus Avoided Felony Charges and Possible Prison Time," *WP*, January 25, 2016; "Petraeus Reaches Plea Deal over Giving Classified Data to His Lover," *NYT*, March 3, 2015.

47. Ackerman, *Reign of Terror*, 209–214; Savage, *Power Wars*, 114–116, 490–492, 512–515; Karen J. Greenberg, *Subtle Tools: The Dismantling of American Democracy from the War on Terror to Donald Trump* (Princeton, NJ: Princeton University Press, 2021), 67–68; David Shamus McCarthy, *Selling the CIA: Public Relations and the Culture of Secrecy* (Lawrence: University Press of Kansas, 2018), chap. 5.

48. Savage, *Power Wars*, 408–409.

49. Erin M. Kearns and Joseph K. Young, *Tortured Logic: Why Some Americans Support the Use of Torture in Counterterrorism* (New York: Columbia University Press, 2020), 2–3.

50. "Cables Detail Torture at Prison Run by Current CIA Chief," *NYT*, August 10, 2018, A8; "Full-on Propaganda from Inside CIA on Pick for Director," *NYT*, April 21, 2018, A11.

51. Patrick Coburn, "Julian Assange in Limbo," *London Review of Books*, June 18, 2020; John Birmingham, "The Man Who Fell to Earth: Julian Assange's WikiLeaks," *Monthly*, October 2, 2010; Ackerman, *Reign of Terror*, 193–199.

52. "Bradley Manning Leaked Classified Documents to Spark 'Debate' on Foreign Policy," *PBS Newshour*, February 28, 2013; Chase Madar, *The Passion of Bradley Manning: The Story Behind the WikiLeaks Whistleblower* (New York: Verso, 2013), 55; Ackerman, *Reign of Terror*, 194–195.

53. Yochai Benkler, "A Free Irresponsible Press: Wikileaks and the Battle over the Soul of the Networked Fourth Estate," *Harvard Civil Rights–Civil Liberties Law*

Review 46 (2011): 315–316; Robert Manne, "The Cypherpunk Revolutionary: Julian Assange," *Monthly*, March 1, 2011.

54. "Microfile," *Guardian*, October 26, 1989, 31; Manne, "Cypherpunk Revolutionary"; David Leigh and Luke Harding, "Julian Assange: The Teen Hacker Who Became Insurgent in Information War," *Guardian*, January 30, 2011.

55. Patrick D. Anderson, "Privacy for the Weak, Transparency for the Powerful: The Cypherpunk Ethics of Julian Assange," *Ethics and Information Technology* 23 (September 2021): 295–308; Manne, "Cypherpunk Revolutionary."

56. Julian Assange, "Conspiracy as Governance," December 3, 2006, https://cryptome.org/0002/ja-conspiracies.pdf.

57. Jeffrey Kuhner, "Assassinate Assange?," *Washington Times*, December 2, 2010; Dianne Feinstein, "Prosecute Assange Under the Espionage Act," *Wall Street Journal*, December 7, 2010; Benkler, "Free Irresponsible Press," 313, 331, 385.

58. Benkler, 323–327; Matthew Weaver, "Afghanistan War Logs: WikiLeaks Urged to Remove Thousands of Names," *Guardian*, August 10, 2010.

59. Benkler, "Free Irresponsible Press," 312, 324; Mark Fenster, *The Transparency Fix: Secrets, Leaks, and Uncontrollable Government Information* (Stanford, CA: Stanford University Press, 2017), chap. 8; "Clinton: Wikileaks 'Tear at Fabric' of Government," NPR, November 29, 2010; Ackerman, *Reign of Terror*, 194–198; Ed Pilkington, "Bradley Manning Leak Did Not Result in Deaths by Enemy Forces, Court Hears," *Guardian*, July 31, 2013; Coburn, "Julian Assange in Limbo."

60. Benkler, "Free Irresponsible Press," 325; Ackerman, *Reign of Terror*, 195–196; Fenster, *Transparency Fix*, chap. 8.

61. Benkler, "Free Irresponsible Press," 338–341.

62. Benkler, 329; Christian Stocker, "Leak at WikiLeaks: A Dispatch Disaster in Six Acts," *Der Spiegel Online*, September 1 2011; Alex Gibney, dir., *We Steal Secrets: The Story of WikiLeaks* (Universal Studios Home Entertainment, 2013); "Julian Assange: Sweden Drops Rape Investigation," BBC, November 19, 2019.

63. Savage, *Power Wars*, 371–373.

64. Ackerman, *Reign of Terror*, 189, 197–198; Madar, *Passion of Bradley Manning*, chap. 5.

65. Charlie Savage, "Soldier Admits Providing Files to Wikileaks," *NYT*, March 1, 2013, 1; Ed Pilkington, "Bradley Manning Verdict," *Guardian*, July 31, 2013; Charlie Savage, "Chelsea Manning to Be Released Early as Obama Commutes Sentence," *NYT*, January 17, 2017; "Chelsea Manning Tried Committing Suicide a Second Time in October," *NYT*, November 4, 2016; "Chelsea Manning Describes Bleak Life in Men's Prison," *NYT*, January 13, 2017.

66. Timothy H. Edgar, *Beyond Snowden: Privacy, Mass Surveillance, and the Struggle to Reform the NSA* (Washington, DC: Brookings Institution Press, 2017), 75; Harding, *Snowden Files*, 122–123; Glenn Greenwald, "NSA Collecting Phone Records of Millions of Verizon Customers Daily," *Guardian*, June 6, 2013.

67. Scott Shane, "Ex-contractor Is Charged in Leaks on NSA Surveillance," *NYT*, June 21, 2013; Edward Snowden, *Permanent Record* (New York: Metropolitan, 2019); Bryan Burrough, Sarah Ellison, and Suzanna Andrews, "The Snowden Saga: A Shadowland of Secrets and Light," *Vanity Fair*, April 23, 2014; Barton Gellman, *Dark Mirror: Edward Snowden and the American Surveillance State* (New York: Penguin Random House, 2020).

68. Glenn Greenwald and Laura Poitras, "NSA Whistleblower Edward Snowden," *Guardian*, June 8, 2013; William E. Scheuerman, "Whistleblowing as Civil Disobedience: The Case of Edward Snowden," *Philosophy & Social Criticism* 40 (2014): 612.

69. Bonnie Raines, "Democracy Needs Whistleblowers. That's Why I Broke into the FBI in 1971," *Guardian*, January 7, 2014; Daniel Ellsberg, "Edward Snowden: Saving Us from the United Stasi of America," *Guardian*, June 10, 2013.

70. Jeffrey Toobin, "Edward Snowden Is No Hero," *New Yorker*, June 10, 2013; Geoffrey Stone, "Edward Snowden: Hero or Traitor?," *Huffpost*, June 10, 2013.

71. Sean Wilentz, "Would You Feel Differently About Snowden, Greenwald and Assange If You Knew What They Really Thought?," *New Republic*, January 19, 2014; David Brooks, "The Solitary Leaker," *NYT*, June 10, 2013.

72. "Snowden Knocks WikiLeaks for Handling of DNC Leak," *Politico*, July 29, 2016; Snowden, *Permanent Record*, loc. 124.

73. "Edward Snowden Is a 'Traitor' and Possible Spy for China—Dick Cheney," *Guardian*, June 16, 2013; John Bolton, "Edward Snowden's Leaks Are a Grave Threat to US National Security," June 18, 2013; Harding, *Snowden Files*, 106.

74. Edward Jay Epstein, *How America Lost Its Secrets: Edward Snowden, the Man and the Theft* (New York: Alfred A. Knopf, 2017); Charlie Savage, "Was Snowden a Soviet Agent?," *New York Review of Books*, December 9, 2017, 16–18; Nicholas Lemann, "Is Edward Snowden a Spy? A New Book Calls Him One," *NYT Book Review*, January 9, 2017; Snowden, *Permanent Record*, 170–172, 219–220.

75. Matt Miller, "Edward Snowden's Grandiosity," *WP*, June 11, 2013; Gellman, *Dark Mirror*, 19; Jason Leopold, "Snowden Tried to Tell NSA About Surveillance Concerns," *Vice*, June 4, 2016.

76. Rodney M. Perry, "Intelligence Whistleblower Protections: In Brief," *Congressional Research Service*, October 23, 2014.

77. Edgar, *Beyond Snowden*, 43–47; Savage, *Power Wars*, 194–213; Arnold, *Secrecy in the Sunshine Era*, 146–151; Granick, *American Spies*, 17, 101, 106–107.

78. Savage, *Power Wars*, 215; Edgar, *Beyond Snowden*, 114–119; Ackerman, *Reign of Terror*, 200.

79. Gellman, *Dark Mirror*, 126.

80. Perry, "Intelligence Whistleblower Protections"; Mary-Rose Papandrea, "Leaker Traitor Whistleblower Spy: National Security Leaks and the First Amendment," *Boston University Law Review* 94, no. 2 (March 2014): 492–493.

81. Yochai Benkler, "A Public Accountability Defense for National Security Leakers and Whistleblowers," *Harvard Law & Policy Review* 8, no. 281 (2014): 299; Edgar, *Beyond Snowden*, 77, 96.

82. Savage, *Power Wars*, 221–223.

83. Perry, "Intelligence Whistleblower Protections."

84. "Third of Americans Take Precautions to Protect Web Presence, Pew Report Finds," *Guardian*, March 16, 2015; "How the Snowden Leak Is Changing the Tech Landscape," *Guardian*, December 2, 2013; "Edward Snowden Offers to Help Brazil over US Spying in Return for Asylum," *Guardian*, December 17, 2013; "Germany's Angela Merkel: Relations with U.S. 'Severely Shaken' over Spying Claims," CNN, October 24, 2013.

85. Granick, *American Spies*, 15; "Fact-checking John Oliver's Interview with Edward Snowden," *Politifact*, April 9, 2015; "NSA Analysts Wilfully Violated Surveillance Systems, Agency Admits," *Guardian*, August 24, 2013; Conor Friedersdorf, "The NSA's Porn-Surveillance Program," *Atlantic*, November 27, 2013; "Snowden, NSA Employees Shared Intercepted Sexts," *WP*, July 27, 2014.

86. Jessica Bruder and Dale Maharidge, *Snowden's Box: Trust in the Age of Surveillance* (London: Verso, 2020), 99.

87. Bruder and Maharidge, *Snowden's Box*, 47.

88. "Claim on 'Attacks Thwarted' by NSA Spreads Despite Lack of Evidence," *ProPublica*, October 23, 2013; Savage, *Power Wars*, 220–221, 584–585; Granick, *American Spies*, 82–85.

89. Granick, 77–80; Priest and Arkin, *Top Secret America*, 100–102; Savage, *Power Wars*, 11–30.

90. Kaeten Mistry and Hannah Gurman, "Paradox of National Security Whistleblowing," in *Whistleblowing Nation: The History of National Security Disclosures and the Cult of State Secrecy*, ed. Mistry and Gurman (New York: Columbia University Press, 2020), 27; Savage, *Power Wars*, 353–356, 370–371, 381–384; Lloyd C. Gardner, *War on Leakers: National Security and American Democracy, from Eugene V. Debs to Edward Snowden* (New York: New Press, 2016), 128–134; Jane Mayer, "The Secret Sharer," *New Yorker*, May 23, 2011; "The Espionage Act: Why Tom Drake Was Indicted," *CBS News*, May 22, 2011.

91. Scott Shane, "New Leaked Document Outlines U.S. Spending on Intelligence Agencies," *NYT*, August 30, 2013, A13; Bernard Harcourt, *Exposed: Desire and Disobedience in the Digital Age* (Cambridge, MA: Harvard University Press, 2015), 70.

92. Shoshana Zuboff, *The Age of Surveillance Capitalism: The Fight for a Human Future at the New Frontier of Power* (New York: PublicAffairs, 2019), 112–121, 308–318; Ackerman, *Reign of Terror*, 33; Max Chafkin, *The Contrarian: Peter Thiel and Silicon Valley's Pursuit of Power* (New York: Penguin, 2021), 154; Sara Morrison, "Everything You Need to Know About Palantir, the Secretive Company Coming for All Your Data," *Vox*, August 26, 2020.

93. Tim Hwang, *Subprime Attention Crisis: Advertising and the Time Bomb at the Heart of the Internet* (New York: Farrar, Straus and Giroux, 2020).

94. Granick, *American Spies*, 91, 96–97; Keith Devlin, "The NSA: A Betrayal of Trust," *Notices of the American Mathematical Society* 61 (June/July 2014): 624–626.

95. Edgar, *Beyond Snowden*, 88; David Ignatius, "Edward Snowden Took Less Than Previously Thought, Says James Clapper," *WP*, June 5, 2014; Epstein, *How America Lost Its Secrets*, 169.

96. "NSA Surveillance: Narrow Defeat for Amendment to Restrict Data Collection," *Guardian*, July 25, 2013; David Kravets, "Lawmakers Who Upheld NSA Phone Spying Received Double the Defense Industry Cash," *Wired*, July 26, 2013.

97. "Obama Touts NSA Surveillance Reforms to Quell Growing Unease over Programs," *Guardian*, August 9, 2013; Savage, *Power Wars*, 566–568, 602, 608, 620–625; Brad Heath, "U.S. Secretly Tracked Billions of Calls for Decades," *USA Today*, April 7, 2015; Greenberg, *Subtle Tools*, 36–37; Edgar, *Beyond Snowden*, 3–5, 81–86, 106, 120–121; Granick, *American Spies*, 31, 113–114; Jack Goldsmith, "Three Years Later: How Snowden Helped the U.S. Intelligence Community," *Lawfare*, June 6, 2016.

98. "Eric Holder Says Edward Snowden Performed Public Service with NSA Leak," *Guardian*, May 30, 2016.

99. Papandrea, "Leaker Traitor," 484; David Pozen, "Edward Snowden, National Security Whistleblowing and Civil Disobedience," in *Whistleblowing Nation: The History of National Security Disclosures and the Cult of State Secrecy*, ed. Kaeten Mistry and Hannah Gurman (New York: Columbia University Press, 2020), 333; "Snowden: Coming Home 'Not Possible' Under Whistleblower Laws," NPR, January 23, 2014; "Edward Snowden Would Be Willing to Return to US for Fair Trial," *Guardian*, February 21, 2016.

100. Laura Poitras et al., *Citizenfour* (Beverly Hills, CA: Anchor Bay Entertainment, 2015).

101. Kerry Howley, "Call Me a Traitor," *New York*, July 20, 2021; Rachel Weiner, "Daniel Hale, Who Leaked Information on US Drone Warfare, Sentenced to 45 Months in Prison," *WP*, July 27, 2021.

102. Jameel Jaffer, *The Drone Memos: Targeted Killing, Secrecy and the Law* (New York: New Press, 2016); Savage, *Power Wars*, chap. 6; Moyn, *Humane*, chap. 8.

103. Oona A. Hathaway, "Secrecy's End," *Minnesota Law Review* 106 (2021): 747; Moyn, *Humane*, 291–292; Jaffer, *Drone Memos*, 14; "The Queen and Her Drones," *Economist*, July 9, 2016, 21; Savage, *Power Wars*, chap. 6; Chase Madar, "Rules of Disengagement," *Bookforum*, December/January, 2017; Hugh Gusterson, *Drone: Remote Control Warfare* (Cambridge, MA: MIT Press, 2016).

104. Ackerman, *Reign of Terror*, 125; "The Unseen Scars of Those Who Kill Via Remote Control," *NYT*, April 15, 2022.

105. Weiner, "Daniel Hale."

106. Priya Satia, "The Defense of Inhumanity: Air Control and the British Idea of Arabia," *American Historical Review* 111 (2006): 16–51; Susan Pederson, *The Guardians: The League of Nations and the Crisis of Empire* (New York: Oxford University Press, 2015), chap. 5; Wray R. Johnson, "Airpower and Restraint in Small Wars: Marine Corps Aviation in the Second Nicaraguan Campaign, 1927–33," *Air & Space Power Journal* 15 (2001): 32–41; Michael S. Sherry, *The Rise of American Air Power: The Creation of Armageddon* (New Haven, CT: Yale University Press, 1987).

107. Andrew Cockburn, *Kill Chain: Drones and the Rise of High-Tech Assassins* (New York: Henry Holt, 2015); Christopher J. Fuller, *See It/Shoot It: The Secret History of the CIA's Lethal Drone Program* (New Haven, CT: Yale University Press, 2017); Kathryn Olmsted, "Terror Tuesdays," in *The Presidency of Barack Obama: A First Historical Assessment*, ed. Julian Zelizer (Princeton, NJ: Princeton University Press, 2018), 216; Greenberg, *Subtle Tools*, 23.

108. Howley, "Call Me a Traitor."

Conclusion: Good-Bye to the Espionage Act?

1. "How Donald Trump Blasted George W. Bush in S.C.—and Still Won," CNN, February 21, 2016.

2. Spencer Ackerman, *Reign of Terror: How the 9/11 Era Destabilized America and Produced Trump* (New York: Viking, 2021), 240–249; "Trump Defends Putin: You Think Our Country's So Innocent?," CNN, February 6, 2017.

3. Yochai Benkler, Rob Faris, and Hal Roberts, *Network Propaganda: Manipulation, Disinformation, and Radicalization in American Politics* (New York: Oxford University Press, 2018), 114, 141–143.

4. Devlin Barrett, *October Surprise: How the FBI Tried to Save Itself and Crashed an Election* (New York: PublicAffairs, 2020), 73, 202, 207; Douglas L. Kriner and Eric Schickler, *Investigating the President: Congressional Checks on Presidential Power* (Princeton, NJ: Princeton University Press, 2016), 233–242, 249–257; "The Conspiracy Theory That Just Won't Fade," *NBC News*, September 11, 2013; "Obama on Clinton's Emails," *CBS News*, April 10, 2016.

5. Barrett, *October Surprise*, 165, 214, 237–238, 263–264; "FBI Was Justified in Opening Trump Campaign Probe, but Case Plagued by 'Serious Failures,' Inspector General Finds," *WP*, December 9, 2019; David Rohde, *In Deep: The FBI, the CIA, and the Truth About America's "Deep State"* (New York: W. W. Norton, 2020).

6. "NSA Leaker Reality Winner Gets Five-Year Sentence," *WP*, August 23, 2018.

7. "Leak Investigations Triple Under Trump, Sessions Says," *NYT*, August 4, 2017; "Ex-CIA Engineer Convicted of Biggest Theft Ever of Agency Secrets," *NYT*, July 13, 2022; Patrick Radden Keefe, "King Josh: The Surreal Case of the Disgruntled CIA Hacker Accused of Exposing the Agency's Digital Arsenal," *New Yorker*, June 13, 2022.

8. "Ex-Pentagon Analyst Sentenced to Thirty Months in Leak Case," *NYT*, June 18, 2020.

9. "Inside Trump's War on the National Archives," *WP*, August 27, 2022; "The Photo of Classified Documents at Trump's Mar-a-Lago Resort, Annotated," *WP*, August 31, 2022; "Takeaways from the Unsealed Warrant for the Search of Trump's Home," *NYT*, August 12, 2022; "Trump Had More Than 300 Classified Documents at Mar-a-Lago," *NYT*, August 22, 2022; Jack Goldsmith, "Thoughts on the Mar-a-Lago Search," *Lawfare*, August 14, 2022, www.lawfareblog.com/thoughts-mar-lago-search.

10. "How Bad Would an Espionage Act Violation Be for a Soldier? What About for Trump?," *Slate*, August 12, 2022; "Mar-a-Lago a Magnet for Spies, Officials Warn After Nuclear File Reportedly Found," *Guardian*, September 7, 2022; "Trump Claims Presidents Can Declassify Documents 'by Thinking About It,'" *Guardian*, September 22, 2022; "Trump Claimed He Declassified All the Documents at Mar-a-Lago. Even If That's True, It Probably Doesn't Matter," *NYT*, August 12, 2022.

11. "Classified Documents Found at Pence's Indiana Home," CNN, January 24, 2023; "The FBI Searched Biden's Home and Found More Classified Documents," NPR, January 22, 2023.

12. Cullen Hoback (dir.), *Q: Into the Storm* (Sausolito, CA: Ro*Co Films, 2021).

13. Craig Whitlock, "Epic Navy Bribery Scandal Shows How Easy It Can Be to Steal Military Secrets," *WP*, January 21, 2016.

14. "Even After Snowden, Quota System on Background Checks May Be Imperiling U.S. Secrets," *WP*, June 14, 2015; Edward Jay Epstein, *How America Lost Its Secrets: Edward Snowden, the Man and the Theft* (New York: Alfred A. Knopf, 2017), 210–212; Oona A. Hathaway, "Secrecy's End," *Minnesota Law Review* 106 (2021): 692.

15. Hathaway, "Secrecy's End," 739; Craig Whitlock, "The Admiral in Charge of Navy Intelligence Has Not Been Allowed to See Military Secrets for Years," *WP*, January 28, 2016; Sam Lagrone, "Former Naval Intelligence Chief Ted Branch Cleared in 'Fat Leonard' Case," *USNI News*, September 22, 2017.

16. *US v. Rosen and Weissman*, No. 445 F.Supp.2d 602 (US District Court, E.D. Virginia, August 9, 2006).

17. Elizabeth Gotein and David M. Shapiro, *Reducing Overclassification Through Accountability* (New York: Brennan Center for Justice, 2011), 33–49; Herbert Lin, "A Proposal to Reduce Government Overclassification of Information Related to National Security," *Journal of National Security Law & Policy* 7 (2014): 443–464; Steven Aftergood, "An Inquiry into the Dynamics of Government Secrecy," *Harvard Civil Rights and Civil Liberties Law Review* 48 (2013): 525–527; Steven Aftergood, "Reducing Government Secrecy: Finding What Works," *Yale Law & Policy Review* 27 (2008): 399–416.

18. Yochai Benkler, "A Public Accountability Defense for National Security Leakers and Whistleblowers," *Harvard Law & Policy Review* 8, no. 2 (2014): 281–326.

19. Margaret B. Kwoka, "FOIA, Inc," *Duke Law Journal* 65, no. 7 (2016); Jason Ross Arnold, *Secrecy in the Sunshine Era: The Promise and Failures of U.S. Open Government Laws* (Lawrence: University Press of Kansas, 2014), 227–232; David E. Pozen, "Transparency's Ideological Drift," *Yale Law Journal* 128 (2018): 100–165; Nicholson Baker, *Baseless: My Search for Secrets in the Ruins of the Freedom of Information Act* (New York: Penguin, 2020); David Pozen, "Freedom of Information Beyond the Freedom of Information Act," *University of Pennsylvania Law Review* 165 (2017): 1097–1158.

20. Jameel Jaffer, Alex Abdo, Meenakshi Krishnan, and Ramya Krishnan, "How the Biden Administration and Congress Can Fix Prepublication Review: A Roadmap for Reform," *Knight First Amendment Institute Policy Papers*, March 11, 2002.

21. Ron Wyden press release, March 5, 2020, www.wyden.senate.gov/news/press-releases/wyden-and-khanna-introduce-bill-to-protect-whistleblowers-ensure-journalists-arent-targeted-for-publishing-classified-information; Gabe Rottman, "How an Espionage Act Reform Bill Would Improve Protections for National Security Reporting," Reporters Committee for Freedom of the Press, March 5, 2020; Ro Khanna press release, July 27, 2022, https://khanna.house.gov/media/press-releases/release-khanna-wyden-massie-introduce-bill-protect-whistleblowers-ensure; "Editorial: Rep. Gabbard Introduces Whistleblower Protection Bill to Reform Antiquated Espionage Act," *Whistleblower Network News*, November 10, 2020; James Risen, "Rashida Tlaib Is Trying to Fix the Espionage Act, but Whistleblowers Are Probably Out of Luck," *Intercept*, July 12, 2022.

22. Gabe Rottman, "Ahead of Daniel Hale Sentencing, RCFP Highlights Concern About Severe Sentences in Leak Cases," July 19, 2021, www.rcfp.org/daniel-hale-sentencing-amicus.

23. Brief of Amici Curiae Scholars of Constitutional Law, First Amendment Law, and Media Law in Support of Defendant at 7-12, *United States v. Albury*, No. 18-cr-00067 (D. Minn., Oct. 4, 2018), https://fas.org/sgp/jud/albury-amicus.pdf.

24. *Edgar v. Haines*, Knight First Amendment Institute, https://knightcolumbia.org/cases/edgar-v-haines#:~:text=Status%3A%20On%20May%2023%2C%20 2022,Case%20Information%3A%20Edgar%20v; *Edgar v. Haines*, ACLU, May 2, 2022, www.aclu.org/cases/edgar-v-haines.

25. Barrett, *October Surprise*, 125; Benkler, Faris, and Roberts, *Network Propaganda*, 160–161; "Seth Rich Was Not Source of Leaked D.N.C. Emails, Mueller Report Confirms," *NYT*, April 20, 2019.

26. "Julian Assange Is Not a Free Press Hero," *WP*, April 11, 2019; Jameel Jaffer and Ben Wizner, "Assange Indictment Is Shot Across the Bow of Press Freedom," *Just Security*, April 11, 2019.

27. "Curious Eyes Never Run Dry," *NYT*, April 11, 2019.

28. "Chelsea Manning Released from Jail on Contempt Charge," PBS, May 10, 2019.

29. Natasha Bertrand, "DOJ Accuses Assange of Violating Espionage Act," *Politico*, May 23, 2019; Ethan Thompson, "Press Freedom and the Espionage Act: A Critical Juncture," *Washington University Journal of Law and Policy* 66 (2021): 198, 204; "Assange Indicted Under Espionage Act, Raising First Amendment Issues," *NYT*, May 23, 2019.

30. "Coalition Letter to the Department of Justice: Drop Assange Prosecution," February 9, 2021, www.hrw.org/news/2021/02/08/coalition-letter-us-department-justice-drop-assange-prosecution; "Groups Press Attorney General to Drop Espionage Act Charges Against Julian Assange," Knight First Amendment Institute, October 19, 2021, https://knightcolumbia.org/blog/groups-press-attorney-general-to-drop-espionage-act-charges-against-julian-assange; "Major News Outlets Urge U.S. to Drop Its Charges Against Assange," *NYT*, November 29, 2022, www.nytimes.com/2022/11/28/us/politics/julian-assange-wikileaks-charges.html.

31. "Amend the Espionage Act," *Pittsburgh Post-Gazette*, May 23, 2019, A10.

INDEX

Sam Lebovic is an associate professor in the department of history and art history at George Mason University. He is the author of the award-winning *Free Speech and Unfree News* and *A Righteous Smokescreen*. His work has appeared in the *Los Angeles Review of Books*, *Boston Globe*, *Washington Post*, and more. He lives in Washington, DC.